לבי ער

A Lightness of BEING

Your Guide to Yom Kippur

RAV DOVBER PINSON

Published by IYYUN Publishing
650 Sackett Street
Brooklyn, NY 11217

www.iyyun.com

Iyyun Publishing books may be purchased for educational, business or sales promotional use. For information please email: contact@iyyun.com

Editor: Reb Matisyahu Brown
Proofreading / Editing: Yaakov Gershon
Cover and book design: RP Design and Development

ISBN 978-1-7367026-4-2

Pinson, Dovber 1971-
A Lightness of Being: Your Guide to Yom Kippur
1. Judaism 2. Jewish Spirituality 3. General Spirituality

RAV DOVBER PINSON

A lightness of BEING

Your Guide to Yom Kippur

IYYUN PUBLISHING

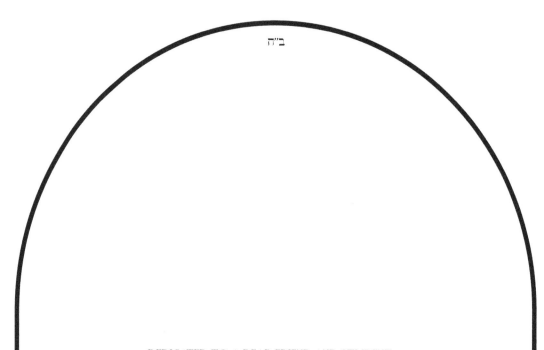

ב"ה

ב"ה

THIS VOLUME IS
IN MEMORY OF OUR BELOVED

CHAYA BISTRITZKY A"H

רווחמה חיה פרומא בת ר' דוב פנחס ע"ה

נפ' ז' כסלו תש"פ

She inspired thousands with her steadfast emunah and her life motto of
"EIN OD MILVADO / THERE IS NOTHING ELSE EXCEPT HASHEM"

Her acts of chesed reverberate still and her presence is constantly felt by us
and her extended family of friends and community.

Yom Kippur is a day of holiness. Its holiness infuses blessings into the entire year.
In her unique way, Chaya did the same.
This extraordinary woman did much for so many in her too short life of
Torah, Mitzvos and Chesed.
May we merit to be with her again with the coming of Mashiach, speedily in our days.

———

WE ALSO HONOR THE MEMORY OF OUR BELOVED MECHUTAN,

PABLO ELKON Z"L

ר' דוב פנחס בן ר' משה ע"ה

נפ' י' ניסן תשפ"א

Berel, *aka*, Pablo, as many knew him, was a person who was very well liked by all.
He was always the first to greet people with an enthusiastic *"good morning!*
I'm fine, how are you?" With emunah and bitachon he overcame his health challenges.
His constant refrain was, "Why should we worry?
Everything will be exactly as HaKadosh Baruch Hu wants."
Through it all, his wife stood by him devotedly.
He personified *'Emor Me'at V'aseh Harbeh'* Speak little, do much.
He always looked to help those in need in a very dignified and quiet way.
He loved learning and it gave him life.
His children, grandchildren and everyone who knew him, loved him, because he loved them all.
His presence and love are sorely missed by all.

JOSEPH AND SHEILA BISTRITZKY

NESANEL AND YEHUDIS GOLD
ARON AND SARAH BISTRITZKY

MARCUS (MOTTY) BISTRITZKY
SHLOMIE AND DEVORAH BROCINER

SHLOMO AND ESTHER R. BISTRITZKY

Contents

PART ONE:

WHAT IS
YOM KIPPUR

Contents

PART TWO:

Teshuvah / Return on Yom Kippur

Contents

PART THREE:

Customs & Tefilos / Prayers for Yom Kippur

PART ONE:

WHAT IS
YOM KIPPUR

Opening

WHO AM I?

YOM KIPPUR HAS AN UNDENIABLE GRAVITAS. IT SPIRI-
TUALLY AROUSES ALL OF US, EACH IN OUR OWN WAY,
AND PULLS US INTO ITS ORBIT. Alas, for many people, Yom Kippur is the only holy day that truly registers. And
yet, this, too, reveals something of the unique essence of this
day. What is Yom Kippur really, and why does it call us so
deeply? Indeed, there is a powerful inner magnetism that pulls
each person towards the heart of Yom Kippur, no matter how
distant or alienated they may be from the depths of life. Something inexplicable happens, and they spontaneously rush into
the embrace of this most unique day.

The truth is that Yom Kippur *seeks us out*. And consciously or not, our souls respond and, in turn, seek Yom Kippur as well. Something deep inside us gravitates toward its light.

We are thus seekers of Yom Kippur. But what is it within Yom Kippur that we are seeking? On the deepest level, we are all *Dorshei Yichudecha* / "seekers of Essential Unity." Most people, living in a world of swirling chaos and disintegration, seek solidity through certainty. On a deeper level, that desire is but a yearning for aliveness, wholeness, and connection with ourselves, with others, and ultimately with the Source and Essence of all life.

While it is possible to mistakenly think that wealth, power, and the accumulation of things will deliver the sense of Unity that we crave, buying that new gadget or achieving that higher accolade never truly makes us feel complete. Our existential yearning to connect to an inner state of Unity cannot be satisfied by such objects. In pursuit of them, one becomes ever more reactive, divided and dispersed, exacerbating one's almost visceral thirst for ultimate truth. One can, in fact, become spiritually dehydrated and parched, as if stranded in a desert. But then, like storm clouds in the summer, one is suddenly greeted again by the lush oasis of Yom Kippur, flowing with its deeply quenching soul-refreshment.

Rosh Hashanah and Yom Kippur, the Days of Awe, inspire within us a burning passion for truth, an equanimous awareness of ultimate unity, and a deep feeling of respect and responsibility for the wellbeing of others. Some may feel this soul-refreshment throughout the Ten Days from Rosh Hashanah through Yom Kippur. Others will feel it mostly on the Yom Tov days, and others maybe just for a few key moments throughout those 24 hours of Awe. However, at some point during the course of Yom Kippur, everyone will be touched by a sense of something deeper, a presence more profound. There will undoubtedly be at least one eternal moment when we realize we are connected to a truth that is greater than ourselves and more real than our daily concerns.

Whether we pause to acknowledge and internalize these moments or we let them pass by to be forgotten, Yom Kippur offers us a vivid encounter with our true self. We are lifted beyond our worldly disguises and facades so that we can experience ourselves as the essential purity, joy and wholeness that we are. This essence of self is our inner *Kodesh Kodashim* / Holy of Holies, our wellspring of *Simcha* / joy, and beacon of *Ohr* / light, leading us beyond all our darkness, uncertainty, brokenness and alienation.

In these moments or periods of deep alignment, we get a glimpse into this essence of who we truly are and a sense of what our purpose on this earth is. We are gradually stripped of the superficiality of our ego self, temporarily detached from identification with money, power, beauty, status, and other attachments. This can ideally open us to experience a point of contact with our true identity beneath all our conditioning and shallow identifications. Naked and bare in front of HaKadosh

Baruch Hu / the Holy Blessed One — whose 'seal' is Truth — our deepest truth emerges. As a result, we are swept up into an ineffable transparency of self and lightness of being.

During this day, we should be ready to identify at least one such moment of transcendence; some experience of deeper connection with our community, our sacred texts, our ancestors, our collective history, a sense of weightlessness, inner purity, or an experience of spiritual sustenance or touching the Divine. Whatever the point of activation, these moments inspire us to live in more alignment with our Neshamah, with HaKadosh Baruch Hu, and with others; in short — they inspire us to come alive.

By consciously receiving and integrating the message of such moments on Yom Kippur, we can focus our lives in the coming year, and even shift the trajectory of our lives forever. Yom Kippur is unabashedly transformative; the power of the day beckons us to work toward fundamental transformation and *Teshuvah* / return to who we really are. Often, the word *Teshuvah* is unfortunately translated as 'repentance'. It is more accurately rendered as 'return', meaning both a return 'from' our states of spiritual alienation and exile, as well as a 'turning to' experiencing our deepest selves. Yom Kippur empowers us to return to our essence, reclaim who we truly are, and live from that place.

We do need to engage in *Teshuvah* / transformative turning inward every day and every moment of life, but Yom Kippur is the nucleus, the axle or center point of all of those moments. On the day of Yom Kippur, we soak in all the *Koach* / energy we will need in order to aspire toward Teshuvah throughout the year.

Preceding Yom Kippur, Rosh Hashanah is a celebration of the birthday of humanity, our collective and individual human origins. On Rosh Hashanah, we are beckoned to wake up to our humanity, to 'self-justify' our existence by coming back to our original intent in being alive. Rosh Hashanah celebrates the fact that *I am*. Then, on Yom Kippur, the question rises into consciousness: '*Who* am I?'

On the 'birthday' of our existence, we reconfirm our dedication to fulfilling the purpose of our existence and progressing toward this purpose in the year to come. With every moment, we need to answer the existential question, "Why was I born?" We need to constantly strive to find the positive answer to the question, "Can I justify my continued existence?"

On Yom Kippur, we need to acknowledge and answer the questions: "Who is the 'I' that was born; who is this existence?" "Can I own my life and my past, forge a higher and deeper life, and be who I really am?"

To truly move forward as a reclaimed self, we need to unload the baggage of the past that is weighing us down. To do this, it helps to make a compassionate but accurate self-evaluation and inventory, or 'spiritual accounting'. This is because we need to own our previous falsehoods and problems before we can let them go and separate from them. Then, from a place of true self-knowledge, connectivity and wholeness, we can transform past problems into tools of future growth.

In the context of Yom Kippur, 'owning our past' means looking back on the previous year and noticing when we were successful in our pursuits and perhaps in which areas we fell short of our potential. When were we not being ourselves? During this day of heightened awareness, we can discern which traits, habits, and activities we should continue and which ones we should release. Think about this and ask: 'Where am I learning, growing, or ascending? 'Where am I stuck, stagnant or even descending?'

Think about how your past has brought you into the present. Where have you been and what have you done? What kind of person did you appear to be last year? Now envision the future. In the coming year, where do you want to go and what do you want to do, and why? Who do you want to be?

When we reach a deep place of wholeness and purity, we transcend our false conceptions of who we are. This allows us to clearly see and own our past, decipher its value, learn from it, and let it go. Then we are inspired and empowered to steer our life toward accurately expressing our Divine soul — the essence of who we really are.

Chapter One
YOM KIPPUR:
RECLAIMING OUR ESSENTIAL SELF

THE DAY OF TESHUVAH / RETURN

AMONG ALL *Yamim Tovim* / HOLIDAYS OF THE YEARLY CYCLE, YOM KIPPUR IS CERTAINLY CONSIDERED THE MOST HOLY AND SUBLIME. On a simple level, Yom Kippur is a day dedicated to *Teshuvah* / returning because, on the original Yom Kippur, Hashem forgave *Klal Yisrael* / the Community of Israel after the episode of the Golden Calf. The natural consequence of that devastating act of idolatry and revolt against Hashem was the destruction of Klal Yisrael. However, through Moshe's fasting and pleading for forgiveness, atonement was attained on the tenth day of the Hebrew month of Tishrei. This momentous salvation made an indelible mark upon the fabric of time, and the day of Yom Kippur became an open portal for Teshuvah, atonement and forgiveness, for all eternity.

THE GREAT WEDDING DAY

Chazal tell us that the verse in *Shir haShirim*, Song of Songs, ביום חתונתו, זה מתן תורה / "'On the day of his wedding' refers to the giving of the Torah" (*Ta'anis*, 26b), characterizing the Sinaitic revelation as a kind of Cosmic Wedding. More precisely, this verse is actually in reference to the day the Second *Luchos* / Tablets of the Torah were given: Yom Kippur (Rashi, *ad loc*). Yom Kippur is thus our spiritual 'wedding day'. Because of this quality, it was once deemed a most opportune time to find one's spouse.*

In Elul, the process is אני לדודי / *Ani l'Dodi* / "I am to my Beloved" — we are working to get closer and closer to our Beloved, to Hashem.

---

* The Mishnah, *Ta'anis*, 4:8, describes maidens dancing in the vineyards on Yom Kippur, to attract attention from the unmarried men. As it is a day of atonement and forgiveness, and a bride and groom are forgiven of their sins on their wedding day (*Yerushalmi, Bikurim*, 3:3), this day is also dedicated to finding a spouse, as the *Yerushalmi* (*Ta'anis*, 4:11) suggests. When people are cleansed of sin, transcending egoic consciousness, as on a day like Yom Kippur, they can choose more effortlessly, accurately and clearly their fitting *Zivug* / spouse. This extends to all choices, and for this reason, certain Chassidic Rebbes would effortlessly choose an Esrog on Motzei Yom Kippur.

Perhaps the knowledge that they were forgiven is what prompted the maidens in this joyful *way* of seeking out a spouse. In the times of the Beis haMikdash, "A thread of crimson wool was tied to the door of the Beis haMikdash, and when the goat reached the wilderness the thread turned white": Mishnah, *Yuma*, 6:8. When it turned white, Klal Yisrael knew they were forgiven. This is also why the maidens danced in white garments. Once there was no longer a Beis haMikdash, this joyful practice was discontinued; however, the inner dynamic remains available.

On the evening of Rosh Hashanah, the sense of *Ani l'Dodi* is even more pronounced, but in the morning, we start shifting into ודודי לי / *v'Dodi Li* / "and my Beloved is to me," sensing Hashem's approaching closeness.

Finally, on Yom Yom Kippur, which is the 40th (today the 39th) day from the beginning of Elul, the stage of ודודי לי is complete. The numerical value of לי is 40, alluding to the completion of marriage, there is an experience of מקודשת לי / "betrothed to me," as the "me" and the "Beloved" are unified on the day of Yom Kippur.

On Rosh Hashanah we tell Hashem, 'I am committed and dedicated to You.' On Yom Kippur Hashem tells us, 'You are Mine, I hereby betroth you to Me. Let this be our wedding day.' Given this 'narrative', the sequence of Rosh Hashanah and Yom Kippur seems backwards. Rosh Hashanah is also the "Day of Judgment," upon which we receive our verdict of 'life or death' for the coming year. Yom Kippur, the day of Teshuvah and cleansing, follows on its heels. Imagine a person is brought to court for an undeniable crime and is awaiting his judgment. Would he not first confess his wrongdoing, show remorse, proclaim repentance and a commitment to changing himself, plead for forgiveness, and then await his judgment? Why would a day of repentance follow the day of his verdict? If Yom Kippur is simply about forgiveness of sin and wrongdoing, then Yom Kippur should come before Rosh Hashanah.*

---

* Rebbe Eliezer and Rebbe Yehoshua debate what day the world was created — referring specifically to the day that humanity was created. Rebbe

MUD-WRESTLING

Another seeming incongruity of the day of Yom Kippur is the fact that on this holiest of all holy days, we choose to re-count all of our (collective) wrongdoings, and do so in great detail and fanfare, many times throughout the day. If we hope to be cleansed and precipitate a *Shanah Tovah* / good year, would we not choose to speak about ourselves more positively on this day, rather than bring up all the spiritual and ethical dirt we have collected over the preceding year? Understand-ably, we need to recall and speak of our negativity for the pur-pose of purging and cleansing it; one cannot forget and let go of something he does not remember and own. Yet it is equally true "that one who wrestles with a muddied person is bound to become muddied himself" (*Tanya*, 28). Why should we risk getting mud and dirt all over our mind and spirit on this most somber and sublime day? While there is a time and place for focusing on negative behavior, perhaps Yom Kippur is not the best time.

Eliezer's opinion is that it took place on the first day of the month of Tish-rei, on Rosh Hashanah. Rebbe Yehoshua, however, asserts that it occurred on the first day of the month of Nisan (*Rosh Hashanah*, 11a). If Adam haR-ishon / the first human, was created on the First of Tishrei, and he sinned and was granted atonement on the same day, it makes sense that the First of Tishrei is the Day of Judgment and humanity is called to task (see *Medrash Rabbah*, Vayikra, 29:1). But if the world was created in Nisan, why is the First of Tishrei a day of judgment? The Ran answers that since the Tenth of Tishrei was chosen as a day of atonement (after the incident of the Golden Calf), the Creator chose the First of Tishrei as a day of judgment, to help humanity prepare for Yom Kippur through introspection and self-evalu-ation. In this way, Rosh Hashanah is there to prepare us for Yom Kippur.

Indeed, it is not! Yom Kippur is actually not about recalling and bringing up all our negative baggage. For that purpose we are given the entire month of Elul, the month of Teshuvah that precedes Rosh Hashanah. In Elul, we need to do an honest soul searching by inspecting our failures and spiritual schmutz, in order to generate an aspiration to right these wrongs. After the month of Elul comes to a close, we are then ready for Rosh Hashanah, the day of our judgment, and hopefully, our vindication.

There are two essential components to Teshuvah: *Charatah* / regretting mistakes of the past, and *Kabbalah* / accepting different behaviors for the future. This is the *Avodah* / inner work of Elul. Once Elul is complete, and we have already cleaned up our lives, only then are we ready to stand before our Creator on Rosh Hashanah with some level of confidence and joy.

So what, then, is Yom Kippur about, if not regretting and dwelling on our past misdeeds?

SEPARATED TIME / SPACE / CONSCIOUSNESS

There are three properties or aspects of this universe: *Olam* / space, *Shanah* / time, and *Nefesh* / soul or consciousness. Whatever we do, we are always in some location, at a certain point in time, and in a particular state of consciousness. These three coordinates are so interrelated that one cannot exist without the others. As is known, time and space are a single continuum. In addition, time and space only have meaning when a conscious observer observes them and defines them as such.

All of space, time, and consciousness emanate from a single point of origin. Furthermore, every particular flow of time, manifestation of space, and extension of consciousness emerges from a particular point of reference within their respective domain (with regards to the time, רבי יהושע אומר בניסן נברא העולם / "Rebbe Yehoshua says the world was created in Nisan (the first month of the year)," רבי אליעזר אומר מנין שבתשרי נברא העולם / "Rebbe Eliezer says, "How do we know that the world was created in Tishrei (the seventh month of the year, i.e., in the middle of the year): *Rosh Hashanah*, 11a. Similarly, regarding space, Chazal also debate *where* the world began to be created: was it from the sides (the 'beginning') of space, or from the 'middle', the center of space (עולם מאמצעיתו נברא או עולם מן הצדדין נברא): *Yuma*, 54b. With regards to the human body, Chazal debate where we consider the creation of a fetus to begin forming — הולד נוצר מטיבורו או מראשו נברא, is it from the 'top' or head, or the 'middle', the navel area: *Sotah*, 45b).

As the domains of time, space and consciousness spread out from their origin, they each function in a universe of separate dimensions. For example, there are practical and perceptual separations between the dimensions of past and future, between 'here' and 'there', and between 'my mind' and 'your mind'. There is also collaborative interaction between diverse dimensions. In *Shanah* / linear time, there is a past that imprints itself upon a present, which in turn affects a future. In *Olam* / space, the dimensions of width, height, and depth combine to form volume and separate discrete physical entities. Domains also interact; a period of time can determine changes in the size of something, and movements in space take certain amounts of time. The *Nefesh* / conscious observer who perceives these diverse interacting dimensions of time and space can project subjective meanings upon them, imbuing events and objects with his or her own feelings or inner state. When a Nefesh interprets certain interactions as fundamentally conflicting and fragmented, that is indeed how they are experienced. Such is the relationship between space, time, and consciousness.

UNIFIED TIME / SPACE / CONSCIOUSNESS

Despite all the apparent diversity and division in creation, there is an original central point that is one, unified and whole, from which all domains, dimensions, interactions, and interpretations emanate. The Center of all reality and existence is the Creator. This Center is ever-present, and can reveal Its presence anywhere in any array of manifestation, representing its Unity and wholeness within diversity. There are central expressions of Unity within time, within space, and within consciousness. From within these central expressions of Unity within time, within space, and within consciousness, infinite oneness begins to stream outward into the finite world.

Yom Kippur reflects the infinite point of Divine Unity and internal unification within all three domains of time, space, and consciousness.

With respect to time, Yom Kippur is referred to as אחת בשנה / *Achas baShanah* / the 'oneness' of the year (*Vayikra*, 16:34). שנה / *Shanah* / year, is related to the word שינוי / *Shinui*, meaning change, as the flow of the year cycle bespeaks diversity and the changing of seasons. Amid the multiplicity of change, Yom Kippur stands as an unchanging point of oneness from which all phases of time emerge and flow. As such, Yom Kippur is always celebrated as one day in all places, even in the Diaspora (where each 'Biblical' or Torah-based *Yom Tov* / holy day is observed for two days).*

Yom Kippur is the central *Nekudah* / point of all time, and thus it stands apart from all flows and manifestations of time. And yet, as the unification of time, it simurltaneously permeates all dimensions of time.**

* יש מחמירים לעשות שני ימים יום כפורים ויש לזה התרה ואין לנהוג בחומרא זו משום דיש לחוש שיבא לידי סכנה / "There are those who are stringent and celebrate Yom Kippur for two days…(but) one should not practice this stringency, because it may be dangerous": Rama, *Orach Chayim*, 624:5. The Diaspora relies (for the purpose of making Yom Kippur a single day) on the fact that Elul is always 'deficient' (having only 29 days), and thus there is no *Safek* / doubt of when it was Rosh Chodesh (Tishrei). Thus, in the Diaspora, in ancient times, the identity of the 10th day of Tishrei was never in doubt. Although see *Rosh Hashanah*, 21a: רבא הוה רגיל דהוה יתיב בתעניתא תרי יומי / "Rabba (who lived in Bavel) was accustomed to fast two days." Says Rabbeinu Chananel, ומלתא רב נחמן יתיב בתעניתא. יתירתא עבד ולא חובה הוא עליו. The Gemara brings a story: כוליה יומי דכיפורי. לאורתא אתא ההוא גברא, אמר ליה: למחר יומא רבה במערבא אמר ליה / מהיכא את אמר ליה: מדמהריא. אמר ליה: דם תהא אחריתו. קרי עליה: "קלים היו רודפינו" / "Rav Nachman had once fasted the entire day of Yom Kippur as usual. In the evening, toward the end of his fast, a certain man came and said to him: 'Tomorrow is the great day, Yom Kippur, in the West (Eretz Yisrael, and it is therefore necessary to fast tomorrow).' Rav Nachman said to him: 'From where do you come?' He said to him: 'From a place called Damihareya.' He said to him, playing on the name of his place: "*Dam* / blood will be his end," meaning Rav Nachman's own end, because due to this information, Rav Nachman would have to fast two successive days, and thereby suffer greatly, as if his blood were being shed: *Rosh Hashanah*, ibid.

** The Mishnah in *Kelim* (1:9) says, קדש הקדשים מקדש מהם, שאין נכנס לשם אלא כהן גדול ביום הכפורים בשעת העבודה / "The *Kodesh haKadashim* / Holy of Holies…only the *Cohen Gadol* / high priest, on Yom Kippur, at the time of the service, may enter it." The meaning of this is straightforward: only on Yom Kippur may the Cohen Gadol enter the Kodesh haKodashim. Yet,

Yom Kippur is also associated with the *Achas baMakom /* Oneness and inner unification of space. As the central Nekudah of all space, Yom Kippur stands apart from all dimensions of space, and yet as the unification of space, it simultaneously permeates all dimensions of space.

When the *Beis haMikdash /* the Holy Temple stood, it was only on Yom Kippur that the *Cohen Gadol /* High Priest was permitted to enter the sacred space of the *Kodesh haKodashim /* Holy of Holies. Within the Kodesh HaKodashim, the *Aron /* Ark of the Covenant (during the first Beis haMikdash) stood over the *Even haShesiyah /* the Foundation Stone, the mysterious, mystical rock from which all of physical space originally extended (*Yuma*, 54b. *Yalkut Shimoni,* Koheles, 2:967).

The holy Aron was as physical as anything else, a manifestation of this material existence with physical measurements of width and height. And yet, when placed in the Holy of Holies, the Aron did not take up any space. If one were to measure from the outside wall of the Aron in any direction, the sum total of the empty areas would be the same as the sum total of the entire width of the Holy of Holies. In other words, al-

---

when the Rambam quotes this *Din /* law, he writes, אין כהן גדול נכנס לקדש הקדשים אלא מיום הכפורים ליום הכפורים / "The Cohen Gadol does not enter the Holies of Holies except from Yom Kippur until Yom Kippur": Rambam, *Hilchos Bi'as haMikdash*, 2:1. It seems from the wording of the Rambam that he is subtly suggesting that when the Cohen Gadol enters on Yom Kippur, the effect of his entrance remains present for the entire year, until the following Yom Kippur.

though the Aron contained a definite measurement, it paradoxically did not take up any space. This is because it melded, unified, and integrated its 'dimensions' into the dimensionless, merging its space into spacelessness, even while it retained its spatial properties.

Just as the central Nekudah of time paradoxically transcends and permeates all times, the central Nekudah and essence of space — the place of the Even haShesiyah — transcends and permeates all space.

Since space and time are one inseparable fabric, the place of the Even haShesiyah, the Kodesh haKodashim, itself transcends and permeates time. This is demonstrated by the Mitzvah to store the *Mon* / Manna in the Aron in the Kodesh haKodashim. The Torah tells us that we are not allowed to keep the Mon for the future: אל-יותר ממנו עד-בקר / "Let no one leave any of it over until morning." (*Shemos*, 16:19). And yet, the Torah also teaches us: "Take a jar, and put one Omer of Mon in it, and place it before Hashem, to be kept throughout the ages." It is true that a positive Mitzvah (keeping a measure of Mon in a jar) can push aside a prohibition (not keeping any Mon until the morning). Yet, from a deeper perspective, the Torah is saying that when the Mon is placed in the Holy of Holies "before Hashem," there is no time, and thus it is not left over 'for the next morning' (ליכא גדר זמן: *Tzafnas Paneach*, Shemos, 16:33).

REVEALING OUR ESSENTIAL SELF

Finally, and most importantly, Yom Kippur is the central, unifying Nekudah of consciousness. In other words, Yom Kippur reveals Unity within our deepest self, the *Achas b'Nefesh*, otherwise known as the *Yechidah* / oneness or uniqueness of the soul (Mitteler Rebbe, *Ateres Rosh*, from Chapter 2 forward) — the pure Self.

As the central Nekudah of consciousness or soul, Yom Kippur stands apart and transcends all other dimensions of soul. Yet, as the unification of consciousness, Yom Kippur simultaneously permeates all dimensions of our being.

Sadly, hopefully infrequently and not intentionally, it may occur that the way we act and behave is not consistent with our inner truth. Our 'outer self' does not accurately reflect our deepest 'inner self'. We may stray from our true path and, in the process, 'eclipse' our essential light, our Yechidah of soul — yet, no matter how alienated we may become, our inner light of Yechidah can never be extinguished. It is the ever-pure and transcendent *Nekudah* / inner point of who we truly are.

Any negativity we have engaged in is not who we are; rather, it is merely what we have done. Our actions occur on the level of manifestation, the level of experience. Beyond or 'prior' to experience is the *experiencer*, 'who we really are'. The consequences of our negative actions can only attach themselves to us as external appendages. True, they may weigh us down, burden us, or cloud our vision, but they can only penetrate just beneath the surface of who we truly are. They can never affect or influence the deepest part of ourselves, which is always present and unified. We, the essential experiencer, remain unscathed and untouched by our mistakes.

Yom Kippur gives us the power to tap into our deepest, infinite, 'non-dual' self. It is a day when we rise above our fractured, divided, heavy ego and fully access the transparency of self and lightness of being — the blissful weightlessness of the Nekudah of consciousness (On Yom Kippur we are pure of all sin, מה מלאכי השרת נקיים מכל חטא כך ישראל נקיים מכל חטא ביום הכפורים :*Pirkei d'Rebbe Eliezer,* Chap. 46).

COSMIC EMPOWERMENT FOR TESHUVAH

Meta-historically, Yom Kippur was chosen as a day of Teshuvah because it was the original day of forgiveness during the formation of Klal Yisrael. A mere six weeks following the monumental Divine encounter at Sinai, when absolute Unity was clear and transparent to all, the newborn nation danced around a Golden Calf and proclaimed, "This is the 'god' that took us out of Egypt." The desire to idolize and worship an image was so powerful, the human need to conceptualize and contextualize so overwhelming, that they were not able to fully assimilate the revelation at Sinai — the revelation that Hashem is imageless, that the *Ein Sof /* the Infinite One is truly Present, and that the perceptual gap between Heaven and earth has been removed. Some eighty days later, after much prayer and beseeching, Moshe secured forgiveness from on High and thus a means for anyone to re-access the highest levels of being even after he or she has fallen. That day was the tenth day of the seventh month of Tishrei, the day of Yom Kippur, as designated by the Torah.

On the day of the creation of Adam and Chavah / Eve, they were banished from Gan Eden — or rather, they banished themselves from a world of perfection, peace, and life. This exile was triggered by their — meaning 'our' — identification with the polarized perspective of the Tree of Good versus Evil. A cloud of separation, death, strife, confusion, and chaos gathered overhead. This cataclysmic event occurred on the original day of Rosh Hashanah, and immediately afterward they began the process of Teshuvah (אדם הראשון חסיד גדול היה, כיון שראה שנכנסה מיתה על ידו, ישב בתענית מאה שלשים שנה: *Eiruvin*, 18b). This is why, ever since, this time is prime for Teshuvah.

Avraham *Avinu* / father of Klal Yisrael, entered into the Divine *Bris* / covenant of *Milah* / circumcision on Yom Kippur.*

---

* The Medrash teaches: אתיא "עצם" מ"עצם" מיום הכפורים, מה להלן כל מלאכה לא תעשו בעצם היום הזה כי יום כפורים הוא, שביום הכפורים נמול אברהם, ובכל שנה ושנה הקב"ה רואה דם הברית של מילה של אברהם אבינו, ומכפר על כל עונותינו / "Not only that, but (it indicates) the tenth day of the month, the Day of Atonement. It is written in connection with the Day of Atonement, 'You shall do no manner of work on that *Etzem* / 'self-same' day, for it is a day of atonement,' and in the present instance the text says, 'On the *Etzem* / 'self-same' day was Avraham circumcised.' Know then that on the Day of Atonement, Avraham our father was circumcised. Every year the Holy One, blessed be He, sees the blood of our father Avraham's circumcision, and He forgives all the sins of Israel": *Pirkei d'Rebbe Eliezer*, 29.

This 'covenant' is the eternal bond that we have with HaKadosh Baruch Hu / the Holy Blessed One, intertwining our Yechidah of soul with the Essence of the Creator. Such a bond is unconditional and transcends 'doing'; no matter what we have done at any point in our life, the essence of who we are remains pure and holy. The everlasting, unchanging Yechidah remains forever one with the Infinite Essence (There are souls who are liable, after passing away, for harsh consequences in *Gehenom* / purgatory, but our father Avraham comes and raises them up and receives them. He does not leave the circumcised behind and allow them to enter Gehenom — ואתי אברהם אבינו ומסיק להו ומקבל להו: *Eiruvin*, 19a).

Yom Kippur is the *Achas baShanah*, the singular *Etzem* / essence of time, connected to the *Achas b'Nefesh* / singular essence of soul or 'consciousness'. Yom Kippur is thus the 'Yechidah' of all space-time-soul. And it reveals our Yechidah so clearly and powerfully that our sages declare, "The Etzem of the day itself brings atonement" (*Shevuos*, 13a. *Likutei Sichos* 4, p. 1151–1152. *Sefer haMa'amarim Melukat* 4, p. 16–17). In other words, the day of Yom Kippur calls forth such a sublime, transcendent, essential light that it outshines all externalities and negativities. Whether we fully consciously participate in Yom Kippur or not makes little difference; so long as we minimally accept the transformative power of the day and do not interfere with it, we can have access to its transcendent "essence."

INSPIRATION & PERSPIRATION

Yet, if we wish to live in the consciousness of Yom Kippur each day of the year, we need to integrate the 'highs' of Yom Kippur into the 'lows' of daily mundane life. To do this, we need to fuse the inspiration above with our 'perspiration' below.

Yom Kippur itself actually includes both higher and lower aspects. On the one hand, "The essence of the day brings atonement." This implies a subtle type of *Avodah* / spiritual inner work in which one affirms there is no Avodah that has to be done, for the day itself achieves atonement for us. On the other hand, Yom Kippur is the culmination of the intense Avodah and personal development regimen begun in Elul. It is the pinnacle of our Avodah. These are both true; we *do* the Avodah of Elul in order to reach a point *beyond* Avodah. Yom Kippur is a fusion of non-doing and doing, Heaven and earth, inspiration and perspiration, "arousal from above" beyond Avodah, and "arousal from below" requiring great effort.

These categories of Avodah and beyond-Avodah are alluded to in the two verses in the Torah which mention Yom Kippur as a *Shabbos Shabbason* — a Shabbos of total rest:

1. שבת שבתון היא לכם / *Shabbas Shabbason Hee Lachem* (*Vayikra,* 16:31), which means "A total day of rest it (literally 'she') will be to you."

2. שבת שבתון הוא לכם / *Shabbas Shabbason Hu Lachem* (*Vayikra,* 23:32), which means "A total day of rest it (literally 'he') will be to you" (see the Alter Rebbe, *Likutei Torah*, Derushim L'Yom HaKippurim, 68a. See also *Chizkuni*, 16:31).

The first verse reveals a cosmic feminine quality, a passive mode of receiving, beyond all Avodah and doing — just being. The second verse reveals the cosmic masculine quality, an active mode of Avodah — intense doing. Yom Kippur joins the two into one.*

A TIME OF IMMANENCE —
A DAY OF TRANSCENDENCE

On Yom Kippur, we have the ability to become 'angelic'. It is a day of rest from acting to meet human bodily necessities. The restrictions of the day are not primarily intended to cause suffering to the body — if inflicting pain was the intention, there would be many much more effective ways of doing so (יכול ישב בחמה או בצנה כדי שיצטער תלמוד לומר / "One might have thought that one should sit in the sun or in the cold to suffer and afflict his soul; therefore the verse states...": *Yuma*, 74b). The focus of the restrictions, rather, is to cease operating exclusively in the physical sphere and ascend to an angelic state of functioning and consciousness. It is a day dedicated to achieving transcendence of the body and world, as well as of all negativity.

---

* On a symbolic level, the feminine represents receptivity, whereas the masculine represents assertiveness. This binary structure is by no means definitive or valuative, nor is it solely gender-based, as all men and women have varying degrees of masculine and feminine qualities. The feminine reflects a passive mode of sensing *Hashgachah* / Divine Providence in our lives, whereas the masculine is the mode of acting through *Bechirah* / free will. Sensing Hashgachah in our lives brings us tremendous faith and 'inspiration', whereas the function of Bechirah is our motivation for 'perspiration', actions. On Yom Kippur there is a total melding of the two into one. On this holy day we move beyond duality and dichotomies, beyond the perceived separation of inspiration and perspiration.

Alternatively, the masculine term refers to the day itself, given to us by Hashem, the "Giver," and the feminine term *Hee* refers to us. We (i.e., our sages) receive and actively reveal what the definition of rest means in the context of Yom Kippur: *Meshech Chochmah*, Acharei, 16:31. In this portrayal, the feminine is active, and the masculine (in terms of our relationship to it) is passive.

The Hebrew word for the Satan, *haSatan*, meaning 'the dividing, confining ego-consciousness', has a numerical value of 364. From this, the sages of the Gemara (*Yuma*, 20a), understood that on 364 of the 365 days of the year, we may struggle with our ego, inner division and spiritual confinement, but on one day, Yom Kippur, we are gifted the power to completely transcend all such division and limitation and exist, in fact, as a bodiless 'angel' (The simple meaning of the Gemara is that on Yom Kippur the Satan has no power to prosecute: שטן ביומא דכיפורי לית ליה רשותא לאסטוני. Alternatively, שליט להלשין בכלן חוץ מיום כפור: *Medrash Rabbah*, Bamidbar, 18:21. Yet, the Chassidic Rebbes read this Gemara somewhat out of literal context to mean that on Yom Kippur man does not struggle with his negative side: see *Be'er Mayim Chayim*, Bereishis, 18:20:2. Although note, *Tosefos haRosh*, Megilah, 31a: משום שזהו דבר שנפשו של אדם מתאוה ונכשלים בהם כל ימות השנה וגם ביום הכפורים. And *Tosefos*, ad loc: לפי שהנשים מקושטות בשביל כבוד היום לפיכך צריך להזכירם (שלא יכשלו בהן).

On Yom Kippur, we achieve self-transcendence through practices of being *Shovess* / at rest (from the root word *Shabbos*): מצות עשה לשבת ממלאכה בעשור לחדש / "There is a positive Mitzvah to 'rest' from all forms of active work on the tenth of the month" (Rambam, *Hilchos Shevisas Asor*, 1:1*).

* Even מלאכת אוכל נפש / work to prepare food, which is allowed on a regular Yom Tov, is not allowed on Yom Kippur, simply because on Yom Kippur we are not allowed to eat; we need to rest from preparing food as well. The Pasuk says, אך בעשור לחדש השביעי הזה יום הכפרים הוא מקרא-קדש יהיה לכם ועניתם את-נפשתיכם... וכל-מלאכה לא תעשו בעצם היום הזה / "Mark the tenth day of this seventh month as the Day of Atonement. It shall be a sacred occasion for you; you shall practice self-denial...you shall do no work throughout this day" (*Vayikra*, 23:27-28). Writes the Netziv, הוא טעם על איסור מלאכת אוכל נפש משום שאסור לאכול: *Ha'amek Davar*, ad loc. But on a deeper level, the reason why even מלאכת אוכל נפש / work to prepare food is not allowed is because the nature of Yom Kippur is a 'Shabbos of Shabbos', thus a day of total rest. Note the words of the Maharsha, וקדושת יום הזה הזה בגדר הז' כקדושת יום השבת

ויה"כ נקרא שבת שבתון כמו השבת משא"כ שאר י"ט שלא נקראו רק שבתון...משא"כ שאר
י"ט שלא נקראו רק שבתון... שהם קצת בדמיון ימי החול שמותר בהן מלאכת אוכל נפש ונתן
לנו יו"ט יום ז' יוה"כ שהוא בדמיון קדושת השבת שאסור בכל מלאכה וכמו שהשבת דוגמת
עוה"ב כן הוא יום הכפורים ויותר ממנו: *Yuma*, 2a. See also *Turei Even*, Chagigah,
18a: כל דטפי קדושתו מחבירו חמיר איסורו, הילכך שבת ויה"כ דקדישי טפי אסור בכל מלאכה.
Indeed, Shabbos and Yom Kippur are one, as the Rambam writes (*Hilchos
Eiruvin*, 8:10), יום הכפורים שחל להיות ערב שבת או לאחר שבת... יראה לי שהן כיום
אחד וקדשה אחת הם / "It appears to me that if a Yom Kippur that falls on the
eve of Shabbos or the day following Shabbos...they are considered to be
one day and one holiness." This is because they contain the same prohibitions: *Maggid Mishnah*, ad loc. Thus, סברת רבינו היא זו נכונה ופשוטה: *Ma'aseh
Rokeach*, ad loc. See also Rebbe Akivah Eiger, *Derush v'Chidush*, Ma'arachah 3, Shabbos, regarding whether a *Mumar* in relation to Yom Kippur is
like a Mumar who is Mechalel Shabbos and thus like a Mumar regarding
the entire Torah: See Rambam, *Hilchos Geirushin*, 3:19. Rama, *Even haEzer*,
123:5. Although a Mechalel Shabbos seems to be a 'Mumar' for a particular
reason: he denies the existence of the Creator: Rashi, *Chulin*, 5a. And since
Yom Kippur is like Shabbos, just as there is חילוק מלאכות בשבת / a division of
labor on Shabbos (if a person has unwittingly performed several prohibited
labors during one lapse of awareness, he is liable to bring one sin-offering
for each labor that he performed), similarly there is חילוק מלאכות / division of
labor on Yom Kippur: *Tzlach*, Sanhedrin, 63b. Rebbe Akivah Eiger, *Derush
v'Chidush* 2, Ma'arachah 7, Beitza. See also *Shu'T Beis haLevi*, 1, Siman
16. Although other Achronim argue: *Shu'T Mahara miPanu*, 123. *Sha'ar
haMelech*, Hilchos Shemitah v'Yovel, 1:1. Note, Yerushalmi, *Shevuos*, 3:3
(this division of labor is not the case on other Yomim Tovim: *Makos*, 21b).
Regarding the entire idea of חילוק מלאכות there are two ways to look at it. Either, it is like doing two separate transgressions (as in eating two prohibited
foods), or it is because it is like doing the same transgression, but with two
different *Gufin* / bodies (as in having relations with two separate married
women), as explored by many Acharonim. See *Marcheshes*, 1, Siman 13.
Minchas Chinuch, Mitzvah 32, Mitzvah 298. *Totzaos Chayim*, Siman 5. As
Yom Kippur is the *Achas baShanah* / Oneness within the year, it represents
the Unity within time, the *Nekudah* / essential point within the diversity,
perhaps, the חילוק מלאכות has more to do with 'separate bodies' than with
'separate transgressions' as the transgression is singular — the violation of
the oneness and unified sanctity of the day.

Practically, this means refraining from physical activities, including eating, drinking, having marital relations, and it could be said even walking or movement, represented by the prohibition against wearing leather shoes. (Without substantial shoes, we are more 'stationary' or restful.)

Many have the custom to stand as much as possible during the *Tefilos* / prayers of the day, as a way to mimic the angels, who only 'stand'. As angels are peaceful towards each other, we, too, ask forgiveness from one another. Accordingly, we wear a *Kittel* / white robe and a white *Talis* / prayer shawl during the Davening of the day in imitation of the angels who are 'enclothed' in pure immaculate white.

RATZU & SHUV / TRANSCENDING AND RETURNING

And yet, the point of all the transcendence and elevation of Yom Kippur is in the 'downward' movement — to draw inspiration down into our day-to-day lives throughout the year.

Once a year, we decisively ascend the 'mountain' of pure being, rest, and perfection, in order that when we descend back to the daily world of imperfection, we can draw from that place of purity.

The Zohar (*see Magen Avraham*, Orach Chayim, 421) says that on Yom Kippur we are asked to remind ourselves of the sons of Aharon who died on Yom Kippur "when they approached Hashem" (*Vayikra*, 16:1). They left their bodies, says the Ohr haChayim, in a spiritual state of rapture and ecstasy — a condition known as *Ratzu bli Shuv*, 'transcendence without return'. By recalling their deaths we are reminded that the most important aspect of the transcendence of Yom Kippur is to make an impression upon our everyday reality. When we soar beyond the world in Ratzu, an angelic state, we must settle back down in Shuv. The word *Shuv* comes from the same root as *Teshuvah* / return, as well as Shabbos. That is why Yom Kippur is referred to as *Shabbos Shabbason*. The purpose of Yom Kippur is to 'return'.

The דרך / *Derech* / path of wholeness requires one to be בקי / *Baki* / expert in both the modes of Ratzu and Shuv. *Baki* is numerically 112, the same value as *Yabok*, the river that Yaakov Avinu needed to 'cross over and return from. *Derech* is numerically 224, which is twice 112 — a person who is a Baki in both Ratzu and Shuv is able to always remain on the Derech, no matter if they are high or low, near or far. "Praiseworthy is one who knows how to *come and go*" (*Zohar* 2, Parshas Vayakhel, 213b).

TURNING LIABILITIES INTO ASSETS

The ultimate Teshuvah is when we can inspire a radical shift in our relationship to the past and its effect upon us, transforming all of life into a perpetual process toward a state of pure positivity in the eternal present. In the language of our sages, "The Teshuvah of love זדונות נעשות כזכויות / transforms willful transgressions into positive virtues" (*Yuma*, 86b).

There is an ancient, mystical tale that records four responses to the question of what should happen to a person when they have deviated from the true path. In the tale, 'Wisdom', 'Prophecy', 'Torah' and *HaKadosh Baruch Hu* / The Holy One Himself, are gathered in discussion. The question is raised: 'What is to be done with a person who has transgressed?'

'Wisdom' offers a wise text, from the book of *Mishlei* / Proverbs (13:21), saying, "To one who has transgressed, evil shall pursue him." 'Prophecy' replies with a prophetic text from *Sefer Yechezkel* / Book of Ezekiel (18:3), saying, "The soul who has transgressed shall perish." 'Torah' suggests a principle of Torah, saying, "Let he who has transgressed bring an offering and thereby be absolved." Finally, HaKadosh Baruch Hu rules, "If a person has transgressed, let him embrace Teshuvah and return to Me; he shall be forgiven" (*Yerushalmi*, Makos, 2:6. *Yalkut Shimoni*, Tehillim, 25, Remez 702. *Pesikta d'Rav Kehana*, Parshas Shuvah. Maharal, *Nesivos Olam*, Nesiv haTeshuvah, 1).

'Wisdom' asserts that people must reap the consequences of their actions. For every action, there is inevitably a reaction — a positive action brings about positive consequences and a negative action brings about negative consequences. In this mechanistic view, there is no way to stop what has been set in motion.

From a purely intellectual and rational perspective, everything is governed by cause and effect. Anything that exists was caused by some other force. In turn, what presently exists will cause something else to come into existence. This is an objective, logical cosmology: evil always begets evil. Wisdom, therefore, maintains that one who has done evil will be pursued by evil. If we inject negativity into this universe, it will rebound upon us. In the realm of intellect and judgment, writes Rebbe Moshe Metrani (*Beis Elokim*, Sha'ar haTeshuvah, 1:98), there is no room for Teshuvah; this is known as *Olam haDin*, the World of Judgment.

In the perspective of **Prophecy**, a person who goes against his nature simply ceases to exist. In a universe of absolute spirit, as perceived from the prophetic point of view, anything that opposes reality has no place in reality, and, as such, it vanishes.

Prophecy is a highly expansive state of consciousness connected with angelic beings, as the Rambam writes (*Yesodei haTorah*, 2:7). A prophet enters a lofty realm of reality, a mystic state undefined by time and space, human comprehension and logic. In this world of undiluted spirituality, past, present, and future merge, and the existence of evil has even less legitimacy than in the logical world of Wisdom. In fact, evil simply does not exist there — everything is only good.

In the angelic realm, beings have no free will to do evil. Therefore, if a person commits a negative act, be it by omission or commission, Prophecy maintains that there is no place for him in existence; one who entertains negativity is automatically 'deleted'. From the perspective of Prophecy, there is no alternative to goodness and no opposite to righteousness.

The perspective of **Torah** introduces a *Chidush* / innovation into the discussion of human agency and responsibility: a person who has erred can rise above causality and remove the future consequences of his mistake. He can bring a sacrificial offering and his transgression can be absolved. Divine law is founded on kindness and compassion (as in *Toras Chesed* / "a teaching of kindness"). Therefore, one who commits an improper action is able to connect to cosmic kindness, compensate for his misdeed and return his life to equilibrium through positive action.

The Torah was revealed within this world of human choice for the purpose of our refinement and elevation, even beyond the level of the angels. From the Torah's viewpoint, human beings are not, nor are we meant to be, angels. We live within the physical world even while simultaneously aspiring to rise above it. The overwhelming temptations and negative states experienced in this world are thus, in a way, understandable, and even potentially valuable. Deviation from goodness is a legitimate possibility in this realm. Anticipating this predicament, the Torah contains a host of 'soul remedies' — when something negative is done, something positive must then be brought into the picture to rectify and rebalance it; this is referred to as *Olam haChesed* / the World of Loving-Kindness.

According to this view, there is a cosmic equilibrium that must always be maintained. When the scales are tilted toward negativity, we must increase positive deeds to correct the imbalance. If one does not fulfill the desire of the Creator, he must compensate for that loss by performing a Mitzvah. 'Torah' therefore suggests that one who transgressed should bring a *Korban* / sacrificial offering, in order to re-establish spiritual balance and be absolved. Connecting to the Creator and 'giving' the Creator a positive act or Mitzvah mollifies the disconnection of a past *Aveirah* / a transgression or act of 'taking away' from the Creator's revelation of Light in this world.

Torah itself is associated with light: כי נר מצוה ותורה אור / "For a Mitzvah is a lamp, and Torah is Light" (*Mishlei*, 6:23. *Sotah*, 21a). As such, from the perspective of Torah, every action that transgresses the directives of the Torah obscures the Divine light that radiates into existence and detracts from the Divine flow that is revealed within Creation. The *Ohr Memalei* / 'permeating light' that illuminates all Creation from within is darkened and reduced by every spiritually destructive action. To replenish that inner light, one must connect with the *Ohr haSovev* / 'surrounding light' that transcends and envelopes Creation. The Mitzvah of bringing a Korban was a way to connect with this Transcendent Light and replenish the diminished *Ohr Memalei*, correcting the imbalance. Today, when there are no longer any physical sacrificial offerings, we accomplish the effects of a Korban through prayer, charity, and other Mitzvos and methods of illumination and 'self-sacrifice'.

Finally, the response of HaKadosh Baruch Hu came forth and presented the ultimate *Chidush* / novel resolution to the debate: "Let the person who has deviated embark on the path of Teshuvah and be absolved." Teshuvah not only absolves the negativity, but replenishes what was cosmically missing by drawing down a new flow of Transcendent Light. Even beyond that, Teshuvah transforms a willfully negative act into a net-positive experience. How this is so will soon be explored.

By giving us the ability to do Teshuvah, HaKadosh Baruch Hu allows negativity, albeit in a transformed state, to exist within the *Achdus Hashem* / Divine Unity. In this context, transgressions of the past become opportunities in the present for growth and development towards a better, brighter future. Teshuvah, as such, transcends conventional paradigms of cause-and-effect, and posits the seemingly miraculous: the transformation of negativity into positive energy. In fact, not just its effect but *the negative act itself* can become positive. The transgression itself can, and will, ultimately be revealed as an authentic merit. This is what awaits all Creation in *Olam HaBa*, the World that is Coming: that all is, and has been, for the Ultimate Good.

All relationships, including deeply loving ones, function in a context of duality: a 'me' and a 'you'. Our essential unity with Hashem, however, is absolute, meaning eternal and non-dual. This means there is no real possibility of ever separating from Hashem. From this perspective, what Teshuvah actually does is simply reveal our unconditional *Achdus* / unity with Hashem. We are always already One; it's just that sometimes we forget. Teshuvah reminds us of this fundamental truth.

On the path of Teshuvah, we return to who and what we truly are, the inner core of self. In doing so, we bypass all views of what should happen to someone who transgresses, until we reveal the transcendent purity that has always been present within us. We uncover the very backdrop and essence of our existence, our pure, transparent soul.

Our essence is forever innocent and pristine, untainted and unaffected by the seemingly discordant nature of the universe or even our own actions. Our deepest self and true identity is totally free of negativity; such deleterious forces simply do not and cannot exist within our soul. This is because it is ultimately one with the Light of Hashem.

In a world of systematic order, everything has its place, and when something is misplaced, there is a way to bring it back into alignment. If we have introduced a negative domino effect into our lives by means of a transgression, the Torah suggests we reassert order and put things back in their proper place. We bring an offering, compensate with a positive deed, and recreate the proper balance. However, there is a deeper world in which disorder and negativity never take hold to begin with: this is *Olam HaTeshuvah*, the world of Teshuvah.

Teshuvah is an incomparably great gift from HaKadosh Baruch Hu, and it is the gift of Yom Kippur. On this day, we are able to experience a total transcendence of all negativity. We are granted the opportunity to rise above our ego-consciousness and shine from the deepest recesses of our soul. On this day, the highest levels of Teshuvah (if we make the effort to access them) reveal the very essence of our being — the core of our soul, where negativity and spiritual disorder have no influence, or even existence.

HIGHER AND LOWER TESHUVAH

On the lower level of Teshuvah, fear is what brings us back from our wayward paths and return to Hashem and to ourselves. When, on this level, we realign with our center, our past willful transgressions are forgiven and viewed as unintentional acts. This is because if we were to revisit the past situation from the perspective of our present state, we might still be at risk of repeating our previous behavior inadvertently.

Yet, on a higher level of Teshuvah, one that is motivated by love, our desire to transform is so overwhelming and absolute that our past transgressions are utterly transformed as well, and they are turned into meritorious actions and positive virtues. They become the existential fuel for our spiritual fire, burning in passionate love for Hashem.

How can this happen? To begin with, it is precisely those past negative actions that are motivating our current deep yearning to return to who we are. The admission and regret of our negative behavior acts as a psychospiritual springboard, propelling us forward toward positive behavior in the present and future. This is the kernel of goodness and light that exists within the seemingly negative and dark aspects of ourselves and experiences of life.

Retroactively speaking, the Divine spark of goodness within the negative action has awakened in the offending individual a deeper desire to return and realign with the One. The Hebrew word for *Cheit* / misdeed is spelled *Ches-Tes-Aleph*. Seemingly, this word could be spelled without the final letter Aleph, as Aleph is silent and superfluous in terms of pronunciation. And yet, *Cheit* is spelled specifically with an Aleph. As the first letter of the Aleph-Beis, and the phonetic opening prior to all sounds, Aleph represents the First, the One, the Only — Hashem (Os*yos d'Rebbe Akivah,* Aleph). Says the Baal Shem Tov, this spelling tells us that even within a Cheit, the Aleph / *Achdus* of Hashem is present, albeit silently.

May we consciously be aware of and tap into the awesomeness of this day, the *Achas baShanah* / Oneness and Unity within the flow of time. May we attain a Teshuvah of love, and reveal the Aleph within Cheit, transforming sin into merit. May this transformation sweeten our entire life and allow us to re-discover our authentic self, our freedom, our essence. May all negativity in the world be subsumed by Divine Goodness, and reconfigured as expressions of pure goodness and life.

Chapter Two

A DAY OF ESSENCE:
BEYOND & INCLUDING BOTH FULLNESS /
EMPTINESS, SOUND / SILENCE,
DESIRE / COMPLETION

YUMA / THE DAY

THERE IS A *Mesechta* / TRACTATE OF MISHNAH AND GE-
MARA FOR ALMOST EVERY MAJOR *Yom Tov* / HOLIDAY.
THE TRACTATE THAT SPEAKS ABOUT YOM KIPPUR IS
CALLED *Yuma* / 'THE DAY'. This is quite an unusual name. For
example, the tractate for *Pesach* / Passover is called *Pesachim*,
and the tractate for Sukkos is called *Sukkah*. Why, then, is the
tractate for Yom Kippur called *Yuma* not *Yom Kippur* or *Kippurim*? (See *Chidushei Agados*, Maharsha, Yuma, 2a: מסכת זו נקראת יומא ע"ש
שיום כפורים הוא יום אחד קדוש בשנה. Note that many early Rishonim did, in fact,
call this tractate *Meseches Kippurim*: Rambam, *Hakdamah l'Mishnayos*. Rav
Sherira Gaon called it both *Seder Yuma* and *Yom haKippurim* — ותנא סדר יומא

הכיפורים יום ובתר ...משום: *Igeres Rav Sherira Gaon*. Yet, the universal title has remained *Yuma*). The deeper reason for this is that Yom Kippur is the *Achas baShanah* / the singular essence of all time. It is 'the Day' among all days of the year.

Yom Kippur is the Day of *Achas* / Unity. When the Torah opens, describing the Seven Days of Creation, the first Day of Creation is not called *Yom haRishon* / 'the First Day', rather it is called אחד יום / *Yom Echad* / "One Day" — "And it was evening and it was morning, One Day." Says Rashi, הפרשה סדר לפי היה לו לכתוב יום ראשון, כמו שכתוב בשאר הימים שני, שלישי, רביעי. למה כתב אחד / לפי שהיה הקב"ה יחיד בעולמו / "According to the regular mode of expression used in this chapter, it should be written here 'the First Day', just as it is written with regard to the other days 'the Second Day', 'the Third…', 'the Fourth…' Why, then, is it called אחד / 'One' on the First Day? Because the Holy One, blessed be He, was then the Only One in His Universe."

In other words, 'Day One' is the Day of Oneness, when only Divine Oneness was (on a revealed level) present. Today, in our present collective and individual state, in which we do not live in a 'Day One' paradigm, the day of the year that we can palpably sense this Oneness of Hashem is the Day of Atonement, or better yet, the day of At-One-ment, the Achas baShanah. Says the Medrash, יום אחד, שנתן לו הקדוש ברוך הוא, ואיזה זה, יום הכפורים / "*Yom Echad*, the 'Day One' that HaKadosh Baruch Hu gave to humanity — what day is that? It is Yom Kippur" (*Medrash Rabbah*, Bereishis, 2:3).

Yom Kippur is a state of being *Lifnei Hashem* / in front of Hashem. It is a day when there is nothing else in our experience besides being spiritual beings in the presence of the Holy Infinite Oneness.

THE עצם / ESSENCE OF THE DAY

Yom Kippur is a day of essence; it is, as it were, the Essence of the Creator revealed in the fabric of time. *Chazal* / our sages tell us עיצומו של יום / "The essence of the day brings atonement" (*Shevuos*, 13a). The day itself calls forth sublime measures of holiness and forgiveness through which all transgressions are covered over, eclipsed and forgiven. In this way, Yom Kippur reveals the essence of who we are, our pure soul, which is always 'at one' with the Creator.

Despite a debate in the Gemara over whether or not the day of Yom Kippur itself absolves one from sin even without them desiring or declaring Teshuvah, all opinions agree that the essence of the day itself brings absolution.*

---

* Even though the Halacha follows the sages, not Rebbe Yehudah, and one needs to do Teshuvah for atonement to be effective on Yom Kippur (וכפרתם לשבים: Ramban, *Vayikra*, 23:10), when one does Teshuvah, it is still the "essence" of the day that brings atonement. In the words of the Rambam, ועצמו של יום הכפורים מכפר לשבים / "The essence of the day of Yom Kippur brings atonement *for those who return*": *Hilchos Teshuvah*, 1:3. In other words, both Rebbe and the sages agree that עיצומו של יום means there is an atoning 'essence' of the day. Their debate, rather, is whether one needs Teshuvah to activate or allow the power of this essence to take effect: *Likutei Sichos*, 4, p. 1150. The sages say that the essence of the day brings atonement *with* Teshuvah. Indeed, all opinions agree that in order to achieve complete Teshuvah, one needs to actively partake in the process of Teshuvah: *Tosefos Yeshanim*, Yuma 85b. In fact, there is a Mitzvah of the Torah to arouse oneself to Teshuvah on

Yom Kippur — ומצות עשה מן התורה להעיר אדם את רוחו לחזור בתשובה ביום הכפורים:
Rabbeinu Yonah, *Sha'arei Teshuvah*, 2:14. According to the Rambam, there
is a *Chiyuv* / obligation to do Teshuvah on Yom Kippur — יום הכפורים הוא זמן
תשובה לכל ליחיד ולרבים והוא קץ מחילה וסליחה לישראל לפיכך חיבים הכל לעשות תשובה
ולהתודות ביום הכפורים: *Hilchos Teshuvah*, 2:7.

The two main components of Teshuvah are *Charatah* / regret and *Kabbalah*
/ acceptance. Indeed, when the Rambam writes about Viduy he writes כיצד
מתודין. אומר אנא השם חטאתי עויתי פשעתי לפניך ועשיתי כך וכך והרי נחמתי ובשתי במעשי
ולעולם איני חוזר לדבר זה / "How does one confess? He states, 'I implore You,
Hashem: I sinned, I transgressed, I committed iniquity before You by doing
the following...and behold, I regret and am embarrassed for my deeds. I
promise never to repeat them again' (*Hilchos Teshuvah*, 1:1). In other words,
in his confession, he speaks about *Charatah* / regret and about *Kabbalah* /
acceptance for the future, "I promise never to repeat this action again."

Yet, within the liturgy of Yom Kippur there is a lot of Charatah and *Viduy*
/ confession, but we do not mention any type of Kabbalah for our future
behavior? Here is what the Rambam writes regarding the Viduy on Yom
Kippur / הודוי שנהגו בו כל ישראל אבל אנחנו חטאנו והוא עקר הודוי "The confessional
prayer customarily recited by all is: 'For we have all sinned....' This is the essence of the confession" (*ibid*, 2:8: ונראה דלאו דוקא חטאנו לבד אלא חטאנו עוינו פשענו
שזהו עיקר הוידוי. *Lechem Mishnah*, ad loc. See also *Tur*, Orach Chayim, 607). In
other words, on Yom Kippur the Viduy is just about Charatah, nothing about
Kabbalah. So what kind of Teshuvah or Viduy is this?

The Ramban (*Devarim*, 31:17) speaks of a type of 'half' Viduy, where there
is just a Charatah: איננו וידוי גמור כענין והתודו את עונם אבל הוא ההרהור וחרטה שיתחרטו
על מעלם ויכירו כי אשמים הם / "This is not a total confession, as in 'And they shall
confess their iniquity,' rather it is a reflection and a regret. They will feel sorry
for their iniquity and recognize that they are guilty" (Indeed, elsewhere the
Ramban writes that when Adam said, גדול עוני מנשא / "My sin is to great to
bear," this was a Viduy, והנכון בפשט שהוא וידוי אמר כי עוני גדול מלסלוח: on *Bereishis*, 4:13. Although, here too there is no Kabbalah for the future).

Perhaps what the Rambam is telling us, and eventually this became the
Halachah and the way it is practiced until today, is that on Yom Kippur, all
we need in order to allow the power of Yom Kippur to take hold and bring
atonement is *Charatah* / regret. (This question will also be explored in a later

In fact, that the essence of the day itself brings atonement is the simple understanding of the *Pasuk* / verse that speaks

---

note on the topic of Viduy, with the opinions of Rebbe Akivah Eiger and the Mabit.)

The reason, perhaps, is the following. Since even according to the Sages, "The essence of the day brings atonement," on Yom Kippur it is sufficient to do the Teshuvah of Charatah. Then one is no longer attached to a negative past, and the power of the essence of the day will take hold and bring atonement.

On a deeper level, the reason for this is as follows. Yom Kippur, as will be explored in great detail, is all about unshackling oneself from the past and its negativity, to make oneself light, malleable, fluid, not weighed down or tied (to vows), angelic and free. As such, the main *Avodah* / spiritual inner work is Charatah and letting go. Only once Yom Kippur is over can we begin to think about our future, hence, the idea of Sukkos, finding our space and being in the place of our dreams. But on Yom Kippur the main idea is simply letting go, and by letting go below, we draw down and assimilate the power of the 'essence of the day' and HaKadosh Baruch Hu 'untangles' us from Above, and gifts us our freedom from the past, as in a Mikvah of time, so we can begin again.

Note the simple meaning of the Pasuk, וכל־מלאכה לא תעשו בעצם היום הזה כי יום כפרים הוא לכפר עליכם / "You shall not do work on this day, for it is a day of atonement, to atone for you," is that it is simply a day of atonement. The Tur writes that fasting is for the purpose of atonement, but he does not mention Teshuvah — והוא מאהבת הקב"ה את ישראל שלא צוה להתענות אלא יום אחד בשנה ולטובתם לכפר עונותיהם וציוה שיאכלו וישתו תחלה כדי שיוכלו להתענות ושלא להזיק להם העינוי: Tur, *Orach Chayim*, 604:1. Similarly, the simple meaning of the Pasuk, כי־ביום הזה יכפר עליכם לטהר אתכם מכל חטאתיכם לפני ה' תטהרו / "For on this day, atonement shall be made for you to cleanse you of all your sins; in front of Hashem you shall be cleansed," is that the essence of the day itself brings atonement. Yet, Rabbeinu Yonah divides the Pasuk into two: כי־ביום הזה יכפר עליכם לטהר אתכם, telling us that the day itself brings atonement on its own, but the words מכל חטאתיכם לפני ה' תטהרו refer to a Mitzvah, the Mitzvah to purify oneself on Yom Kippur through Teshuvah: *Sha'arei Teshuvah*, 4:17.

about Yom Kippur: כי־ביום הזה יכפר עליכם לטהר אתכם מכל חטאתיכם לפני ה' תטהרו / "For on this day, atonement shall be made for you to cleanse you of all your sins; in front of Hashem you shall be cleansed" (*Vayikra*, 16:30). The Pasuk says, "You *shall* be cleansed" not 'You *may* be cleansed.' This suggests that spiritual cleansing occurs on its own (see also *Aderes Eliyahu*, ibid). The argument is only whether we need to activate this dimension through participation, by desiring change, or if the day atones without any human effort whatsoever.

Every day has an inner *essence*, an עצם / Etzem, and a revealed *quality*, a גילוי / Giluy. The essence of each day of the year is exactly the same; what changes is the *quality* of the days. One day there is a special quality of Freedom (the Yom Tov of Pesach), and another day is imbued with ecstatic joy (the holiday of Purim). Yom Kippur, however, is a Yom Tov when the *essence* of the day itself is revealed, not just the *quality* of the day. It is therefore not merely a quality of atonement that is available on Yom Kippur, but rather, the essence of Yom Kippur *is* atonement. On Yom Kippur, the Giluy and the Etzem are one and the same. There is no distinction between the quality of Yom Kippur and Yom Kippur itself.

SEPARATING FROM MUNDANE 'LIFE' AND ENTERING THE MIKVAH OF HASHEM

In the Mishnah, *Meseches Yuma* begins with "Seven days before Yom Kippur the *Cohen Gadol* / High Priest is separated from his home...," and concludes with "'Rebbe Akivah says, 'fortunate are you Israel! Before whom are you purified and who purifies you? Before your Father in Heaven'…It is also written מקוה ישראל ה' / 'Hashem is the *Mikvah* (hope) of Israel' (*Yirmiyahu*, 17:13). Just as a Mikvah cleanses the impure, so does the Holy and Blessed One cleanse Israel."

This Mishna alludes to the inner reality of Yom Kippur: *Mikvah Yisrael Hashem* / "Hashem is our Mikvah, our purifying ritual bath." Additionally, on Yom Kippur, we are each given the ability to be like the *Cohen Gadol* / High Priest (as the Rambam writes, every person can reach the level of the Cohen Gadol, if he so desires*). In the image of the Cohen Gadol, we too need to separate ourselves, albeit only on Yom Kippur itself, from our "physical" attachments. We need to separate ourselves from our "home"; no eating, drinking, or physical intimacy, as we immerse in the Mikvah of 'Hashem' throughout the 26 hours of Yom Kippur.

Just like Shabbos, Yom Kippur spans pre-sunset to the next evening's nightfall. This adds up to about 25 hours. There is a Mitzvah to add a little time to Yom Kippur, both before and after the contours of the day, which is called *Tosefes Yom Kippu*r

---

* ולא שבט לוי בלבד אלא כל איש ואיש מכל באי העולם אשר נדבה רוחו אותו והבינו מדעו להבדיל לעמד לפני ה' לשרתו ולעבדו לדעה את ה' והלך ישר כמו שעשהו האלקים ופרק מעל צוארו על החשבונות הרבים אשר בקשו בני האדם הרי זה נתקדש קדש קדשים / "Not only the tribe of Levi, but each person from among all living beings, whose spirit moves him to separate himself and devote himself to the service of Hashem and to know and serve Hashem, and has walked uprightly after casting off his neck the yoke of many a cunning wile that men have contrived, is sanctified as the Holy of Holies…": *Hilchos Shemitah v'Yovel*, 13:13.

/ adding to Yom Kippur (*Rosh Hashanah*, 9a. וצריך להוסיף מחל על הקדש בכניסתו וביציאתו: Rambam, *Hilchos Shevisas Asor*, 1:6). As such, for the most part, everyone is in the state of Yom Kippur for approximately 26 hours. The number 26 corresponds to the unpronounceable Name of Hashem: Yud/10, Hei/5, Vav/6, Hei/5=26. During these hours we are totally immersed within the Mikvah of the Name 'Hashem'.

When one immerses in a Mikvah, one ceases to 'be', as it were, while underwater. Human life exists on dry land; this is where we breathe, build and blossom. Underwater, with no oxygen, we cease to breathe and act in the world, and in this sense, we cease to 'exist'. Similarly, on Yom Kippur we immerse in a Mikvah of 'time', a time capsule of 26 hours in which we separate, as it were, from the world, and transcend the 'human' activities of food, drink, physical intimacy, tending to outward appearance. We enter a spaceless space of *Ayin* / no-thingness, self-emptiness, as we silently submerge in the Transcendent Light of Hashem.

Under the Infinite 'waters' of Hashem's Presence, immersed in a Divine Mikvah-in-time, we shed our old, misaligned, tangled *Tzurah* / form and existence. We become Tzurah-less, formless and infinite. When we re-emerge from this day, and 'dress' ourselves again in the 'garments' of regular human life, we are palpably pure, clean, and unburdened.

ANGELIC REALITY

During the times of the Beis haMikdash, the only time a person was allowed to enter the Holy of Holies (besides for repairs and maintenance) was on the holiest day of the year, Yom Kippur, and only the Cohen Gadol could enter. This is the most private, intimate moment of the yearly cycle, being at one with the One, in the singularity of the holiest space at the holiest time of the year.

Speaking of the entry into the Holy of Holies by the Cohen Gadol on Yom Kippur, the Torah says, וכל אדם לא יהיה באהל מועד / "And there shall be *no man* in the Tent of Meeting when he goes in to make atonement in the holy place…" (*Vayikra*, 16:17). Asks the Medrash (*Medrash Rabbah, Vayikra*, 21:12), וכהן גדול לא אדם היה / "Is not the High Priest a man?" The verse says, "there shall be *no man*," yet the Cohen Gadol is an אדם / *Adam* / man.

The Medrash also recounts that when the Cohen Gadol would enter the Holy of Holies, he would be transformed; his face would burn like flames, and he would take on the appearance of an angel (בשעה שהיה רוח הקדש שרוי עליו היו פניו בוערות כלפידים עליו, הדא הוא דכתיב כי שפתי כהן ישמרו דעת וגו׳: *Vayikra Rabba*, 21. See also *Moed Katan*, 17a).

At the peak of the Yom Kippur service, the Cohen Gadol was no longer (an ordinary) אדם / *Adam* / man. Their *Tzurah* / form of an Adam — a human being with failings — had been shed. As he entered the Holy of Holies, he also entered his own deepest, most inward place and lost all attachment to external forms. His nature as an Adam was transcended, and he existed as a pure, transparent angel, as it were.

Actually, as taught in the *Yerushalmi* / Jerusalem Talmud, the Cohen Gadol became even more than an angel on Yom Kippur: והכתיב כל־אדם לא־יהיה באהל מועד בבאו לכפר בקודש עד־צאתו. אפילו אותן שכתוב בהן ודמות פניהם פני אדם לא יהיה באהל מועד / "'And there shall be no man in the Tent of Meeting when he goes in to make atonement in the holy place, until his departure....' This means that even angels may not be present, even those who have a human appearance" (*Yerushalmi, Yuma,* 5:2). An angel is a conduit, an intermediary between Heaven and earth, moving pure spirit into matter, and vice versa. But on Yom Kippur, the Cohen Gadol attained a level beyond both man and angel: *Deveikus* / unity with HaKadosh Baruch Hu, without any barrier, intermediary, or movement.

Divested of any sense of separation, the Cohen Gadol experienced deep spiritual intimacy with the Creator. This is one reason the Kodesh HaKodashim is referred to as חדר המטות / the Bedroom (*Melachim* 2, 11:2. Rashi, Radak, *ad loc.* In general, the Beis haMikdash is called 'the Bed' — הנה מטתו, זה בית המקדש: *Tanchuma,* Nasso, 9. *Yevamos,* 109b, Rashi, *ad loc:* מטתו בית המקדש). This image suggests holy marital intimacy, which is an act that is performed without any physical barriers, garments, or even mental or spiritual divisions (*Kesuvos,* 48a. *Tikkunei Zohar,* Tikkun 58). In the same manner, the Cohen Gadol was divested of any spiritual 'garments' between himself and the Infinite Beloved. Nothing 'else' was present, not even himself as a human or angelic entity. His essence, his core above, beyond, and within all his manifest qualities, was revealed. In the essence of time and space, the essence of soul was intimately embraced within the Essence of the Creator.

יצא ובא לו בדרך בית כניסתו, ומתפלל תפלה קצרה בבית החיצון / "He then exits and comes out the way that he entered. And he recites a brief prayer in the outer chamber" (Mishnah, *Yuma*, 5:1). In the Kodesh HaKodashim there is no prayer to be uttered. The Cohen Gadol has so transcended his humanness that there is no longer any room for self, nor words, nor even an expression of the desires of Klal Yisrael. Only once he exits that space of Infinite Oneness, can he utter a short prayer. Only when he leaves the Holy of Holies does his humanness return to him, and then he is able to pray and break the silence of perfect transcendence. Only then is he able to re-enter the world of *Cheser* / lack and need, the world of prayer.

ESSENCE: BEYOND ANGELIC TRANSCENDENCE, YET INCLUDING HUMAN LACK

On the deepest level, Yom Kippur is simply Essence, beyond being and non-being, silence and sound, completion and lack, perfection and imperfection. Yet being beyond all opposites, Essence also includes all opposites. In this sense, Essence may be called 'Inclusive Transcendence'.

On a practical level, we can only become 'aware' of our essence by 'being' our essence. Our essence is not a separate phenomenon nor a part of us to which we relate; it is *who we really are*. However, in order to be experientially aware that we are the essence of our being, we often need to stop 'doing' and just 'be'. This is why we do not eat or drink, and so forth, on Yom Kippur.

On Yom Kippur, the holy Torah says we are לפני ה' / *Lifnei Hashem* / "in front of Hashem." This also means 'before Hashem', in the sense of being 'prior to' or 'beyond' the Name Hashem. Like the Cohen Gadol in the Kodesh haKodashim, on Yom Kippur we reach beyond all our names, external functions and revealed qualities. We return to and become again our essence, prior to our name.

To explain: every גילוי / *Giluy*, particular revealed quality, has a name. A table is called 'a table' because the formation of the pieces of wood functions for us as a 'table'. We may call someone 'kind', or 'charming'; these are qualities of the person, but they are not the person in himself. A person's name is really only needed in the context of interpersonal relationships, where an external point of reference is needed to identify them and call their attention. The person himself, when all alone, does not need a name, and in a sense, does not have a name.

Similarly, when two long-time spouses are spending time together, they do not necessarily call each other by name. In a sense, they may not always view each other as a separate individual with separate qualities or descriptions. They are a 'we', with no perceptual distance between them.

The Ineffable, Infinite Name of Hashem refers to the Infinite 'quality' of Hashem, as it were; it does not 'describe' Hashem in

Himself. Each Name of Hashem represents what is being re-vealed to us; each indicates a particular Divine attribute. They are all in the world of Giluy. Hashem's Essence is 'before' or beyond His Names, his *Giluyim* / revelations. On Yom Kippur, we stand in our own essence, in a posture of לפני ה' / *Lifnei Hashem*, 'before' or beyond all *Giluyim* — in the infinite light of 'We', the Oneness of עצם / *Etzem* / Divine Essence.

KESER: THE SPACE THAT MAINTAINS THE PARADOX OF BEING AND NON-BEING

ועשרת הימים שבין ראש השנה ליום הכפורים ירמוז לעשר ספירות / "And the ten days between (and including) Rosh Hashanah and Yom Kippur, represent the Ten *Sefiros* / Divine attributes." These are the words of the great sage, the Ramban, Rabbeinu Moshe ben Nachman of the 13th Century (Ramban, *Vayikra*, 23:24). These Se-firos are like 'screens' through which the Infinite Light of the Creator penetrates and flows into finite Creation.

The system of the Sefiros is visualized as a sort of 'tree' with a right-left-middle column structure. The 'right column' Sefiros (*Chochmah* / Wisdom or Intuition. *Chesed* / Lovingkindness and Giving. *Netzach* / Victory and Perseverance) are forces of giving, expanding, and reaching out. The 'left column' Sefiros (*Binah* / Understand-ing, Reason or Analysis, *Gevurah* / Strength or Restriction. *Hod* / Humility or Compromise) are qualities of receiving, restricting, and mov-ing inward. The 'middle column' of Sefiros (*Da'as* / Knowledge or Awareness, *Tiferes* / Balance or Compassion, *Yesod* / Foundation or Connec-tion) balances between the characteristics of the right and left paradigms.

The first Sefirah is *Keser* / Crown or Desire, visualized as the highest point of the middle column. It is the highest root of all manifestations, the transcendent 'space' that includes, balances, and maintains the right and left sides of the "tree" and all its fruitful paradoxes.

According to the Ramak, Rebbe Moshe Cordevero, the famed *Mekubal* / Kabbalist, the progression of the Ten Days and corresponding Sefiros is from the lowest level to the highest level, and thus, on the tenth day, Yom Kippur, the Sefirah is Keser (*Siddur*, Pirush al Seder Avodas Yom haKippurim, Os 16. See also Shaloh, *Asarah Hilulim*, Os 7. The first day of the Ten Days corresponds to Malchus, as Rosh Hashanah is Malchus, and the tenth day of the month, Yom Kippur, to Keser. The Tzemach Tzedek, *Ohr haTorah*, Shabbos Shuvah, writes that the two days of Rosh Hashanah are Chochmah and Binah. The seven middle days are the emotional Sefiros, from Chesed to Malchus, and Yom Kippur is Keser).

Yom Kippur is characterized by the phrase, לפני ה' / *Lifnei Hashem* / "before Hashem." In terms of the four letters of the Name *Hashem* (Yud-Hei-Vav-Hei), the Yud corresponds to Chochmah. The upper Hei is Binah. The Vav is the six emotional Sefiros, from Chesed until Yesod. The final Hei corresponds to Malchus. In this way, *Lifnei Hashem*, means 'before the Four Letters and their corresponding Sefiros' — referring to Keser. The realm 'before' the Name, is the Crown and *Etzem* / Essence of Reality (See the Rebbe, *Basi leGani*, Chaf Tes).

BEING ETZEM

On Yom Kippur, the Cohen Gadol attains and reveals the state of Etzem, a state in which human and angelic postures are maintained simultaneously. As a human being, the Cohen Gadol is attached to this world and all its lack, and therefore prays for the atonement and betterment of Creation. As an 'angel', he is utterly detached from all the mundane qualities of this world, and blends into a world of perfect silence and perfection. Etzem is what unites these opposites.

The Mishnah says, "Seven days before Yom Kippur, the Cohen Gadol is separated from his home." The Sages interpret the term 'his home' as 'his wife'. "Rebbe Yehudah says: The Sages designate another wife for him lest his wife dies, as it is stated in the Torah, "And it will atone for him and for his house." In other words, it is imperative that the Cohen Gadol be a married man, and at no point on Yom Kippur may he be unmarried.

One's spouse represents one's home, one's groundedness, the fullness and structure of their own human-ness. So on the one hand, he is separated from his wife and is 'not at home', and on the other hand, he must be married, and therefore connected to his 'home'. He needs to fast and refrain from food, drink, and spousal relations, and yet, he must also be married and pray even about the weather. Throughout the Avodah of Yom Kippur, the Cohen Gadol needs to be both "no-man" and every-man. He needs to be both 'before' the Name Hashem, in Keser — and at the same time 'in front of Hashem' as a 'man', a separate individual, in Malchus. He must be detached, beyond the world, like an Angelic presence, yet he needs to be attached to every human being to pray for their ultimate good. He needs to be immersed in the Divine as in a Mikvah, underwater, as it were — and yet, standing strong on dry land. And so must *we* be, on this most holy of days.

Yom Kippur is the perfect expression of Etzem, and its paradoxical integration of all opposites. On Yom Kippur we can sense the utter transcendence within the immediacy of the moment, the Infinite Light shining through our all-too-human mind and heart.

Chapter Three

THE YIRAH / AWE & AWESOMENESS OF YOM KIPPUR

THE DAYS OF ROSH HASHANAH AND YOM KIPPUR, THE HIGH HOLIDAYS, ARE KNOWN AS *Yamim Noraim* / DAYS OF AWE, ALTHOUGH THE ACTUAL TERM *Yamim Noraim* / ימים נוראים IS POST-TALMUDIC. While this term is not used by Chazal, it appears during the early period of the Rishonim, in the 12th Century (The Ra'avyah / ראבי״ה, Rebbe Eliezer ben Yoel haLevi (Bonn, 1140–1225) speaks about ימים נוראים: *Ra'avyah*, Berachos, Siman 39:1. Note, *Tanchuma*, Vayishlach, 2). To understand what the phrase *Yamim Noraim* refers to, we have to delve into what נורא / *Nora* / 'awesome' means, and what it means to be 'in awe.'

Many may assume that the reference to awe indicates that the High Holy Days require a type of 'fear' — since this is the Time of Divine Judgment — that we should have awe and fear about what our judgment will be. This is not invalid, and it may be the experience of many people. Yet, fear of being judged unfavorably is somewhat shallow spiritually, as it is based on an egoic perception of life and egoic anxieties. The truth is, over-emphasizing this type of fear is actually negative, stifling, and depressing, and it ultimately demonstrates a lack of *Emunah* / faith and trust. If so, why did many great *Tzadikim* / exalted souls speak of being paralyzed and unable to move a muscle in Davening on the Days of Awe? It was certainly not from fear of having a 'bad' year, as they would have been ready to give up their lives for HaKadosh Baruch Hu, and their deepest pleasure would be to serve Hashem under any conditions, 'good' or 'bad'. Insofar as a difficult coming year did not faze them, what does 'fear' or 'awe' mean to these Tzadikim?

WHAT IS AWE?

Forty days before Yom Kippur, the first day of Elul, is the beginning of the Days of Awe. On this day, says an old Yiddish expression, the 'winds of Elul' begin to blow and awe is palpable in the air. Forty is a powerful number that reminds us of both repentance and revelation. Moshe was up on the mountain for 40 days to receive the first set of *Luchos* / tablets, and 40 days for the second set as well. During the 40 days of the Yamim Noraim, we strive to receive the revelation that results from true repentance and authentically 'turning around' to face our lives and to face HaKadosh Baruch Hu. During these days, we open our hearts, minds, and souls, and stand before Hashem, humble, raw, and vulnerable.

But what does all this have to do with awe? 'Awe', in this context, refers to a moment when you stop being defined by or contained within your limited self, and you enter into a state of being that is much larger and more expansive. Let's say you chance upon a magnificent sunset, and your eyes become so entranced by the indescribable beauty that you become immobilized and speechless. In that moment, before you attempt to conceptualize why you are feeling awestruck, and before your rational brain can make sense of the experience, you are completely lost in the majesty of the sunset. The Yamim Noraim induce this type of awe. It is a time when we become lost in a reality that is much bigger than our personal self. It is an experience of sensing the numinous mystery of being in the presence of the Ineffable. It is being existentially overwhelmed by the unfathomable immensity and luminosity of the All-Sovereign Creator.

If you were walking along an unfamiliar forest path and suddenly the trees parted, revealing a sheer thousand-meter sea cliff and a vast, panoramic view, your hair might stand on end or your knees might begin to buckle from the beauty or imposing expanse. You might step back in awe. Only once you have found a stable place to sit and settle your nerves might you then begin to delight in the subtlety of the scene, but at this moment, your conventional sense of self is absent. Similarly, *Yirah* / awe and wonder result from an experience of the shockingly vast panorama of the Divine Presence.

There is יראת שמים / *Yiras Shamayim* / 'fear of Heaven', and there is יראת הארץ / *Yiras haAretz* / 'earthly fear'. Yiras haAretz is a fear of being punished or threatened in relation to matters of the earth and the earthly self. Yiras Shamayim is 'awe of Heaven', of Hashem's Infinite Presence (*Aderes Eliyahu*, Bereishis, 1:1,4). The lower Yirah, as Rabbeinu Yonah explains (on *Mishlei*, 2:5), is based on reward and punishment, whereas the higher Yirah is based on the soul sensing the awesomeness of Hashem and His limitless power. The experience is standing before vast Mystery, in the presence of the Infinite One. We tremble from this, and yet we are fascinated by it; we recoil from the immensity of this presence, yet counterintuitively feel attracted to it and pulled forward into it.

Unresolved or subconscious fears can cause a person to grasp at objects and at the earthly ego itself. When these self-preservation instincts are enfolded within a relationship to Hashem, they are called *Yiras haAretz*. For example, someone installs Mezuzos because they are afraid of robbers, or someone starts wearing Tefillin because they are afraid of losing their income. There is obviously nothing wrong with these reactions; indeed, the 'by-product' of performing Mitzvos does protect us, and Hashem's will was done in the Mitzvah, no matter the motivation. However, *Yiras Shamayim* means releasing instinctual self-preservation strategies and earthly anxieties within the Heavenly majesty of Creation and the Creator. This is the experience of losing yourself in the vast, overwhelming Presence of HaKadosh Baruch Hu.

The illusory thought that somehow one can control every situation is in fact the root of all one's fear. The idea that one can control life at all is the fruit of the ego's twisted root, a threatening sense of separation from life and from the Source of Life. All control really belongs to Hashem, the Master and Guide of the Universe. The deeper we see our fear for what it is, the more it dissolves into awe, surrender, and loss of self within the Divine Guidance. This is *Yirah Ila'ah* / higher Yirah. In the words of the Maharal (*Nesivos Olam*, Nesiv Yiras Hashem, 1), "Yirah means to make oneself as if he did not exist." Higher Yirah is the sensation of the collapse of the ego.

Awe descends at the moment that we surrender the self in an *aha* (or 'awe-ha') moment. At that moment, there is very little self-awareness. There is only the sense that HaKadosh Baruch Hu is here, holding us and giving us space.

Higher Yirah is the awareness that we are held and upheld by Divine love alone, that the Creator has carved out a space, as it were, for us to exist. The Creator makes for us a *Makom* / space in this world, and without it, we have no place. When Moshe asks Hashem to show him His Face, so to speak, to show him His Essence or Inwardness, Hashem tells him, "You cannot see My Face," but, הנה מקום אתי / "There is a place with Me...station yourself there...and you will see My Back" (Shemos, 33:21–23). Says Rashi, יש מקום מוכן לי לצרכך שאטמינך שם שלא

תזוק ומשם תראה מה שתראה / "There is a destined *Makom* / space prepared for you by Me for your sake. You can hide here and not be hurt, and can see what you can see." Hashem tucks us away and places His hand over us, so-to-speak, so our existence is not overwhelmed by the Infinite Light or simply the intensity of life itself. We are tenderly protected, yet the experience of this Divine intimacy and care stimulates great awe.

To see the Divine "Back" means to perceive the Infinite One's expression, the Divine Presence or Divine providence within life and history, *in retrospect*. This, too, is a form of protection; if we were to see Divine providence and perfection in everything unfiltered and as it unfolds in the moment, it could be too much for our minds to bear. We might not be able to retrieve our sense of individuality, choice, agency or productivity. Therefore we predominantly see Divine providence when we 'look back'. HaKadosh Baruch Hu exposes us only to the amount of awe that is beneficial to us.

Yiras Shamayim is life-sustaining, for after losing our individual self in nearness to Hashem, we are given the space to be ourselves. Earthly, lower fear, by contrast, is life-threatening, feeling that we are losing our footing or retreating from life, like we have no place, no shelter. When we view such responses honestly, we can see they are mostly imaginary, fake, or unnatural. Earthly fear is debilitating, and devastating to one's health and wellbeing. It feels intrusive and invasive. Yiras Shamayim is invigorating, grounding, liberating and expansive, even when we are filled with sacred trepidation.

Rebbe Yonasan Eibshutz, speaks about this form of *Yirah* / awe, its innate nature and thus its life-giving nature: כי יותר שמתחיל ביראת השם יותר יוסיף לירא את השם כי אין קץ לגדולתו ובכל זה לא יחלה ולא יגיע במדרגת מרה שחורה או שום בלבול בדעתו וכדומה אדרבה יהיה כולו מחמדים ואהוב ומיושב בדעתו וזה כי ביראה כזו בחר הנפש וזהו טבעו של אדם ולכך נוצר ועל דבר זה נכרת ברית טבע הבריאה ולכך הטבע מסייעתו משא"כ ביראה של שטות שאין הטבע הוסד לכך א"כ עושה דבר נגד טבעו ולכך יצר לו ויחלש כחו וזהו מאמר הפסוק (משלי י' כז) יראת ה' לא תחליש רק תוסיף ימים ואדרבה תחזיק גופו ותוסיף לו בריאות / "The more one sets out (on the path) of awe of Hashem, the more he will *continue* to be in awe of Hashem, for there is no end to His greatness. (And by engaging in awe) he will not make himself sick, nor descend into melancholy or mental confusion, etc. To the contrary, he will be (in a state of) affection and love, and mentally settled. This is because our soul has chosen (the path of) awe — this is the nature of a person and for this we were created. A covenant was made with the inner nature of Creation, and this is why nature will always help one (in this path). This is not the case with the nonsensical (worldly) fear. Nature was not founded on that. Therefore, if one does something against his nature, against the way he was created, his strength weakens. And this is the meaning of *Mishlei*, 10:27 — יראת ה' תוסיף ימים / 'Awe of Hashem adds to one's days….' Awe never weakens a person; it only adds to his life. And furthermore, it strengthens his body and increases his health" (*Ya'aros Devash*, 4:6).

Normal fear causes a contraction of life. People get literally sick from fear. Living in fear, anxiety or paranoia eventually shortens one's life. By stark contrast, Yiras Shamayim increases the life force in us. This is because through awe, we become less egoic, making more 'room' for the Divine life force to expand in us, which prolongs both our lifespan, and our 'length of days' or quality of life.

THE AWESOMENESS OF YOM KIPPUR

The ultimate experience of awe, self-negation and self-transcendence is to be touched by Infinity, and to sense the palpable Presence of HaKadosh Baruch Hu, the holy 'Other'. When we are *Lifnei Hashem* / in front of our Creator, we feel real 'awe' (*Toldos Aharon*, Re'eh). This is the deeper sensation of *Yirah* / awe that we experience during these days: "Everyone feels this *Pachad* / urgency and trembling, during these days" (*Yosher Divrei Emes*, 52). It is the experiential practice of *Shivisi Hashem* / placing yourself before Hashem, literally and viscerally.

Imagine the awe you would experience if you were to stand in front of an all-powerful king, in all his glory, and in whose hand was life or death. Your senses would become sharp; your mind and attention would become clear; your entire Gestalt would become centered, present, alive and focused. Admittedly, this metaphor is hard to understand for modern people, as we have not experienced royalty in this sense. Similarly, the modern mind struggles with simple Yirah, reverence for another, and sadly even respect for others. Nevertheless, we can try to imagine living 1,000 years ago, when absolute monarchy was the way of rule. Just for a moment, picture yourself living in a small, impoverished town, and one day you are granted an audience with the resplendent king, the absolute ruler, in whose hands is your very life and livelihood. Try to feel the awe, the trepidation, the hyper-vigilance, and the instinctive urge to honor him.

This is a mere *Mashal* / metaphor of what it means to stand in the Presence of the King of Kings, the Infinite Power of the Creator of all life. If you truly sense this *Kirvas Hashem* / proximity to the Infinite, everything suddenly changes; you are overwhelmed yet electrified, focused and ready to serve. Your limitations drop away, your self-oriented narrative is silenced, your ego falls away, and you cannot even move from your own initiative, as you are absorbed in the existential embrace of the Unmoved Mover.

On these Days of Awe, all superficiality and ego is shed, and our raw, inner self can emerge. Yom Kippur is the peak of this process, the day when we must let go and allow all trivial pursuits to fall away. In this induced state of awe, nothing matters any longer but being close to HaKadosh Baruch Hu, the Sovereign and Essence of All Existence.

For this reason, Yom Kippur can be the most existentially challenging day of the year. It is a day when we are invited and given strength to open into our essence, stripped from superficial ego and petty attachments. If we allow, Yom Kippur temporarily 'deletes' all of the external qualities of our life, and everything that is not technically necessary to our existence on this day, such as food, drink, possessions and power. We are then able to deeply reflect and consider: who or what is left when everything that can be deleted has been deleted? On this day, we intensively ask ourselves, 'Who am I before my Creator?'

As higher Yirah is the absence of self, the loss of egoic, observing self, it may serve us well to ponder and imagine that today, on Yom Kippur, is the last day of your lives. In these final moments, what would we hold onto and what would we let go of? What is fundamental to your identity? What is essential to your existence? Who are you really?

NEXT YEAR IN YERUSHALAYIM

At the end of this day-long meditation, as Yom Kippur comes to a close, we blow the Shofar one last time and declare, *L'Shanah haBa'ah b'Yerushalayim* / "Next year in Jerusalem!"* After the entire process of Rosh Hashanah and Yom Kippur, we conclude with firm resolve and Emunah that this coming year will be good, as it always already is, right now. The new year begins at this very moment.

almost alwaysIt is significant that the word *Yerushalayim* is the congregation's final exclamation on Yom Kippur. Yerushalayim is the eternal city, the eye of the world. The Torah tells us that Malki-Tzedek (who was actually Shem, the son of No-

---

* Note that the word *Shofar* in numerical value is 586, the same value as the word ירושלם, which is ירושלים without the Yud, the way *Yerushalayim* is almost always written in Tanach, as for example ויהי כשמע אדני־צדק מלך ירושלם: *Yehoshua*, 10:1. *Esther*, 2:6.

ach) first named this city, of which he was king, "Shalem." Following this, Avraham named the city in reference to the place of the Akeidah, "*Hashem Yireh* / the Infinite will see" (*Bereishis*, 22:14). So now this city had two names, "Said the Holy One, blessed be He, 'If I call the place 'Yireh' like Avraham did, the righteous Shem will complain. However, if I refer to it as 'Shalem', the righteous Avraham will complain. Rather, I will call it 'Yeru-shalayim', and that name will combine the ways it was called by both of them: *Yirah-Shalem*'" (אברהם קרא אותו יראה,

שנאמר: ויקרא אברהם שם המקום ההוא ה' יראה. שם קרא אותו שלם, שנאמר ומלכי צדק מלך שלם, אמר הקדוש ברוך הוא אם קורא אני אותו יראה כשם שקרא אותו אברהם, שם אדם צדיק מתרעם, ואם קורא אני אותו שלם, אברהם אדם צדיק מתרעם, אלא הריני קורא אותו ירושלים כמו שקראו שניהם, יראה שלם, ירושלים :*Medrash Rabbah*, Bereishis, 56:10).

Yirah Shalem also means 'Complete Awe', implying the higher, deeper form of Yirah as explored above. At the end of the process that began on Rosh Hashanah and culminates on Yom Kippur, we proudly and triumphantly declare that we have attained *Yirah Shalem*, and in the coming year we will live in this state. Furthermore, living with Yirah Shalem, we will be living 'spiritually' in *Yerushalayim*. And in this way, G-d willing, we will merit to live in Yerushalayim physically as well, in the rebuilt holy city, the lower Yerushalayim of brick and mortar, which mirrors the higher Yerushalayim (*Ta'anis*, 5a), speedily in our days.

We have a choice: we can live in fear and apprehension over the unknowable future, plagued by uncertainty and racked with anxiety, or we can live in awe and surrender to HaKadosh

Baruch Hu's plans and live in wonder from moment to moment. Having gone through the process of these ten days of Teshuvah, primed by the preceding month of Elul, we have made this choice and transformed any egoic fear of the unknown into mighty awe within the Transcendent Source of Life. Thus, we proclaim, 'This coming year, we will be in *Yerushalayim* / complete higher Yirah!'

Shalem also means *Shalom* / peace and wholeness. Therefore, we proclaim that in this coming year, our lower Yirah and anxieties will become elevated, allowing us to reside in the *Shalom* / peace and wholeness of Yiras Hashem.

This final Shofar blast was also the signal of the beginning of a *Yovel* / Jubilee year. At the moment the Shofar was heard, the slaves or indentured servants would go free and return home. A piece of land, too, would revert to its original owner. For us today, this blast signals our freedom from servitude to limited images of what should or should not be. Ultimately, it signals our "freedom from sin" (הוא סימן חירות...חירות מעבירות הגופות: *Levush*, Orach Chayim, 623:5). With this blast, our apprehension about our future disappears, and the chains of lower fear fall away forever. We can live fearlessly and sinlessly, as we have returned to our 'original', true Owner.

May we merit to experience the literal meaning of the words "Next year in Yerushalayim," with the revealing of Moshiach and the building of the Beis haMikdash, soon, in our lifetimes.

Chapter Four

BUMPING UP AGAINST THE IMMANENCE OF DEATH

O N YOM KIPPUR THERE IS A CUSTOM TO WEAR WHITE GARMENTS, SUCH AS A WHITE *Kittel* / ROBE, AT LEAST DURING THE *Tefilos* / PRAYERS OF THE DAY. Commenting on the *Shulchan Aruch* / "the Code of Jewish Law," the Rama writes: נהגו ללבוש בגדים לבנים ונקיים ביוה"כ דוגמת מלאכי השרת וכן נוהגין ללבוש הקיטל שהוא לבן ונקי גם הוא ונקי גם הוא בגד מתים ועי"ז לב האדם נכנע ונשבר / "The custom is to wear white, clean clothes on Yom Kippur, in the likeness of the ministering angels. And the custom is to wear the Kittel, which is white and clean. And it is also the garment in which a person is buried, and thus (while wearing it) the heart of man is humbled and broken open" (*Shulchan Aruch*, Orach Chayim, 610:4).

Essentially, there are two reasons for wearing white: a) we affirm that our soul is like an 'angel', pure and clean of negativity and sin, and b) we remind ourselves of our death when our body will be wrapped in a white shroud, in order to stimulate remorse and to humble the ego. These two reasons can also be seen as the two dominant themes and perspectives of Yom Kippur.

The Shulchan Aruch writes (*Orach Chayim*, 610:4), נוהגים בכל מקום להרבות נרות בבתי כנסיות ולהציע בגדים נאים בבית הכנסת / "We are accustomed, in all regions, to increase candles in synagogues and spread nice fabrics in the synagogue." These practices suggest festivity (Indeed, נשים מקושטות בשביל כבוד היום: Tosefos, *Megilah*, 31a). On the other hand, the Rama writes that every person should light a "soul candle" for Yom Kippur: גם נר נשמה לאביו ולאמו שמת / "also a candle for a mother or father who has passed away" (Rama in the name of the *Kol-Bo*, since Yom *haKippurim*, 'atonements' in the plural, means atonement of both the living and the deceased), and doing so reminds us of our own mortality. Again, this reinforces this dual dynamic of Yom Kippur: on the one hand, we are festively celebrating our 'angelic' transcendence, our eternal pure soul, and on the other, we are humbly contemplating our limitations and our mortality.

Yom Kippur is a day of forgiveness, this is clear from the Torah. The question is how should we enter this day, and what mindset will allow us to align ourselves with it? Are we to think of ourselves as ever-pure, 'angelic' souls, transcending sin — or should we think of ourselves as limited, fallible and mortal in order to stimulate remorse for our sins? Which of these opposites are the Mitzvos and customs of Yom Kippur supposed to provoke in us? These questions will help clarify the deeper nature of Yom Kippur. For now, let us explore the focus on mortality.

DEATH PRACTICES

Without going into the details of the prohibitions of Yom Kippur, we refrain from eating and drinking, washing, wearing leather shoes, and anointing ourselves. Couples also refrain from physical intimacy and the act of procreation. Each of these prohibitions can be understood as symbols of dying. In the process of departing from this world, a person naturally stops eating and drinking, stops washing, walking around, treating or perfuming their skin and hair, and procreating.

Fasting from foods and liquids is one of the most visceral symbols of dying. The difference between fasting one day and fasting one hundred days (and literally dying) is merely a quantitative difference, not a qualitative one. Fasting is essentially a miniature form of death, and can feel a little bit like dying. In this way, refraining from the five 'life-promoting' activities makes us face, in quite a palpable way, the fickle and transient nature of our lives. The five prohibitions are a 'death practice', as it were, in which you 'ritually', contemplatively, and viscerally sacrifice yourself, meaning let go of your life as a limited individual self so that you can be regenerated anew in the highest way (In fact, the Mekubalim also write that the Akeidah, the ultimate self-sacrifice and demonstration of a willingness to die, occurred on Yom Kippur: *Rekanti, Asarah Ma'amaros. Yalkut Reuveni*).

Other practices leading up to Yom Kippur also induce consciousness of the fickleness of corporal life and the transient nature of our existence.

Many have the custom of performing *Kaparos* / 'Atonements' over a live chicken. This *Minhag* / custom, which originated in the times of the Geonim (גם שמעתי כי נשאל לרבינו האיי גאון ז"ל ואמר שכן נהגו: *Teshuvos haRashba*, 1, 395), is followed by Ashkenazim who adhere to the ruling of the Rama and follow the teachings of the Arizal, as will be later explored. Basically, a man buys and takes a rooster in his hands, and a woman a hen, and they circle the bird over their head while reciting a short *Tefillah* / prayer. Following this, the bird is ritually slaughtered, preferably in front of the person who performed the ritual, and the meat is given to charity.

In Medieval Europe, before the industrial food revolution, the bird that was taken for Kaparos was most probably one that you raised yourself or saw your neighbor raising in your own back yard or local coop. In this way, there was some level of personal connection between you and the bird. Either you fed and protected it, or knew the person who did. The slaughter would, in this way, be felt quite personally. Today as well, the intention of Kaparos is for you to take personally the immediacy of death. In one moment, you vividly feel the aliveness of the animal in your hand, an animal you 'know' and own, and in the next moment, it is being slaughtered.

This subtle 'brush with death' is meant to inspire you to Teshuvah, to refocus your life and think about what really matters in life. In the words of the Rama, עי"ז לב האדם נכנע ונשבר / "... and through that, the heart of man is humbled and broken open." You are supposed to feel pained or disturbed by the sensation of holding a living being that is pulsating and flapping about, and then, the next minute, seeing its head removed. This should make us shudder, breaking us out of our spiritual stupor and complacency, and awaken us to Teshuvah and a deeper way of living.

As such, Kaparos is not, *Chas v'Shalom* / Heaven forbid, a 'superstitious" act, where you do one act and hope for an unrelated reaction due to some magical power. Rather, there is deep symbolic and innate value in this personal encounter with death. The holy Arizal speaks of the four kinds of capital punishment that were once in effect for severe sins. The penalty of *Sekilah* ("stoning") is symbolically invoked when the chicken is placed on the ground and one tosses a handful of dirt or pebbles in its direction. When the *Shochet* / slaughterer holds the chicken down by its neck, this symbolizes the capital punishment of *Chanikah* / choking. When the Shochet cuts through the neck, it symbolizes the punishment of *Hereg* / beheading. Finally, the penalty of *Sereifah* / burning occurs when the chicken is cooked and eaten by the poor. We should contemplatively receive these four forms of capital punishment — and the atonement that they were meant to bring — by fully identifying with our chicken. We need to think, 'That should have been me.' This morbid thought is meant to sharpen us and awaken us to Teshuvah.

ויש מקומות שנוהגין לילך על הקברות / "There is a custom to go visit a gravesite on Erev Yom Kippur," the Rama also writes (*Orach Chayim*, 605:1), as is the custom to kindle a special flame on Erev Yom Kippur for the souls of our departed loved ones, a candle that will burn throughout the entire day of Yom Kippur (*ibid*, 610:4). These practices force us to take stock of our lives and look at ourselves and the way we are living, with honesty and openness.

Before Yom Kippur enters, there is a custom to immerse oneself in a Mikvah (Rosh, *Yuma*, 8:24. *Shibbolei haLeket* 283. *Manhig*, 52. Tosefos, *Berachos*, 22b. *Tur, Shulchan Aruch*, Orach Chayim, 606:4. Perhaps this is an 'obligation', and one should even recite a *Beracha* / blessing before the immersion: Rosh and *Shibbolei haLeket*, ibid). Immersion in a Mikvah is another visceral 'death practice'. As with all mammals, oxygen is essential to us, and without breathing we would cease to live. When we are fully submerged underwater, we cease to breathe and lack this vital sign of life (*Yuma*, 85a. Rambam, *Hilchos Shabbos*, 2:19. *Shulchan Aruch*, Orach Chayim, 329:4). Again, the difference between remaining underwater for more than a few minutes (and literally expiring), and remaining underwater for just a few moments, is not a qualitative difference rather a quantitative one. We die a little bit, as it were, when we are underwater and suspending our life-breath.

Immersing ourselves in a Mikvah on *Erev* / 'the Eve of'

Yom Kippur is for the purpose of spiritual cleansing. Poignantly, such spiritual cleansing is also the reason a dead body is immersed in a Mikvah before it is interred. Thus, our immersion is a direct reminder of our own death. Following the Mikvah, one dresses in a white garment, again similar to the one in which he will someday, 'after 120 years', be buried.

After we have immersed Mikvah and donned a white garment, we pray the וידוי / *Viduy* / Confession, the exact prayer one prays right before he passes from the world if he is conscious that he will pass. Saying Viduy as Yom Kippur is about to enter, and throughout the entire day of Yom Kippur, arouses within us a stark awareness of the transience of our physical life.

Indeed, there is an urgency to this moment of life because it is all we have. All ambitions and drives, and all the pleasures of this world, are *Hevel* / vanity and emptiness. Nothing is permanent, and as *Sefer Koheles* / 'The Book of Ecclesiastes' concludes, סוף דבר הכל נשמע את־האלקים ירא ואת־מצותיו שמור כי־זה כל־האדם / "The sum of the matter, when all is said and done: revere Hashem and observe His commandments. For this is the totality of man" (*Koheles*, 12:13).

DAY OF NAKED TRUTH

Yom Kippur is a day of truth. Stripped away from all externalities, both external externalities, such as food, drink, beauty, and inner externalities, such as sin and negativity, we can come face to face with our deepest self. One should pause to consider: 'If I had only these 24 hours to live, who would I be? How would I think and act? What would be my priorities, goals and ambitions? How would I relate to the people in my life? What would be different?' This is a proper mindset to adopt as we enter into the day of *Emes* / truth. If Rosh Hashanah is the time of our birthday, Yom Kippur is the moment before our death. In the sharp focus on facing our mortality, all of life can become sweetened. On Yom Kippur, the urgency of the day allows for such a sweetening.

A Mishnah in *Avos* teaches, "On three things does the world depend: justice, truth, and peace." Rosh Hashanah is a time of judgment or 'justice'. Sukkos is a time of peace, as everyone in Klal Yisrael sits together, so-to-speak, under one *Sukkas Shalom* / canopy of peace." Yom Kippur is our moment of 'truth', stripping away all the externalities of life, such as food and drink, and bringing us face to face with our deepest self so we can ask ourselves, 'Who am I? Am I truly living?'

Once we have induced ourselves into this mindset of Emes, we can let go of egoic fears and live life more deeply. With an understanding that everything in this world is empty and transient, there is actually nothing in the world to fear, nothing can hold us in its grip, and nothing can truly overwhelm us. This is the deeper reason why Sukkos follows Yom Kippur.

Once we are free of fear, we can leave the security and comfort of our walls, roof and indoor amenities, go outside, and live in a temporary, insubstantial shelter, exposed to the elements. This demonstrates our fearlessness in action and puts it to the test. We show ourselves that we can embrace the fact that this life is a 'temporary structure', like a Sukkah. Because of this, we spontaneously become joyful, released, free and at ease. Ultimately, we sense that we are surrounded by the infinite embrace of HaKadosh Baruch Hu.

ROSH HASHANAH / BIRTH; YOM KIPPUR / DEATH

On Rosh Hashanah we celebrate our collective birthday, and therefore, on Rosh Hashanah the questions we ask ourselves are, "Does the fact that I was born benefit the world?" "Can I justify my existence before the King of the Universe?" "Can I stand in Judgment favorably? "Do I have the clout and power to request from my Creator a good new year and future?" These are questions of 'birth'. On Rosh Hashanah we need to think about *why* we exist, whereas on Yom Kippur, we need to think about *how* we exist. Have I lived honestly and authentically? Therefore, on Yom Kippur we need to bump up against our own mortality and the transient nature of life to stimulate these questions.

If we lived with an awareness of the reality of death every day, how many of the trivial fights and grudges — and how much internal nonsense, silliness and pettiness — would simply fall away. A long-lost friend you have avoided speaking to, a sibling you are arguing with, a petty financial quarrel you are having with a business associate, all mean nothing in the face of looming death. In this recognition, you will be motivated to make peace and amends. Even more subtle or inner pursuits, such as gaining a sense of acceptance, personal productivity or success, lose their importance in the face of imminent death. All shallow emotions and narratives melt away. What really matters becomes clarified, magnified and urgent to the one who knows their end is near.

This is what Yom Kippur is meant to achieve; we allow ourselves to be shaken by the matter of death so that we will wake up and actively engage in what is truly important in life.

LIFE REVIEW & SWEETENING

Standing vulnerably before the Ultimate Truth, we get honest with ourselves. We can then begin to answer our existential questions and commit to what truly matters to us.

In this induced end-of-life consciousness, you can take a 'snapshot' of our entire life, own the positive points, and do Teshuvah for the negative points. You can make a summary of your entire life, bringing your past into the present moment, and create a Tikkun and *Hamtakah* / sweetening for it all. Looking back, you can see that everything that you ever experienced and did was 'meant to be', for it has led you to sincere Teshuvah. It has made you into the person you are right now, with your sharp focus on what is real and genuine, true and holy. Therefore, everything is being swept up into the deep positivity of Yom Kippur. This day reveals a great Hamtakah of one's entire life.

Yom Kippur plunges us into Teshuvah in such a way that it can generate *Ta'anug*, a spiritual pleasure that soars beyond all forms of physical and finite pleasure such as those of luxury, food, drink and intimacy. This is because Yom Kippur is a cosmic revelation of *Lifnei Hashem* / before or 'beyond' the Name of Hashem, as it were — meaning beyond all 'nameable' or definable experiences. In this way, Yom Kippur is the revelation of the highest level of *Keser* / the 'Divine Crown', which is called *Ta'anug* / Perfect Bliss.

Chapter Five

ANGELIC TRANSCENDENCE:
LIVING BY AIR

A S EXPLORED EARLIER, WEARING WHITE AWAKENS IN US AN AWARENESS OF THE IMMEDIACY OF DEATH, BUT IT ALSO INDUCES A MORE ANGELIC, PURE, TRAN-SCENDENT STATE OF BEING. Similarly, fasting mimics angelic life, as angels do not eat or drink. During Yom Kippur, there is a custom to stand as much as possible in the services, also mimicking the angels who 'stand'* (ונתתי לך מהלכים בין העמדים האלה /

---

* Yom Kippur is a day when a person functions as an angel — מה מלאכי השרת אין להם קפיצין כך ישראל עומדים על רגליהם ביום הכפורים. מה מלאכי השרת אין להם אכילה ושתיה כך ישראל אין להם אכילה ושתיה ביום הכפורים. מה מלאכי השרת נקיים מכל חטא כך ישראל נקיים מכל חטא ביום הכפורים. מה מלאכי השרת שלום מתווך ביניהם כך ישראל שלום מתווך ביניהם ביום הכפורים / Just as angels do not have divisions in their legs and I will permit you to move about among those who stand": *Zechariah*, 3:7. העומדים – שרפים ומלאכי השרת שאין להם ישיבה. Rashi, *ad loc*. Angels are called 'standing ones' because they do not experience free choice, and thus they do not 'walk', move or progress from level to level).

On Yom Kippur, we engage in 'angelic practices' embodying angelic consciousness, meaning transcendent of negativity and sin. These practices focus on the lightness and purity of being, dwelling 'above' physicality and all the trappings of the ego's need to survive.

THE TWO PASSAGEWAYS, THE KANEH AND VESHET

Chazal tell us that the 365 prohibitive commands of the Torah correspond to the 365 days of the year (שלש מאות וששים וחמש

(i.e., they do not bend their legs, as it says "their legs are straight" *Yechezekel*, 1:7. In other words, they are always standing), we too stand on our feet on Yom Kippur. The angels do not eat or drink, nor does Klal Yisrael on Yom Kippur. Just as angels are clean of sin, so are we clean of sin on Yom Kippur. Just as peace rests between the angels, peace rests between us on Yom Kippur": *Pirkei d'Rebbe Eliezer*, 46. As the Ramban writes, אמר לפני הקב"ה רבון כל העולמים יש לך עם אחד בארץ כמלאכי השרת שבשמים מה מלאכי השרת יחפי רגל כך הן ישראל יחפי רגל ביום הכפורים מה מלאכי השרת אין בהם אכילה ושתיה כך ישראל אין בהם אכילה ושתיה ביום הכפורים מה מלאכי השרת אין להם קפיצה כך ישראל עומדין על רגליהם ביום הכפורים מה מלאכי השרת שלום מתווך ביניהם כך הן ישראל שלום מתווך ביניהם ביום הכפורים מה מלאכי השרת נקיים מכל חטא כך הן ישראל נקיים מכל חטא ביום הכפורים: Ramban, *Vayikra*, 16:8. The Rosh (quoting the Medrash above) suggests that asking forgiveness from one another is also angelic behavior, as angels exist in peace without strife: Rosh, *Yuma*, Siman 24. See also Rebbe Yoseph Ya'avetz, *Toras Chesed*, Derush al Yom Kippur, p. 528, where he explains that everything on Yom Kippur, even for example not wearing leather shoes, is done to mimic angelic behavior. See also *Sefer haKuzari*, Ma'amar 3:5. Removing our shoes represents being divested of physicality, as is an angel: *Drisha*, Orach Chayim, 606.

לאוין כמנין ימות החמה: *Makos*, 23b. *Tanchuma*, Ki Seitzei, 2). The Zohar (*Zohar* 1, 170a) teaches that each of the 365 prohibitive commands corresponds to one of the sinews, the main veins and arteries (or passageways) of the body. Yom Kippur corresponds with the קנה / *Kaneh* / 'windpipe' or trachea.

There are two 'pipes' or passageways through which we receive fuel for survival from the outside world: the Kaneh, through which we inhale oxygen, and the ושט / *Veshet* / esophagus or 'food pipe' through which we ingest nutrients.

These two passageways represent a portal to two types of worlds. The Kaneh, the windpipe, is associated with *Olam haBa* / the World to Come and Ya'akov, the man who dwelled in tents of Torah study. The *Veshet* / food pipe is associated with *Olam haZeh* / this material world and Ya'akov's brother, Eisav, the hunter and the man of the field (*Zohar* 3, 231b). By its very function, the Veshet is connected to the world of death and aggression, and the survival of the physical and egoic self. To feed our life, we need to cut off or detract from another life, whether a fruit, plant or animal. Even when we eat something that has on its own fallen from its source of life, it is already 'dead'. The very act of eating destroys or 'kills' it even further, breaking down its form more and more with the grinding of our teeth and processing of our stomach. In this way, life feeds off death. The function of the Veshet, in particular, is to 'take' from life. By contrast, the Kaneh merely brings in life-giving oxygen and releases carbon dioxide. This process is vastly more peaceful and gentle, and is more about 'sharing' than 'taking'.

Since the וושט / Veshet is based in 'taking from life', the potential of the שטן / Satan / adversarial force, which is also identified as one's own *Yetzer haRa* / negative inclination and the *Malach haMaves* / Angel of Death. The potential for this adversarial or negative force resides with the Veshet. When a person overeats, they over-use their Veshet and subtly awaken this force. For example, when one eats too much bread — and "eating bread" is sometimes used as a metaphor for indulging physical pleasures for their own sake — one ends up sinking lower and lower into the realm of the *Yetzer haRa* / ego-driven reality, and ultimately the self-destructive energy of the שטן.

שטן and וושט have similar letters, sharing the Shin and Tes (שט). The dissimilar letter is the Vav ו of וושט / *Veshet* and the final Nun ן of שטן / *Satan*. The ו and the ן are graphically almost aligned; the only difference is that the ן extends further down, below the baseline. Through overeating, says the Zohar (*Ibid*, see also, Shaloh, *Sha'ar haOsyos, Os Kuf, Kedushas haAchilah,* 232), the ו descends (below the 'baseline' of life), and the *Veshet* becomes like a *Satan*.

Our own Veshet can become our own 'Satan', that which entices us to negativity, and eventually our own 'angel of death', which kills us, *Chas veShalom* / Heaven forbid.

שטן is also related to the word שטות / *Sh'tus* / foolishness (*Shaloh*, ibid), which refers to the trivial temptations of the fleeting, transient moment. Momentary 'satisfaction', if it can be called satisfaction at all, can cause a person to sink further and further from his true self, until he is enmeshed in the domain ot the Yetzer haRa and the Angel of Death. Indeed, as the Rambam emphasizes, overeating can lead to all types of health issues and eventually shorten a person's life. Besides being a metaphor for materialism in general, overeating is a gateway to other materialistic indulgences and compulsions.

We are in fact meant to 'take' from this world, rather than to deny our physical and psychological needs, but we are meant to do so in a balanced way. We need to consume fuel and resources, to be married, to work in this world, to 'take in' and digest elements of the external world. We do all of these activities with the power of our Veshet. Yet, to live a balanced life with healthy intake, we need an equally healthy out-take. As we receive from life, we need to give even more back. If, however, taking becomes dominant and we begin to become obsessed and then possessed by the need to take and possess more and more, we will sink lower and lower into the abyss of unquenchable desire and perpetual emptiness. And then, instead of the Vav of *Veshet*, which is a letter that concludes on the baseline, what we create is a Final Nun, extending below the human realm, where it invokes the Satan.

A Vav does naturally descend from its high point, but it stays above the baseline, within the borders of a healthy ego and a balanced fulfillment of instinctual needs. A Final Nun descends below the baseline of what is healthy, degrading our lower instincts in an attempt to satisfy bottomless, insatiable desires. When we are possessed by cravings and lose control of our intake, they end up 'sinking us'.

"Rav Yochanan said, 'A man has a small organ (used for physical intimacy). If he starves it (does not overindulge), it is satiated. If, however, he satiates it (and overindulges), it 'starves' and desires ever more" (*Sukkah*, 52b).

Such is the nature of physical desire. Physical desire belongs to a world of 'incompleteness' and is, by its very definition, incomplete and hence insatiable. In fact, the more one tries to fill a physical desire — the more he believes he is "satisfying" it — the more it 'starves' and craves even more fulfillment. Attempting to fill a sense of lack, in the world of lack, he only creates more lack, and more lust for yet another substance, object or person. It is a loop or 'self-fulfilling prophecy' of ever-greater lack.

Trying to fill existential emptiness with empty things creates even greater emptiness. What's more, every time a desire is temporarily satisfied, the 'vessel' of that desire only expands and enlarges, and craves even more. And as the vessel expands, so does the 'empty space' within it, along with deeper feelings of a void and a restless need to fill it.

Such is the nature of *Olam haZeh* / this world, the realm where the Veshet is dominant and where the hunter, Eisav, roams and rules. "And Eisav said to Yaakov, 'Give me some of that red stuff to gulp down (into my Veshet), for I am famished' — which is why he was named *Edom* (Red)" (*Bereishis*, 29:30). *Edom* is also the name of Rome, and by extension, the Westernized world. In a world where indulging the cravings of the Veshet is promoted and celebrated, we have to be especially vigilant. We need to ensure that the natural 'taking' of our healthy Veshet does not become imbalanced and fall below the line into the abyss of the emptiness and transience of the outer world, the realm of the Satan and the Yetzer haRa, and ultimately into the grip of the Angel of Death.

YOM KIPPUR AS ANGELIC, LIGHT, AIR: THE DAY OF THE קנה / WINDPIPE

Chazal / our sages tell us (*Yuma*, 20a) that the word השטן / 'the Satan' is numerically 364, suggesting that the Satan has sway during 364 days of the year, but not the 365th day, which is Yom Kippur. Throughout Yom Kippur we have no connection to the world of the Satan[*] nor to the Veshet for that matter, as <u>we literally do </u>not feed our physical cravings via our Veshet.

[*] There is no Satan on Yom Kippur': *Yuma*, 20a. See also *Nedarim* 32b, Ran and Rashi, *ad loc. Zohar* 3, p. 63a. *Chibur haTeshuvah*, Meishiv Nefesh, Ma'amar 2:9. In the lunar calendar there are only 354 or 355 days, not 364, as in the solar year. Does Klal Yisrael not count lunar years? Rebbe Yonason Eibschutz asks this question and offers a few answers. ומקשים הא אנו מונים ללבנה ושנותינו רק שנ"ד או שנ"ה וא"כ נפיש יו"ד ימים בזה בכמה בחינות כי באמת נודע כי המ"ם ונו"ן מתחלפים: *Ya'aros Devash*, Derush 6, 5. Now, although the Gemara (*ibid.*) merely says that on Yom Kippur the Satan does not accuse, שטן ביומא דכיפורי לית ליה רשותא לאסטוני — clearly even on Yom Kippur we do have a Yetzer haRa, as the Gemara (*Yuma*, 19b) also records: והא האידנא יומא דכיפורי הוא, ואבעול כמה בתולתא בנהרדעא. See also *Gittin*, 57a. Yet, in various sources this statement of the Gemara comes to mean that on a very deep level, and if one truly believes that one is a Tzadik on Yom Kippur, there is no Satan at all on Yom Kippur. At the very least, this means that on Yom Kippur the *Shelita* / dominance of the Satan is *less*: See *Gilyonei haShas*, Rav Yoseph Engel, Yuma, 20a, quoting *Shu'T Mahariv*, Siman 192. *Meshech Chochmah*, Nitzavim. ומסתמא כן הוא באדם שאין היצה"ר שהוא השטן שולט בו: *Sefas Emes*, Yom Kippur.

Yom Kippur is the day of the *Kaneh* / 'windpipe', when we are nourished only by breathing and uttering words (breath) of *Tefillah* / prayer. Yom Kippur is the day of רוח / *Ruach* / 'wind' / spirit, and the day of *Neshamah* / soul. *Neshamah* comes from the word *Neshimah* / breath. We demonstrate that we do not *essentially* rely on food, rather we live off breath and spirit. The Arizal teaches (*Eitz Chayim*, Yom Kippur. *Machberes haKodesh,* Sha'ar Erev Yom Kippur) that on Yom Kippur, Malchus, which is often a code word for our existential reality, receives its food directly from Binah, which is called the *Hevel haElyon* / the Supernal Breath.

On Yom Kippur, we are like angels who exist without food, drink or the need to procreate and perpetuate. We don white garments to symbolize that we are as pure as angels, following our immersion in the life-purifying Mikvah. We are transcendent, transparent, light and bright.

There are four primary elements in physical matter: fire, wind (or air), water, and earth. These can also be classified as hot, moist, cold, and dry, or in modern parlance, hydrogen, nitrogen, oxygen, and carbon. Fire, wind, water, and earth are not meant to be taken literally, as in a clod of earth, a bucket of water, air in the atmosphere, and a candle flame. Rather, they are to be regarded as primary 'qualities' of matter. Everything in our created world consists of these basic four elements, albeit some creations have more of the 'water' quality, and some more 'fire'. Angels, on the other hand, do not contain the tangible properties of 'earth' or 'water', and only contain fire and wind

(Ramban, *Toras haAdam*, Sha'ar haGmul. *Sodei Razya*, Hilchos Malachim, p. 163. Alter Rebbe, *Siddur Im Dach*, p. 275). Indeed, the *Pasuk* / verse reads, בדבר ה' שמים נעשו וברוח פיו כל צבאם / "With the word of Hashem the Heavens were created, and with the רוח / *Ruach* / wind within His mouth, all the angels" (*Tehillim*, 33:6).

Angels are created by Divine *Ruach* / 'wind' and are therefore creatures of the wind, as it were. Angels are weightless, do not contain the grounding and gravity-pulling elements of earth and water, representing depression, laziness and insatiable desire, and they are thus certainly unburdened by the gravitational pull and burden of sin and negativity.

"For my iniquities have overwhelmed me; they are like a משא כבד / *heavy burden*...." (*Tehillim*, 38:5). Physical life, with its desires to sustain itself, can weigh a person down, and certainly when the ugly head of sin rears its head. Besides being pulled down by laziness and depression, which in many ways is the worst 'sin', one can be devastatingly burdened by literal negatives and sin, and then collapse under the stress of life. Comes the Divine gift of the day of Yom Kippur, and we are released from the burdens of sin, for "the essence of the day brings acquittal." Yom Kippur makes us feel so light that we can soar upward like angels.

THE LIGHTNESS OF BEING

Besides the spiritual lightness we can experience on this day, many people feel physically lighter by refraining from food. Some feel like they are floating above the world during the later hours of Yom Kippur, just from having been detached from the downward pull of the Veshet, and the heaviness of material needs. It can be argued that we do not 'fast' on Yom Kippur at all; we do not *refrain* from food or drink and other needs — rather, we are *free* from food and drink and other needs. For 26 hours, we are liberated from the *Bechinah* / paradigm of the Veshet, and nothing can bring us down.

Yom Kippur commences with the recital of the Kol Nidrei service. The reasons and details of this service will be explored later on, but the basic function of Kol Nidrei is the annulment of our vows, a letting go of all verbally self-imposed attachments to certain actions. In other words, we begin Yom Kippur by freeing ourselves from anything that can weigh us down, and rising into a lightness of Being.

Similarly, the tractate that deals with the laws and practices of Yom Kippur, *Yuma* / 'The Day', begins thus: "Seven days prior to Yom Kippur, the *Cohen Gadol* / the High Priest would be removed from his home" (*Yuma*, 1:1). As explored earlier, the same Mishnah teaches us that for the Cohen Gadol to serve on Yom Kippur he must be married and his wife must be alive. And yet, he is 'removed' from his wife and from his home seven days prior to Yom Kippur. He returns back home in great joy after he concludes his last service of Yom Kippur. He is married but 'removed', meaning detached, from his wife, home, and family life. While he needs to be a family man, well grounded in the world of Veshet, yet even just to prepare for Yom Kippur, he also needs to become 'free' from his identity as a worldly person. He needs to be a person of the Kana, as free as the whirling wind, a person of *Ruach* / spirit and *Neshamah* / soul and Supernal Breath.

As we pass through the gate of Kol Nidrei, we are similarly removed and unbound from the world of physicality and the needs of the ego, and we are lighter. Like the Cohen Gadol, we can now soar into the higher realms of purity and light.

On Yom Kippur we ask HaKadosh Baruch Hu for סליחה / *Selichah* / forgiveness. The root of the word סליחה could be seen as לח / *Lach* / dampness or moisture. Having been stuck in hardened negative patterns of behavior, with actions that pull us down and leave us spiritually parched, we ask Hashem to forgive and free us, and soften us with the moist, pure dew of Heaven. All sin and negativity that may have clung to our mind and body from our past actions slides off us so we can start over again, fresh and light. Yom Kippur is a day of atonement, liberation from our past and our negative actions and states of mind. We begin anew, perfectly clean, like a freshly laundered white garment (In addition to wearing white to mimic angels, the custom for all is to specifically wear "clean" garments: *Magen Avraham,* Orach Chayim, 610:5).

And in order for us to enter fully into the fluid-like power of Yom Kippur, and be washed of all externalities, we ourselves need to be malleable or fluid, or air-like, like angels who are created through the *Ruach Piv* / wind of the Creator's Mouth, as it were. Regarding them, the *Nusach* / liturgy of Shacharis

says: וכלם מקבלים עליהם על מלכות שמים זה מזה, ונותנים באהבה רשות זה
לזה, להקדיש ליוצרם בנחת רוח / "And all of them (the angels) receive
upon themselves from one another the yoke of the Sovereignty of Heaven, and they lovingly give one another permission
and space to sanctify their Fashioner with a pleasant spirit
(wind)...."

The reason they are able to lovingly give one another the
space to sanctify Hashem is that they are rooted in the open
space of 'breath' — the cyclical give and take of the Kaneh,
rather than the 'grabbing' of Veshet.

YOM KIPPUR & THE WINDPIPE VS.
TISHA B'AV & THE SCIATIC NERVE

As mentioned, Yom Kippur is a "full-day fast" of 25 to 26
hours. The other full-day fast of the year is the fast of *Tisha
b'Av* / the Ninth Day of the Month of Av. Yom Kippur is connected with *Kana* / trachea or 'windpipe'. Tisha b'Av, the only
other day of the year that the Zohar reveals as being connected
with a body part, is connected to the *Gid haNasheh* / sciatic
nerve (*Zohar* 1, p. 70b), namely the Mitzvah not to eat this nerve.

In the Pasuk that delivers this Mitzvah (*Bereishis*, 32:32),
"Therefore the Children of Israel do not eat את גיד הנשה / *Es
Gid haNasheh* / the dislodged vein," the word את / *Es* / the
(spelled **Aleph-T**av) is a reversed acronym for *Tisha Av* / the
Ninth of Av (*Akeidas Yitzchak*, Vayishlach, Sha'ar 26). Furthermore,
the numerical value of the words את גיד הנשה / *Es Gid haNasheh*

is the same as the words *Tisha b'Av* (Rebbe Pinchas of Koretz, *Imrei Pinchas*, p. 7).

The Gid haNasheh is a part of the animal that we do not eat; in fact, we must completely remove it. The Gid itself has no taste, as our Sages teach *Ein b'Gidim b'Nosein Ta'am* / "Nerves do not transmit taste" (*Chulin*, 101a. *Tur* and *Shulchan Aruch*, Yoreh De'ah, 100). The sciatic nerve represents *Cheser* / absence or 'lack', on every level: it is an existential Cheser as it must be eliminated, and it is a sensorial Cheser, as it is tasteless (More- over, ואינו ראוי לאכילה / "and it is not considered food": Rashi, *Beitza*, 12a).

Tisha b'Av is all about Cheser, absence, mourning the de- struction and absence of the Beis haMikdash, and feeling our collective and individual loss. Abstaining from eating on Tisha b'Av is connected to the mourning for the Cheser in the world. Indeed, who *could* eat on this day? It is like when a person is in mourning and feeling the Cheser, the void in their life, they lose their appetite. They cannot eat even if they want to.

Yom Kippur is not about Cheser at all; quite the opposite, it is about transcendence. It is not about refraining from eating, but rather being beyond eating. Yom Kippur is a time of the windpipe; food and eating are irrelevant to us, as the Berditch- ever Rebbe once said, "on Yom Kippur who *wants* to eat!" We are beyond being anchored by food, and for that matter, all physicality. None of it is an issue for us. We are simply borne aloft, breathing in the ever-pure Supernal Breath.

On Yom Kippur, we un-hinge ourselves from the stuckness of negative attachments, sins and modes of thought that oppress and compress our souls. We take full responsibility for what we have done and neglected to do, yet no longer identify ourselves with our negative actions or omissions. We identify with our soul, our spirit. Liberated from the influence of the worldly *Veshet* / esophagus and all its associated *Yeshus* / limited being, we release our anchor in the 'animal self', unfurl our spiritual wings, and become *LuftMentschen* / 'people of the air'. We fly aloft in the wind of spiritual הבל / *Hevel* / breath, and take off into the Divine *Ayin* / emptiness, soft, open, expansive, transparent, and transcendent.

On this awesome day of light, we are nourished from the Breath of HaKadosh Baruch Hu alone (*Kaviyachol* / so-to-speak). We open to receive the 'exhale' of the Divine Presence into our inhale, and we release our exhale into the Divine 'inhale' (see *Kedushas Levi*, Kedushas Shelishis, Purim). In this way, we become one with the Supernal Breath itself, as it cycles through us, lifting us higher and higher.

Chapter Six

THE FIVE FORMS OF REST: FOOD, SHOES, WASHING, INTIMACY & ANOINTING

Pushing Ourselves to Our Limits Reveals Our True Potential

O N YOM KIPPUR, WE ARE IMMERSED IN RIGOROUS *Avodah* / SPIRITUAL WORK FOR AN ENTIRE DAY. AS THE DAY UNFOLDS, PERHAPS HUNGER AND EXHAUS-TION SET IN, EVEN IF WE DO FEEL LIGHTER. Yet, we continue to push ourselves in our Avodah beyond what we think is possible. We continue to stand like angels for many hours in deeply focussed prayer, even if our feet hurt or we feel a desire to go to sleep. We break our physical cravings by forcefully rising above them, even when it creates sharp discomfort.

Paradoxically, the more we push ourselves beyond our comfort zone in these ways, the freer and lighter we become on this day. Doing so frees us from all false perceptions of self and our maximum potential.

Once a year, we are asked and invited to forget about our job, money, position, influence, status — forget about all the externals of life, and deeply ask, 'When I peel away all superficial layers of my identity, what is left?' Once everything external is gone, our question becomes, 'Who am I really? What am I, in essence?'

On Shabbos, we rest from work in order to enjoy family, food, spirituality and study. It is a day on which we are able to 'elevate' all of our actions and experiences, even the most physical, up to the realm of the spiritual. On Shabbos, the act of eating becomes a spiritual experience — it has a totally different quality than eating during the six days of the week. Externally oriented enjoyments become vehicles for spiritual elevation and elation.

Yom Kippur is to Shabbos what Shabbos is to the six days of the week; it is "the Shabbos of Shabboses," when we 'rest' even from *Shabbosdik* forms of rest. Whereas on Shabbos we are using eating and enjoyments to realize our intimacy with the Creator, on Yom Kippur we are *Shovess* / resting from food, drink and other bodily needs, desires and enjoyments, as the Rambam writes: מצות עשה אחרת יש ביום הכפורים והיא לשבת בו מאכילה ושתיה / "There is an *additional* Mitzvah on Yom Kippur: to rest from eating and drinking" (*Hilchos Shevisas Asor*, 1:4). On

Yom Kippur, we rest even from 'elevating' or 'sweetening' our normal human activities — we separate ourselves from them completely for one day. By the conclusion of the day, these activities are sweetened and elevated.

FIVE LEVELS OF REST

Overall there are five aspects of human life that we need to rest from on Yom Kippur: eating, bathing, wearing leather shoes, using oils and lotions, and physical intimacy (Mishnah, *Yuma*, 8:1). These are known as the five types of עינוי נפש / *Inuy Nefesh*, the 'afflictions of the spirit' that we endure on this day. The phrase *Inuy Nefesh* can be understood as 'making ourselves poor', as the word עינוי / *Inuy* is related to the word עני / *Ani* or 'poor'. This indicates that we are diminishing, or impoverishing, our lower, surface levels of self so that we can reveal, or enrich, the deeper, higher levels of self.

Yom Kippur is not a time, in the language of our sages, to simply 'pain' ourselves. If that were the goal, maybe one should "sit in the sun or in the cold" (*Yuma*, 74b). Rather, Yom Kippur is a day of 'transcendence' of food, drink, and the normative life that these five practices represent.* And the 'impoverishment'

---

* In the words of the Maharal, וכן כל המצות שצוה השם יתעלה ביום הגדול והקדוש הכל לסלק לסלק הגופניות שבאדם עד שהוא כמו מלאך לגמרי, ולפיכך צוה לענות נפשו, הכל לסלק עינוי את הגוף עד שיהיה האדם קדוש כמו מלאך: *Derashos*, Shabbos Shuvah. The Gemara, *Shabbos* 115a, tells us, מפצעין באגוזים ומפרכסין ברימונים מן המנחה ולמעלה מפני עגמת נפש, thus, it is clear that Yom Kippur is not about עגמת נפש, rather, עינוי נפש, which can be experienced as 'transcendence of spirit', or 'poverty of normative pleasure'. The Chasam Sofer writes that the idea of עינוי is not pain, rather it means an awakening, a time of spiritual arousal. *Toras Moshe*, Nitzavim, Derush, 27th Elul.

of these five activities is meant only to reveal and enrich the five levels of our soul.

Yet, the Torah warns us, "Any person אשר לא-תענה / 'who will not be afflicted' on that very day shall be cut off" (*Vayikra*, 23:29). Says the Chasam Sofer, this can also be read as follows, 'Any person who does not *feel* afflicted or moved on that very day (should know that he is already) *Kares* / cut off" from the Source of All Life.

If we are not moved to yearn or tears during the course of Yom Kippur, if we do not tremble at the ways we have been spiritually and ethically asleep, it could indicate that we are living *as if* we are separate from the Source of all Life. It could mean that — even on Yom Kippur — we are still so insensitive that we are disconnecting from being truly alive, may Hashem have mercy.

On the deepest level, however, by transcending these five physical needs, we attain the level of *Ta'anug Pashut* / pure pleasure, transparent bliss. These five forms of refraining or rest are not a form of suffering, but rather, moods of pleasure beyond the superficial world of appearances. (*Inuy* is spelled Ayin, Yud, Nun, Vav, Yud. Taking the three root letters, that are Ayin, Nun, Vav, and instead of the two Yuds placing a Hei, the word *Onah* / 'physical intimacy', emerges. This is because on the higher or deeper level, Inuy *is* Onah, a deep form of pleasure; it is just when manifested in this world it could appear as *Inuy* / affliction or hardship. And actually, the way we see something is the way it appears; if we view the Inuyyim as forms of spiritual pleasure, we can experience them this way. Again, as the Berditchever Rebbe said, "Who *wants* to eat on this day," as the fast is, in a deep sense, much more pleasurable than eating.)

FIVE PARALLEL FIVE

Since the Torah mentions the word עינוי / *Inuy* (in singular or plural forms) five times, we learn that there are five forms of *Inuy* (*Yuma*, 76a: הני חמשה ענויין כנגד מי אמר רב חסדא כנגד חמשה ענויין שבתורה). This is the simple reason for these five forms of rest. The Gemara (*Yuma*, 74b) proves that the term *Inuy*, as used in the Torah, refers to some type of depriving oneself of eating and drinking. All major Halachic opinions agree that the prohibition of eating and drinking is a Torah-based law. The debate among the Rishonim, the early commentators, is whether the other four are prohibited by the Torah itself, or by the sages. The latter is the opinion of most Rishonim (Rashi, *Yuma*, 74a. Tosefos, *Yuma*, 77a. Rosh, *Yuma*, 8:1. *Chinuch*, Mitzvah 313. *Tur*, 611. An early source, Rav Hai Gaon, maintains that all five are from the Torah, directly indicated by the five times the Torah writes the word *Inuy* regarding Yom Kippur. *Yuma*, 76a. See also, the Netziv, *HaEmek She'elah*, 167).

The five prohibitions correspond to the five books of the Torah, the five senses of the body, the five immersions of the Cohen Gadol on Yom Kippur, and of course, the five *Tefilos* / prayers that we pray on Yom Kippur. The five Tefilos of Yom Kippur are: 1) *Ma'ariv* / evening prayers, 2) *Shacharis* / morning prayers, 3) *Musaf* / additional prayers, 4) *Mincha* / afternoon prayers, and 5) *Neilah* / closing prayers (וחמשה עינויים הם אכילה ושתיה ורחיצה וסיכה ונעילת הסנדל ותשמיש המטה. כנגד ה"פ נפש דכתיבי בפרשה וכנגד ה' שמות טבילות לכ"ג ו ה' תפילות: *Baal haTurim*, Vayikra, 23:27. See also *Shach al haTorah*, ad loc).

On a deeper level, these five prohibitions correlate to the five levels of our soul, explains the Maharal, Rebbe Yehudah Loew: 1) *Nefesh* / the functional self, 2) *Ruach* / the emotional self, 3) *Neshamah* / the intellectual self, 4) *Chayah* / the spiritual self, and 5) *Yechidah* / the essential self.

The Alter Rebbe writes that the five prohibitions correspond to the five levels of *Gevuros* or 'restrictions' of *Malchus* / 'Kingdom' or physical reality, which all experience an elevation of Yom Kippur (*Siddur Im Dach*. See also Arizal, *Sha'ar haKavanos*, Derush 1).

Let's unpack and explore these correlations. The five prohibitions or 'restings' represent the nullification of the external factors of our lives that we tirelessly pursue and define ourselves by. For it is only when we strip away these external aspects of self that the real Self can emerge.

JOB, MONEY, APPEARANCE, STATUS & POWER

There are five aspects of worldly or social life that most people crave or pursue at certain ages or states of spiritual maturation. These give one a sense of *Yeshus* / existence or value as an individual ego. Sadly, for many, these pursuits become their self-definition and they lose touch with who they really are. The five aspects are 1) job, 2) money, 3) appearance, 4) status, and 5) power.

1) *Job* — Many people define themselves by their profession or avocation. They may become so associated with their work,

position, or role in life that they begin to identify with it not as 'what they do', but rather, 'who they are'. This is often indicated by the way people introduce themselves, for example, 'My name is Dr. Yaakov, I'm a pediatrician,' or 'Hi, I'm a stay-at-home mom," or, "I'm a student."

2) *Money* — Some people tend to define themselves by how much money they have in their bank accounts. As a result, the money they have or lack builds them up or pulls them down. The more money they have in their account, the more confident they feel, and the less money, the less confident. For some reason, people who are materially very wealthy feel entitled to have an opinion about everything and everyone, even things completely unrelated to their sphere of knowledge or experience.

3) *Appearance* — Another way that people define themselves is by how they look or don't look, as if their external appearance defines who they are. Unfortunately, some people's identity and self-worth is so entangled in appearances that they obsessively strive to manipulate their image through clothes, dieting, grooming and even cosmetic surgery. A perceived disapproval can seem devastating. Someone with a physical abnormality may shy away from certain social interactions or life-pursuits. Both tendencies can be rooted in the fact that they have made their self-worth dependent on their external appearance.

4) *Status* — Some people tend to define themselves by their inherited status or perceived 'birthright'. Through their ances-

tral lineage, or even their progeny, they may feel entitled or privileged over others. The opposite is also true; for example, people may also feel disenfranchised or 'less than' due to their genealogy or immediate family. A person who has famous figures in their *Yichus* / lineage may feel a greater sense of belonging or entitlement, while someone defining themselves as a convert or the child of *Ba'alei Teshuvah* / returnees to faith, may feel less rooted or at home. People may also derive a sense of status from their university degrees, their past successes in an art, sport or hobby, or even just from having been part of a certain club or group longer than other members.

5) *Power* — People may also define themselves by their positions of perceived power or powerlessness. That is to say that they define themselves by how much influence they have over others, whether in a company, a community, family, or culture. This self-image may be rooted in the person's gender, personal charisma, or other elements of the four categories above. Their power 'over others', whether imagined or real, informs and shapes their self-worth and identity. If their power is denied, they may erupt in rage, for without it they feel they are nothing.

WHO ARE WE TRULY?

On Yom Kippur we receive the gift of 'rest' from such external definitions and identifications. This allows us to find out who we truly are, underneath all of them. Yom Kippur is the day of Truth; as we are stripped of all foolish, trivial or harmful facades, our deepest truth can emerge and give us focus for the entire year to come. Yom Kippur is the foundation upon which all the days of the year stand, so the depth of our self-revelation on this day makes a great impression on the rest of our life.

On Yom Kippur we are offered the gift of clarity that forces us to ask, 'Without my job, my money, my appearance, my status, my power — what am I left with? Who am I without all that?' Imagine not even subtly judging or defining yourself by your function, your income, your image, your social status or your influence — you are just you.

On a given day, many people place a great deal of focus and energy on the foods they eat, their physical cleanliness and scent, and even their experience of, or pursuit of, physical intimacy. On Yom Kippur, a person is suddenly left without any such projects. All that remains is the ultimate Divine question asked to Adam and Chavah in the Garden: *Ayekah* / "Where are *you*?" Where is the real 'you' amid the multitude of distractions in life?

This Holy Day of Yom Kippur is a time to reclaim our priorities, reaffirm what really matters in our lives, and just be ourselves.

THE FIVE PROHIBITIONS & THEIR CORRELATIONS IN GREATER DEPTH

On Yom Kippur we experience a form of ritual death, as explored earlier. We go to the Mikvah or 'ritual bath' (as does a body after death), we wear a white garment (as does a body about to be buried), we cease eating and drinking, and we are not physically intimate with our spouse. Our 'vital signs' are flat-lined, as it were.

Experiencing a state of 'death' while still alive is similar to a deep meditative state in which we are 'asleep' while awake. As such, we can consciously experience our subconscious mind and access levels of consciousness that are not readily available to our normative state. It is like 'lucid dreaming', or rather lucid waking. This state of consciousness is very useful, as with it, we can clearly see our subconscious attachments and identifications and let them go. Even if we are not normally aware of being attached to our looks or our power, for instance, these are pulls that are embedded in the human subconscious mind, and we are certainly affected by them on some level. On Yom Kippur, in our induced transparent state of being, we can see our hidden identifications and let them dissolve in the light of truth.

The five aspects of ego-identification correlate to the five prohibitions specific to Yom Kippur in the following way: 1) job – no shoes, 2) money – no food, 3) appearance – no bathing, 4) status – no marital relations, 5) power – no anointing with lotions or oils.

To further expand this idea, we will detail the correspondences between these five categories and the five senses, and finally, the five levels of the soul.

1) NO LEATHER SHOES; JOB; SENSE OF TOUCH; NEFESH

Historically, not wearing leather shoes has had different meanings. Nowadays, it is meant to effect a humbling of self. Leather shoes are often considered 'dress' shoes as opposed to casual shoes. By not wearing leather shoes, we are refraining from 'dressing up' on Yom Kippur. But in its original application, at a time when most shoes were made out of leather — before the advent of synthetic materials — the intention was that a person would actually be barefoot, or closer to the earth.* We can, of course, still use this original meaning in our contemplation and inner experience of Yom Kippur. As one example among others, the B'nei Yissaschar, the great Chassidic Rebbe, was known to go without shoes altogether on Yom Kippur, even though he had the option of wearing shoes crafted from other materials.

Spiritually speaking, on Yom Kippur it is important that we feel and touch the ground, or at least be closer to it. This prohibition is connected with the sense of touch. Shoes separate a person from the ground, but without shoes or with thin-

---

* The prohibition of wearing leather shoes is not to create discomfort, as wearing non-leather shoes is permitted, even if there is comfort. As the Gemara says, אמר ליה רבא: ומשום תענוג בלא מנעל ביום הכפורים מי אסירי והא רבה בר רב הונא כריך סודרא אכרעיה ונפיק / "Rava said to him: 'But is footwear that is not considered to be shoes forbidden on Yom Kippur due to the pleasure one derives from wearing them?' But Rabba bar Rav Huna would wrap a scarf on his feet and go out on Yom Kippur so his feet would not be injured." This implies that there is no prohibition against wearing something comfortable on one's feet as long as it is not defined as 'shoes': *Yevamos*, 102b.

ner shoes, one is lowered, humbled. One is literally in touch with the ground and the fact that "you are dust from the earth, and you will return to the earth." Not only do shoes 'separate' you from the ground you are walking on, they also raise you 'above' it. Certainly, if you are wearing fancy heeled shoes, you are raised above the ground. Taking off your shoes ensures that you feel connected to the earth to which your body will return.

Refraining from wearing shoes thus awakens the awareness that we do not dominate our physical reality and selves. We do not 'own' the earth we walk on, rather it 'owns' us, so to speak; we will one day give back to it the physical bodies which we have on loan. Relinquishing our shoes for the day is an embodied act of giving up our aloof posture and sense of mastery over the physical world and our physical life.*

In this way, shoes are a sign of mastery. When Yoseph's brothers sold him into slavery, with the money they received on the sale they bought shoes to demonstrate their mastery over his life. A student should not put his teacher's shoes on for him, say our sages. People may mistake the student for a slave,

---

* From another perspective, not wearing shoes is simply due to the great holiness of the day. After eating from the Tree of Knowledge, the earth was cursed. Due to this, there was a custom not to walk directly on the earth, but rather to wear shoes. "On Yom Kippur," says the Dinover (*Agra d'Pirka*), "there is no curse; we are holy and so are our surroundings. The earth is holy, so we do not need to avoid stepping on it, thus there is no need to wear shoes." Moshe is told that when the earth is holy there is no need for shoes: "Remove your shoes from your feet, for the place upon which you stand is holy ground" (*Shemos* 3:5).

helping his 'master' put on his shoes, which is a classic form of subservience.

On Yom Kippur we surrender our sense of mastery, and rest from our assumed control over the world of *Asiyah* / the physical plane, and over our *Nefesh* / active spirit.

We rest as well from our sense of identity as it is connected to our work. We cease defining ourselves by the job we have or how 'masterful' we are in our position. We refrain from manipulating our environment and ourselves, and let go of the shallow identity that is forged by what we do in this world. We let go of 'climbing the corporate ladder', and all the other ways we human beings try to raise ourselves above the level of earth.

2) NO EATING OR DRINKING; MONEY; SENSE OF TASTE; RUACH

The prohibition against eating and drinking on Yom Kippur is related to the sense of taste, to the world of *Ruach* / spirit, as well as to the sense of identity that is generated by our relationship to money (Although keep in mind that generally, eating and drinking are related to taste, and a prohibition regarding foods is an issue of הנאת גרונו, the pleasure of the throat: *Chullin*, 103b. Rambam, *Hilchos Ma'achalos Asuros*, 14:3 — שאין החיוב אלא על הנאת הגרון בכזית מדבר האסור. Yet, with regards to Yom Kippur, perhaps we rule (also) as does Reish Lakish, the main issue being הנאת מעיו / the pleasure of one's stomach: *Shu"T Chasam Sofer*, Orach Chayim, 127. *Minchas Chinuch*, Mitzvah 313:2. See also *Sha'agas Aryeh*, 76, regarding eating לא כדרך אכילתן / not in the usual manner of eating).

A major component of our relationship to food is taste. Yes, we eat to survive, but eating is also an immensely pleasurable activity for most people. The same is true of money. Arguably, we need money or some other form of value-exchange to survive in our world. Yet, money can also be the key to accessing a wide array of pleasures beyond the immediate needs of our survival. Both food and money can give us access to what we need, or enjoyment of what we desire.

The difference between eating simply for nutrition and eating for taste, is the element of enjoyment, pleasure. The world of Ruach is the spirited world of emotions, desires, and pleasures.

Throughout the year, people are steeped in the pursuit of pleasures; hopefully they are all permitted and healthy on physical, emotional and spiritual levels. Often, people define themselves by their ability to satisfy those desires, namely, their access to money. Naturally, one pursues not only what is *Tov* / good for them, but also what is, or appears to be, *Nechmad* / pleasing to them.

On Yom Kippur we fast completely from all foods and liquids, whether tasty or bland. In this way, we remove ourselves completely not just from pleasure, but also from the *possibility* of pleasure. And in this way, we remove ourselves from desire.

3) NO BATHING OR WASHING;
APPEARANCE; SENSE OF SIGHT; NESHAMAH

Refraining from bathing and washing is related to the sense of sight and the world of physical appearances. In order to appear aesthetically attractive, one will often need to bathe, groom, and pamper oneself to highlight and draw out the innate beauty of the body.

On Yom Kippur we are invited and empowered to let go of this superficial definition of who we are. We are enabled to let go of focussing on outer appearances and to look deeper, to get a glimpse of the Neshamah — our soul and our life's purpose. Nullifying the importance of outer appearances allows for the inner quality, the Neshamah, to shine forth. Without the distraction of thinking about how others see us, we glimpse our true, eternal beauty — the humble, ever-pure soul.

4) NO MARITAL RELATIONS; STATUS;
SENSE OF HEARING; CHAYAH

Physical intimacy is connected with the 'living soul' — known in Hebrew as *Chayah* / 'alive', and this is related to the sense of hearing. To be truly intimate with another is to be able to hear them, and to express oneself in a way that they can hear. Any lack of listening is bound to cause a fracture in communication, which leads to the weakening of the relationship. Open, clear listening, and speaking on the basis of open, clear listening, creates unity and strengthens the bond.

On Yom Kippur we rest from bodily relations so that we can be free from identifying ourselves by our relationship. By creating a temporary distance between each other, each partner is able to reorient their hearing. They can take time to focus inwardly and listen to their inner voice.

We rest from the physical aspect of our spousal relationship to demonstrate to ourselves that our partner is not the source of our self-worth. We let go of attributing our wellbeing to another person, and re-clarify our own inner point and purpose.*

---

* The Mishnah says, מקום שנהגו להדליק את הנר בלילי יום הכפורים מדליקין. מקום שנהגו / שלא להדליק אין מדליקין "In a place where people were accustomed to kindle a lamp in the house on Yom Kippur evenings, one kindles it. In a place where people were accustomed not to kindle a lamp, one does not kindle it": *Pesachim*, 53b. And as the Gemara adds, בין שאמרו להדליק ובין שאמרו שלא להדליק / שניהן לדבר אחד נתכוונו "Both in a place where the Sages said to kindle and in a place where they said not to kindle, they both intended to achieve the same objective" (to distance people from physical intimacy, which is prohibited on Yom Kippur. This is the ruling of the Shulchan Aruch; מקום שנהגו להדליק נר בליל יום הכפורים מדליקין מקום שנהגו שלא להדליק אין מדליקין / "In a place where the custom is to light, we light; in a place where the custom is not to light, we do not light": *Orach Chayim*, 610:1. Yet, the Mechaber adds, יש מי שאומר שמברך על הדלקת נר יום כפורים / "And there are those who maintain that we kindle a candle in honor of Yom Kippur, and we do recite a blessing," this is also, as the Rama, adds, the custom in these lands (of Ashkenaz). The root of this ruling is the Rosh (*Yuma*, 8:27). However, we do not recite a blessing on a *Minhag* / custom (*Sukkah*, 44b — מנהג נביאים היא בגבולין ולא יסוד נביאים הלכך אינה צריכה ברכה: Rashi, *ad loc*) and the Mechaber himself rules this way (ונוטלים ערבה ביום זה מלבד ערבה שבלולב ואין מברכין עליה: *Orach Chayim*, 664:2, ויש אומרים שאף הצבור אין מברך עליו לא בתחילה ולא בסוף זה. *Orach Chayim*, 422:2. דעת הרמב"ם וכן נוהגין בכל מלכות ארץ ישראל וסביבותיה And the reason is because דעיקר ההלל בר"ח אינו אלא מנהגא ולא מן הדין וכנ"ל ואמנהגא לא מברכין: *Mishnah Berurah*, ad loc), so why recite here?

This question was asked of the Radbaz, שאלת על מה שכתב הרא"ש שמדליקין נר בליל י"ה במקום שנהגו להדליק ומברכין עליו והא קיי"ל אמנהגא לא מברכינן מידי דהוה אערבה ונ"ל בטעמו של הרא"ש ז"ל דמשום שלום. He answers, שהוא מנהג נביאים ולא מברכינן

5) NO ANOINTING ONESELF WITH PERFUMES & LOTIONS; POWER; SENSE OF SMELL; YECHIDAH

Perfumes and lotions are connected to our sense of smell, they are also connected to a sense of power.

The sense of smell is connected to our deepest self. The Gemara says that our soul takes pleasure in the sense of smell (*Berachos*, 43b). Smell is the only sense that was not damaged or distorted by the Tree of Knowledge of Good and Evil — as it is the only sense not mentioned in the story: "And the woman *saw*...and she *took* (touch)...and she *ate* (taste)...and they *heard*...." (*Bereishis*, 3:6–8). Therefore, even today, our sense of smell remains connected with the state of consciousness that we experienced in the Garden of Eden. It can transport us back to the Tree of Life, into Unity-consciousness.

Smell can also awaken our earliest personal memories. This is because the sense of smell is free from the obscurations of duality, it can tap into the unity of the past, present and future.

הבית קבעוה חובה שהרי בליל שבת אין שם מצוה מפורשת אלא שהוא בכלל כבוד שבת ונצטוינו על כבוד שבת ביוה"כ נמי כתיב ולקדוש ה' מכובד ואמרינן בגמרא זה יוה"כ וכיון שאנו מצווין לכבדו הדלקת הנר בכלל מצות כבוד הוא ומצי לברוכי :Shu'T Radbaz, 6, Teshuvah 2, 209. Essentially, the Radbaz answers that lighting a candle on Yom Kippur night is because of *Shalom Bayis* / peace in the (lit) home, and also, because it is for the purpose of *Kavod* / honoring Yom Kippur, which the Gemara in *Shabbos*, 119a, says is applicable on Yom Kippur. But this answer is a little problematic, as the Gemara in Shabbos where it speaks about Kavod on Yom Kippur only mentions wearing nice clothes, but does not mention lighting a candle. Besides, the Rosh writes that lighting the candle for Yom Kippur is for Shalom Bayis, not Kavod, and Shalom Bayis, not to stumble in darkness, is part of Oneg not Kavod, and on Yom Kippur there is no Mitzvah of Oneg.

Regarding Moshiach it is said, "He shall smell the awe of Hashem" (*Yeshayahu*, 11:3), and "He shall judge by smell" (*Sanhedrin*, 93b). What you cannot judge by sight, you may still be able to judge by sound. But what you cannot judge by either sight or sound, you may still be able to judge by smell.

Moshiach is called Moshiach because he is *Mashuach / 'anointed with oil'*. The supreme power over a nation is the king. In the period of the Tanach, kings were anointed with sacred oil (כשמעמידין המלך מושחין אותו בשמן המשחה...ואין מושחין מלך בן מלך: Rambam, *Hilchos Melachim*, 1:7–12).

On Yom Kippur we need to strip ourselves of all (illusions of) 'rulership'. We should stop thinking about our power to influence others, whether real or illusory, and ask ourselves: 'Without any power over others, who am I?' You may be a very influential business person or leader, but just for now, delete from your mind, feelings and self-image, any sense of command or supervision. Now, look at yourself: who are you, really?

On Yom Kippur we are invited to stop identifying with human hierarchies. This includes identifying as a person at the bottom of a hierarchy, or one who lacks power, honor or sovereignty, subject to the decisions of others. If we consider ourselves powerless, we will eventually blame others for our experience of life. We may even dedicate ourselves to angrily resisting their presumed power. On this day of introspection, we can look inward and imagine our life without any sense of disempowerment or servitude. We can take the Divine question to heart: *Ayekah* / "Where are you?" If you deleted all sense of human hierarchy, where would you stand? If you subtract the influences of others, who are you?

AYEKAH / WHERE ARE YOU?

Free from all externalities is the essence of Yom Kippur, the day of naked truth. Resting on Yom Kippur from trivial identities frees you from these shallow perceptions of self. Forget about your job, money, position, influence, status, and desires — forget about all conventional maps and coordinates, and ask yourself "Where am I?" Are you standing in front of human concepts and definitions, or are you standing in front of Hashem?

When we stop allowing external influences to define us, we can begin to choose our real, G-d given identity. This is the empowering beginning of genuine *Teshuvah* / return to our true place, our true self, our sense of being 'here'.

The most devastating episode in the Garden of Eden was not just the mistake of eating the fruit of the Tree of Knowledge, itself. To begin with, Adam and Chavah were so lost and vulnerable in the face of outside influences, that they deferred to a voice that was not their own: the voice of the Snake. They had already vacated their own 'presence' when they listened to the reasonings of a separate, external influence. After they gave into their lower base instincts, Hashem asked them *'Ayekah*, Where are you? Where is your I? Are you present in your life?

Have you lost your center?' This compassionate question was answered by a deafening silence. Adam and Chavah were 'not there' — there was 'nobody home' to answer that question.

When Adam finally spoke, he pointed at his wife, Chavah, and when Chavah spoke, she pointed at the Snake. They were incapable of assuming responsibility for their own predicament. They surrendered their G-d-like creative ability of free choice, and claimed to be powerless. This is, arguably, the most devastating part of the narrative.

Ayekah is the existential question which HaKadosh Baruch Hu is asking all of us at every moment. When we point our finger outward with blame, or ascribe our inner experience to external forces, we lose contact with our true 'location'. When we are reactive, it is as if we are displaced — we are 'over there', rather than 'here'. We are in a self-imposed exile.

On Yom Kippur we are given the gift of at-one-ment, the gift and power *Teshuvah* / re-alignment and redemption. *Bechirah* / free-choice is the root of this Divine gift. Without the ability to freely choose, our actions seem predestined or externally imposed, and there is no room for Teshuvah. Teshuvah is taking responsibility for our life by acknowledging that we have Bechirah. As such, the Rambam describes the human ability to choose freely in the Laws of Teshuvah. On Yom Kippur, this innate, Divine-like power is restored to us. We discard the notion that we are powerless in the face of external influences, labels and desires, and we reconcile with the fact that they do not determine our choices. We break free from identifying ourselves with what we do, and we come to identify with who we are.

When we release all contingent, conditioned identities and imagine that this is our last day on earth, with nothing to hold onto — then who are we? We are unconditional purity, purpose, and light. Our Divine soul is revealed.

In the Torah, we find the practices of not eating, not wearing shoes and not having marital intimacy with regards to Matan Torah, which is a *Giluy haShechinah* / revelation of the Divine Presence:

- Moshe does not eat or drink when he is on Mount Sinai (*Devarim*, 9:9).

- He is told to take off his shoes when he first encounters Hashem (*Shemos*, 3:5).

- The nation of Israel is instructed not to have intimacy during the three days before they receive the Torah (*Shemos*, 19:15).

Yom Kippur is *Shabbas Shabboson* / the Resting of All Resting. When we rest from giving our freedom of choice away in exchange for promises of position, wealth, beauty, status, and power, we reveal what we really are: a part of the Divine, *Mamash* / literally (*Tanya*, Chapter 2).

May we all be blessed with the clarity to answer the thundering Divine question, *Ayekah*, with the words *Hineini* / 'I am here, I am ready!'

THE FIVE PROHIBITIONS & THEIR CORRELATIONS						
Prohibition	Definition	Senses	Divine Name	Tefillah	Torah	Consciousness
Shoes	Job	Touch	Hei	Ma'ariv	Bereishis	Nefesh
Eating & Drinking	Money	Taste	Vav	Shacharis	Shemos	Ruach
Bathing & Washing	Appearance	Sight	Hei	Musaf	Vayikra	Neshamah
Intimacy	Status	Hearing	Yud	Minchah	Bamidbar	Chayah
Perfumes & Lotions	Power	Smell	Kotz Shel Yud	Neilah	Devarim	Yechidah

Chapter Seven

MIKVAH OF TIME & THE QUESTIONS OF MI / 'WHO' & MAH / 'WHAT'

IN THE FINAL MISHNAH IN *Yuma*, REBBE AKIVAH EXCLAIMS: אשריכם ישראל, לפני מי אתם מטהרין, ומי מטהר אתכם, אביכם שבשמים... מקוה ישראל ה', מה מקוה מטהר את הטמאים, אף הקדוש ברוך הוא מטהר את ישראל / "How fortunate are you, Israel! Before מי / *Mi* / Whom are you purified? And מי / *Mi* / Who purifies you? It is your Father in Heaven: 'The *Mikvah* / 'ritual bath' of Israel is Hashem!' Just as Mikvah purifies the impure, so too, the Holy One, Blessed be He, purifies Israel" (Mishnah, *Yuma*, 8:9).

Yom Kippur, as Rebbe Akivah teaches us, is also similar to a Mikvah. Just as there is a Mikvah in space, an actual 'ritual bath' of water, there is a conceptual Mikvah within the world of time: Yom Kippur. The first and last letters in the word מקוה / Mikvah spell the word Mah / מה / 'what'. The middle two letters in מקוה spell the word Kav / קו / line. In this way, a מקוה is a Kav Mah / 'a line of what', or 'a line towards what'. Indeed, Yom Kippur is a 'direct line' to Mah / 'self-nullification', as Moshe tells Klal Yisrael, V'Nachnu Mah / "And we (Moshe and Aharon) are nothing" (Ramban, *Shemos*, 16:7). This nullification refers to freeing ourselves of our limiting identities and conditions, which is the function of a Mikvah. Yet this step is just a preparation to approach the *Mi*, 'before *Whom* I am purified', and also to discover 'who' we really are.

MIKVAH IN TIME

In order to honestly answer 'What am I', we need to be willing to confront ourselves and search our soul with absolute honesty and vulnerability. We need to shed all our shallow concepts of what is real and be ready to let go of everything that we are not. When we ask 'What am I,' we should look within and notice: I am *not* just a role, I am *not* just a utensil of wealth or aesthetic beauty, nor am I just a statistic of social status or interpersonal power. I am not just a body; certainly not a 'food-pipe', an ego or a Yetzer haRa. None of these define me.' When we see 'what' we are not, we are purified on a deep level.

A Mikvah is a place where we totally let go of what is not

essential to us. As we are submerged under the water there is a release of self, since humans need oxygen to exist. There is a *Bitul* / nullification or transparency of our *Tzurah* / assumed form within the formless and 'infinite' waters of the Mikvah. This is also the nature of the 'Mikvah in time', Yom Kippur. On this formless, 'infinite' day, we let go of all sins, all negativity, all false ideas of what we are. In the all-cleansing 'Mikvah' of Divine Presence we ask the question *Mah Ani* / 'What am I?' and release all our false identities and separateness.

WHO & WHAT

The *Hakdamah* / Introduction to the Zohar speaks of two types of questions: *Mah* / 'What?' and *Mi* / 'Who?' The question 'What?' asks for a fact, as in "What is going on here?" But the question of 'Who?' is a question of relationship, of trying to know the Infinite and Ultimate Hidden One (ועל דקימא לשאלה

ואיהו בארח סתים ולא אתגליא, אקרי מ"י...ואית אחרא לתתא ואקרי מ"ה. מה בין האי להאי,

אלא קדמאה סתימאה דאקרי מ"י קימא לשאלה :*Zohar* 1, 1b).

'What' is a much less sophisticated question than 'Who'. 'What' is an 'it' question; a utilitarian question, rather than a question of deeper relationship. As referenced in the Haggadah of Pesach, the Torah says the *Tam* / 'simple child' merely asks, *Mah Zos* / "What is this" (*Shemos*, 13:14)? Says Rashi, זה תינוק טיפש שאינו יודע להעמיק שאלתו וסותם ושואל מה / "This is the question of a dull child who has not sufficient understanding to question very profoundly and who therefore asks in an indefinite fashion, 'What...?'"

Sometimes simplicity is more profound than sophistication; the simple question of *Mah* can, in fact, be the deeper one. When one acknowledges that they know nothing, and they do not even know what to ask, they are open to a new understanding. His not-knowing opens him up to a knowing that is greater in *quality* than that of an 'expert'. Only an empty glass can be filled. A cup that is already filled with a large quantity of water is not fundamentally changed by a little bit more water. The additional water is seen through the prism of what was already present; it's merely more of the same.

When we are open, and ask, 'What is my life really about? I know nothing,' then everything that I've ever thought about myself I can put aside. I am ready to be existentially and honestly challenged. I am like *Ayin* / no-thing-ness, empty of all inner formations of the past. I am surrendering my sense of selfhood in the Mikvah of HaKadosh Baruch Hu, praying, 'Hashem, cleanse me! Purify my heart, opening me to something more wonderful, deeper, more real!' At that moment, true *Selichah* / forgiveness is granted. The deepest form of Divine forgiveness, which completely washes away one's old forms of life and allows one's very existence to be renewed, is rooted in the Thirteen Attributes of Divine Mercy. These attributes are expressions of the Transcendent qualities of Keser called *Ayin* and *Atik* / Primordial Being, and even the Divine Essence beyond all qualities.

When we sense the *Koach haMechadesh* / Divine power of renewal which continuously brings all manifestations from

Ayin to Yesh, then we too can be a *Soleach* / forgiver of others and ourselves. By immersing ourselves here and now in the 'Mikvah' of pre-existence, we empower ourselves to let go of any resentment, suffering, darkness, trauma, sin, anger, and any form of *Tuma* / stagnancy or 'impurity'.

And yet, this *Bitul* / emptying of our false Tzurah is only for the sake of allowing us to be filled with the deepest mystery of the *Mi*, the 'Who-ness' that is continuously re-creating us and giving us life. Once we have totally let go of everything, we are empty of 'what' and ready to be filled with 'Who'. We are able to move from the 'emptying' question of *Mah* to the 'filling' question of *Mi*.

Ultimately, we are given the understanding that אשריכם ישראל, לפני מי אתם מטהרין, ומי מטהר אתכם / "You are so fortunate, Israel; before מי / *Mi* / 'Whom' you are purified, and מי / *Mi* / 'Who' purifies you — it is your Father in Heaven." True purity comes from being *Lifnei Mi* / in front of the ultimate 'Who', and knowing that *Mi*, the deep, hidden 'Who-ness' of our Divine Father and King is what fills us with purity.

The *personal* question of 'Who am I,' is connected to 'Before Whom am I standing; in Whose presence am I living?' And the answer is, *Lifnei Melech Malchei haMelachim HaKadosh Baruch Hu*. We need to ask ourselves *Mi Ani* / 'Who am I,' and recognize that we are a pure soul-essence standing before the Transcendent King of Glory.

The answer to מי הוא זה מלך הכבוד / "Who is this King of Glory?" is omnipresent "Who-ness": ה' צבאות הוא מלך הכבוד / "Hashem, the Owner and Essence of Myriad Manifestations, is that King of Glory…" (*Tehillim*, 24:10). Hashem is beyond being a King, yet manifests as a King for our sake. The ultimate *Mi* is vast beyond all manifestation, yet also *Karov* / close: קרוב אתה יותר מכל קרוב / "Close are You, closer than any closeness" (*Even Ezra*, Tehillim, 119:151). HaKadosh Baruch Hu is our nurturing Parent, our intimate Beloved, and also the Omnipotent, Infinite, All-Transcendent Sovereign — and yet HaKadosh Baruch Hu is not defined by any of these roles. The Divine 'I' is simply אנכי מי שאנכי / *Anochi Mi sheAnochi* / "I am Who I am," I am Myself, prior to all roles and qualities.

On Yom Kippur we repeat the passage אבינו מלכנו אין לנו מלך אלא אתה / "Our Father, our King, we have no King but You." There are alternative ways of reading these words: אבינו מלכנו אין לנו מלך — אלא אתה / 'Our Father, our King, we have no king — rather, we have You!' In this sense, we cry out, 'Yes, You are our Parent and You are our King — but we really just want *You*, alone.' Or, 'Dear Father, we do not have a king, all we really have is You.'

Atah / 'You' refers to the Divine Self or 'Essence', which can manifest as Melech or Av, or both simultaneously, even though these contradict each other from a human perspective. A father cannot be a true king over his children because *Melech sheMachal al Kevodo Ein Kevodo Machul* / "A king cannot forgo his honor (and remain a king)." A father naturally has *Rachamim*

/ compassion for his children and forgoes his honor out of affection. A Melech holds up the world of *Din* / judgment and *Eimah* / fear: *Som Tasim Alecha Melech* / "Place a king over yourselves…" (*Devarim*, 17:15) — *Shetehei Eimaso Alecha* / "…so that his awe will be upon you (Sota 41b, *Aderes Eliyahu, ibid*). In this way, there is no Rachamim in Din. Yet *Atah*, the Divine 'Who', can be both our Father and our King, as It is also transcendent of these definitions. It is both infinitely far and yet infinitely close, totally transcendent yet deeply imminent; It is Ungraspable Ayin, yet the Being-ness that fills our every cell. And none of this can even begin to describe 'Who' Reality really Is.

LETTING GO OF WHAT HOLDS US DOWN & BECOMING LIGHTER

Once we have let go of 'what' we think we are, and discovered 'who' we really are, there is yet another step.

As we entered the 'Mikvah' of Yom Kippur, we first immersed in *Mah* / non-existence, and let go of 'what' we seemed to be, a form, a *Yesh* / ego. Thus open and transparent, we found ourselves *Nochach Pnei Hashem* / "before the Presence of the Vast Mystery, the Ultimate *Mi*, Who is also our 'Loving Friend', closer than close. The next step is to emerge from that 'Mikvah'….

One enters a Mikvah 'impure', stuck in self-definitions and shut down, but leaves the Mikvah purified, alive, and expansive. One enters with an old, limited form, but leaves as a *Beriah Chadasha* / a new, refreshed, revitalized *Yesh* / existence.

In this way, the Mikvah of Yom Kippur washes us clean of all impurity, sin, stuckness, smallness, pettiness, anger, aggression, and self-loathing. It 'magically' transforms us, so long as we allow it to and believe in its healing power, and we become new again, alive, free, light. We are open to assume a new form of life, a fresh, wholesome, holy, noble identity, and positive role and purpose. We feel alive, having confirmed our mission and purpose in the world; we are now clear about what we are supposed to be doing with the awesome gift of life that we have been given. This new form is the living answer to *Mah Ani* / 'What am I?

The physical sensation of lightness from having fasted, which dawns upon us as Yom Kippur comes to a close, represents the lightness and unburdening of being forgiven. Negativity pulls us down, and makes us feel inwardly heavy, and even physically lethargic. כי עונתי עברו ראשי כמשא כבד יכבדו ממני / "For my iniquities have passed over my head (overwhelmed me); they are like a heavy burden, more than I can bear" (*Tehillim*, 38:5). Besides fear and dangerous travel, one of the things that מכחישים כחו של אדם / "diminish a person's strength," is sin, as it says (*Tehillim*, 31:11), כשל בעוני כחי / "My strength fails because of my sin" (*Gittin*, 70a). In contrast, forgiveness lightens and strengthens us. As such, the sense of joy, elation, and lightness of being, is felt not merely because you did not eat and weigh your body down with food for 25 to 26 hours. Rather, this is a symptom of something deeper, that you are forgiven and freed of the weight of your entire negative past.

Amazingly, following the intensive *Avodah* / spiritual inner work of Yom Kippur, and arduous fasting and prayer, most people do not feel exhausted, depleted, empty, or ready to collapse. Rather, after the fast, people usually feel light and empowered, sharpened and focused. This is similar to the feeling of coming out of a refreshing Mikvah clean, elated, elevated, empowered, mission driven, focused, unburdened and invigorated. This is the new you.

A new you has emerged; you are unburdened by the weight of the past, you are free, empowered to live in the present and to move forward into a bright future.

Chapter Eight

THE MEANING OF THE WORD
כיפור / KIPPUR

Yom *Kippur* simply means 'the day of *Kippur* / atonement'. The Torah (*vayikra*, 23:27) uses the plural, יום הכפרים / the Day of *Kippurim* / Atonements: אך בעשור לחדש השביעי הזה יום הכפרים הוא / "Mark the tenth day of this seventh month as the Day of Kippurim." What is the deeper meaning of כיפור / *Kippur*, and why does the Torah use a plural term to name this day?

On one level, the simple linguistic answer for the pular is as follows. *Kippurim* is a *plurale tantum*, a type of noun that appears only in the plural form, denoting an abstract idea — such as the concept of atonement. Yet, since every detail in the Torah is highly significant, even a linguistic construct like this must contain a *Peshat* / literal reading and a *Sod* / hidden meaning answer, as well. This is because Peshat and Sod are always inseparably linked (כי באמת הפשוט והפנימיות הן בדרך א': *Meor Einayim*, Shelach. See also *Meiras Einayim* (Rebbe Yitzchak d'Min-Aco), Bechukosai. *Eitz haDaas Tov* (Rebbe Chayim Vital), Tehillim, 45. Arizal, *Sha'ar Ma'amarei Chazal*, Chagigah. Gra, *Even Sheleimah,* 8:21). One of the great later Rishonim, the Mahari Veil or "Mahariv," writes that the reason the Torah uses the plural for Yom Kippur is that it is a day which brings atonement for more than one category of souls: the living and those who have passed on (See *Ba'eir Heitev,* Orach Chayim, 622:8: ולכן נקרא יום הכפורים בלשון רבים ר"ל לחיים ולהמתים. מהרי"ו).

Many sources support this idea. The *Shulchan Aruch* (*Orach Chayim,* 622:6) writes, "There is a custom to give charity before Yom Kippur in honor of those who have deceased." And the Rama adds (in the name of the Mordechai), ומזכירין נשמותיהם דהמתים ג' / כ"כ יש להם כפרה ביה"כ / "And we recall the memory and pray for those who have passed on, for the dead to attain atonement on Yom Kippur." Similarly, it is brought down by the Rishonim to light a special candle in honor of the *Neshamah* / soul of a departed one (*Kol-Bo,* See *Darchei Moshe,* Orach Chayim, 610:4. *Nishmas Chayim* (Rav Menasha ben Yisrael), Maamar 2, 28), again the reason being that Yom Kippur brings atonement for the living and the dead (Rabbeinu Yerucham, *Mishnah Berurah,* 621).

Not only do we pray for the souls of the departed, but as the Chasam Sofer writes (*D'rashos,* Parshas Nitzavim), "We have received a tradition that on Rosh Hashanah and Yom Kippur the holy souls of those who have already passed on, and the souls of our ancestors, *join us* in our *Tefilos* / prayers."

MEANING OF THE WORD KIPPUR

What exactly does the word *Kippur*, from the word *Kaparah* mean in the context of the Torah? The root of the word כיפור is כ-פ-ר / *K-P-R* and the first time this root appears in the Torah is in the story of Noach and the Ark.

A flood is about to wash civilization and Hashem tells Noach to go ahead and build an ark, to protect himself and his family. The instructions he was given is עשה לך תבת עצי־גפר... / וכפרת אתה מבית ומחוץ בכפר / "Make an ark out of gopher wood... וכפרת / and you shall coat it from within in and from without with כפר / *Kofer* / pitch (a protective coating)" (*Bereishis*, 6:14). Since the waters of the flood were rough waters, he had to cover it with pitch inside as well as outside (as Rashi explains).

In this way, the basic idea of *Kippur* is to protect, as the Rambam writes; Teshuvah is כתריס לפני הפרענות / "a coat of armor against punishment" (*Hilchos Teshuvah*, 6:2). How does this 'protection' fit into the other times that *Kippur*, and its root, are mentioned in the Torah? For example, the *Kapores* / 'cover' of the *Aron* / Ark of the Covenant, may perhaps serve as a protection to what lies therein, but *Kofer* is also used in the form of a 'ransom', as in אם־כפר יושת עליו / "If ransom is laid upon him" (*Shemos* 21:30). *Kofer* also indicates a form of purification, as in וכפר אהרן על־קרנתיו אחת בשנה / "Once a year Aharon shall perform purification upon its horns (protruding corners of the altar)" (*Shemos*, 30:10), and of course, the root appears often in the term *Kaparah* / atonement, as in לכפר על־נפשתיכם / "to atone for your souls" (*Shemos*, 30:15).

What connects all these various forms of the root of *Kippur*? Is there an underlying principle related specifically to Yom Kippur?

In the context of transgression and Teshuvah, Rashi, the classic commentator on the Torah, writes that the root of the word *Kaparah* means to 'wipe away'. When Yaakov is about to encounter his embittered and estranged brother Eisav, he sends for gifts to Eisav and reasons to himself, אכפרה פניו במנחה / "I will appease him with gifts..." (*Bereishis*, 32:21). Says Rashi, אבטל רוגזו וכן וכפר בריתכם את מות לא תוכלו כפרה. ונראה בעיני שכל כפרה שאצל עון וחטא ואצל פנים כולן לשון קנוח והעברה הן / "'I will appease him: I will remove his anger.' This is similar to 'And your covenant with death shall be *annulled* (וכפר),' and 'One should not be able to *put it away* (וכפרה).' I (Rashi) am of the opinion that wherever the verb *Kaper* / כפר is used in association with iniquity and sin or with anger, it always signifies *wiping away* or *removing*."

The Even Ezra (ibid) writes that the meaning of the word *Kaparah* means to אכסה ואסתיר / to cover up and hide. This is an alternative understanding of the word. When a person transgresses or is steeped in *Tumah* / impurity, the purpose of Kippur is to 'cover over' those inequities or failings, so that they can draw closer to HaKadosh Baruch Hu despite those potential spiritual impediments.

Commenting on Rashi, the great Spanish sage Ramban writes (ibid) that *Kaparah* means פדיון / ransom, as in a ransom for a soul. In the context of this story, Yaakov tells his messengers, "Say in a respectful manner, 'Behold, he is also behind us.'" The Ramban interprets: "'Behold, your servant Yaakov is also behind us, and he has sent us before him in order to give *a ransom* for his life....' Just as servants present their ransom when they are given permission to see the king's face." In this sense, the Kaparah of Yom Kippur could be a sort of ransom or exchange. In place of a punishment — an objective consequence of one's negative actions — a Kaparah brings a more positive consequence. The seemingly inevitable consequence is 'exchanged', and one is spared punishment.

Kippur is related to the ideas of washing away, removing, covering over and exchanging consequences. Yom Kippur ties all these interpretations together; all the above meanings relate to the power of this day. On a simple level, Yom Kippur can be said to 'cover over transgressions' but not necessarily transform them. In this sense, the day 'protects' us from our sins, so that we will not reap their negative consequences and feel impeded from experiencing intimacy with the Divine. At the same time, Yom Kippur certainly has the power, when coupled with 'Teshuvah of love', to completely cleanse and wipe away all negativity at its root.

On the deepest level, Yom Kippur can bring about a 'ransom', 'exchanging' negative consequences with positive consequences; to transform זדונות...כזכיות / the liabilities of intentional sins into merits.[*] As an illustration, Rebbe Levi Yitzchak

---

רבי אומר על כל עבירות שבתורה בין עשה תשובה בין לא עשה תשובה יום הכפורים מכפר חוץ *

of Berditchev once met an infamous sinner and with a smile exclaimed, "I am so jealous of you. Imagine the holiness of your transformed sins! Do you even realize the potential merits you have?"

KIPPUR, PAR = 280

The *Sod* / inner, secret meaning (which, as mentioned, is fundamentally one with the *Peshat* / literal meaning) of the word *Kippur* is as follows. כיפור / Kippur (and its root, כפר) contains the letters פר / Par, which numerically is 280 (Pei/80,

---

מפורק עול ומגלה פנים בתורה ומפר ברית בבשר / "Rebbe says, 'For all transgressions that are stated in the Torah, whether one does Teshuvah or whether one does not, Yom Kippur atones, except for one who divests himself of the yoke of Heaven....'" The Sages then argue and conclude that Yom Kippur atones only for the one who does Teshuvah: *Shevuos*, 13a. *Yuma*, 85b. The Rambam rules as the Sages, ועצמו של יום הכפורים מכפר לשבים / "The essence of the day of Yom Kippur brings atonement for those who return": *Hilchos Teshuvah*, 1:3. Yet, the Rambam also rules, שעיר המשתלח מכפר על כל עברות שבתורה, הקלות והחמורות, בין שעבר בזדון בין שעבר בשגגה, בין שהודע לו בין שלא הודע לו, הכל מתכפר בשעיר המשתלח. והוא שעשה תשובה. אבל אם לא עשה תשובה אין השעיר מכפר לו אלא על הקלות / "Moreover, the Azazel-goat (an essential Avodah of Yom Kippur in the times of the Mishkan and the Beis haMikdash, as will be explored) atones for all transgressions mentioned in the Torah, both minor and major, whether one committed it in spite or whether he committed it in error, whether it was done by him knowingly or unknowingly. For all, the Azazel-goat creates atonement, provided the sinner does Teshuvah. But if he does not do Teshuvah, the Azazel-goat does not create atonement, save for his minor sins": *Hilchos Teshuvah*, 1:2. In other words, there is some level of atonement on Yom Kippur (via the Azazel) even *without* Teshuvah, while with Teshuvah there is much greater atonement — and גדולה תשובה שזדונות נעשות לו כזכיות / "So great is Teshuvah that one's intentional sins become merits... כאן מאהבה / (when one does Teshuvah) out of *Ahavah* / love": *Yuma*, 86b.

Reish/200). The number 280 is also the sum of the values of *MaNTzePaCh* / the five 'final letters' in the Aleph-Beis. These are the five letters that change shape when they appear at the end of a word (MaN-Tze-PaCh: Mem/40, Nun/50, Tzadik/90, Pei/80 and Chaf/20 = 280). Because these shapes appear only at the ends of words, the five MaN-Tze-PaCh letters are considered 'limiting' letters; they end or 'restrain' words. If they were not there to establish the ends of individual words, all the letters on a page would be read as one long word. Thus, they represent the five expressions of Gevurah (Gevurah of Chesed, Gevurah of Gevurah, Gevurah of Tiferes, Gevurah of Netzach and Gevurah of Hod) or *Dinim* / judgments, the five basic forces of constriction and concealment in the universe.*

These five letters are connected with the five letters of the Name *Elokim* (Aleph, Lamed, Hei, Yud, Mem). This is the Name of Hashem connected with the world of nature and apparent finitude, as well as the five senses, which allow us to participate and interact in this world of finitude. Our senses are the portals through which we connect to the outside world.

---

* In *Sha'ar haKavanos* (Inyan Rosh Hashanah, Derush Zayin), Rebbe Chayim Vital explains that the 320 Kelipos are the feminine aspect of Kelipah and the 280 are the masculine aspect of Kelipah. Yet, in other places in *Kisvei Ari* it says the opposite, that the 320 Dinim are the masculine aspect of Kelipah, rooted in the level of Chochmah (i.e., the dark or flip side of *Chochmah* / wisdom), and the 280 Dinim from the feminine aspect of Kelipah, coming from the level of Binah (i.e., the dark or flip side of *Binah* / comprehension): *Eitz Chayim*, Sha'ar Te'n'ta, p, 23b. Of course, there are aspects of the masculine within a generally feminine phenomenon, and feminine aspects within a generally masculine phenomenon.

As such, they are instruments of apprehension but also of division and separation. For example, when we look at one object and focus on it, we simultaneously exclude the vast majority of our scope of vision. When we listen to one sound, we block out other sounds. In this way, our senses function more as filters or reduction valves than as sponges.

These last two consonants in *Kippur*, Pei and Reish, appear in the roots of many words, such as *Pru'ah* / to reveal, or *l'Pharek* / to break apart. *Par* is therefore considered a force of breaking open, dividing and damaging; it represents a force of Din and Kelipah, judgment and concealment.*

The remaining letters of *Kippur*, when spelled in full, are כ / Chaf, י / Yud and ו / Vav (or just the letter Chaf remains when the word is spelled as in the Torah: כפר). Chaf/20 Vav/6 is the *Gematria* / numerical value of the Name Hashem (Yud/10, Hei/5, Vav/6, Hei/5 = 26. Chaf Vav spelled out (Chaf/20, Pei/80. Vav/6, Vav/6) is 112, the Name YaBok, the Yichud of Hashem/26 and Elokim/86=112). And Yud/10 represents the tenth day of Tishrei.

This reveals the idea that on the tenth day of Tishrei we are "*Lifnei Hashem* / in front ('before' or 'beyond') Hashem."

פ-ר / *Par* is both the root of *Kippur* and the root of the word *Shofar* / שופר. In the word Shofar, the other two letters are ש-ו / Shin-Vav, which spell *Shav* / equal. Rosh Hashanah, the day of <u>blowing the S</u>hofar, 'equalizes', or neutralizes negativity. Yom

---

* The word כפור / Kippur can be rearranged into two pairs of letters: כ-ו, פ-ר. The letters כ-ו equal 26, which is the same as the Name of Hashem. Add 26

Kippur, however, carries the power of the Name Hashem, which transforms the negative into positive. In other words, after we have traversed the Ten Days of Teshuvah we have the power to not only protect ourselves from the negative effects of past actions by 'covering' them over (like the *Kapores*), but ultimately we can transform all negativity into virtue by 'ransoming' (*Kofer*) or 'exchanging' bad for good. (On Yom Kippur there is a *Hamtakah* / sweetening of Par / 280, the Gevuros of *MaNTzePaCh* as they are elevated to the mindfulness place of Binah: *Siddur haArizal*, Rebbe Shabtai, Yom Kippur. Rosh Hashanah is a time of Din, whereas Yom Kippur is a time of Divine Rachamim, compassion and mercy: Ramban, *Vayikra*, 23:24.)

SELICHAH, MECHILAH, AND KAPARAH

In general, there are types of forgiveness that we ask for: *S'lichah* / סליחה / pardon, *Mechilah* / מחילה / forgiveness, and *Kaparah* / כפרה / atonement.

On Yom Kippur, we say throughout the day, many times, סלח לנו, מחל לנו, כפר לנו / *S'lach Lanu, Mechal Lanu, Kaper Lanu* / "Forgive us, pardon us, atone for us." This triplicate suggests that there are three distinct levels of forgiveness and return to intimacy with the Creator.

Mechilah means simply 'pardon', as in למחול על חוב / 'to pardon a debt'. In the context of Yom Kippur, *Mechilah* means

to 280 (פ-ר) and the sum is 306, (ש-ו / Shin-Vav). Thus, *Kippur* also carries the 'neutralization' of *Par: Bris Kehunas Olam*, Eilo Shel Yitzchak, 39.

that the debt (negative effect) incurred by our actions is over-looked and effectively erased. In this way, *Mechilah* is a type of forgoing an obligation, as in מחל על כבודו / *Mochal al Kevodo* / who 'forgoes his honor'. For example, you 'owe' your teacher honor, but in a certain situation he is *Mochel* / he 'pardons' his honor, and you do not need to show him the customary etiquette. The obligation does not exist under those conditions, as the teacher has nullified it.

Selichah is deeper than Mechilah: it is not merely a nullification of negative consequences. While spiritual debt is canceled for a recipient of Selichah, there is a positive element extended as well: a holistic acceptance of the person and a desire to reconnect to them.*

In our daily Davening we ask, סלח לנו אבינו כי חטאנו, מחול לנו מלכנו כי פשענו / *S'lach Lanu* / "Forgive us our Father because (we acknowledge that**) we have sinned," *Mechal Lanu* / forgive us our King for (we acknowledge that) we have intentionally

---

* On the other hand, without making a distinction between *Selichah* and *Mechilah*, the Ramban writes, והנכון בעיני כי סליחה הנחת העונש כדברי אונקלוס / "The correct interpretation appears to me to be that the term *Selichah* means 'remittance of punishment', as Onkelos rendered the phrase *S'lach Na* — 'Let go, please'": Ramban, *Shemos*, 14:17.

** As Chazal tell us, שכל מי שחוטא ואומר חטאתי אין רשות למלאך ליגע בו / "Whoever sins and confesses and says that they have sinned, no angel (force) can do him harm": *Medrash Rabbah*, Bamidbar, 20:15. Or, as the *Yerushalmi* teaches, ויאמר שמואל חטאנו לה לבש שמואל חלוקן של כל ישראל. אמר לפניו: רבון העולמים, כלום אתה דן את האדם אלא על שהוא אומר חטאתי, הני נשפט אותך על אמרך לא חטאתי, ואלו אומרים לפניך חטאנו: *Ta'anis*, 2:7

transgressed." We speak of Hashem as our King, our Ruler and Master, when we ask for *Mechilah*, as we are asking pardon for our debts toward the royal honor. This is not about a personal relationship; it is a kind of official transaction that changes a supplicant's status in the court of the King. The One who created us gave us orders; when we deviate or disobey, we incur consequences.

When we ask for Selichah in the daily service, we speak of HaKadosh Baruch Hu as our loving parent, our Father in Heaven. This is because Selichah is not asking to simply cancel the debt, but rather to restore the warmth of the relationship (This is also why we proclaim in the Yom Kippur liturgy, סלחן לישראל ומחלן לשבטי ישורון / "Hashem is the One who gives Selichah to (Klal) Yisrael, and offers Mechilah to the Tribes of Yeshurun." 'Yeshurun' is connected with Kingship, Hashem as King — ויהי בישרון מלך בהתאסף ראשי עם יחד שבטי ישראל / "Then (Hashem) became King in Yeshurun, when the heads of the people assembled, The tribes of Israel together": *Devarim*, 33:5. 'Yisrael' is connected with being a child of Hashem, as in, כה אמר ה' בני בכרי ישראל / "So says Hashem: Yisrael is My child, my firstborn": *Shemos*, 4:22).

Kaparah is an even deeper level. It affords us the ability not only to cancel the negative consequences of our deed and repair the positivity of our relationship, but to reframe our deed as a meritorious act. In this way, we can transform all the Din in our lives and surroundings. By revealing the positivity in apparent negativity, we can establish a wholeness that includes, encompasses and heals all experiences of brokenness and fragmentation.[*]

---

[*] Selichah, Mechilah, and Kaparah can be seen as benefiting three different entities: 1) Selichah benefits the *Gavra* / person who perpetrated the

TWO-LETTER ROOTS

The three-letter root of the word *Selichah* is ח-ל-ס / *S'lach*, and its two-letter root can be considered to be ח-ל. The letters לח spell *Lach* / wet or moist.

Similarly, the three-letter root of *Mechilah* is ל-ח-מ, and its two-letter root can be considered to be ל-ח. The letters חל spell *M'chal* / nullified, as in the Pasuk לא יחל דברו / "He shall not *Yacheil* / חל / break his pledge" (*Bamidbar*, 30:3), which the Targum translates as, לא יבטל פתגמיה / "He shall not nullify his pledge." Another Pasuk says, ולא-אחל את-שם-קדשי עוד / "And never again will I let My holy Name be profaned" (*Yechezkel*, 39:7). This suggests that *Mechilah* is related to a type of 'making light' of something, nullifying its importance, rendering it חול / *Chol* / non-sacred, and perhaps even treating it like חול / *Chol* / sand (Note, *Shu't Noda biYehudah*, 1, Siman 33. אף אני אומר כאשר פשפשתי למצוא סמך ללשון מחילה בלשון הקודש לא מצאתי לו שום שורש לא שורש חול ולא לשון חלה (וגם לשרש אחל א"א לדמותו... ולא מצאתי לו שום סמך רק שורש יחול והוא מלשון מצפה).

Both *Selichah* and *Mechilah* are thus rooted in the letters Lamed and Ches — only in different sequences and with different derived meanings, as above.

When we act out of *Selicha* / forgiveness, we become more fluid, more malleable in mind and body. Forgiveness is an ability to flow, to let go of rigidity, let things slide off like water.

transgression and rebelled against the command. Mechilah 'benefits' the King, the commander of the Mitzvah, Whose honor was insulted. Kaparah repairs the spiritual damage, created by the transgression, in the world and one's surroundings.

This is the quality of being לח / *Lach* / 'wet', as it were. It does not mean we forget how the other person hurt me, however, we nonetheless release the negativity in a 'soft' posture.

When we act out of *Mechilah* / pardon, we forgo our honor, allowing it to be temporarily 'non-sacred', so-to-speak. We make ourselves like *Chol* / sand, pardoning the other person for having 'stepped on us' a little. *Chol* also means hollow, empty. To render an act as Chol means to hollow it or empty it of its sting. In this sense, we grant pardon by taking the hurt or drama that occurred, and relating to it as if it is empty of negativity or insult.

Mechilah can be the beginning of deeper stages of forgiveness. Ultimately, the bitterness of what was hurtful can be transformed into sweetness. In the language of the Gemara, *Mechilah* is related to the word *Machlia*, which means 'to sweeten' (as in, אגב חורפיה דחילתיתא מחליא ליה / "...because the sharpness of slicing it with a knife enhances its taste": *Avodah Zarah*, 39a. Says Rashi, מחליא ליה — ממתקו, this means 'sweetens it').

If someone speaks insultingly to us, we have the power to pardon them, to forgo being victimized by it. We can respond flexibly, let it slide, and empty the words from their sting. When we are taking our honor seriously and the insult seriously, we become rigid and reactive. We take on the role of a victim, which only increases and prolongs the pain. But if we can be like water and 'flow' around the incident, then the 'insult' becomes like *Chol* / sand — simply inert words.

Similarly, the root of the word *Kaparah* is *Kaper* / כפר, and the two-letter root can be considered to be כ-ר / Chaf-Reish. These two letters spell רך / *Rach* / weak or soft. Our sages tell us, לעולם יהא אדם רך כקנה ואל יהא קשה כארז / "A person should always be *Rach* / soft like a reed, and not rigid like a cedar" (*Ta'anis*, 20a).

One who lives in a state of rigidity is brittle and fragile. The slightest impact creates unbearable resentment. Without letting that anger slide off, it can solidify and cement itself into their psyche. The more that resentment becomes ingrained in their personality, the harder it is for them to stop being a victim and move forward in life; they are always stuck on old grudges and brokenness. This is why Chazal warn us to be as soft as a reed.

MECHILAH / MACHOL / HOLY DANCE

At the end of the Gemara *Ta'anis*, the Mishnah says, "There were no greater days of joy than *Tu b'Av* / the Fifteenth of Av and Yom Kippur... On these days, the daughters of Yerushalayim would dress in white garments which they borrowed in order not to shame anyone who had none... and they would יוצאות וחולות בכרמים / go out in *Macholos* / circle dances in the vineyards, exclaiming, 'Young man, lift up your eyes and see who you choose for yourself'" (*Ta'anis*, 26b). Later on, the Gemara adds, עתיד הקדוש ברוך הוא לעשות מחול לצדיקים / "Hashem will make a *Machol* / a circle dance for the Tzadikim... and Hashem will, so to speak, sit with them and all will point with their finger and say, 'This is Hashem, I will rejoice in Him'" (*Ta'anis*, 31a).

מחול / *Machol* is related to the word *Mechilah* / pardon. What is the connection between dancing and pardon? In a Machol, many people join hands to dance and turn in a circle. To do this, each person needs to be in sync and in rhythm with the others in the group. In a dance of many parts moving as one, each is required to be soft and open and pardoning of one another. 'Protecting one's own honor' by pushing back on someone when they stumble or tread on your toe can cause the whole circle to fall apart.

Mechilah leads to *Selichah*, to be *Lach*, fluid, allowing yourself to flow along with another person's rhythm. You need to empty yourself, a little like a selfless person, in order to stay warm and responsive to other people's steps and missteps. If someone is departing from the circle, you draw him back in. Then the circle remains unbroken. And this is the definition of a holy dance, a dance of the unity of many.

In an 'unholy' dance, a person dances by himself, self-absorbed, self-oriented and 'rigidly' isolated from others. In a holy dance, each individual holds someone else's hand, honoring the other and rejoicing together. Each person is equally important and equally embraced within the circle. As a result, Hashem's presence is there, uplifting the whole.

This is why they danced in a Machol on Yom Kippur, and

the young men and women courted their soulmates. It is the Day of Mechilah, the perfect day to find your spouse, with whom you intertwine your lives in a circle of pardon and forgiveness — with a sense of Transcendence revealed at the center of your relationship.

BEING SOFT AND LIGHT
AND THE ABOVE RESPONDING IN KIND

Every day of the year, we ought to dispense Selichah, Mechilah, and Kaparah towards our fellows, but certainly on Erev Yom Kippur, a day set aside for others to ask our forgiveness, and on Yom Kippur itself. We need to demonstrate that we are 'soft' and fluid, not rigid, stuck in the past, or unforgiving. By doing so with others, we elicit a corresponding response from Above.

דע מה למעלה ממך / "Know what is Above you," instructs the Mishnah (*Avos*, 2:1). This is interpreted to mean, 'Know that all that happens Above is *from* you' (*Tzavaas haRivash*, 142. See also *Nefesh haChayim*, 1:4, Note). ה' צלך / "Hashem is your shadow" (*Tehillim*, 121:5), and your shadow mimics your actions (*Shaloh, Sha'ar haGadol*, 22a. *Keser Shem Tov*, Hosafos, 60). If we show fluidity and softness to others, Hashem shows softness to us as well, so-to-speak. By forgiving others, we are inviting Hashem to forgive us.

This is the deeper meaning of the teaching of Chazal, כל המעביר על מדותיו מעבירין לו על כל פשעיו / "Whoever forgoes his reckonings with others (for apparent injustices done to him) the Heavenly court in turn passes over all his sins" (*Rosh Hashanah*, 17a. See also *Sha'arei Kedusha*, 2:3). To illustrate this teaching, the Gemara offers a story: Rav Huna, the son of Rav Yehoshua, became sick, and Rav Pappa went into his home to inquire about his well-being. He saw that the world was growing weak for Rav Huna (he was dying). Rav Pappa said to his attendants: 'Prepare his provisions and his shrouds.' In the end, Rav Huna recovered and Rav Pappa was very embarrassed to go and see him, as it seemed as if he had decreed Rav Huna's death. Rav Huna's friends said to him: 'What did you see when you were lying there suspended between life and death?' Rav Huna said to them: 'Yes, it was so, I was truly close to dying, but the Holy One, Blessed be He, told the Heavenly court that since he (Rav Huna) does not stand on his rights (he is ready to waive what is due to him), you too should not be exacting with him in his judgment,' as it is stated: "He bears (*Noseh*) sin and forgives transgression." Whose sins does He bear? The sins of one who forgoes his reckonings with others for injustices committed against him."

KIPPUR AS PROTECTING THE SCATTERED

If we act fluidly, allowing offenses to roll off us and not letting them affect our positive judgment of others, Hashem lets our own offenses roll off and not affect His positive judgment on our lives. Not eating and drinking on Yom Kippur is a way to lighten and soften us on a physiological and emotional level. Without the constant input of food, our defenses and habitual rigidity lose energy and we let go more easily.

Yom Kippur is a Mikvah in time, as explored earlier. Underwater, we become free-flowing like water. We lose ourselves and our grip on our physical cravings, our honor and our narratives. Our deeply encrusted negative patterns of behavior are released into the waters of the *Ohr Ein Sof* / the Infinite Light of HaKadosh Baruch Hu. We bask and revel in the מי הדעת טהור / 'waters of pure, higher awareness' (in the language of the Rambam, *Hilchos Mikvaos*, 11:12).

Yet, the purification of a Mikvah is not achieved while one is immersed in the Mikvah, rather, when one emerges from the Mikvah.* Our transformation does not manifest in the first step, the letting go of the old. It manifests when we have gathered up all our good points, re-congealed our sense of self, and emerged from Yom Kippur with a greater sense of wholeness.

Par, the root of the word *Kippur*, shares a root of words that mean to 'burst' or 'crumble', as in פירורים / *Pirurim* / crumbs. The *Navi* / Prophet declares that in the future, פרזות תשב ירושלם מרב אדם ובהמה בתוכה / "Jerusalem shall 'burst open' (as a city not enclosed by walls) from the many people and cattle it contains" (*Zecharya*, 2:8. See *Chabakuk*, 3:14, ראש פרזו). On the one hand, *Kippur* means to burst, disperse and crumble everything that is hardened to make them flowing and soft: מפרר וזורה לרוח / "to crumble and throw into the wind." Yet *Kippur* also means 'covering over with a protective shield'. A shield needs not to burst

---

* *Kesef Mishnah* on the Rambam, *Hilchos Avos haTumah*, 6:16. Perhaps an earlier source is *Tosefos, Shabbos*, 35a, "*VeYarad*." See, however, *Pri Yitzchak*, 2, Siman 35. *Avnei Neizer*, Choshen Mishpat, Siman 72. *Devar Avraham*, Hashmatos, 2:15.

or crumble, but to have rigidity and firm integrity in order to enclose and protect its contents. As such, *Kippur* also highlights the second and essential step in the purification process of Yom Kippur: stepping out of the day with a re-configured, firm wholeness of self.

In the final moments of the day, a long, 'whole' blast of the Shofar expresses our new self-confidence and even holy pride. We have transcended ourselves, and now we victoriously return to ourselves, like a sea-farer returning to solid land, knowing that we have been forgiven and purified. We are like the Cohen Gadol, after the conclusion of his service of self-sacrifice, as he donned his civilian clothing and returned triumphantly home to his wife and family, celebrating having achieved his mission of national atonement, and rejoicing in the fact that he emerged from the Holy of Holies alive and intact.

Chapter Nine

KOL NIDREI / ALL VOWS: NULLIFYING ALL SUPERFICIAL ATTACHMENTS

I N THE LUMINOUS MINUTES BEFORE YOM KIPPUR ENTERS, JEWS THE WORLD OVER AND FROM ALL WALKS OF LIFE ARE ALREADY GATHERED EXPECTANTLY IN THEIR SYNAGOGUE, their *'Beit Knesset'*, *'Shul'*, or *'Shtiebel'*. They are about to embark on a 24- to 26-hour journey together to forgiveness, atonement, transformation and communal elevation.

One can be deeply touched by the aura of enthusiasm, hope, dread and inner joy as Yom Kippur descends. Yet, we do not begin the services with an eloquent piece of poetry describing Yom Kippur, nor with some holy chapters of Tehillim highlighting the meaning of forgiveness, nor the stirring story of

HaKadosh Baruch Hu forgiving Klal Yisrael in the Desert. Rather, we begin with a recital of *Kol Nidrei*, a technical-sounding legal text in which we formally annul our vows.

A few simple and obvious questions therefore come to mind: why begin Yom Kippur with an annulment of our vows? Why is this important? And how is it related to Yom Kippur?

The irony is even deeper, since as we are about to embark in petitions and pleadings for forgiveness, we begin by seemingly breaking our promises, canceling the binding effect of our hopeful statements of intention and the positive resolutions that we take upon ourselves. This may seem counterintuitive — if not contradictory to this day of complete honesty and positive hopes. Kol Nidrei seems the *opposite* of what Yom Kippur is all about, especially the idea of being responsible and accountable for our life.

And not only do we not recite this legal text quietly, but we sing it openly and proudly, with emotional fervor and a beautiful melody. There seems to be a disconnect between the singing and the words. Why do we *sing* Kol Nidrei, and why just before the beginning of Yom Kippur?

THE ORIGIN OF KOL NIDREI

The very origin of the liturgy of Kol Nidrei is itself mired in obscurity. Chazal do tell us (*Nedarim*, 23b) הרוצה שלא יתקיימו נדריו כל השנה יעמוד בראש השנה ויאמר כל נדר שאני עתיד לידור יהא בטל / "The person who desires that his vows not be binding should declare in the beginning of the year that all future vows (meaning that vows in the coming year should be void: Tosefos, *ad loc.* Whereas some commentaries say that this is an annulment of past vows: Rosh, *Yuma,* 8:28. Tur, *Orach Chayim,* 619) be rendered void and non-binding." But who composed the *Kol Nidrei* text that we have today, and when?

Some state that the introduction of the Kol Nidrei liturgy, or its prominence as Yom Kippur's opening service, took place during the Ninth Century, a period of Byzantine persecution. Others argue that it was composed as early as the Sixth Century, when the King of Spain ordered all the Jews in his domain to convert to his religion or suffer the consequence of death. The story is that those under duress and coercion to convert (or at least to make it appear outwardly that they were converting) would publically annul any statements implying an intent to abandon Yiddishkeit, and re-confirm their faith in Hashem and His Torah.

Yet, there are others who assert that Kol Nidrei can be traced to the Men of the Great Assembly some 2,000 years ago. And in fact, it may have been originally composed in Hebrew, not the Aramaic text we have today — as Kol Nidrei is found in Hebrew in one of the earliest Siddurim, the Siddur of Rav Amram Gaon (although he comments, שמנהג שטות הוא זה ואסור לעשות כן). According to this theory, it was only later translated into Aramaic, the language that most Jews spoke at that time.

Yet, a bigger question remains. One would expect that the first Tefillah of Yom Kippur expresses the theme of the day. It would be appropriate to sing of our soul's deep yearning to connect to HaKadosh Baruch Hu, or of our steadfast commitment to the intent of the day. But instead, Kol Nidrei speaks of retracting the force of our promises, suggesting perhaps that they were or will be made in a state of spiritual immaturity and inconsistency, and perhaps even that we want to avoid responsibility for them.

There is emotional resonance in the speculation that the Kol Nidrei service first gained prominence during the Dark Ages of Medieval Europe when many Jews were forced to relinquish their faith or die, and as a result, many outwardly converted. On the eve of Yom Kippur, these Jews would secretly gather and declare that the vows they made in the previous year were totally null and void, reaffirming their complete devotion to their Jewish roots. Whether this speculation is true or not, it provokes an intense emotional response in us, and this does set the tone for the whole-hearted repentance of Yom Kippur, its contemplations on death, and its stimulus to increase in devotion and love for our Creator. However, none of these historical narratives can be the *only* reason that Kol Nidrei has such power.

HASHGACHAH / PROVIDENCE

It is important to keep in mind that the text of Kol Nidrei is indeed technical and legal, and it deals only with the *laws* of vows and their nullification. For example, if a person made a vow not to overeat, he would have incurred a transgression if, in a moment of weakness, he broke his vow. Therefore, as the day of letting go of transgressions is beginning, and we are not allowed to annul vows on a *Yom Tov* / holy day, it is vital to annul the legal force of that broken vow just before the beginning of Yom Kippur, when people are already gathered. It is arguably only because the composers, cantors, and *Ba'alei Tefillah* / prayer leaders adorned this text with intricate melodies and choral arrangements that Kol Nidrei has become a dramatic, aesthetic service.

Yet, everything that occurs in life is *Hashgachah Peratis* / Divine providence, and all the more so phenomena connected to the spiritual customs embraced by the majority of Klal Yisrael. The fact that we sing Kol Nidrei with powerful and stirring melodies suggests that there is a deep *Ohr* / light in Kol Nidrei, beyond its technical dimensions. It also suggests that Kol Nidrei is intricately related to the theme of Yom Kippur, and it is not merely a strategic opportunity to observe the laws of vows.

We must say that Kol Nidrei's concept of releasing ourselves from certain self-imposed conditions is inwardly associated with one or more central themes of Yom Kippur.

LETTING GO OF INTERNAL NEGATIVE PROMISES

On one level, the idea of nullifying vows refers to unshackling ourselves from 'negative' declarations or vows that we may have taken upon ourselves over the past year.[*]

---

[*] There are various Hebrew words used to mean a vow or promise. Two of the principle words are *Neder* / vow and *Shevuah* / oath. The major difference between a Neder and a Shevuah is that a Neder is on the *Cheftza* / object, while a Shevuah is on the *Gavra* / person: *Nedarim*, 2b. For example, when

Sometimes a person is traumatized by the difficult breakup of a relationship, for example, and because of that, he or she might promise never again to open their heart to another person. Or a person has a nasty argument with a boss, and says to himself, 'After I quit, I will have nothing to do with this company.'

Such experiences could have happened this past year, or even many years ago. It could be that when you were 10 years old, a class bully made fun of the question you asked your teacher, and you made a silent promise never to ask teachers a question. Or you tried to sing in public and someone made fun of you, and you swore to yourself never to sing in public again.

Or maybe, this past year you tried to establish a discipline to learn more Torah, or focus more attention on your Tefillah,

---

a person makes a vow, they might say, "This *object* will be forbidden to me as if it were an offering in the Beis haMikdash." With that declaration, that object becomes forbidden to the person, like *Hekdesh* / an item consecrated to the Beis haMikdash. A *Shevuah* on the other hand, is an oath upon oneself to do, or not do something. The source of the power to create נדרי איסור / vows that make objects forbidden is from נדרי הקדש / vows to consecrate objects. In the words of the Ran, היכא שהתפיס ואמר הרי ככר זה עלי כקרבן חייל נדריה ועיקר נדר הוא זה: Ran, *Nedarim*, 2a. In other words, it would be similar to kindling another second or third candle from the same flame. On a deeper level, a נדר / *Neder* is Nun-Dar, drawing down the *Ohr* / light and level of נ / Nun / Binah, and making it דר / 'dwell' below in the world. Hence, a Neder transforms the object of the Neder, placing it in a category similar to Hekdesh. Annulling a Neder thus comes from an even more transcendent space, the level of Chochmah (*Ko'ach-Mah* / the power of 'no-thing'), as in חכם מתיר נדר / "A *Chacham* / person wise in Torah can nullify a Neder": *Machberes haKodesh,* Sha'ar Erev Yom Kippur.

but it did not go as well as you anticipated, and you gave up. Maybe you made a subtle promise not to fool yourself again, and to avoid attempting such goals.

When Yom Kippur is about to arrive, its aura of truth, honesty, openness, and transparency is already shining in us, and we are moved to bring up such promises, let them go, and declare them null and void. We courageously discard all promises with which we bound and stifled our own soul, and we set our vision on soaring to new heights in life, untethered and free.

WHY ANNUL A POSITIVE VOW?

Releasing ourselves from ties and constructs that hold us down liberates our heart, mind, and spirit; it makes perfect sense to annul internal 'negative' vows at the gate to Yom Kippur. But Kol Nidrei refers to "all vows" — both positive and negative ones. If a person promises that he will be a better person, will act more kindly and seek to help others, why should he nullify these positive promises? And why should he do this specifically on Erev Yom Kippur, as this holy "Day of Judgment" is entering? As we stand trembling before the Awesome King, knowing that our lives are being evaluated, shouldn't we *own* our commitments to kindness rather than disown them?

WHO WE ARE AND ARE NOT

Yom Kippur is the point of oneness in time that reveals the unity of all dimensions of time, space, and soul. Within this point, our soul-essence can be freely accessed. Although our soul-essence can be accessed on any day and at any moment of the year, on Yom Kippur this availability is heightened. In fact, throughout the year, whenever we have the inspiration to connect deeply with who we essentially are, that is properly called 'a Yom Kippur moment'. Yom Kippur is the inner light that helps us transcend our identification with obsessions such as food, drink, luxury, pleasure, position and power, and to live from the essence of who we really are.

With the help of Yom Kippur, we reveal who we are without all our externalities, superficialities, and negativities. We are not the negative self, the one who is angry, lustful, judgmental or despondent. All these traits appear only in the world of duality, where there seems to be an 'us' and a 'them', a 'me' against a 'you', a realm where it seems I need to control or be controlled, to manipulate my experiences, to take advantage of others — all in order to feed my own self-image and narrative, and to try and fill my gaping sense of emptiness with desires and stimuli.

In our essence, we are actually perfectly unified, whole, and complete. In our soul, we really lack and desire nothing. The core of who we are is an abstract space that is utterly unified, beyond plurality or fragmentation. Here we are at one with all reality and with our Divine Source. External pressures and desires have no effect on this level of soul; it remains pure and in its perfect state, under all circumstances and conditions.

Many of us, sadly, live for the most part in an external reality, in which we are primarily connected with our lower self, the self of ego and fragmentation. Because of this, when it comes to keeping our word, we feel morally, ethically and spiritually compelled, as if 'forced' to keep our word. If we promise someone we will do them a favor, we feel the honorable thing is to do it; even if we no longer feel up to it, we feel a pressure to keep the promise. Our conscience tells us that an honest person must keep his word, even against his own will.

FROM 'I MUST' TO 'I CAN'

Of course, we should keep our word and do as we say. Yet Kol Nidrei reminds us that although our words are binding, the fact that we feel 'forced' to keep our word indicates that there is a misalignment between our mind, heart and actions. If we are doing something good today *only* because of the verbal commitment we made yesterday, there is an inconsistency in our conviction and faith.

If you feel you have to use force or threats to motivate yourself to fulfill a past commitment, you are living from a 'I must' paradigm. However, there is a higher level you can access. Yom Kippur inspires us to live from an 'I can' paradigm. As we begin the holiest of days, and begin delving deeper and deeper into our essential self, we annul our future (and according to the Rosh, which is the way we rule, our past) vows. We affirm to ourselves that we no longer need the external pressure of promises to enforce good behavior. For the coming year, we aspire to live mindfully and integrate our actions and words with our deeper moral convictions and inner knowing. We are ready to live a life in which our minds and hearts will be in sync, in which we can act without pressuring ourselves against our will.

We are stepping out of the paradigm of 'I must,' and into the paradigm of 'I can.' I can do good because it is my *true will* to do good; it is of my essence to be and do good.

Yom Kippur gives us an ability to reveal the essence of who we are, and then live accordingly. This is a deeper reason we begin with Kol Nidrei. We only need to take a vow when there is a possibility of *not* keeping our word, and thus the vow forces us. But if we are ready to authentically live from the essence of who we are, we do not need the crutch of a vow. I don't 'have to' keep my word, 'I want to,' because it is who I am.

We can only begin to walk on our own power when we let go of our crutches. We might think, 'I must' use my spiritual crutches; I am not strong enough, I don't trust myself. But on Kol Nidrei Night, when we are invited to let go, we realize 'I can' rely on who I really am — and right now this can be my sole source of motivation to do good. At that moment, we are ready to stride courageously into Yom Kippur.

Freeing ourselves from reliance on external support and motivation is related to the name of the month of Yom Kippur, Tishrei. Says the Medrash (*Vayikra Rabba*, 29:8), *Tishrei* means to 'unbind', to let go. As Yom Kippur approaches, we 'unbind' ourselves, releasing ourselves from all of our self-imposed limitations and constrictions, and rendering them unnecessary.*

* Yom Kippur is a time of transcendence. Yom Kippur night is a unique time
in that a *Talis* / prayer shawl is worn during Kol Nidrei and Ma'ariv, the
night service. (Still, we should make sure to put on the Talis before sunset,
as the Mitzvah of wearing a Talis is fulfilled only during daylight, with a
garment that is customarily worn by day. The reason why a Talis is worn at
this unusual time is that during Ma'ariv, the Thirteen Attributes of Divine
Mercy, transcendental attributes rooted in the deepest levels of Keser, are
recited — and tradition has it that a Talis should be worn when reciting
these — א"ר יוחנן אלמלא מקרא כתוב אי אפשר לאומרו מלמד שנתעטף הקב"ה כשליח
צבור והראה לו למשה סדר תפלה אמר לו כל זמן שישראל חוטאין יעשו לפני כסדר הזה ואני
מוחל להם / "Rebbe Yochanan said: 'Were it not (explicitly) written in the
verse, it would be impossible to say that this (verse) teaches that the Holy
One, Blessed be He, wrapped Himself (in a Talis) like a prayer leader, and
showed Moshe the order of prayer.' He said to him: 'Whenever the Jewish
people sin, let them act before Me in accordance with this order (let the
prayer leader wrap himself in a Talis and publicly recite the Thirteen Attributes of Mercy,) and I will forgive them'": *Rosh Hashanah*, 17b.

As explored earlier, Yom Kippur is both a day of awareness of the immediacy of death, and a day of transcendence of that which dies. We thus wear
white both to act as transcendental angels, and remind ourselves of our
burial shrouds — נהגו ללבוש בגדים לבנים ונקיים ביום"כ דוגמת מלאכי השרת וכן נוהגין
ללבוש הקיטל שהוא לבן ונקי גם הוא בגד מתים ועי"ז לב האדם נכנע ונשבר: Rama, *Shulchan Aruch*, Orach Chayim, 610:4. In the context of the Gemara, a Talis is
considered a white garment — אמר אמימר מאן מלאכי השרת רבנן...ואמאי קרו להו
מלאכי השרת דמצייני כמלאכי השרת / "Who are the ministering angels... And
why are the Sages called ministering angels? Because they stand out like
ministering angels (as they are recognized by their clothing)": *Nedarim*,
20b. Says Rashi, שעטופים בציצית / "They wrap themselves in a Talis with
Tzitzis." Thus, a Talis is also worn throughout the prayers of Yom Kippur to
mimic angels, as they are said to be 'dressed' in pure white. The Tzadikim in
Gan Eden also 'wear white garments', so-to-speak: *Nidah*, 20a, Rashi: שמא
אזכה – לגן עדן והצדיקים מלובשים לבנים.

While some people can reach Teshuvah by simple inner reflection and introspection, others need a push, something external to inspire them. For
some, then, a Talis is worn as a sign of an induction into transcendent consciousness. For others, the Talis is a stark reminder of death and the transient nature of physical existence. Customarily, the dead are buried in a Talis

AS BELOW SO ABOVE:
ANNULLING ALL RESTRICTIONS

As the Zohar explains, the principle of "As below so above" means that every action below on earth is mirrored by a re-action in the upper realms and throughout all realms of exis-tence. And as mentioned earlier, דע מה למעלה ממך / "Know that all that exists Above is *from* you," and that ה' צלך / "Hashem is your shadow." This means our annulling of external motivating factors below stimulates, as it were, an annulling of external motivating factors Above. We turn to HaKadosh Baruch Hu, the Master of the universe, and say, 'True, we have led a life full of dubious behaviors, and we know that our spiritual alienation from You, the Source of Life, causes us physical, mental, emo-tional and spiritual conditions of exile, and estrangement and alienation throughout Creation. However, this predicament is partially because You have taken an oath, as it were, to respond according to our behavior "as below so Above," and to run the world on a system of judgment of cause and effect and mea-sure-for-measure consequences. But now that we are annulling

---

and a Kittel (white robe), and so on Yom Kippur, these garments are worn to inspire (if needed) a will for Teshuvah.

Beyond the dimension of transcendence that the whiteness of the Talis represents (although a Talis can technically be any color), the idea of a Talis represents the transcendent light of *Makif* / 'surrounding', encompassing light which hovers above the *Penimi* / the immediate, 'inner' or hidden light. What's more, a unique aspect of Yom Kippur is that the Divine *Nukva* / dimension of receiving (manifest as 'night') is elevated into higher dimen-sions. This is why the garment of *Makif*, the Talis, may be worn on this night.

our personal oaths, we ask that You too do the same, and once again allow Your Divine Presence to rest among us unconditionally.'

In the Zohar, Kol Nidrei is explained not just in terms of allowing human vows, but also in terms of annulling all *Divine decrees*. If a person is facing a Divine decree against him — a Divine 'oath' as it were — it means his negative actions have created a binding negative result, and the impurity of the past has impregnated the present moment. On Yom Kippur, however, we have the power to unshackle ourselves from negative consequences by reaching a point of *Teshuvah* / return which is beyond causality, beyond the world of cause and effect. As a reflection of this transformational point beyond causality, we proclaim that all vows and oaths are null and void. Teshuvah effectively nullifies the oath or 'decree' below and invites the Divine 'oath' or 'decree' Above to also be nullified.

During Kol Nidrei, we reenact a court of law. The *Chazan* / prayer leader is flanked by two people holding Torah scrolls. This is done to mimic a *Beis Din* / court of law of three people, as three are needed to annul vows. Besides simply annulling vows, we are, in a sense, also defending ourselves in front of the *Yeshivah shel Ma'alah* / the High Court Above. By our posture of Teshuvah, we are erasing our past misdeeds and, in effect, annulling the effects of our past actions. As a Beis Din, we are thus annulling the Divine vow, as it were, to follow the principle of cause and effect in which every negative action 'must' have a negative reaction. We proclaim that through Teshuvah, even our negative actions 'can' eventually have positive outcomes.

LINE VERSUS CIRCLE

The Creator's Light manifests in two ways. There is a light that surrounds all worlds, the *Ohr haSovev Kol Almin*, also called *Sovev* for short. This is a transcendent Light that 'hovers' above Creation, as it were. There is also a light that fills all worlds, the *Ohr Memalei Kol Almin*, or *Memalei* for short. This is an immanent and all-pervasive light that 'fills' the universe, permeating all Creation.

Clearly, the terms 'surrounding' Creation and 'filling' Creation are spatial metaphors that should not be taken literally; they are actually distinguished by the degree of their revelation within our experience. The Divine Light of *Sovev* is called 'encompassing' because it is indirectly revealed and remains beyond us. Only in a moment of awe do we realize that there is much beyond what we can understand or articulate. The Light of *Memalei* can be directly observed and felt as the unifying Divine orchestration of the details of our lives.

In the process of Creation, the transcendent Sovev quality *gives rise* to the substance of a thing, while the imminent Memalei quality *forms* the substance into a particular structure or configuration. Sovev allows something to be, while Memalei animates it. Memalei is intimately enclothed in the universe like a soul is enclothed in a body.

In the world of Memalei, the natural order is rigid and predictable; everything happens within a particular sequence and structure. There is an organic, linear unfolding of time, space, and individual consciousness. Every action has an inevitable reaction.

Teshuvah allows us to 'override' this rigid system and connect with the non-linear light of Sovev. In this way, we can undo the linear, causal effects of our past actions. In the linear world, every spiritually destructive action perceptually obscures the Divine Light that radiates into existence, diminishing the Light within Creation, the *Ohr Memalei*. To replenish that imminent Light, we must connect with the non-linear Light that transcends and encompasses Creation, the *Ohr haSovev.**

On Yom Kippur, using the power of Teshuvah, we tap into the transcendental light of Sovev, and remove our-

---

* When we commit a transgression, we blemish the Divine Light apportioned to existence, distorting as well as reducing the Divine flow immanent within Creation. To replenish what our transgression has taken away requires reaching the *Ohr haSovev* / a Transcendent and encompassing Light, the Light of the Circle, as explored earlier. The first letters of סלח לנו, מחל לנו, כפר לנו ("Pardon us, forgive us, atone for us") comprise the phonetic spelling of the word סמך, *SaMeCH* (the circular letter ס). *Forgive us* for closing our eyes to G-d's Presence and not connecting to It. *Pardon us* for not humbly fulfilling our obligations to our King and His honor. *Atone* for our insensitivity to our Beloved, for blemishing our deep-rooted mutual love through a lack of awareness. And therefore, Hashem, *forgive, pardon and atone for us* — through the Ohr haSovev, symbolized by the letter Samech.

selves from the destructive reverberations of our transgressions that would influence our subconscious mind in the present. Therefore, as Yom Kippur is beginning, we nullify those 'oaths', those negative reverberations, and move beyond the 'linear reality' of Kav into the 'circle reality' of Sovev. This allows us to repair all negative reverberations at their source.[*]

SPEECH & ESSENCE: DUALITY & UNITY

Ohr / light, whether transcendent and Infinite or vested in immanence and finitude, is an expression of the Source of Light, the עצם / *Etzem* / Essence. Etzem is actually 'Hashem Himself', although It is described as the Essence which transcends and includes both the finite Light of Kav and the Infinite Light of Sovev. Yom Kippur is connected with Etzem, in the words of Chazal: עיצומו של יום מכפר / *Itzumei Shel Yom Mechaper* / 'The essence of the day of Yom Kippur brings atonement.'

---

[*] The custom is to take out the Torah scrolls from the *Aron* / Ark for Kol Nidrei, and this is done to inspire the congregants, and to ensure that our *Tefillah* / prayer is linked to the Torah. As explained previously, the Chazan leading the Kol Nidrei is flanked by two people holding Torah scrolls to form a *Beis Din* / court of three judges, as a Beis Din is required to annul vows. Just as Moshe was flanked by Aharon and Chur when he Davened for the victory during the war with Amalek, so too, on fast days, such as Yom Kippur, these three people stand together. In a way, Yom Kippur is a battle against our own inner Amalek / the voice that cools us down spiritually and divides us. The ideas of a wrapped Torah scroll, its round image and the idea of three, are all related to the world of Keser, the singularity that unifies dualities, the world of Sovev.

Essence is the unmanifest Manifester. In the world of manifestation, a higher reality becomes the immediate source or cause of a lower reality, and this lower reality, in turn, becomes the cause, for an even lower reality. Such is the world of cause and effect, the world of duality, our perceptual world.

This manifest world is created via Divine speech, as it were: "The world was created with ten utterances" (*Avos*, 5). Speech is a modality of manifestation, and it is therefore an expression of the dual principle of cause and effect: "Elokim said, 'Let there be a…' and so it was." The very concept of a Creator implies the duality of Creator-and-Creation, or cause-and-effect.

Human speech does not create actual reality *Yesh meAyin* / something from nothing, rather it merely quantifies reality and contextualizes it. Yet in this sense it too 'creates' things. As such, human speech functions in a world of cause and effect, 'causing' events to occur.

Divine speech conceals and condenses, as it were, the Essence of the Creator, in order to reveal a glimmer of light or power, which eventually gives rise to physical matter. Human speech, too, is a form of concealment and condensation; we take undifferentiated sound and articulate it. First, breath rises up from the lungs, it vibrates in the vocal cords, and then the *Kol* / undifferentiated sound fills our mouth, where we shape it using the five 'organs' of articulation: the throat, palate, tongue, teeth, and lips. Finally, speech emerges. The letters of speech are composed of sounds that come from the throat (gutturals), from the palate (palatals), from the tongue (linguals), from the teeth (dentals), and from the lips (labials). Since, in the articulation process, these five kinds of letters create constrictions and limitations on the undifferentiated sound, they are connected with the five kinds of *Gevurah* / 'constriction'.

A vow is the most binding type of speech, creating the greatest constriction in terms of cause and effect. In other words, why keep a vow? A vow is a powerful 'cause' of an action in the present moment, i.e., the fulfillment of the verbal commitment.

In order to annul such powerful Gevurah, we need to tap into the Essence prior to the differentiation of causes and effects. Teshuvah affords us this ability, taking us beyond the accountability of our dualistic relationship with the transcendent Cause. All of our past negativity is then atoned, and its projected future effects are removed. All vibrations in the atmosphere are exposed and transformed, and all Divine 'oaths' are nullified, unbinding us and everyone around us.

LETTING GO OF OLD GRUDGES

On the level of inner development, the meaning of Kol Nidrei, and why it is established as an opening to Yom Kippur, is as follows.

To move forward in life, we need to let go of old grudges and hurts. Many times we get hurt by another person and we inwardly make a sort of 'vow' that we will never forget the hurt they caused. But today, holding onto that hurt is at least subconsciously crippling us. When Yom Kippur arrives, we declare that we are letting go of all our 'vows' and all the hurts and grudges we have stubbornly clung to. We are starting over again, with vulnerable innocence.

Yes, you may have had a difficult relationship with your parents, maybe it is true they did not treat you well, but now that you are an adult, it is only you, yourself, that you are hurting by holding onto your grudges, your defenses, or your self-image as a victim.

Yom Kippur is a time of cleansing, letting go. We let go of everything, our food and drink, our shoes, our attachment to possessions, honor and power, and we start over again.

Of course there's no need to let go of or forsake healthy attachments, commitments and responsibilities. But we certainly need to let go of attachments that are detrimental to our growth, whether physical, emotional, mental, or spiritual. We need to lay down our arms and remove our armor, and we need to drop our heavy stories about who we are, what we want and what we deserve — and just rest into the Divine Presence.

REDEMPTION OF THE SHECHINAH

As "Hashem is our Shadow," and Heaven mimics our *Avodah* / spiritual efforts below, activating the personal transformational quality of Kol Nidrei has repercussions. Kol Nidrei is a plea that the *Shechinah* / Divine Presence, which is in exile, be returned to Her proper place and be made whole again with *Kudsha Brich Hu* / the Holy Blessed One, as it were. There is a Divine "oath" in effect, so-to-speak, that Hashem's Presence will not enter and rest within the heavenly Yerushalayim above until the earthly Yerushalayim (meaning the Beis haMikdash) is rebuilt, so that Hashem's Presence can enter the Yerusha-layim below (the wording in the Gemara is אמר הקב"ה לא אבוא בירושלים של מעלה עד שיבוא בירושלים של מטה: *Ta'anis*, 5a. However, the Zohar writes that HaKadosh Baruch Hu "swore," *Kaviyachol* / so-to-speak — הקב"ה נשבע שלא יבא בירושלים של מעלה עד שיבא בירושלים של מטה: *Zohar* 3, Naso. *Shaloh*, Vayishlach, Torah Ohr, 2). The Heavenly Yerushalayim above mirrors the earthly Yerushalayim below, meaning that our individual ac-tions have a macrocosmic effect. There cannot be wholeness in the Divine Presence until there is wholeness in our own lives.

As we chant Kol Nidrei and annul our oaths, we are Dav-ening that the Divine 'oath' be annulled and the Shechinah be immediately liberated from exile. We are asking that there should be a revealing of Hashem's Presence and kindness, the annulment of all restrictions and concealments Above as well as below. And this is one reason that we sing the seemingly 'dry legal text' of Kol Nidrei with a stirring melody and deep feel-ing and hope. And this is why many shed a tear, and feel im-mediately softer and lighter. As we are letting go and soaring upward, and the holy Shechinah is descending into our minds and hearts, and we are experiencing a foretaste of the coming Complete Redemption, may it be soon and in our days.

BUILDING THE DIVINE KINGDOM

In addition to the above insights, the nullification of vows fits with one of the overarching themes of the *Yamim Noraim* / Days of Awe (*Ra'avyah*, Berachos, Siman 39:1), including the days between Rosh Hashanah and Yom Kippur (otherwise known as the Ten Days of Teshuvah). That is the theme of *Binyan haMalchus* / the rebuilding of the Divine desire for Kingship. The "rebuilding" is the re-awakening of a *Ratzon* / desire within Hashem, so to speak, to be the Creator, the King, the One who nurtures, nourishes and sustains all existence.

Malchus is the attribute of 'kingship', a quality that is intricately connected with the world of *Dibbur* / speech. After all, a king rules through his words, which are received as commands.

The Ten Sefiros are the channels through which the Infinite Formless Creator creates the world and continuously permeates reality. Malchus is the final or 'lowest' Sefirah, and the 'crown' of our lower universe. In this sense, it can be considered the most important of the ten. Each Sefirah is like a hologram, reflecting within itself all ten, yet Malchus is also a 'receptacle' in relation to the light of the Sefiros above it. Thus, in addition to being a Sefirah in its own right, Malchus can receive, include and reveal the other nine Sefiros: *Chochmah* / wisdom, *Binah* / understanding, *Da'as* / knowledge, *Chesed* / loving-kindness, *Gevurah* / strength, *Tiferes* / beauty, *Netzach* / victory, *Hod* / thanksgiving, and *Yesod* / foundation.

Since the fullness of Malchus is when it includes all the Ten Sefiros, we are given ten days — from Rosh Hashanah through Yom Kippur — to accomplish Binyan haMalchus. During each one of these ten days, we seek to build the Malchus of another Sefirah. On one day, we aspire to awaken within HaKadosh Baruch Hu a new desire to manifest Chochmah within His *Malchus* / Kingship. In other words, we strive to awaken Hashem's desire to rule with Divine wisdom. On another day, we aspire to awaken the Chesed within Malchus, to awaken Hashem's desire for a sovereignty of kindness.*

We also aspire to build our own personal Malchus by correcting and rectifying our speech. Every time we promised to do or not do something, we formed a reality through our words. For the most part, human words define and 'shape' reality, while Divine words 'create' reality. Yet, with the Divine power vested in our capacity to speak, when we promise something, our words 'create' binding conditions — vows closely mimic the creative power of Divine speech. Subsequently, if our actions do not match those conditions, an emptiness emerges. Vows that are uttered but not fulfilled are *Chol* / void, meaning, they lack vessels of fulfillment. In order to repair this lack — to

---

* According to the Arizal (*Siddur*), the first day of Rosh Hashanah corresponds to Keser, the second day of the month (the second day of Rosh Hashanah) corresponds to Chochmah, and so forth. The tenth day, Yom Kippur, corresponds to Yesod and Malchus together. According to the Ramak (*Siddur*), the first day corresponds to Malchus, and the tenth day corresponds to Keser. Similarly, the Tzemach Tzedek (*Ohr haTorah*, Shabbos Shuvah) writes that the two days of Rosh Hashanah are Chochmah and Binah. The seven middle days are the six emotional Sefiros (Chesed through Yesod) and Malchus, and Yom Kippur is Keser.

'build' the necessary vessels — we need to remedy our way of speaking. This rebuilding begins with becoming conscious of our words.

This is why there is such an emphasis on annulling vows during the Yamim Noraim (On Erev Rosh Hashanah there is a custom to annul our vows in preparation for the first day of the Yamim Noraim, and on Erev Yom Kippur, during Kol Nidrei, we annul vows again as a preparation to enter the last day of the Yamim Noraim). In order to build Malchus Above, we need to correct and put in order our Malchus below. Throughout the day of Yom Kippur, much time is spent recalibrating or 'rebuilding' our speech, our Malchus, by means of speaking the words of *Davening* / prayer.

As Yom Kippur enters, may we nullify all decrees, pierce the Heavens, break all limitations, and bring down a year of blessings and goodness for ourselves and the entire world.

Chapter Ten

THE THREE STAGES: SUBMISSION, SEPARATION, SWEETENING

ELUL — ROSH HASHANAH — YOM KIPPUR

ALL SPIRITUAL AND PSYCHOLOGICAL DEVELOPMENT EVOLVES IN THREE STAGES, SAYS THE BAAL SHEM TOV. Every collective and individual process of redemption unfolds in these three stages as well:

1) הכנעה / *Hachna'ah* / Submission

2) הבדלה / *Havdalah* / Separation

3) המתקה / *Hamtakah* / Sweetening

These steps unfold as three stages of Teshuvah, as manifest in three distinct time periods: 1) the month of Elul, 2) the day of Rosh Hashanah, and 3) the day of Yom Kippur. Elul embodies the quality of *Hachna'ah* / submission, Rosh Hashanah the quality of *Havdalah* / separation, and Yom Kippur is the culmination of the three stages of Teshuvah, the quality of *Hamtakah* / sweetening.

ELUL: SUBMISSION

Hachna'ah is humble submission and acceptance that comes from looking honestly at our life up until this present moment and fully acknowledging and embracing ourselves as we are. The *Avodah* / spiritual work of Elul involves fully acknowledging all our past and current mistakes and shortcomings, and humbly accepting them as our own doing. This includes accepting our body, identity, status, thoughts and feelings, as they are. *Hachna'ah* means to humbly accept all aspects of yourself, and to accept responsibility for them. What you are in this moment is the sum total of the ways you have been living up until now.

In Elul, a person needs to take responsibility for their life and claim, or reclaim, their past as their own. Only then can they progress to the second stage, 'separation' from mistakes and shortcomings. Even if we feel we have risen to a higher spiritual level in this past year, we should 'submit' to the Teshuvah process. The son of the Rambam, Rebbe Avraham recounts: "Once my father heard one of the important members of the community boasting on the Eve of Yom Kippur, 'I am so flawlessly righteous that I do not know why I would need any form of Teshuvah.' Hearing this, my father interjected, 'Perhaps he needs Teshuvah for the mere fact that he thinks he has no need for it!'" (Sefer *haMaspik LeOvdei Hashem*, Erech haAnava, p. 68. See also *Lev Dovid*, 12, p. 82).

In Elul, we take full accountability for our actions. As a metaphorical example, we need to say, '*I* spilled the milk,' not simply, 'The *milk* spilled.' We should also avoid dishonestly dodging accountability by implicating others: 'Yes, I spilled the milk, but he's the one who placed the milk on the edge of the counter,' or 'Well, if he hadn't asked me to get the milk, I wouldn't have spilled it....'

This month is a time of soul-searching, evaluation and submitting to *what is*. Owning responsibility for what we are honestly responsible for is the first step of Teshuvah. Elul is the *Achris Shanah* / end of year, and the word *Achris* is related to *Achrayus* / responsibility. When we look back at the past year, we own it, take full Achrayus, and say, 'That difficult situation did not just happen to me, but rather, I was a critical part of it.' The way we react to an event is largely our experience of that event. We need to gather up the past year and see where we abdicated responsibility, and own up to our part in it, no matter how small.

Say a young professional began a lucrative job earlier in the year, but as it turned out, the job did not utilize his talents as he had expected. In addition, he did not get along well with his supervisor, who was asking him to do tasks which did not come naturally for him — and he was not able to quickly learn the new skills he needed. Finally, in the summer, he frustratedly resigned. Even though the job was never a fit, he felt badly about the loss of income, and blamed his supervisor for the challenging experience. In Elul, however, he worked on gathering and contemplating the details of this experience, and owning his part in them. It was not his fault that the job was not right for him, but neither was it the supervisor's fault. In the end, it became clear to him that resisting and blaming his supervisor, and himself, was actually the bulk of his suffering. He realized that letting go of blame relieved him of his sense of victimization, inability and loss, and he was able to go forward, open-hearted, into a hopeful new year.

Remembering and gathering the details of our past year is like an 'inhale'. In Elul we 'inhale' the entire past year, take it in, process it, and assume full responsibility for our actions and mindset.

We cannot release and forget that which we do not remember. First, there needs to be Hachna'ah, an acceptance of the past, a submission to 'what is'. Only then can we experience a real *Havdalah* / separation, release, and 'forgetting' of all that was undesirable or contrary to our ultimate intention and direction in life. Only when we acknowledge the darkness that we have created and accept responsibility for all of it, can we ascertain a complete and accurate 'diagnosis'. Only then can we effectively apply the 'treatment' of Havdalah, and rise above all that is toxic to our soul or against our most authentic desire.

We also need to accept and 'submit' to our deepest potential, our soul's desire in coming down into this world. We need to embrace the fact that we are a *Shliach* / emissary of HaKadosh Baruch Hu in this world, and our deepest intention is to bring light and make this world a dwelling place for the Divine Presence. In Elul we need to submit, on a new level, to our general and specific purposes in being alive, and we need to humbly admit our essential greatness.

False humility manifests as self-denigrating denial of our goodness and our power to fulfill our mission. Real humility is based on inwardly admitting the brilliance of who we really are — and then proceeding to investigate how we may have been avoiding or blocking our true self, our gifts and our unique light. Part of the *Cheshbon haNefesh* / written self-evaluation that we perform during Elul should be appreciating and celebrating our positive actions, revealing our good points, and accepting our exalted purpose in being alive. For in this light, we can clearly see our shortcomings without resorting to self-deprecation.

ROSH HASHANAH / HAVDALAH, SEPARATION

Rosh Hashanah is a time of Havdalah, completely separating ourselves from our failures and anything negative or incomplete in our past. *Rosh Hashanah* / the 'Head of the Year' is the 'headwaters' of our life in this world; it is a new beginning, a fresh start for us. Not just the year, but we ourselves become 'new' and present in the now, and in this sense, separated from the past.

Our movement into a state of Havdalah is propelled by the sound of the Shofar. While the Shofar orients us to the spiritual task at present and the urgency of the moment, it also pushes away all distracting 'static' of the past. This is much like when a person claps their hands or hears a sudden noise — their entire focus is on that noise to the exclusion of all other thoughts or noises.

Imagine walking down the street distracted by an onrush of thoughts, and then suddenly a loud noise is heard and your entire mind becomes fixated on it. In this way, the sound of the Shofar sharpens our mind, allowing us to cut ourselves free from lingering scattered thoughts, and to focus on the urgent immediacy of the present moment. Similarly, if a person is suffering from *Machshavos Zaros* / distracting thoughts during *Davening* / prayer, he should clap his hands (*Likutei Eitzos*, Tefillah, p. 157. *Likutei Moharan*, 1:46. *Noam Elimelech*, Shemini. *Degel Machaneh Ephrayim*, Noach). This piercing sound focuses his scattered thoughts and energies. A sudden sound can pull our wandering mind back to centeredness and presence.

Rosh Hashanah is the "Day of Judgment," meaning 'Day of Alignment'. When we cleanly break off or cut away all negativity from our consciousness, we become unified and singularly focused upon our purpose, mission and destiny. This Havdalah is accomplished through the sound of the Shofar, which both orientates us in the moment and cuts away all other (distracting) noises.

This piercing sound of the Shofar is called *Teru'ah*, the same term that the Torah uses to refer to Rosh Hashanah; "the Day of *Teru'ah*." The word *Teru'ah* comes from the word *Ra'uah* / broken. *Teru'ah* thus means to break or smash, as in *Tero'em b'Shevet Barzel* / "You will *smash* them with an iron rod" (*Tehillim*, 2:9. Ritva, *Rosh Hashanah*, 33b). This relates to the second stage of our spiritual work, Havdalah. We focus on the good and present, while smashing, cutting away and severing ourselves from all negativity. This severance is accomplished through the Shofar blast.

All the Torah says of Rosh Hashanah is that "It shall be a day of *Teru'ah*." But what exactly is the Torah referring to? We know that Teru'ah is the sound of the Shofar, but which sound? Is it a sound of joy, jubilation, wailing or crying? Our sages explain that this sound is derived from the wailing and sobbing of the mother of Sisera, a powerful non-Jewish general (*Rosh Hashanah*, 33b). While waiting for her son to return from battle, when he was late, she began to worry: "The mother of Sisera looked out the window and cried through the lattice, 'Why is his chariot so long in coming? Why do the hoofbeats of his chariots tarry?'" (*Shoftim*, 5:28). In fact, according to the *Aruch*, all of the 100 sounds of the Shofar correspond to the 100 sounds that the mother of Sisera cried while waiting for her son's return, but deeply knowing that something was amiss and he might have been killed in battle (Tosefos, *Rosh Hashanah*, 33b).

A mother's cry for her child is a complete sound; she is totally present and unified with her cry. There are no other thoughts that enter the mother's mind when she is crying, for nothing exists outside her immediate pain; this essential sound negates all inner noise. This is the dynamic of the stage of Havdalah; to focus exclusively on the present good, and to 'blast' away all negativity in our consciousness.

This is also the dynamic of *Tashlich* / 'casting away' our sins; walking to a body of water with fish on Rosh Hashanah and symbolically throwing our sins into the water (a German *Minhag* / custom that has become a universal practice. For the earliest sources, see the German late Rishon, the Maharil, *Minhagim*, Hilchos Rosh Hashanah, 9. Quoted later by the Rama, *Orach Chayim*, 583:2. Note, Rashi, *Shabbos*, 81b).

We call this practice *Tashlich* / 'cast away', based on the verse in *Michah* (7:19): "...And 'cast' (*Tashlich*) into the depths of the sea all of their sins." Inwardly, this practice triggers a psychological and spiritual 'throwing away' of, and 'separation' from, our negative thoughts, emotions, words and even actions. Totally discarding all our negative past, and throwing it into the abyss of the sea.

On Rosh Hashanah, we recognize that there is 'what' we did or did not do, and there is 'who' we are. We may have sinned and perpetuated negativity during the past year, but on Rosh Hashanah, we stand in front of HaKadosh Baruch Hu, the Master of the Universe, and cast away all negativity and sin, courageously declaring, "I may have done such and such, but that is *not who I am.*"We therefore practice a *Havdalah* / separation between ourselves and what we may have done.

In Elul we claimed full responsibility for our thoughts, words and actions. We owned our past as we 'inhaled' the previous year. Comes Rosh Hashanah and we smash and cast away all negative or unholy past behaviors, cast them into the sea, and become decisively aligned with positivity in the unfolding new present moment. As we 'exhale' into the Shofar, we become fully aligned with and focused on the good. This is why on Rosh Hashanah we are all like Tzadikim and there is no mention in our Davening of penitence or regret for negative actions. There are also no *Tachanun* / penitence prayers on Rosh Hashanah (*Magen Avraham*, Orach Chayim, 584:2). This is in sharp contrast to the days of Elul, whose prominent feature is the *Selichos* / prayers of penitence focused on drawing down *Selichah* / pardon for misdeeds. Rosh Hashanah is the spiritual 'surgical removal' that follows the 'diagnosis' given in Elul.

Beyond the fact that we do not say *Al Cheit* / 'For we have sinned,' there is in fact no mention of sin whatsoever on Rosh Hashanah. We even go so far as to refrain from eating nuts. This is because אגוז / *Egoz* is numerically 17, and while the word חטא / sin is actually 18, we can subtract the Aleph (1), leaving חט, which is still phonetically equal to חטא / *Cheit* / 'sin' (*Shulchan Aruch*, Orach Chayim, 583:2, Rama: אגוז בגימטריא חט). In other words, on Rosh Hashanah we are so *Muvdal* / separated from the idea of sin that we do not even eat an item that has a numerical value of a word that only *sounds* like the word for sin.

The Medrash recounts that we go into Rosh Hashanah dressed in our finest, most elegant attire, trimmed, showered and prepared for our judgment (*Medrash Rabbah*, Vayikra, 29. Quoted in Tur, *Orach Chayim*, 581: לובשים לבנים ומתעטפים לבנים ומגלחין זקנם ומחתכין צפרניהם ואוכלין ושותין ושמחים בר"ה לפי שיודעין שהקב"ה יעשה להם נס).

In other words, we come with confidence and certainty, for we firmly trust that the coming year will unfold in the most favorable ways possible. This is, in part, because of all the work and responsibility that we have taken upon ourselves during the preceding month of Elul. On a deeper level, it is because we are in the state of Havdalah; we are confidently defining ourselves by 'who we are', rather than 'what we do' or what we have done.

On Rosh Hashanah we dress festively to confirm that we are ultimately beyond sin; this 'perfection' is who we are, and although we may have done 'imperfect' things in the past, that is not ultimately who or what we are. Therefore, we 'separate' ourselves from our past actions to the point that they no longer even come to mind.

YOM KIPPUR: SWEETENING

Ultimately, from that place of separation and detachment from the dramas and entanglements of the past, the deepest stage of Teshuvah is revealed: *Hamtakah* / sweetening.

Similar to Rosh Hashanah, on Yom Kippur, we dress in our finest garments. Men, in addition, don a pure white Kittel.

However, in the context of Yom Kippur, this is not so much an act of confidence, but rather to honor the day of itself. מאי דכתיב ולקדוש ה׳ מכובד? אמר ליה זה זה יום הכפורים, שאין בו לא אכילה ולא שתיה, אמרה תורה: כבדהו בכסות נקיה / "What is the meaning of the words, 'The holy one of Hashem is honored?' He said to him: 'That is Yom Kippur, when there is no eating or drinking, and so the Torah says to honor it with a clean garment'" (*Shabbos*, 191a). Giving *Kavod* / honor is to give weight (*Koved*) and value to that which is being honored. On Yom Kippur, we are honoring the power of the Day of Atonement.

Having arrived at the *Achas baShanah* / the unity within the rhythm of time, we can integrate and assimilate all of our past into a higher context in the present. We can experience a full reclamation of self by teasing out the slivers of light that reside in our past, even those ensconced in darkness. This is a form of spiritual 'composting', in which the energy that had been stored in the 'waste' of unsavory past actions returns in a purified form to nourish and vitalize a beautiful new flower. In this sense, we don fine garments and a white robe to give Kavod to the pure essence within our past mistakes. We are honoring Yom Kippur's powers of integration, redemption and sweetening.

On the one hand, the light of this day pushes us to our physical limits making us transcend our normal needs. This helps us demonstrate to ourselves that we can extend ourselves and achieve our innate greatness. On the other hand, there is an acute humility caused by the acknowledgment of our failures. This paradoxical state of consciousness is an expression of the *Achas* / oneness of this day. We hold both the highest and lowest aspects of ourselves, at the same time, uniting our transcendent detachment and our entanglements, our empowerment and our embarrassments, our present freedom and our past enslavements. From this place of *Yichud* / unity, we sweeten our entire life.

As the days of the *Yamim Noraim* / Days of Awe come to fruition on Yom Kippur, many layers of selfish obsession have been peeled away, and our inner core and essence are revealed. Trivialities and nonsense no longer hold sway for us, allowing us to dip back into our past, without stimulating trauma or drama, and redeem it. We are strong enough to look back upon our negative past, and sincerely recite Tachanun and Al Cheit over it, confessing it and turning it over to HaKadosh Baruch Hu.

From this deeper perspective, we can honestly look back upon all our past and proudly recognize that it is the cause of our present state of empowerment. This is the beginning of sweetening and integration, in which even "intentional negative actions are transformed into merits" (*Yuma*, 86b. The sins become like a *Hechsher Mitzvah* / a necessary preparation for a Mitzvah. See *D'rush b'Inyan Arvus Yisrael*, Pesicha, *Chidushei v'Shiurei Reb Baruch Ber*, p. 7–8).

There is a way of seeing every past mistake and failure as a merit: acknowledging that it got you to the place that you are now. It was the waste that has become compost, which is now fueling the blossoming of your higher consciousness or more refined character traits in the present. On Yom Kippur 'who we *were*' is becoming 'who we *are*'. Our mistakes are becoming Mitzvos.

Let us explore this idea more deeply.

GREATER LIGHT REVEALED THROUGH THE DARKNESS

וראיתי אני שיש יתרון לחכמה מן־הסכלות כיתרון האור מן־החשך / "And I saw that wisdom has an advantage over folly, as the advantage of light over darkness," proclaims the wise Shlomo haMelech / King Solomon (*Koheles*, 2:13). The simple meaning of the words "I saw that wisdom…the advantage of light over darkness," is 'I recognize the value of light through its contrast with darkness.' For example, if a person was injured and experienced difficult pain, but now the pain has disappeared, he values the absence of that pain more than ever before. This type of insight is the topic of the dialectical teachings called *Toras haHipuch* / 'the Torah of Opposites'. The Maharal explores such concepts at great length. He begins his *Sefer Netzach Yisrael*: "A good thing is really known by its opposite…from the color black we can know what is white" (*Netzach Yisrael*, 1. *Be'er haGolah*, 5. See also the teaching of Reb Aharon haLevi of Strashelye).

Chassidus reveals an even deeper meaning of Shlomo haMelech's verse by noting that the word מן usually means 'from' rather than 'over'. As such this quote means, 'I have seen...the advantage of light מן־החשך / *from* the darkness.' This implies that there is a greater light that comes 'from' the darkness itself — an 'advantageous' light comes from within and through the experience of darkness.

In this way, *Geulah* / redemption comes 'from' *Galus* / exile. Not only is a redemption the 'absence' of exile, but the redemption is only reached *through* the exile. There is an 'advantage' in this perspective, because the exile itself becomes 'sweet'; it is 'seen' as valuable, meaningful or luminous in its own right. Indeed, on Yom Kippur, a *Hamtakah* / sweetening manifests through revealing the hidden light within the darkness of sin, transforming malice into merit.

GREAT IS A SIN FOR A HIGHER PURPOSE

Our sages tell us גדולה עבירה לשמה ממצוה שלא לשמה / "A sin performed with good intentions is greater than a good deed performed without good intentions" (*Nazir*, 23b. *Horayos*, 10b). What is the source of this teaching? It comes from the story of Yael, who was intimate with the powerful general, Sisera, in order to assassinate him. Regarding Yael, a verse in *Nach* / Prophetic Writings proclaims, תבורך מנשים יעל... מנשים באהל תבורך מאן נשים שבאהל שרה רבקה רחל ולאה / Blessed above all other women shall Yael be... above the 'women in the tent' shall she be blessed" (*Shoftim*, 5:24). "Who are the 'women in the tent'? They are Sarah, Rivkah, Rochel, and Leah, the holy Matriarchs of Klal Yisrael" (*Nazir*, ibid). Because of her deeds, even though they were controversial, Yael is lauded as blessed above all women.

Sisera features prominently in Halachic and mystical expositions of Rosh Hashanah, as we know what a *Teru'ah* should sound like from the anxious cries of his mother, as explained above. But who is Yael and who is Sisera?

Sisera was the powerful general of the archenemy of *Klal Yisrael* / People of Israel, in the times of the prophetess Devorah. During this tenuous period in Jewish history, the time of the Judges and Prophets before the establishment of Kings in Israel, Klal Yisrael was very vulnerable to attacks from their neighboring states. One such state was headed by Sisera, the chieftain of the army of Yavin, the king of Canaan. He was young and extraordinarily powerful. In fact, his power seemed to be from 'beyond this world'. He struck terror, say our sages, even in the animals roaming the fields (*Yalkut Shimoni*, 247. *Gevuras Hashem*, Hakdamah, 3).

Devorah summoned the Jewish general, Barak, and said to him "Rise, for this is the day which Hashem has given Sisera into your hand...." And indeed that is what he did, until Yael was able to trick Sisera into her tent and eventually kill him, to quote, "And Barak went down from Mount Tabor, with ten thousand men after him. And Hashem confused Sisera and all the chariots and all of the camp with the edge of the sword before Barak; and Sisera alighted from his chariot, and fled on foot...And Yael went out to meet Sisera and said to him, 'Turn in, my lord, turn in to me; fear not.' And he turned with her into the tent, and she covered him with a garment. And he said to her, 'Give me now a little water to drink, for

I am thirsty.'"And she opened the flask of milk and gave him to drink, and covered him. And Yael…took the tent-pin, and placed the hammer in her hand, and came to him stealthily, and thrust the pin into his temple, and it pierced through into the ground. And he was in a deep sleep and weariness, and he died" (*Shoftim*, 4:14-21).

Besides giving him milk to drink which made him sleepy and lethargic (*Shevuos*, 23a. Rambam, *Hilchos Bi'as Mikdash*, 1:2), Yael, a married woman, actually had physical relations with him, committing adultery with him seven times (שבע בעילות בעל אותו רשע באותה שעה). Although this was a severe sin, her only intention in doing it was to weaken and exhaust the general so that she could safely kill him and end the widespread bloodshed. Strangely enough, because of this she is blessed beyond even Sarah, Rivkah, Rochel and Leah, the holy matriarchs of Klal Yisrael. Yael's story is an example of the principle גדולה עבירה לשמה / *Gedolah Aveirah Lishmah* / "Great is a sin for a (higher) purpose," otherwise known as "redemption through sin." It is possible, but of course certainly not preferable, that through an encounter with darkness or even committing a dark act, one can attain a greater light than could have been attained without that darkness.

WHEN DOES THE PRINCIPLE OF GEDOLAH AVEIRAH LISHMAH APPLY?

It is very rarely permissible to apply the radical principle of *Gedolah Aveirah Lishmah*. The simple reason is that the human

Yetzer haRa can easily justify any action it takes, and claim its sins to be sacred. When can it be applied? The *Nefesh haChayim* (7, Miluim) writes that it is a "dangerous" principle, and it was only valid before *Matan Torah* / the Giving of the Torah, and it is no longer applicable at all. However, this interpretation is a bit troubling, since the story of Yael and Sisera occurred many decades *after* Matan Torah, and indeed Yael was Jewish, already a convert at that time, making her liable to receive the Torah's consequences for these cardinal sins (*Yalkut Shimoni*, Yehoshua, 1, Remez 9: יש נשים חסידות גיורות — הגר, אסנת, צפרה, שפרה, פועה, בת פרעה, רחב, רות, ויעל אשת חבר הקיני).

Nefesh haChayim brings, in a note, that the principle of *Gedolah Aveirah Lishmah* is only applicable if the act was done "for the rescue of the entire Community of Israel"— not just for the rescuing of an individual. The story of Yael was indeed for the entire Klal Yisrael, and therefore it was allowed (ועשתה עבירה לשמה כדי להציל את ישראל: *Tosefos*, Kesuvos, 3b. See also Rav Elchanan, *Kovetz haOros*, Siman 48. *Shu'T Shevus Yaakov*, 2, Siman 117. *Shu'T Maharik*, Siman 167. This is the opinion of the Meiri in *Sanhedrin*, as well).

According to the Ramchal (*Kinos Hashem Tz'vaos*), *Gedolah Aveirah Lishmah* applies only in the realm of *Ishus* / marriage and *Zenus* / forbidden relationships, but nowhere else. In other words, a person cannot steal, murder, or commit any other sin, even for the greatest positive intention. The end cannot justify the means (Indeed, the Gemara in *Nazir* mentions only cases of Ishus. Interestingly, on the verse, "And Rochel stole her father's household idols" (*Bereishis*, 31:19), Rashi seemingly quotes *Medrash Rabbah*: להפריש את אביה

מע"ז נתכונה / "Her intention was to wean her father from idol-worship." Yet, the terminology in *Medrash Rabbah* (*Bereishis*, 74:5) is והיא לא נתכוונה אלא לשם שמים / "And her intention was only for the Sake of Heaven"— Rashi changes the wording, apparently because he does not wish to write that theft can be לשם שמים / 'for the sake of Heaven'. Note, however, the language of *Tanchuma*, Vayeitzei, 12: כדי לעקור עבודה זרה מבית אביה נתכונה).

A student of the Baal Shem Tov, the Toldos Yaakov Yoseph, writes (*Ki Seitzei*) that this principle can only function if the individual performing the sin has absolutely no pleasure from the sin, and if he or she is in fact disgusted by the act. Then and only then does the principle of *Gedolah Aveirah Lishmah* have any relevance (זה הכלל יהי' לאדם, אם אינו נהנה מעבירה עצמו, שהיא רעה אצלו ומתביייש מעבירה ומצער עלי', רק שצריך לעשותה כדי שיבא מזה תכלית טוב שהיא לשמה, אז שרי, ואם לאו לא יעשנה אם נהנה מעבירה עצמו).

In any case, in the story of Yael, the deed was a) for the sake of Klal Yisrael, b) it was in the area of Ishus, and c) she had no interest or desire to be physically intimate with him,* in fact, all she wanted the entire time was to kill him and end the battle.

THE COSMIC PROCESS OF REVEALING LIGHT THROUGH DARKNESS

Yael and Sisera are important examples for understanding

---

* Additionally, with regards to women in a prohibited relationship, there is a principle of *Isha Karka Olam* / "The woman is 'mere land', i.e., she is inert and not an active participant": Tosefos, *Sanhedrin*, 74b. The Rambam holds differently: *Hilchos Yesodei haTorah*, 5:5; see *Chidushei Rebbe Chayim al ha-Rambam*, ad loc.

this idea of 'redemption through sin' — and how a higher light can be revealed through darkness. In order to better understand this dynamic in relation to Rosh Hashanah and Yom Kippur, the power of higher Teshuvah to transform intentional malice into merit — and ultimately the full redemption of all sin — let us explore the cosmic process of Creation.

'Initially', there is only the Infinite Light and Oneness of Hashem (this is a temporal and spatial metaphor and should not be taken literally; Infinite Oneness remains eternally unchanged). Then (in a manner of speaking), in order to 'make space' for an 'other' to exist, for a creation to emerge, there is a *Tzimtzum* / cosmic contraction and withdrawal, a perceptual 'setting aside' of the Infinite Light, allowing a *Chalal* / apparently empty space to emerge. This is the 'place' of void, perceptual darkness and emptiness. Once the space is emptied, there is then a *Chazar veHe'ir* / a return of Divine Light which fills and illuminates Creation. This process of emptying, returning and re-filling is all for achieving a greater purpose and attaining a level that could not have been reached without it.

Again, first there is only the Infinite Light, a state of infinity, perfection and unified being. Then, a 'lack of perfection' is introduced as a result of the Tzimtzum. Once the Light returns, it creates the context for a different kind of perfection: perfection in a state of 'becoming', creating the conditions for a deeper revelation of Infinite Light. Whereas before the Tzimtzum the Infinite Light *excludes* finitude, after the Tzimtzum the Infinite Light is revealed as well as *within* finitude. This is an integral dimension that is deeper than 'Infinity', as Infinity and finitude are paradoxically coexisting without canceling each other out.

Being and becoming, perfection and 'imperfection', are mysteriously conjoined in a revelation of Unified Light within the place of duality and separation. It is 'the perfection of imperfection', as it were.

Yom Kippur is about *Hamtakah*, the full reclamation and integration of all the past darkness within a higher and deeper context. It is the full sweetening of 'coming full circle'. It is the redemption of all our past, the interinclusion of all 'darkness' within the Light, the subsuming of all 'duality' within the context of 'Unity'. This is the nature of the Teshuvah of Yom Kippur, which follows the *Hachna'ah* / submission of Elul — when we circled back and revisited our negative past, recited Selichos, mention our 'sins' and confess *Al Cheit* — and the *Havdalah* / transcendence of Rosh Hashanah. Now there is a great sweetening and integration, in which even "intentional sins become merits."

All of our past creates our present. There is a way of looking at every past mistake and failure as a merit, as it got you to the place that you are now. Again, this is a sort of 'spiritual composting', in which all the energy stored in what is discarded (sin) now returns to vitalize the blossoming of something new and beautiful (merit). Our past is fueling the blossoming of our present Teshuvah. In the moments of deep Teshuvah and high aspiration on Yom Kippur, 'who you were' is becoming 'who you are'. Your mistakes are becoming Mitzvos.

Yom Kippur's nature of *Achas* / oneness allows us to unify our states of transcendence and detachment with the light hidden in our lowest states. Yom Kippur peels away all the superficial layers of our experience, revealing our paradoxical essence. We discover that we are like pure angels, and yet like dust and ashes. We are frail, fallible human beings, and yet we are Hashem's beloved. The more this full-spectrum, unified reality becomes revealed, the more elated we become, until we realize we are the *Yechidah* / the 'singular' essential soul which both transcends and includes all soul levels and bodily experiences.

Gedolah Aveirah Lishmah, in the above exploration of Yael's encounter with Sisera, was the dynamic in which light and higher purpose were revealed precisely through the darkness of sin. When Yael achieved this, it brought a *Hamtaka* / sweetening of the negativity of her sin within a greater context of positivity (Again, her acts were to save all of Klal Yisrael and she had no personal pleasure or gain from the act, and therefore it was not 'sinful' in the normal sense). The advantage of light was revealed precisely through darkness.

THE LIGHT OF REBBE AKIVAH SPARKED FROM WITHIN THE HEART OF DARKNESS

Our sages tell us, "Among the descendants of Sisera there were those who studied Torah in *Yerushalayim* / Jerusalem" (מבני

בניו של סיסרא למדו תורה בירושלים: *Sanhedrin*, 96b). In the version of Rabbeinu Nisan Gaon, it continues: "And who was that descendant? Rebbe Akivah" (*Berachos*, 27b).

In other words, Rebbe Akivah, the great light of Klal Yisrael, was a descendant of the infamous enemy of Klal Yisrael, Sisera, and from the murkiest of unions (*Pesach Einayim, Sanhedrin*, ibid. *Asarah Ma'amaros*, Ma'amar Chikur Din, 5:10–11). On the third of the seven acts of intimacy, Yael became pregnant with a child who became a grandparent of Rebbe Akivah: "The spark of Rebbe Akivah was brought down into this world on that ominous night" (*Ibid, Megaleh Amukos*, 88, Va'eschanan).

Mahara miFano, the great Italian *Mekubal* / Kabbalist, writes that from the unholy union between Yael and Sisera, eventually Rebbe Akivah was born, whom the Master of the Universe placed in that generation (of the destruction of the Second Beis haMikdash and the beginning of the current exile) to protect the entire world and the secure the flowering of the Torah that it not be, G-d forbid, forgotten (*Ibid*, Ma'amar Chikur Din, 5:11. See also *Pri Tzadik*, Rosh Hashanah). The light of Rebbe Akivah had the advantage of emerging out of darkness — and because of this, he could go on to illuminate one of the darkest experiences in the history of Klal Yisrael.

REBBE AKIVAH AS THE HIDDEN LIGHT

Rebbe Yitzchak ben Moshe of Vienna, an early *Rishon* / Medieval Rebbe (13th Century), was unsure whether the name *Akivah* should be spelled with a Hei at the end as in עקיבה, or with an Aleph, as in עקיבא (in the *Bavli*, Babylonian Talmud, Akivah is mostly spelled with an Aleph [עקיבא], and in the *Yerushalmi*, the Jerusalem Talmud, it is always spelled with a Hei [עקיבה]. This is related to how vowels are used in Hebrew and Aramaic). One night, as he was pondering this issue, he had a dream, and in the dream he beheld the verse אור זרע לצדיק ולישרי לב שמחה / *Ohr Zaru'a laTzadik ul'Yishrei Lev Simchah* / "Light is sown for the righteous, and for the upright of heart, gladness" (*Tehillim*, 97:11). The last letters of the words of this Pasuk spell ר׳ עקיבה / "R(ebbe) Akivah" with a Hei, and he thus knew that Hei was the appropriate ending, and this prompted him to entitle his major work *Ohr Zarua* (*Seder haDoros*. Today we write Akivah with a Hei: *Beis Shmuel*, Even haEzer, 129, Ayin. The Chasam Sofer writes that we name people Akivah with a Hei, as not to be reminded of Rebbe Akivah's death when pronouncing the Aleph of the word *Echad* in the Shema — דגם רמ"א מודה דאין קורין שם על מי שלא הי' סופו טוב ומודה רמ"א דיש לכתוב עקיבה בה"א בסוף ולא באלף אע"ג דכל ר"ע בש"ס באלף ר' בסוף מ"מ מפני שסרקו בשרו במסרקות של ברזל וזה נרמז באלף שיצאה נשמתו באחד ע"כ כותבי' ה"א בסוף שמרמז על שמחה הנרמז בס"ת אור זרוע לצדיק ולישרי לב שמחה כמו שגילה בחלום לרבנו יצחק אור זרוע: *Shu'T Chasam Sofer*, Even haEzer 2, Siman 25:5).

This illustrates the spiritual fact that Rebbe Akivah is the אור זרוע / *Ohr Zarua* / the 'Light that is sown'. There is a deeper teaching that suggests that Rebbe Akivah at first spelled his name ending with the letter Aleph, and only later in life, when he had reached a higher level, was it spelled with the letter Hei, as in the verse of *Ohr Zarua* (*Likutei haGra*, Pirush Be'er Yitzchak [Rav Yitzchak Chaver], Erech, *Ohr Zarua laTzadik*). This means that at some stage, Rebbe Akivah 'became' the Ohr Zarua, the great luminary of Torah, embodying the *Ohr haGanuz* / 'Hidden Light' of the First Day of Creation, which had been set aside or 'sown' for the righteous of the future (*Chagigah*, 12a).

Rebbe Akivah is the embodiment of *Torah she-b'al-Peh* / Oral Torah, and the Ohr haGanuz was set aside and hidden throughout the Torah, and especially in the Torah she-b'al-Peh (*Degel Machaneh Ephraim*, Bereishis. *Yosher Divrei Emes*, 3. See also *Nefesh haChayim*, end of Sha'ar 1, Hagaha. Note, *Zohar* 1, p, 264a. *Tanchuma*, Noach). Historically speaking, he was the Ohr Zarua in his generation and the light of all generations to come. Today we are still basking in his illumination.

Rebbe Akivah is a 'redeemed soul'. A poor, uneducated shepherd boy and child of converts became the greatest Talmudic sage and embodiment of the entire Oral Torah, in which it is said, "The law always follows the opinion of Rebbe Akivah." This holiest of men, the most exalted of all sages, rises up from the most unholiest and precarious of unions, that of Yael and Sisera (Thus, it was specifically Rebbe Akivah who was able to declare, שכל הכתובים קדש, ושיר השירים קדש קדשים / "All the writings are holy, but *Shir haShirim* (which is seemingly about mere romantic, lower love) is holy of holies": *Yadayim*, 3:5).

"Through the window, the mother of Sisera looked forth" (*Shoftim*, 5:28). "The mother" refers to the holy Shechinah, the

'Mother of the World' who was "looking" to make sure that the holy spark residing deep within the soul of Sisera — the seed of the great Rebbe Akivah — would not be snuffed out in the battle. The light of Rebbe Akivah was still 'hidden' within Sisera and he needed to survive until this spark could be released into Yael and eventually produce Rebbe Akivah.

Torah she-b'al-Peh / the Oral Torah is referred to as 'the Torah of Rebbe Akivah'. He is the *Nefesh* / soul of the Torah she-b'al-Peh, and it is named after him in the same way that the *Torah she-b'Kesav* / the Written Torah is named after Moshe: '*Toras Moshe*' (*Asarah Ma'amaros*, ibid). Moshe was born into the priestly *Sheivet* / tribe of Levi, whole and circumcised, and as he was born the entire home became filled with light. Thus he embodies the Torah she-b'Kesav, the immediately revealed light. Rebbe Akivah was born in a lowly state, lived for years as an uneducated person, and only later on in life did he become the greatest of sages. As such, he embodies Torah she-b'al-Peh, the light that emerges from darkness. Our sages tell us that Yael's beauty was connected with her voice (יעל בקולה: *Megilah*, 15a). The Oral Torah, the Torah of the 'voice', is rooted in Yael and revealed by her descendant, Rebbe Akivah.

In the dark depths of the sin of Yael's intimate act with Sisera, the seed of Rebbe Akivah was released. From the soil of depravity a great light sprouted, the Light of the Ohr Zarua, the soul of redemption from all darkness.

100 CRIES OF BIRTH, 100 CRIES OF SISERA'S MOTHER, 100 BLASTS OF THE SHOFAR

Symbolically speaking, a mother cries out 100 cries during childbirth (Medrash, *Vayikra Rabbah*, 27:7). The first '99 cries' are during labor, and with the one-hundredth cry the child emerges from the womb, and the mother then knows (*b'Ezer Hashem* / with Hashem's help) that she and the child are going to live (*Tanchuma*, Tazria, 4. *Meshech Chochmah*, Emor).

Sisera's mother's cry, which she emitted while Sisera was cohabiting with Yael, represents the cry of the Shechinah and the emerging of the spark of Kedushah that lay deeply hidden within the body of Sisera, with its transmission into Yael (*Resisei Laylah*, 46). Her cries were like startling wordless prayers that accomplished the *Zarua* of the *Ohr*, the sowing of the Hidden Light in Yael, which would become the *Tzadik*, Rebbe Akivah.

These cries, in our own lives, are the 100 blasts of the Shofar on Rosh Hashanah, birthing us as the Tzadik we could be, and revealing the light that can come from our own inner darkness.

YOM KIPPUR:
THE HAMTAKAH & REVEALING OF THE LIGHT OF TORAH SHE-B'AL-PEH & REBBE AKIVAH

Rebbe Akivah, the light that comes from within and through the darkness, is unleashed on a 'seed level' on Rosh Hashanah, and becomes fully manifest on Yom Kippur. Yom Kippur thus manifests the power of Teshuvah, which is the redemption of light from darkness and the *Hamtakah* / sweetening of all judgments — a radical transformation of sin into merit.

Yom Kippur was chosen as a day of atonement because of an episode and its aftermath that occurred in the Desert with Klal Yisrael after leaving *Mitzrayim* / Egypt. A short while after leaving Mitzrayim, Moshe went up Mount Sinai to receive the First *Luchos* / Tablets. In the estimation of the People, he tarried in coming down, and with the help of Aharon, many of them fashioned an *Egel Zahav* / a Golden Calf, and eventually served it as an idol. After beholding this, the *Cheit haEgel* / sin of the Golden Calf, Moshe smashed the Luchos. He then returned to the mountain and pleaded with *HaKadosh Baruch Hu* / the Holy Blessed One for forty days, and then an additional 40 days — and finally on Yom Kippur atonement was manifest. A higher light and connection with the Divine was revealed, one that remains intact despite seeming obstacles and sins, and one that has the power to transform negativity and sin into positivity and merit. Ever since that event, this day is gifted to us as an eternal Day of Atonement. The day of Yom Kippur continues to be a 'redemption' that comes after sinning, a great light that emerges from the depth of darkness.

On Yom Kippur we were given the *Luchos Shniyos* / Second Tablets which Moshe had carved *himself*, signifying the idea of Torah she-b'al-Peh, the Torah of toil and human participation and ingenuity. If we had received only the First Luchos we would only have Torah she-b'Kesav (and *Sefer Yehoshua*: *Nedarim*, 22b). There would have been only an *Ohr Yashar* / direct light', transmission or revelation. The *Cheit haEgel* / sin of the Golden Calf, brought about the *Sheviras haLuchos* / breaking of the First Luchos. However, it was also the cause of the Teshuvah of Klal Yisrael, which eventually led to the revelation of a greater light revealed in the Oral Torah. The master key of Teshuvah, the Thirteen Attributes of Mercy which were revealed through Moshe, are inwardly aligned with the Thirteen Principles of Torah she-b'al-Peh — enumerated by Rebbe Yishmael.

Torah she-b'al-Peh consists of answers that are revealed through questions and uncertainties, human toil and mental exertion, representing a light that emerges from within darkness. "The people who walked in darkness saw a great light" (*Yeshayahu*, 9:1) refers to the light of the Oral Torah. "Darkness" refers to the questions and debates of the Oral Torah, and "great light" refers to its answers and resolutions (*Tanchuma*, Noach, 3). Torah she-b'al-Peh is the *Ohr Chozer* / 'reflective light' that comes *through* the darkness of questions.

Our sages tell us that the verse במחשכים הושיבני כמתי עולם / "He placed me in darkness like those long dead" (*Eichah* 3:6), refers specifically to the Talmud of *Bavel* / Babylon (*Sanhedrin*, 24a. The sages of Bavel are connected with 'darkness' [*Zevachim*, 60b], and the light that comes from darkness [Ritva, *Yuma*, 57a]). Talmud is a type of learning in which wisdom and clarity, light and resolution, are attained by means of toiling in questions, debates, and being persistently present with 'not-knowing'.

This is a "great" light specifically because it is revealed through resolving doubts, difficulties and lack of knowing. It is "the advantage of light from darkness," for darkness allows us to perceive the light that is deeper than the pure, 'unbroken' light of what is already known. And this is the ultimate redemption of Sisera himself; he unknowingly becomes the progenitor of the great revealer of Torah she-b'al-Peh.

Tishrei / תשרי, the month in which Yom Kippur occurs, is spelled Tav, Shin, Reish (Yud). These are the last three letters of the Aleph-Beis in reverse order, as the month of Tishrei embodies a reverse or backward flowing light, the *Ohr Chozer* that passes through darkness. Indeed, Yom Kippur reveals a more comprehensive illumination, a light that is much greater and sweeter than the original, direct light (עריבים עלי דברי דודיך יותר מיינה של תורה / "The words of Your beloved ones (the sages of the Torah she-b'al-Peh) are more pleasant and sweet to me than the wine of the (written) Torah itself": *Avodah Zarah*, 35a).

From Rosh Hashanah, with the 100 blasts, we are empowered to move on to Yom Kippur, to revisit our past, redeem and sweeten all of it — to retrieve the sparks from within the darkness to convert them into even greater light.

REBBE AKIVAH PASSES AWAY ON YOM KIPPUR

Appropriately, the culmination of Rebbe Akivah's life, which is his full redemption from the darkness of Sisera, and from his early years lacking Torah knowledge, was on Yom Kippur (*Ben Yehoyadah*, Berachos, 61b), the day of Ultimate Transformation.

Tragically, at the end of Rebbe Akivah's life, he was put into prison for teaching Torah in public. The Gemara (*Berachos*, ibid) relates: "When they took Rebbe Akivah out to be executed, it was time for the recitation of Shema. And as they were raking his flesh with iron combs, he was reciting Shema, accepting upon himself the yoke of Heaven. His students said to him: 'Our teacher, even now? (Even as you suffer you are reciting the Shema)?' He said to them: 'All my days I have been troubled by the verse, *With all your soul*, meaning, "even if Hashem takes your soul." I said to myself, when will the opportunity be afforded me to fulfill this verse? Now that it has been afforded to me, shall I not fulfill it?' Then, היה מאריך באחד עד שיצתה נשמתו באחד / he prolonged his uttering of the word *Echad* / אחד / 'One', until his soul left his body. A voice descended from heaven and said: 'Happy are you, Rebbe Akivah, that your soul left your body (as you uttered) Echad / אחד / One!'"

As the First Day of Creation comes to a close, the Torah says, ויהי־ערב ויהי־בקר יום אחד / "And it was evening and it was morning, day *Echad* / One" (*Bereishis*, 1:5). As the sages ask, why call it 'day one', and not the 'first day'? 'The first day' is the normal way of listing the first one in a series. Indeed, the Torah enumerates the rest of the days of Creation as the 'second day', the 'third day', and so on. Says the Medrash: *Yom Echad* / 'Day One' refers to Yom Kippur (יום אחד שנתן לו הקדוש ברוך הוא, ואיזה זה, יום הכפורים: *Medrash Rabbah*, Bereishis, 2:3).

Yom Kippur is the *Echad*, the Day of Oneness, of ultimate Unity, the day of *Yehi Ohr* / "Let there be Light," which sweetens and transforms all darkness and negativity and turns it into light. אחד / *Echad* is the level that Rebbe Akivah attained at the moment his soul soared from this world on Yom Kippur. He completed his journey in an enlightened state of אחד on the day of אחד.*

Most appropriately, the final words of the Mishnah in *Yuma*, the laws of Yom Kippur, are the words of Rebbe Akivah. "Rebbe Akivah said, 'How fortunate are you, Israel: before Whom are you purified, and Who purifies you? It is your Father in Heaven,' as it is stated: 'And I will sprinkle purifying water upon you, and you shall be purified' (*Yechezkel*, 36:25). And it says: 'The ritual bath of Israel is Hashem' (*Yirmiyahu*, 17:13). 'Just as a ritual bath purifies the impure, so too, the Holy One, Blessed be He, purifies Israel'" (*Yuma*, 85b).

---

* Rebbe Akivah is actually connected to the world of elevated *Katnus* / smallness or immaturity (as in 'darkness'). In the name of עקיבא there is the word עקב / heel, which numerically is 172. This, says the Arizal (*Sha'ar haKavanos*, Sefiras haOmer, Derush 7), is connected to the two levels of the Name אלקים, which is 86 (86 + 86 = 172), as it is in a state of Katnus. The remaining letters of Akiva's name (as spelled with an Alef), אי, represent the two ways that the letter א / Aleph can be fashioned, when using a י (Yud / Vav / Yud or Yud / Vav / Dalet). The Rashash writes in the *Siddur*, that in the Avodah of the *Sa'ir haMishtaleach* / 'scapegoat', which will be explored in greater detail later on, is connected to יעקב (and all the letters of יעקב are in the name עקיבא) and to Eisav. And when the goat was thrown off the mountain, the Divine Name אא-ללההייסם (which is twice אלקים) was the intention. This is a very powerful Name and the first Name that was revealed in Creation: Ramchal, *Adir baMarom*, p. 334. The Avodah of Rebbe Akivah, as later revealed in his main student Rebbe Shimon bar Yochai, is the elevation of the place of *Sham Aven* ('Shimon') / 'There is sin' (*Toldos Aaron* [Zelichov], Pinchas). In other words, the place of *Safek* / doubt (*Mei haShiloach*, Toldos) was elevated into the realm of Kedushah. Darkness became light, as in *Yehi Ohr*.

The Nefesh of Rebbe Akivah, the light of the Oral Torah, which is deeply seeded within the darkness of Sisera and the darkness of the acts of Yael, shines forth with the power of redemption from exile. Rebbe Akivah confirms that we have the power to be purified, elevated, illuminated, and totally redeemed even now, in the midst of our own darkness. So may it be, soon and in our days.

PART TWO:

TESHUVAH

Chapter One

THE ESSENCE OF TESHUVAH
ALL OF CREATION IS IN A PERPETUAL
STATE OF TESHUVAH

TESHUVAH IS ONE OF THE PHENOMENA THAT WAS CRE-ATED 'BEFORE CREATION' (*Pesachim*, 54A. RAN, *Nedarim*, 39B). On one level, this is because Teshuvah is a precondition for the existence of an 'imperfect' Creation, and especially of the human being (*Zohar* 3, 69b. *Reishis Chochmah*, Sha'ar haTeshuvah, 1). "There is not a just person on earth who does good and does not err" (*Koheles*, 7:20, Tosefos, *Shabbos*, 55b). As such, a world without Teshuvah is a hopeless world. And without a means to unshackle ourselves from our negative past behavior, we human beings would be forever crushed by the burdens of our past errors. It is only through Teshuvah that we are able to be relieved of our past or to reframe and transform our past.

This is the only means by which one can truly live in the present and move forward.

On another level, the fact that Teshuvah precedes Creation means that it is the bedrock and foundation of everything, from conscious and sentient life to inanimate objects. It is the essential component of reality itself. It is the healing and re-unifying force embedded within every atom of space and every moment of time, the power which draws all creations back to their Creative Root (תשובה היא החזרת הבריאה אל שורשה האלוקי, כל דבר בעולם חפץ להידבק בשורשו ובמקור החיים: *Yosher Divrei Emes*, 137).

The yearning to return to wholeness, to realign with the inner world of 'perfection', is innate and all-consuming. This is because the creation of finite space-time-consciousness occurs by means of a perceptual severing and *Tzimtzum* / contraction of the Infinite Light of Unity. As a result, one has the sense of having left original Perfection and Wholeness and being 'exiled' in a finite, fractured state. As the creation process is continuous, every finite creature feels this lack of wholeness at every moment and longs only to return to Infinite Unity. Teshuvah is the pervasive desire and deepest will within each and every creature.

Even beyond human beings who have free will to deviate from their innate Divine nature, every animal, insect, plant, and mineral is in a perpetual state of Teshuvah, returning to its 'original pre-creation' status. Much like human Teshuvah, which brings a person to a greater state of integration and wholeness than before 'sin' even occurred, the universe's un-folding 'path' of Teshuvah brings it to a greater state of inte-gration and wholeness than it had before its creation occurred. Before creation, Divine Unity was expressed only as Infinity. Now, engaging with Teshuvah, the universe of multiplicity is gradually becoming a revealed expression of Divine Unity. The finite world will return to Infinity even while remaining finite and physical.

All of Creation is in a state of perpetual Teshuvah — always moving upwards towards greater *Yichud* / unity. Like a plant that gradually turns toward the sunlight while its roots make every effort to reach toward their source of water, all forms of life are naturally turning and reaching toward their higher evo-lution. Only the human being, the microcosm of Creation, the one endowed with free choice, has the ability to choose or not choose Teshuvah. We are not governed by natural evolutionary forces alone; it is up to us whether or not we decide to move toward greater states of Yichud.

HUMAN BEINGS & TESHUVAH

A world imbued with Teshuvah is a world of possibility, op-timism, life, and genuine opportunity. Regardless of our current state, Teshuvah gives us the ability to leap over any obstacles that we have generated through our deeds, words, thoughts, and past decisions. Teshuvah empowers us to liberate ourselves from our exiles and to begin anew with vitality and hope.

If we ever sense that we are 'not in the right place' or even 'not the right person', Teshuvah alleviates this syndrome and restores us to authenticity. Genuine realignment with what is right for us requires profound sensitivity and honesty. It requires awareness of the true nature of our past desires, intentions, and needs. We need to sift through many competing and conflicting narratives, choose what is truly healthy, and let go of what is not healthy. This inner work may create a tenuous sense of self and an unsettling feeling of fluidity, but ultimately, when some level of Teshuvah is attained, one feels grounded, rebirthed, and reawakened to life and the true brightness of the future.

While to be human is to err, we need not despair. The possibility of reorienting our life, and ultimately transfiguring our existence, is always available to us. What we did yesterday is by no means an inevitable cause of what we will do today. What we do today does not predict what we will do tomorrow. The future is not an absolute consequence of the past, and time is not stuck in a rigid linear flow. There is always hope.

If there were no way to unshackle ourselves from the past, we would be imprisoned by our errors. Without the power of disengagement, we would be resigned to a hamster wheel of relentless, inevitable causes and reactions, preventing any real advancement. Someone who thinks that there is no way out can sink deeper and deeper into the gaping abyss of their predicament. One who thinks that everything they ever did from early childhood until now is permanently ingrained within them will be tempted to give up and simply continue with their negative patterns of behavior.* Without the hope that we can alter the course of our life, we fall onto a long slippery slope to the depths of despair. Life is drained away in a world of inevitable causality. Conversely, life imbued with Teshuvah is a life of optimism and vitality, a world of endless possibility. Regardless of who we were and the imprints of the past, we always have the power to reorient our life and choose life in the present.

RE-ENTERING LIFE & REINTEGRATION

Teshuvah offers us the freedom of rejuvenation, of beginning anew, of a quantum leap in our spiritual, intellectual, and emotional evolution. This self-transformation is essential for our wellbeing and that of the world.

Our sages speak of this universe as being created with the letter ה / Hei (*Menachos*, 29b). The design of this letter consists of three lines: a vertical line on the right, a horizontal line on

---

* In the words of the Rambam, מפני שבהכרח אדם טועה ונכשל, או שמתוך בורותו הוא מעדיף דעה או מידה שבאמת אינם עדיפים או שתאווה או כעס גוברים עליו. ואילו האמין האדם שֶׁשָּׁבַר זה לא ניתן לאיחוי לעולם, היה מתמיד בתעייתו, ואולי היה מוסיף על מריו מכיוון שלא נותרה לו עצה. אבל עם האמונה בתשובה הוא ימצא את תיקונו ויחזור למצב טוב יותר ושלם יותר ממה שהיה בו לפני שעבר עבירה / "For it is impossible for man to be entirely free from error and sin; he either does not know the opinion which he has to choose, or he adopts a principle not for its own merits but in order to gratify his desire or passion. If we were convinced that we could never make our crooked ways straight, we should forever continue in our errors, and perhaps add other negative acts to them since we did not see that any remedy was left to us. But the belief in the effect of Teshuvah causes us to improve, to return to the best of the ways, and to become more perfect than we were before we sinned": *Moreh Nevuchim*, 3:36.

the top, and a shorter, disconnected line on the left. As the left line is not touching the top horizontal line, it leaves a small gap above, like an open passageway. The bottom of the Hei is also open, making the letter like a box with no floor. This openness on the bottom indicates that it is possible for someone to fall out of the Hei, so to speak. However, the gap on the upper left side of the formation indicates that even if one does fall out of the bottomless 'box', it is possible to leap up and reenter the Hei through that upper passageway.

Very similar to the Hei is the letter Ches / ח. Both letters look like a three-walled box with no floor. The distinction between them is that in the Ches there is no gap on its left line. In the paradigm of Ches, one could fall through the bottom, yet there is no gap above, which could serve as a re-entry point.

In the Ches paradigm, there is only one way to go, and that is to fall out of the bottom. When a person deviates from his innate self and sins, he feels as if the 'floor' has fallen out of his life and there's no way to return and get back 'into' a state of holiness. As such, the word 'Ches' sounds similar to the word חטא / Cheit / 'sin', or more accurately, 'missing the mark' (*Shoftim*, 20:17: קלע באבן אל־השערה ולא יחטא / "Sling a stone at a hair and not miss the mark").

Return is possible in the paradigm of Hei, albeit not via the same route from which one fell. When a person has drifted off course and lost his way, the most effective route of return is often to take an entirely new route, and a higher one, like through the upper gap in the Hei. In the quest for transformation and re-integration, it may be necessary at first to shift perspective and not to deal directly with the activity or interaction that drove you off course to begin with. You may need to find a new — and sometimes opposite — focal point in order to proceed forward and move on with life.

For example, a person who is suffering from emotional depression (as opposed to clinical depression, which needs to be dealt with clinically), due to a lack of positive actions and mindset, or because one has stepped into negative patterns of behavior and feels terrible and depressed because of this, needs a radically new focal point to pull him out of his depression. Depression of this sort arises because of an over-indulgence with his sense of self. Internal statements such as, "I am not feeling well," "I am not a good person," "I feel trapped," "I feel incapable," are often evidence of over-occupation with the 'I', one's egoic self.

A remedy to break out of such an egoic stupor or depressive rut is to redirect one's attention outside of oneself. One very effective way to do this is to focus on the needs of others, and make efforts to help them. Directing our attention and energy toward other people makes us feel productive and needed, and builds our resiliency after a fall. Ultimately it will help us climb back up from where we have fallen and re-enter the world from a higher vantage point, as the opening in the Hei. Even a subtle positive feeling created by giving to others may awaken within a depressed individual a sense of joy and purpose. In the quest for self-rediscovery, the road that leads the person back home may be, in fact, the opposite of that which led him astray.

In the above examples, the word *Teshuvah* means 'returning' and reintegration; reentering the path of life after having fallen from it. While *Teshuvah* is often translated as 'repentance' or even 'penitence', a translation is never the precise meaning. A translation is more like the backside of a tapestry, where there is only a semblance of the intended design. In this sense, the meaning of *Teshuvah* includes but goes far beyond the translation 'repentance'. It is difficult to compress its vast implications into one English word or phrase, but a more accurate translation is 'returning from…', or 'turning towards'. The same word also means 'response' or 'answer'.

Teshuvah returns and restores the *human being* to the state of *being human*, to the state of integration within oneself and with the Source. It is also the 'answer' to the deep questions of life.

TESHUVAH AS 'RESPONSE'

Teshuvah, in its alternative meaning of 'response' or 'answer', implies that there is first a question or a need, and then an answer or resolution. The existential questions that call forth Teshuvah include 'What is the meaning and purpose of my existence?' 'Why is life so difficult?' 'Why does suffering exist?' 'Am I alone?' 'Who am I?' Such questions have always vexed human beings, causing them to turn inward in hopes of finding solace. The response of Teshuvah is an inner movement toward wholeness and self-discovery and, ultimately, a return to a life intimately connected to the Source of all Life.

Sadly, there are many for whom turning to HaKadosh Baruch Hu is 'the last straw', the final option, or an act of desperation prompted by a seemingly 'hopeless' or extremely challenging or negative experience. Pain, depression, loneliness, or alienation drive many to search for something larger than themselves for meaning, direction, purpose, and peace. Suffering can also break down the ego's resistance to the experience of the Transcendent. Thus, tragedy, even more than joy, seems to bring people closer to spirituality, introspection, self-evaluation, and positive change.

Oftentimes, happy experiences reinforce arrogance. How many can trace their downfall to 'high times' or a false sense of self-confidence and invulnerability? And how many people trace their discovery of a life with deeper meaning and connectivity with a Higher Power to a tragedy, a time of vulnerability, a sense of great need, or of letting others down? The process of Teshuvah is often ignited because one's desire for change is in accordance with the measure of his devastation. But Teshuvah is much more than a knee-jerk reaction to suffering and tragedy. Teshuvah is not in itself a derivative of desperation; rather, it is an expression of our deeper underlying self-worth. Teshuvah is a *healthy* response to life; it entails a full acceptance of self-accountability and some recognition of our essential dignity.

In truth, every person has a 'question' that bothers them, and the way they live their life is the response to that question. For some people, their question is, 'Why am I not rich?' Their primary drive in life then becomes making ever-increasing amounts of money. For others, the question is, 'Why am I disliked?' Their primary reason for being then appears to be amassing accomplishments or creating appearances that attract admiration and honor. Teshuvah is to respond directly to life's deepest questions: 'Who am I really?' 'What is the purpose of my existence?' 'Why do I continue, despite my efforts, to act in ways that I know are spiritually harmful?' A life of Teshuvah is a life of revealing your deepest truth of who you are, knowing who you are and why you exist. It is actively taking responsibility, or 'response-ability', for everything in your life.

As a 'response', Teshuvah answers the questions, 'Am I living with the awareness of the constant presence of the Omnipresent One? Does my behavior reflect the fact that I am always in the presence of Ultimate Greatness and Goodness? Am I honestly engaging in my own greatness and developing my gifts to the best of our ability?'

Of course, sometimes Teshuvah is about the details: 'I have done this or that, I have neglected this or that, I would like to fix such-and-such aspects of my character,' etc. There is, however, a deeper level of Teshuvah, which addresses a much bigger picture and answers much more comprehensive questions. This is the affirmative response to the questions of our life as a whole; 'Are we aligning ourselves with Hashem's vision of what we can be?'

When we engage in the practice of Teshuvah and self-examination from this deeper, holistic perspective, it is not so much about the details but rather about returning our entire being to be present before the King and Master of the world. 'Is my basic and fundamental desire to live with the awareness that I am in the presence of the King?' Without this bigger picture or core vision, we can get lost in dealing with endless minutiae and trying to fill in the ever-widening pockets of emptiness in our lives. To be healthy, a tree needs to be watered at its roots; it doesn't help to sprinkle each leaf with a few drops of water.

We do need to be detail-oriented and practical in our spiritual path. Yet, if we get carried away by the details — doing one good deed and then another, fixing one negative attribute and then another, following an array of precise customs and codes of behavior — there still may be no cohesiveness across all our actions and choices. Our good actions will still be good, but they might not be performed within the unity and wholeness of who we are and before Whom we stand. There will still remain an emptiness at the root level of life. Without revealing an overarching theme to our lives, even our well-intentioned or meticulous good deeds might lack a coherent trajectory.

The bigger picture of our relationship to the King infuses our individual spiritual works with a greater overall purpose. This faithful relationship to our Source connects our seemingly isolated experiences, mistakes, and good deeds. A redemptive wholeness embraces all the myriad details of our perceptions, activities, practices and efforts at self-improvement.

Teshuvah is the response to the most all-embracing vision of our reality, namely, the acute awareness that there is a King and Master of the Universe, and we live in the Divine Presence. The rest is commentary.

'TURNING AWAY FROM' & 'TURNING TOWARD'

Teshuvah also means 'turning', as in 'turning away from' or 'turning toward'.

'Turning away from' means departing from and letting go of a path of sin, deprivation, or negativity. It is releasing the past and our old modes of life. 'Turning toward' means turning toward Hashem, toward truth, toward a good future, or toward one's soul, mission and purpose. We turn 'from' what we are not and turn 'toward' who we really are.

'Turning toward', implies that there is an origin from which one was exiled and to which one can return. What is this origin? It is one's own deepest self, the self prior and above sin (Maharal, *Nesiv Olam*, Nesiv haTeshuvah, 8). While being led down into exile, the Prophet Yechezkel says, "...And *I* was within the exile" (*Yechezkel*, 1:1). The most devastating form of exile is the estrangement from our own inner 'I', when 'who we are' itself is in exile. Teshuvah begins when we decide to reclaim our rightful place in relation to our deepest 'I'. Teshuvah is a process of returning to the root of our soul, to the core of who we truly are (The Rebbe, *Likutei Sichos*, 2, p. 409. Teshuvah is return to oneself: The Mashgiach, *Da'as Chochmah uMusar* 3, 161). It is fundamentally a return to our existence, a redemption of the 'I' within.

RETURNING THE HEI TO HASHEM'S NAME

The Zohar divides the word *Teshuvah* into two parts: *Tashuv* / 'return', and *Hei*. The final letter Hei in the four-letter Name of Hashem, Yud-Hei-Vav-Hei, represents Hashem's Presence in this world (*Zohar*, 3:122a), as the world is created by the letter Hei. When the Hei seems disconnected from the Divine Name, there is exile, and we are called to return and reconnect the world to Hashem.

When we consider what it means to 'return the Hei' in our personal life, we can appreciate the discrepancy between the term *Teshuvah* and its colloquial translation as 'repentance'. While 'repentance' accurately describes recognizing one's past errors, regretting the past and resolving to do better in the future, *Teshuvah* is also concerned with reintegrating the 'Hei', Hashem's Presence, more deeply within our consciousness and, by extension, the world around us. Teshuvah can embrace, therefore, both an individual who habitually strays and an individual who is consistently upright, noble and righteous. The Teshuvah of every person contributes to returning the cosmic Hei to Hashem's Name, bringing greater reconnection and wholeness to the entire world. To return our inner spark of Divinity, the Hei within us, to our Creator, is relevant for everyone and at all times.

TESHUVAH AS LEARNING FROM OUR PAST

This is the deep work of Teshuvah: looking back into our past and redeeming everything from the 'other side.' We have to learn from all our experiences, and derive wisdom from our past mistakes.

No matter how difficult a challenge may be, whether it be a lost job, a broken relationship, or even the death of a loved one — if we wish to live in the present with wisdom, we need to learn to ask productive questions. For instance, it is not necessarily productive to ask, "*Why* did this happen to me?" Nor does it help to explain a negative situation away by blaming it on external causes. A better question is *What* — 'What could I possibly learn from this situation?' or 'What is the deeper meaning of this event?' Perhaps you will realize that, 'This is happening now so that I can learn something for the future.'

When we ask 'Why' in an attempt to find a logical reason or cause for events in our life or in history, we are focussing solely on the past and thus living in the past. For some people, this focus becomes an obsessive-compulsive fixation on the past. We can never truly know 'why' things happen. Only the Creator knows every side of the story, the hidden causes and reasons. Knowledge that is existentially relevant to our lives is knowledge of what is existing now and what patterns may play out in the future.

Instead of focusing on the *Lamah* / 'why', we should train ourselves to focus on the *leMah* / 'towards what end'. Rather than trying to trace an event's 'genealogy,' we should try to intuit the potential trajectory of the event in the present. We should resist the illusion of false certainty within mythological histories, and remain vulnerable and open to the infinite possibilities of the future by being fully present in the now. When we ask, 'Why', we are looking to lay blame for something that is past, something that no longer exists. When we ask, 'towards what end', we are claiming responsibility for the co-creation of what does exist: the now and potential future 'now.'

All of this is part of returning toward your true self; 'turning away from' old concepts of yourself, and 'turning toward' a new sense of self. Doing so is the foundation of returning toward your soul's journey.

RETURNING TO YOUR SOUL'S PURPOSE IN DESCENDING INTO A BODY

All souls embodied within physical forms yearn for Teshuvah, re-connection and ever deeper integration with Divine Presence. Enfolded within body and ego, our infinite soul longs to return to its root in Divine Infinity. Yet, Teshuvah while embodied is very different from a disembodied, purely spiritual Teshuvah. While nested within a body, the soul acknowledges the body's ultimate purpose. Then Teshuvah becomes a 'return' to Source while remaining in the body, without the body expiring or the soul leaving the body, as can happen in ascetic, body-denying spiritual practices. On the contrary, the soul realizes it must return to Divinity *by means of* physical embodiment. To accomplish this, the soul needs to harness the power of the body to manifest and actualize the presence of *Atzmus* / the Divine Essence. Atzmus transcends all definitions, even that of being Infinite, and hence It includes the infinity of the soul as well as the finitude of the body, allowing the two to remain linked. The soul recognizes the great advantage in returning to Essence (via the body) over returning to Infinity (by separating from the body). Essence is incomparably greater than Infinity.

As Teshuvah is an authentic homecoming to oneself, the path is specific to each individual. Each person's journey is tailored according to the uniqueness of their own soul and psyche. Just as no two people are physically identical, no two people are spiritually identical. In fact, our physical diversity is a manifestation of our spiritual diversity. Teshuvah is a return to our unique self and our distinct purpose.

In the initial stages of Teshuvah, many people need to shift their perspective or transcend their egoic past by conforming to particular dress codes and behavioral patterns, specific musical choices and ways of speaking, and so forth. Such changes in personality are means of 're-entering the Hei' by a different passageway than the one through which they fell. However, these are not in themselves Teshuvah nor the goal of Teshuvah; they are merely tools. Dressing differently can help elevate a person's consciousness temporarily and give them a new opening into life, but it cannot transform them. The Creator designs each and every individual with different experiences, inner struggles, gifts and purposes. Teshuvah is authentic when we re-embrace our past and our unique self in a higher context. The goal of Teshuvah is to reconnect *yourself* to Hashem, not someone else.

Throughout our journey through life, we may look to our fellow travelers for assistance, advice, encouragement, or inspiration, but ultimately, we must trek our own path. We may observe the accomplishments and setbacks of other travelers, but we can only grow according to our own range of comfort and challenge. Blazing our own trail might be more difficult than imitating another's, but it is ultimately the only way we can be true to ourselves and to real Teshuvah. This is called "the longer, shorter way." It is "longer" since we may encounter more tests and doubts and times of loneliness, but it is "shorter" since it is the only route leading all the way to our destination. By contrast, the seemingly 'shorter' but actually longer path is to permanently walk in someone else's footsteps and conform to their forms of personality and appearance. This may seem 'easier', less fraught with uncertainty and unsettling surprises, yet, it is longer, as it will never take you to the place you really need to go.

When Avraham first heard the Divine call, on a deeper level, it was a Divine call to each and every one of us. Hashem called him to embark upon his soul quest and journey with the words *Lech Lecha*, meaning, 'Go to yourself — for yourself, and by yourself' (*Bereishis*, 12:1). He understood that leaving his home and land and family was for his own benefit, and that he needed to go on this journey to find himself 'by himself'. No one else could accomplish this for him. As descendants of Avraham, we must also make a journey back to our true self, and we must do this independently. Ultimately, no one else in the world can help us make the final step into who *we* are.

The Divine voice calls out to us every day: 'You want to become someone in this world; deep down, you want to discover who you really are and what you are here for. So *Lech Lecha*, go on the hero's journey of self-discovery. Rediscover your original self. Only you can do this, and only by yourself, by truly being yourself.'

Your Teshuvah is yours alone. You should not compare your journey to another's. Of course, it is essential to find a reliable community of like-minded people, a spiritual home where you are welcomed, recognized for who you are, and encouraged to grow. But even there, your calling is not merely to fit in — nor is it to stand out. 'Fitting in' and 'standing out' pertain only to outer appearances, not to who you really are. Even within a close community, your journey is yours alone. You can never measure your growth or service of Hashem in comparison to others, even to the most like-minded ones, or people with a similar background. True growth and true service of your Creator are relative to your own inner life.

Always remember that *Teshuvah Sheleimah* / complete return is the total reintegration and reorientation of our entire self; our talents, unique qualities, and distinctive ways of thinking and feeling and processing the world. Everything about you will be rebirthed in a higher, deeper way of life. Even your particular mistakes and shortcomings, born of your unique challenges and unmet needs, will, in the end, be illumined and revealed as merits. Hashem made you unlike anyone else so that you can shine an entirely new light into the world.

Chapter Two

LINEAR TIME, TIMELESS PRESENCE, AND THE POWER TO CHANGE

THE GREAT 13TH CENTURY CASTILIAN REBBE AND MOR-
ALIST, RABBEINU YONAH, WRITES: "THE FOUNDATION
OF TESHUVAH IS CONSIDERING TODAY AS THE VERY DAY
YOU WERE BORN, THE FIRST DAY OF YOUR LIFE, AND YOU HAVE
NO DEMERITS OR MERITS" (ועשה עצמו כאלו בו ביום נולד ואין בידו לא זכות ולא
חובה). This state of consciousness, this sense of the newness of
this moment, is unaffected neither by the negativity nor the
positivity of the past. This timeless newness is the foundation
and the goal of Teshuvah.

כי המצוה הזאת אשר אנכי מצוך היום / "For this Mitzvah which I have commanded you today…" (*Devarim*, 33:11), "this Mitzvah" refers to the Mitzvah of Teshuvah (Ramban, *ad loc. Otzar haGeonim*, Sanhedrin, 514. *Baal haTurim, Seforno, Abarbanel*, and *Kli Yakar*, ad loc. *Sefer haIkarim*, Ma'amar 4:25). This is the essential Mitzvah of the Torah and it is one that is commanded "today." "Today" literally means at that time in history, but Teshuvah is also always about "today," the present moment.

Chazal / our sages say, אין ועתה אלא תשובה / "The word *v'Atah* / 'and now' (in Torah) means Teshuvah" (*Medrash Rabbah*, Bereishis, 21:6). The time for Teshuvah is always 'now…and now' — but more deeply, Teshuvah is about the now, being present in the current unfolding moment. When we are consciously in the 'now', we are basically unaffected or influenced by the past, nor worried or anxious about the future. This moment is always pure and new.

QUESTIONS

Let us unpack this idea of newness and living in the present moment, and its fundamental relationship with the world of Teshuvah, self-transformation.

Firstly, the present moment is the only place we actually live. However, we may not always be conscious of this, and our mind and actions may stray from its timeless purity.

Mistakes and misaligned actions, thoughts, or feelings seem to be almost inevitable, as "There is not a just man on earth who does good, and does not err" (*Koheles*, 7:20). However, part of being a mature and responsible human being is owning your life and your mistakes — bringing them into the light of the present and resolving them through Teshuvah. The trouble with 'owning your life' is that sometimes the past can seem so overwhelming that it swamps the person. It may seem that the present moment is crowded out, inhibiting one's ability to stand firm in the pure present and choose Teshuvah.

If one takes full responsibility for his past while viewing the present moment as a continuation of the past, how can he access Teshuvah in the present moment? The present moment is then still completely weighed down by the past, and there is no room for a new choice. How can he choose now to act in a way that will affect the past if he is living in a paradigm where the past inevitably affects the present?

On the other end of the spectrum, a person might try to 'live in the present' in a way that dissociates from the past and future. In this way, he may shirk all responsibility by denying the reality of his past mistakes, fail to 'own' his life in the present, and avoid steering toward a more righteous future. This, too, inhibits one's ability to make Teshuvah.

How can we balance living in the unsullied present with taking responsibility for our past and future? This is an existential dilemma.

THE GIFT OF THE PRESENT

Rebbe Yoseph Albo, the 15th Century Spanish philosopher and rabbi, writes העבר אינו נמצא והעתיד לא יצא עדיין אל הפעל וההוה / "The past no longer exists, אינו אלא העתה הקושר בין העבר והעתיד and the future is yet to exist; the present is only the now which the connects the past with the future" (*Sefer haIkarim*, Ma'amar 3:27. See also, *Ralbag*, Melachim 2, 4:16. *Peleh Yoetz*, Erech Da'agah). The past is just a memory, the future is yet to come, and the only true moment we have is the now, the present moment. And this moment paradoxically welcomes the past and the future without being burdened by them.

We cannot actually experience the past or the future. Even if it were theoretically possible, that 'past' or 'future' would be experienced in the present. In this sense, past and future do not exist; they are but fragments of memory and imagination that are appearing in the now. The only true moment is now, and we can never leave it or escape it.

Of course, the anomaly of the present moment is that while everything only exists in the now, there is actually no such 'thing' as the now. The now is not a 'thing', for as soon as you become aware of the present moment or try to grasp it, that moment is already past and you are no longer in it.

This present moment is not an object; it is not a point in time or the 'content' of your awareness. Rather it is the 'container' — the awareness itself — in which all points in time and all contents appear. Living in the now is deeper than merely being with what is *happening* in this moment. It is being present with the fullness of the now itself.

'Now' is the one and only constant in life. It is the context in which life-forms flow and transform, appear and disappear. Whatever happens in our life and whatever changes we may undergo, we are always here, now. This moment is therefore not an action after which we must chase, but rather it is the eternal, pure, open field upon which all actions unfold.

It is this present moment of pure awareness that makes Teshuvah possible, since the present stands uninfluenced by past behavior and experiences and by what may happen in the future. Teshuvah is about *you*, right now. Only by fully being *you* in the present moment, can you birth yourself anew at any given moment. Otherwise, you may be limited by or enslaved to fixed self-images of who you were in the past. A fixed self-image blocks the possibility of real transformation.

If we believe that we were not successful yesterday, and therefore we cannot make a new beginning and be successful today, then our past imprisons our present. In this state of 'exile' or constricted consciousness, change is never a possibility and any real movement is unattainable. Living this way, the future is already closed before us, for it means that what we are now, and what we will be in the future, is always going to be the same as what we were in the past.

RENEWAL EVERY MOMENT:
THE AYIN OF EXISTENCE

Another word for the 'content' of experience is *Yesh* / existence or 'thing'. Another word for the context of experience, the present awareness, is *Ayin* / 'no-thing' or empty of real, separate existence or 'content'. The present moment offers the possibility of untangling oneself from the shackles of past negative behavior, from the Yesh of the past, because it is the content-free 'Ayin' dimension in time. In the present, the past is not a real 'existence'. On the other hand, one needs to do Teshuvah precisely because of his or her past behavior. In this way, the Yesh dimension of experience compels us to make Teshuvah, while the Ayin dimension of experience offers us the ability to do Teshuvah.

Creation is a continuous act of recreation, a movement from the Divine Ayin into Yesh — every moment, there is a new Creation of *Yesh meAyin* / 'something' from 'Nothing'. As such, within Creation there remain these two ingredients, as it were, the Ayin and the Yesh. There remains a dynamic of the 'Ayin', the newly revealed formless present, as it is being filled with the Yesh of form. The *Koach haHischadshus* / the power of renewal is present within every moment, every 'now' of Creation, as Creation continually manifests out of an Ayin state of non-being into a Yesh state of being.

Since this dynamic is always present, we can tap into the root of this recreative Ayin at any moment in order to instantaneously refresh our lives. We can unburden ourselves of past experiences, which are within the realm of 'something-ness', by entering into a state of 'no-thing-ness'. Immersed in the fluid and formless present moment of Ayin, we can choose a radically different form of life.

YESH AND AYIN WITHIN OUR CONSCIOUSNESS

Just as the past is Yesh and the present is Ayin, and the content of experience is Yesh, and the context or empty awareness of experience is Ayin, within our own consciousness, there is a state of Yesh and a state of Ayin. Our Yesh is our finite, egoic identity, our narrative self, and our Ayin is our infinite, Divine-like, pure awareness or soul.

Our Yesh identity is self-absorbed and self-conscious, always seeking its own survival, propagation and expansion. It views itself as devastatingly separate from everything and everyone else, and considers all as potential enemies that have the power to infringe on its survival and perpetuation. When we identify as a Yesh, all others appear to us as a Yesh, and everything is viewed as 'me-versus-you', or 'us against them', or even 'the whole world is conspiring against me.' This is the source of all lust, greed, anger, violence, despondency, ignorance, and spiritual sleep.

Our Ayin self, or rather 'no-self', is our deeper, higher, Divine soul dimension. Forever in a state of absorption in the Source, the pure soul has no sense of separate self; rather, all appearances of separation are seen as 'nothing' in the Infinite embrace of Oneness. The Ayin is our stainless, selfless aware-ness or being-ness. It is the un-experienced experiencer, dis-tinct from anything that can be experienced. It is the un-felt perceiver of feelings, the inconceivable knower of concepts.

Our past is our Yesh, the narrative content of our lives, and our Ayin is the witnessing presence in the eternal present, empty of all narratives.

All of this explains why our Yesh, our ego is fixated on our self-image. A self-image is a product of past actions, experi-ences, thoughts, feelings, and impressions. It is the pictures and stories that our mind presents to us of who we are and what we have experienced. If, G-d forbid, as a youth, a person has a traumatizing experience with an older authority, this narrative may define his self image, who he thinks he is. The freshness and possibility of the present moment is then clouded and blocked. We get to live in an imaginary world, a world that does not exist any longer. It only seems to exist as long as we are choosing to overlay our stories of a muddied past upon our unmuddied, ever-present being-ness.

Instead of being open to the infinite possibilities of the pres-ent, the 'narrative self' pulls us to cling to a fixed, conditioned, limited self-image.

Our 'Yesh' reality is the sound that echoes against the back-ground of our silent present-ness. That transcendent silence, free of content and image, is our Ayin reality. We can allow our expansive, 'infinite' Ayin self to surface when we are fully present in the ever-unfolding formless moment, when we let go of superimposing labels and opinions, but just listen and witness life from a deep inner stillness and unity.

When we live from a worldview of the separate ego, we are identifying with a self-image from the past. Sadly, we may *think* that we are actually experiencing the present, but we are actually just looking at images that are past and no longer exist. When the ego pretends to 'be present', in truth, it is merely regurgitating Yesh content from the past. The ego cannot actually be present; the ego itself is nothing more than a finite, separate self-image spilling over from the past.

In attempting to be present, the ego focuses on the content of the experience of that moment rather than the timeless context, the endless moment itself. This is merely exchanging one form of Yesh for another Yesh — trading the finite story of a past or future for a finite story of a so-called 'present moment'. Yet, even this false 'present' is better to focus on than egoic ruminations about the past or future. Although the false present does not approximate the infinite story-less spaciousness of Ayin, at least it is a better 'story' in that it produces less anxieties, illusions and transgressions.

Teshuvah involves returning to our pure, innocent state of Ayin, while alive in this world. This is the reason that Yom Kippur involves contemplations of our mortality. We must 'die', so-to-speak, to all that is subject to death — our Yesh. In so doing, we can come to identify with the eternal component of our being that transcends death — our Ayin.

It is important to note that there is an essence of self that is beyond and inclusive of both Yesh and Ayin. Our essence is beyond our narrative self and our selfless stillness, beyond our fullness and our emptiness, beyond life's content and life's context. As such, the ultimate goal of life is not to reject our Yesh or our narratives. Ultimately, we embrace our narratives, our ambitions, and our drive and desire to better ourselves and the world. We are not meant to remain forever silent, unmoved, selfless, and aloof from the world. Our deepest calling is to consciously be our essence, both in the world and beyond it at the same time. However, for the purpose of Teshuvah, full immersion in the transcendent Ayin state is key. To be in a state of Teshuvah requires that we let our old, false self-image 'die' so that we can embrace who we really are. We need to detach from the sticky past and its seemingly inevitable future in order to return to full presence in the infinite potential of this moment, and from there, to re-embrace our essence.

RESPONSIBILITY FOR OUR PAST, RENEWAL IN THE PRESENT — HOLDING BOTH AWARENESSES

Meditating on the present moment, the Ayin, we intuit the newness of every moment. We sense our *Koach* / ability to begin again at any time, right now. This is true *Chochmah* / intuitive wisdom, as חכמה / *Chochmah* means כח-מה / *Koach-Mah* / 'the power of no-thing' or Ayin. Yet, without an awareness of the

Yesh, the content of our lives as effects of our past, we would not take, or need to take, responsibility for our past actions. Indeed, if in this present moment there is no past nor future, then why would we need to assume responsibility in life? This is why we need to maintain both these paradigms, the Yesh and Ayin, simultaneously. The power of 'no-thing-ness' gives us the wisdom and *ability* to change, while awareness of the Yesh of the past gives us a *reason* to change.

Seemingly conflicting, these perspectives actually compliment each other. Without the ever-unfolding flow of Ayin, there would be no room for change, just stuckness and despair. And without any type of Yesh and form, with no desire to develop and move, we might have great Koach and abilities, but nothing of it would come to fruition.

From the perspective of Ayin, every moment and everything in it is new; there is only now and at any point, you can begin life all over again. Ayin provides the spaciousness and freedom to transform, however a return to Yesh reintroduces accountability. Ayin and Yesh thus complement and complete each other. Yesh without Ayin is self-referential and rigid, with no potential for actual change. Ayin without Yesh is a dis-embodied state of limitless potential, without substance or sense of tangible manifestation.

Divine Light and Life flow into the world continuously, from Ayin to Yesh, and then the Light 'returns' to its Source, from Yesh back into Ayin. This macrocosmic process of 'back and forth' is mirrored and reflected in the microcosmic process of breathing in and out. As we exhale, we disappear subtly into Ayin, and as the new inhale is given to us, we re-appear as Yesh. Teshuvah is to hold these two states simultaneously — metaphorically like the moment of breath retention between every inhale and exhale and between every exhale and inhale. To be in a state of Teshuvah — certainly to be in a 'turning away from' negative patterns of behavior — is to be in that retention space, embracing both the Ayin of our timeless purity and the Yesh of our accountability.

THE MEASUREMENT OF THE 'YESH' OF TIME AS MOVEMENT AWAY FROM THE PAST & PREPARING FOR THE FUTURE

In Hebrew, time is called *Z'man*. On one level, the only way to measure time is by seeing it moving from the past into the present. Time can also be viewed as the present preparing for the future. זמן / *Z'man* is thus also related to the word הזמנה / *Hazmanah* / preparing, inviting (הזמנה מילתא היא: *Sanhedrin*, 47b). These are both 'Yesh' perspectives of time; causality, form, and content rule, and whatever happens earlier 'invites' what happens later. The present, as it is pulled toward a future, is a 'preparation' for the future.

Z'man in numerical value is 97 (Zayin / 7, Mem / 40, Nun / 50 = 97). In the terminology of *Sod* / deeper teachings of the Torah, *Z'man* / '97' is connected to the two Divine Names *Mah* and *Ban*. The numerical value of מה / Mah (Mem/40, Hei/5) is

45 (this is the 'filling' of the four letter Name of Hashem with the letter Aleph: יוד-הא-ואו-הא / Yud-Vav-Dalet=20, Hei-Aleph=6. Vav-Aleph-Vav=13, Hei-Aleph=6, totaling 45). The numerical value of בן / Ban (Beis/2, Nun/50) is 52 (the 'filling' of the four letter Name of Hashem with the letter Hei: יוד-הה-וו-הה / Yud-Vav-Dalet=20, Hei-Hei=10, Vav-Vav=12, Hei-Hei=10, totaling 52). Mah and Ban together are 97.

Representing two forms of Divine expression vis-a-vis the Sefiros, these two Names are channels of Divine flow into our world. Mah is connected with the higher, more transcendent six emotive *Sefiros*, the 'attributes' of *Chesed* / kindness, Gevurah / restriction, *Tiferes* / compassion, *Netzach* / perseverance, and *Hod* / glory. Ban is connected with the Sefirah of *Malchus* / immediate Presence, already vested within manifest existence.

In terms of our personal life, these two Names symbolize parts of ourselves, Divine dynamics reflected within our body-mind-soul dynamic. Our soul, our transcendent, formless self, is associated with the higher transcendent Name Mah, whereas our finite, defined, physical body is connected with the Name Ban. As such, אדם / Adam / mankind is numerically 45 (Aleph/1, Dalet/4, Mem/40 =45), as Adam refers to the higher dimension of self, our soul (note, *Yevamos*, 61b: אתם קרויין אדם. *Tosefos*: דיש חילוק בין אדם להאדם, ad loc). And בהמה / *Beheimah* / animal is numerically 52 (Beis/2, Hei/5, Mem/40, Hei/5 =52), corresponding to our lower 'animal soul', our ego that is vested in our physical body and created for the sake of our physical survival.

In the world of *Z'man* / time, the Name Mah is connected to the present moment as it is open toward a future. *Mah* literally means, 'What?' It is a question that opens us up to a possible or unknown future, a mystery, a coming surprise. Ban, which is Malchus, on the other hand, represents what already is, what is immediately manifest and revealed in the now. In other words, 'Ban' is the quality of a present that is a manifest effect of the past, and 'Mah' is the quality of a present that is still a mystery pulled toward a yet unrevealed, undefined future.

One phenomenal distinction between an animal and a human (from our perspective) is our ability for true growth. "A day-old ox is (already) called an ox" (*Baba Kama*, 65b); there is very little qualitative difference between a baby ox and an adult ox, for the adult is just quantitatively bigger. A small lion, too, is a complete lion, just physically smaller and with less physical strength and experience. Humans, on the other hand, are able to experience, if they so desire, real qualitative growth and advancement. Even if a person is born with less physical capabilities than his fellow man to lift heavy objects, with practice, determination, resolve and perseverance, he can build muscle and outlift someone who is naturally strong. This is a physical metaphor, but for humans, it also applies to mental and emotional capacities, communication and learning skills, and the ability to advance in all areas of life, financial, emotional, intellectual, and spiritual. A human being is called a *Mehalech* / a creature who 'progresses', grows, dreams, aspires, and reaches for the stars, and attains what is beyond its inheritance from the natural world, beyond the natural paradigm of cause-and-effect.

An animal lives in the present, but remains, relatively speaking, exactly what it was in the past. Its future, too, is just a linear trajectory based on its present. Human beings can choose at any moment to break from a linear, natural trajectory, and radically change for the better (or, G-d forbid, for the worse). We can rise above biological and neurological causality and create for ourselves a much brighter future than our past. To be human, a physical being with a transcendent human soul, is to live unshackled by your past and live and choose freely in the present. An 'Adam' is *Adameh l'Elyon* / 'a resemblance of the Transcendent One', a likeness of the Divine Ayin.

To be human is to quest, to ask, '*Mah*, what is life?', 'Who do I want to be?' A human being is a seeker, one who yearns and strives more and for better, who is capable of innovating ways of improving his or her wealth, stability, knowledge, wisdom, and spiritual enlightenment; who is capable of making Teshuvah and creating a brighter future for themselves, their family and the world at large.

The word בהמה / *Beheimah* / animal, says the Maharal, is composed of two words בה / (swallowed) 'within her' is מה / the question 'What'. The existential question 'What' is hidden from her. Thus, in a sense, a בהמה lives contentedly, grazing on what is already there growing from the earth, and living without real questions, existential dilemmas or drives to change.

The animal is 'what' the animal is and will be. The 'what' of an animal as it is; there is no perception of a future and no potential for creating a paradigm shift in her life. There is no capacity for change and no real emotional, mental or spiritual growth for the ox, since the 'what' is already manifest and fixed within the ox from birth. What you see is what you get.

We, too, can become a little less human, and a little more like a בהמה / animal, if our מה / *Mah*, our longing, our drive and dreams for a new 'What', have become swallowed בה / 'within ourselves'. Unfortunately, some people never transcend their natural patterns or grow, and the exact same struggles they had when they were 20 are what they have when they are 120. They remain 'what' they are, for they do not ask deeper questions or challenge the 'content' of their lives. Tragically, one stops evolving when one gives up striving for elevation and settles for 'animal comforts' alone. A potential 'Adam' then ceases to *Adameh l'Elyon* / 'to resemble the Transcendent One', and becomes like *Adamah* / inert, lowly 'earth', even below the level of a land animal.

To be a true Adam, we need to constantly grow, and to live with the mystery of what the future will bring. We must dream, yearn, hope, aspire and even push ourselves, to reach ever-greater heights in all areas of life.

To reiterate, Ban is the present as an effect of the past and with no possibility for any different outcome in the future. Mah is the present as it opens into a possible, new future — in other words, the power of *Hischadshus* / renewal. And we need both, a unification of these Names. The dimension of Ban stimulates us to take responsibility for our past, and the dimension of Mah gives us the ability to break free, do Teshuvah, radically change our patterns of behavior and produce a radically new future.

In a dimension of Ban without the contextualization and contribution of Mah, the effects of genetics, environment, education, and childhood are so solid that they hold an absolute grip on one's life. Life is predictable and change is impossible. Yet, when the context of 'Adam' or 'Mah' is united with the content of Ban, the present is not the inevitable effect of the past. Rather, the greater context of infinite possibility draws the best from the past and the present. As a result of this unification, we have the ability to release ourselves from the weight of the past and see every moment as a new moment with limitless potential.

Simply speaking, we need to be conscious of our mortal body and also our eternal soul. Without soul-consciousness, we will live in the past, robbing ourselves of the Infinite unfolding of the present. Not only will we not dream, we will not be truly alive in the human sense; we will live in a 'dead' world, a dead-end, where "nothing is new under the sun."

Even if we can look back at our past and see that we have accomplished amazing things in our life, the moment our focus is fixed upon a nostalgic past, we have stopped aspiring to a new future. To live in the past is to become a 'living corpse'. The presently unfolding possibility of the future dies.

We discover the real 'fountain of youth' when we 'turn away' from dwelling on nostalgia and what we have already achieved, and resist the temptation to sit back, rest on our laurels and 'retire'. We must arise and stand in the newness of the present, open to the unprecedented possibilities of the future, and dream of what we want to accomplish while we are still alive.

THE ETERNAL PRESENT OF AYIN THAT IS EXPRESSED IN THE PAST / FUTURE OF YESH

To live as a Yesh firmly within the context of Ayin, the eternal now moment, is to be utterly transparent and free, fresh and empowered to change. We are informed by the past but not defined by it. We can alter our future in a way that is completely beyond our past achievements and identities. More deeply, from this presence, we can alter our past and transform the trajectory of our old negative behaviors into a positive trajectory, from liability to merit.

One of the names of Hashem is המקום / *HaMakom* / the Place. "He (Hashem) is מקומו של עולם / *Mekomo Shel Olam* / the Place of the world, and the world is not His place" (*Medrash Rabbah*, Bereishis, 68:9. *Nefesh haChayim*, Sha'ar 3:1).

Hashem, 'the Name' of the Infinite and Ineffable One, is composed of four Hebrew letters: Yud, Hei, Vav, and Hei (י-ה- ו-ה). These four letters can be rearranged to spell the words היה

/ *Hayah* / 'was', הוה / *Hoveh* / 'is', and יהיה / *Yihyeh* / 'will be' (Additionally, in the future, the Vav of the Name will rise up to become a Yud, thus instead of י-ה-ו-ה it will be spelled יהיה / *Yihyeh*). The Name thus expresses the idea that Infinity transcends but also encompasses the past, present, and future as one unified whole.

Numerically, the value of the Name 'Hashem' is 26 (Yud/10, Hei/5, Vav/6, Hei/5 = 26). Another way of calculating the numerical value, called the 'full value', involves multiplying each letter, in which case the Name 'Hashem' is 186 (Yud/10x10, Hei/5x5, Vav/6x6, Hei/5x5 =186). This is the same numeric value as the name מקום(ה) / *(Ha)Makom* (Mem/40, Kuf/100, Vav/6, Mem/40 =186). This correspondence between the Names 'Hashem' and 'HaMakom' suggests that Infinity is expressed in the immediacy of this place, precisely in this moment — right here, right now. As such, the most important place to be is right here, and the most important time is right now.

This four-letter, ineffable Divine Name can also be read as י-הוה / *Yud-Hoveh*, meaning 'the Yud of the present moment'. The letter Yud is a small point, symbolizing the first infinitesimal point of manifestation that encompasses all further articulations. Yud, therefore, represents the pure potency of what is to unfold. In this way, the small point is like the Ayin, nothingness, that comes before the Yesh, the fullness of existence. Indeed, the writing of every Hebrew letter begins with a small Yud, the point where the quill first touches the parchment before the ink flows and expands downward, and only then continues into various horizontal or vertical lines to form other letters.

Furthermore, when the letter Yud appears at the beginning of a word, it creates a grammatical sense of continuity. For example, עשה means 'did', and יעשה means 'will do', or 'always does', as in ככה יעשה איוב כל-הימים / "This is what Iyov always used to do" (*Iyov*, 1:5. Rashi, *ad loc*. Alter Rebbe, *Tanya*, Sha'ar haYichud ve-haEmuna, 4). In this way, the Name Yud-Hei-Vav-Hei is *Yud-Hoveh*, the ever-unfolding, continuous act of bringing the present moment into being. And as the Yud-Hei-Vav-Hei also embodies the quality of Infinity as it embraces the past, present and future, it demonstrates that Infinity, which is beyond all dimensions of time, is also expressed and experienced within the *Hoveh* / the now. It is an Eternal present-ness that is 'beyond' time, yet includes and embraces past and future.

In other words, the Ayin, the Infinite possibility of the moment, is 'found' within the immediacy of this moment in time, in a way that unifies the past, present and future. In the infinite eternity of Ayin is a dimension that includes finite time.

ETERNAL LIVING IN THE NOW VS. LIMITED LIVING FOR THE NOW

This helps us understand the important distinction between living 'in' the now versus living 'for' the now.

Living 'for' the now is limiting one's scope to the immediate present and one's current desires and impulses. This is actually the opposite of the liberating posture of living '*in* the now'. To act spontaneously, yet with no consideration for the motivation or outcome of one's actions, is to discard intentionality, openness, awareness, and responsibility. Living for the now is like eating an entire tub of ice cream without considering your memory of the negative effects of your past acts of gluttony, and your knowledge that you will experience a stomach ache in the near future. This is the dynamic of all momentary urges and cravings.

By distinction, to live *in* the now is to behold the eternally expansive present, which transcends but also encompasses your past and future, and the causes and effects of your actions. This authentic freedom includes mindful clarity, morality, responsibility and accountability.

'Living in the now' is obviously deeper than just being with what is *happening* in this moment. It is also being present with the fullness of the 'now' itself. Happenings are the 'content' of the moment, while the present itself is the 'context', the aware 'space' in which everything happens. The present is an infinite openness that contains all finite expressions, experiences and occurrences (Note *Chochmah uMusar*, 1:252). Now-ness is a portal into all-inclusive wisdom, engagement and aliveness.

While living *in* the newness of the present offers a fresh start, a sense of redemption, living *for* the now is the cause of chaos, confusion, and crisis, and ultimately, ennui, emptiness and exile.

True, the entire process of redemption from Egypt, its slavery, and the depth of existential and spiritual stuckness began with the Mitzvah of "sanctify the new moon." The first Mitzvah Klal Yisrael received in Egypt was, החדש הזה לכם ראש חדשים / "This month shall be to you the first of the months" (*Shemos,* 12:1-2). The word *Chodesh* / month comes from the word *Chidush* / new. The moon represents a paradigm of renewal and the potential for novelty that breaks the monotony of linear time. 'Newness' is a major ingredient of redemption. The eternal newness of the present is a powerful gift that liberates us from the past and gives us a new future.

On the other side, when the Torah begins to describe Klal Yisrael's deeper descent into slavery, it says, ויקם מלך־חדש על־ מצרים אשר לא־ידע את־יוסף / "And a new king arose in Egypt, who did not know Yoseph" (*Shemos,* 1:8). This refers to a king who did not remember the kindness and benevolence that Yoseph bestowed on Egypt in the past, during the years of famine. This king, in a sense, was 'living for the present'. Extremely impactful historical events were not a concern to him. As a result, there was a deeper exile, and eventually, the king himself lost everything. Living for the now with no consideration of past or future consequences is a kind of enslavement. This type of now erases awareness, memory and gratitude.

Redemptive, grateful, aware living is in the presence of the now; not a now that erases the past or denies the future, but that learns from the past and chooses a future.

LIVING WITH A SENSE OF RENEWAL
AND NEWNESS IS REDEMPTION

In the beginning of his book, the Prophet Yechezkel (Eze-kiel) relates visions revealed to him during the beginning of the Exile, on the banks of נהר כבר / the River Kvar. In Hebrew, *Kvar* means 'already'. Subtly, the Torah is associating exile with the notion of 'already', as in a 'been there, done that' attitude. One who 'already knows' cannot learn or grow. This person leaves no space for disengaging from his fixed patterns of the past or beginning anew. Exile is the burdensome clinging to the old, one's old ways, perceptions or habits, with no freedom of movement. In a redemptive state of consciousness, nothing is *Kvar*, 'already' or old; everything is fresh and meaningful. Every moment is a brand-new opportunity.

In terms of Teshuvah and Yom Kippur, there is a way of transforming the negative sense of *Kvar* into a positive one. The Rama rules in Shulchan Aruch that on Motzei Yom Kip-pur, after Yom Kippur, "we eat and are joyous, as it is a minor *Yom Tov* / holy day (אוכלים ושמחים קצת במוצאי יום הכפורים דהוי קצת יום טוב: *Orach Chayim*, 624:7). What is this Yom Tov, and why the cele-bration? On Motzei Yom Kippur, a *Bas Kol* / heavenly voice rings out and says, לך אכל בשמחה לחמך ושתה בלב-טוב יינך כי כבר רצה האלקים את-מעשיך / "Go and eat your bread with joy, and drink your wine with a glad heart, because Hashem has כבר / *Kvar* / already forgiven your (negative) actions" (*Koheles*, 9:7. *Biur haGra*, *Mishnah Berurah*, ad loc. Note, בת ובשעה שישראל נפטרין מבתי כנסיות ומבתי מדרשות *Medrash* קול יוצאת ואומרת: לך אכל בשמחה לחמך, כבר נשמעה תפלתכם לפני כריח ניחוח *Rabbah*, Koheles, 9:7,1).

244 | A LIGHTNESS OF BEING

What this means is that after Yom Kippur, there is a transformation of all negativity — even the *Kelipah* / the negativity
of *Kvar*. Following the deep atonement of Yom Kippur, the
at-one-ment with the deepest levels of our soul and deepest
levels of *Deveikus* / revealed unity with HaKadosh Baruch Hu,
a sense of "already forgiven" sets in. We have come to realize
our inner perfection and wholeness, that we are *already* whole
and perfect. With this high level of consciousness, we are ready
to enter as-it-were into a *Chuppah* / wedding canopy with our
Beloved. We are ready to be embraced by our Beloved in the
all-encompassing hug of the Sukkah.

Yet, in general terms, *Kvar* refers to the negative sense of
oldness and exile, while *Chadash* / new and *Chidush* / renewal refers to redemption. So whereas *Geulah* / redemption and
freedom begin with the recognition of the new moon and the
new months, the descent back into exile with the destruction
of the Beis haMikdash and the exile from the Promised Land,
begins כי־תוליד בנים ובני בנים ונושנתם / "When you will have children and grandchildren, and you will get *old*..." (*Devarim*, 4:25.
ונושנתם comes from the word ישן / sleep and נושן / very old). In this way,
one's 'exile' begins when their enthusiasm for Torah and Mitzvos, or any area of life, becomes old, stale and sleepy. Without
engaging with passion and excitement in life and *Avodas Hashem*, there is no sense of *Hischadshus* / renewal and freedom.

LIVING IN WONDERMENT AS A CHILD

When one's present is nothing more than a commemoration

of their glorious or not-so-glorious past, routine, drudgery, and stagnation set in. As a result of this deadening effect, one often begins to live 'for' the moment and rely on the stimulation of the vain desires of this world until he becomes addicted and enslaved to them. This underscores the great spiritual importance of rekindling our passion, excitement, and sense of Hischadshus in life. And one effective way to do this is to observe innocent children.

Children live in a state of wonderment. Everything in their lives is literally new, fresh, exciting and a potentially fascinating exploration. When we are younger, a year seems to pass much more slowly than when we are older. This apparent stretching of time happens because our perception of self and world is not yet fixed or routine. Our days are full, and every moment is novel. As every experience is new, each one leaves a strong impression and impact, forming deep, foundational memories. As our memories accumulate, however, our constant state of awe gradually diminishes. As years go by, we become more set in our ways. More and more experiences fall into the category of 'already', and time seems to speed up, as nothing is new and noteworthy. As we stop living with wonder, our awareness begins to close down, and walls start to go up, boxing us in.

תִּינוֹק / *Tinok* / 'child' has the same five letters as the word תִּיקוּן / *Tikkun* / 'rectification'. This is hinting to us that part of our personal soul elevation and rectification, part of our personal Tikkun, is to reconnect in adulthood with our inner child. Part of our Tikkun is to recapture the enthusiasm, the wonderment, the childlike awareness of wonder, awe, and excitement that we lived with as children, and to live with this now, as a mature and thoughtful adult.

Living on autopilot or with jadedness and cynicism gives us a sense of 'already'. Then, instead of living in the state of תינוק / Tinok and תיקון / *Tikkun,* we live in a state of ניתוק / *Nituk* / disconnected, separated, from self, from others, from life itself, and ultimately from the Source of all Life and Renewal.

The Source of Life commands us to choose life, to be alive, to be awake, to be present in the moment and to consciously create a future: החיים והמות נתתי לפניך...ובחרת בחיים למען תחיה אתה וזרעך / "Behold I place before you life and death...choose life so that you (in the present) and your offspring (in the future) will live" (*Devarim,* 30:19). Choosing death would be no choice at all; it would be the opposite of a choice. To not choose is to live as a passive effect of the past and not as the cause of the future. To not choose is to be not truly alive, not truly connected to the Source of Life. To choose is to be alive, connected, consciousness and renewed.

ALWAYS FEELING YOUNG AND RENEWED

In the Yom Kippur *Davening* / prayers, we repeat a passage from *Tehillim* / Psalms: אל־תשליכני לעת זקנה / "Do not forsake me when I am old" (*Tehillim,* 71:9). The simple meaning of this verse is, of course, 'Hashem, please give me strength even in my old age.' A deeper meaning taught by the Baal Shem Tov is, 'Please, Hashem, give me the strength and wisdom that my

Divine service should never become "old," habitual, lethargic or stale. May I always live with passion and desire' (*Baal Shem al haTorah*, Noach, 68. See also *Ohr haMeir*, Yisro. *Degel Machaneh Ephrayim*, Ekev, 1). May we always be 'young', enthusiastic, wide-eyed, and open to the wonders of the Creator.

"It is prohibited to be old," proclaim the Chassidic Rebbes (*Likutei Halachos*, Tefillin, 5:5). To observe this spiritual 'prohibition', we must be open to the Divine Presence of the present moment. If we can remain open, nothing in our lives and religious practices will get mired in automatic routine or mimicry of the past. Such a way of living is untrue to life and reality. In reality, all of Creation is flowing out of no-thing-ness, continuously, right now, and every moment is new, with radically new opportunities and vistas.

"This Mitzvah that I commanded you *today* is not hidden from you, and it is not distant" (*Devarim*, 30:11). According to the Ramban and many other classic interpreters, "this Mitzvah" refers to the Mitzvah of Teshuvah. With regards to Teshuvah, "today," meaning 'now', is the most important element of time. This is not only true of Teshuvah but of all our activities and way of being in this world. Therefore, according to Sifri, this verse implies that we should perform all Mitzvos as if they were given to us anew every day. Newness or 'nowness' is essential to all our spiritual practices, and in fact, to the way we approach life in general.

Every moment is new, fresh, exciting, loaded with possibility. Nothing is old or 'already'. What was done or not done yesterday is history. Now is a new, un-content filled present; choose it.

SEIZE THE DAY

'Seize the day' is the attitude to adopt when approaching Teshuvah and transformation on any level. At any moment, we can take hold of the vast opportunity that is here and now, as the present moment is existentially unrelated to the past and is yet to define a future. We have a clean slate, right now...and again, right now....

A Sixteenth Century prisoner was granted permission to choose one day out of the year to fully practice his *Yidishkeit /* Judaism. This presented him with a unique dilemma. Being a devout Jew, he did not know which day of the year would be the *Eis Ratzon /* the most propitious time in which to invest his efforts; should he choose Shabbos, so he could recite the Kiddush? Perhaps he should wait until Rosh Hashanah? Or better yet, maybe he should choose the holiest day of the year, Yom Kippur? Unable to reach a decision, he sent letters to the leading sages seeking their counsel. Some time later, the Radbaz, a prominent Rebbe of the era, wrote and instructed him to choose the first opportunity that presented itself; to choose 'today', whether it be Shabbos, a weekday, or a holiday.* In oth-

---

* *Teshuvas haRadbaz*, 4, Teshuvah 1087: אנן קיימא לן, דאין מעבירין על המצות ואין חולק בזה כלל. הלכך המצוה הראשונה שתבא לידו שאי אפשר לעשותה והוא חבוש בבית האסורים קודמת, ואין משגיחין אם המצוה שפגעה בו תחלה היא קלה או חמורה, שאי אתה יודע מתן שכרן של מצות, וזה פשוט מאד אצלי. Chida, *Chedrei Beten*, Shabbos Teshuvah, p. 369. *Nemukei Orach Chayim. Hilchos Megilah*, 695:4. The principle is ושמרתם את המצות. כדרך שאין מחמיצין את המצה כך אין מחמיצין את המצוה, אלא אם באה

er words, the specialness of the day is irrelevant — the most important thing is not to delay doing a Mitzvah. According to Torah, the moment that is presenting itself *right now* is the most consequential moment of your life, for this is the only time when we are truly in contact with life and the Creator of Life.

Each day and each moment, we can explore our lives as if for the first time. The simple act of awakening to a new day, or any awakening to the moment throughout the day, is an encounter with our great capacity for Teshuvah and personal growth.

מצוה לידך עשה אותה מיד / (read) "'And you shall watch over the Mitzvos.' Just as Matzos are not permitted to become Chametz (i.e., to sour), so a Mitzvah should not be permitted to become Chametz, rather if the opportunity of a Mitzvah presents itself to you, perform it immediately": *Mechilta*, 12:17:1. Rashi, *Shemos*, 12:12. And in general, the principle of Reish Lakish is that אין מעבירין על המצות / we do not bypass a Mitzvah: *Pesachim*, 64b. *Yuma*, 31a. 58b. 70a. *Megilah*, 6b. *Menachos*, 64b. Ran, *Moed Katan*, 30a. The Chacham Tzvi argues that it's better to wait and perform the Mitzvah with more Hidur or if it is a 'greater' Mitzvah — כתב מהרדב"ז בתשו' י"ג מי שהיה חבוש בבית האסורין ונתנו לו רשות לצאת פע"א בשנה אין חוששין למצוה קלה או חמורה אלא כיון דקי"ל אין מעבירין על המצות הראשונה שתבא לידו וא"א לעשותה בבית האסורין יעשנה ויש להקשות על זה דקמבעיא לן בפ' התכלת דף מ"ט ציבור שאין להם תמידין ומוספין איזה מהן קודם ומוקי לה במוספין דהאידנא ותמידין דלמחר תדיר עדיף או מקודש עדיף ואי כסברת הרב ז"ל אף אי תדיר עדיף מוספין קדמי מטעם דאין מעבירין על המצות א"ו דלא אמרינן אין מעבירין עה"מ אלא בשתיהן שוות אבל לא בדחד מינייהו עדיף: *Shu'T Chacham Tzvi*, Teshuvah 106. See also, *Ba'eir Heitev*, Orach Chayim, 90. *S'dei Chemed*, Kelalim, Klal 1–3. 80, Klal 39. *Turei Even*, Megilah, 7b, regarding the opinion of Tosefos (Although see *Shu'T Divrei Malkiel*, Orach Chayim, 8). Alter Rebbe *Shulchan Aruch*, Orach Chayim, 85:5.

Cheshbon haNefesh / evaluating our mental, emotional and spiritual status is not just to analyze our past. And Teshuvah is much more than merely rectifying past behaviors. Self-evaluation and Teshuvah involve coming to a sensitive understanding of how we can move forward in the present and eventually evolve into who we truly are. Yesterday may have brought certain successes, but today is a new day, and we are a 'new person'; we have a new manifestation of self to refine today. This means we need to analyze and choose in the present moment how we wish to live right now and in the future. This is essential to Cheshbon haNefesh and Teshuvah.

'PAST' IS SIN

To be in an exile and constricted state, and deeply to live in an עבירה / *Aveirah* / 'sin' state is to live in the *Avar* / past. The word עבירה has the same root as the word עבר / *Avar* / 'past'. Sin is about staying stuck in the past, marred in the mistakes of the past that do not let one move forward in the present. Images of our mistakes or faulty decisions sometimes come back to haunt us and cloud out any redemptive possibilities in the present. Our sins can shackle us to our past and hinder everything that is actually available to us in the now.

Our actions do have consequences, and our sins and traumas do have a magnetism that draws us back into our past; however, in the state of Teshuvah, we can affirm, "I am not a slave to my past; Hashem is continually creating the world anew, every split second. I can tap into this perpetual renewal and begin again, right now!"

In general, holding on to the past is a minor 'sin' of sorts. This is certainly true of holding on to old hurts and grudges. But even to wander in the past, to sadly reminisce and say, "Those were the good old days" subtly transgresses your soul, as it robs you of the opportunities of the unfolding, infinite present. A living memory that inspires positivity in the present is obviously beneficial, but dwelling on the past for its own sake can be trivial and unfruitful. When present life seems unsatisfying, to attempt to gain comfort by idealizing life in the past, restlessly roaming through a maze of memories in a search for a richer or more promising reality, is actually robbing oneself of the Divine gift of life given right now.

LIVING IN THE PAST IS AMALEK

My dear grandfather, the beloved *Mashpia* / spiritual guide Reb Avraham Mayorer, would say in jest that the Hebrew word עמלק / Amalek, the archenemy of Klal Yisrael and everything it stands for, is related to the Yiddish word אַמאָל / *Amal*, 'it once was.' Amalek is the Kelipah, the negative, destructive force of living in the past. This idea is hinted at when it says in the Torah that Amalek attacked Klal Yisrael "from behind" (*Devarim*, 25:18). Our inner Amalek, or inner saboteur, attacks us by using thoughts of what is 'behind' us, drawing us to live in the false world of our memories, instead of focusing on the present with its endless possibilities.

If there is no present, there is no future. If only the past is valid and real, then the present is merely the effects of the past, and there can be no vision of a future. It is a world of inevitability and predictability. Regarding Amalek, the Torah says, ואחריתו עדי אבד / "But his fate is to perish forever" (*Bamidbar*, 24:20). This is because Amalek is all about living in the past, which is forever perishing. If we relegate our life-force to the perishing past, there is a deadness also to today, and the future seems dark and doomed. We become tired and weak, straggling 'behind' the now, vulnerable to the cold, negative attack of our inner Amalek.

In numerical value, עמלק / *Amalek*, is 240. This is the same gematria as the word פעמים / *Pa'amayim* / 'twice', as in repetition. Amalek says, 'Why get excited or hopeful? Your future will be just a repetition of the past. You'll never really change much. Teshuvah is a fantasy.' Amalek whispers to us: 'The אחרית / end is עדי אבד / doomed; the future is lost, and you will never change.

Indeed, without a living, viable, expansive awareness of the present moment, there is really no ability to change. Our future then seems predetermined and hopelessly doomed to be a repetition of our past. This is a deeper reason the Torah tells us, "Go and wage battle with Amalek מחר / tomorrow…" (*Shemos*, 17:9. *Yuma*, 52b: מחר...הכרע חמש מקראות בתורה אין להן הכרע...מחר). We need to fight Amalek's worldview that robs us of our tomorrow by insinuating that there is no hope for transformation or growth.

Mitzvos, and specifically the essential mitzvah of Teshuvah ("this Mitzvah"), are the ultimate weapons in fighting apathy, hopelessness, and inevitability. To be engaged in Mitzvos, especially the רמ"ח / *RaMaCH* / '248' positive Mitzvos, is to confirm that there is indeed a positive potential for מחר / tomorrow — the letters of רמח / *RaMaCH* are the same as the letters of the word מחר / tomorrow. Mitzvos and good deeds, in the present, confirm our deep belief that every act of goodness and every Mitzvah brings us one step closer to personal and world redemption. They confirm our steadfast inner knowing that our life and the world are moving forward and evolving toward greater and greater goodness. Even when it feels like this evolution is only inching forward, we can still sense the presence of its ultimate destination: the full redemption of humanity in a state of *Yichud* / unity.

OWNING THE PAST AND THEN LETTING IT GO

As explored earlier, the first step in Teshuvah is owning the past, a state of *Hachna'ah* / submission based on recognizing and accepting the trajectory of the past and what we have done. But then we need to move forward to the state of *Havdalah* / transcending the past, by committing ourselves to the present and future and actually 'forgetting' the past. Only by 'forgetting' can we truly transition into the newness of the present with empowerment and joy.

Rabbeinu Bachya, the Late Tenth Century Spanish moralist and Rabbi, writes that while memory-recall is a tremendous gift, so is the ability to forget (*Chovos haLevavos, Sha'ar haBechinah*, 5). Without an ability to forget, no sorrow could ever be healed, and no tragedy would be put to rest. In a world of total recall, life as we know it would, in fact, be unbearable. In the context of Teshuvah, if every past negative experience were a lucid, present memory, how would we access the enthusiasm needed to change?* One would live with *Yi'ush* / despondency. Certainly, a person who has had a checkered past would become depressed if everything they had ever done was a fresh memory. They might mistakenly think that change is impossible, knowing what they have done.

Yet, life has a clever survival mechanism called 'forgetting', a built-in mechanism that can free a person from the chokehold of his past actions. Lapses in negative memories allow one to come to life in the present moment, with empowerment and alacrity. Without forever carrying heavy images of the past, one becomes light, fresh, and full of the vigor and enthusiasm needed to tackle life. A wise Chasidic Rebbe once said, "The world thinks that forgetfulness is just a negative quality; I, however, think it has great value" (*Sichos haRan*, 26). This value

---

* True, we need the posture of כי-פשעי אני אדע וחטאתי נגדי תמיד / "For I know my sins, and my sins are before me at all times" (*Tehillim*, 51:5). Yet, the appropriate word is *Negdi* / נגדי / "before me," not 'in me'. "Before me" implies distance, as the Alter Rebbe explains, אלא נגדי דייקא, כמו ואתה תתיצב מנגד, מנגד סביב לאהל מועד יחנו, ופירש רש"י מרחוק / "Rather, (the term used for "before me" is) specifically *Negdi*, which implies being 'opposite' but at a certain distance, as in the verse that says, "You shall stand at a distance (*Mineged*)"; or "At a distance (*Mineged*) around the Tent of Assembly shall they camp." Rashi defines *Mineged* (lit., "opposite") as "at a distance": *Tanya*, Igeres haTeshuvah, 11. While we need to recognize our tendencies to sin, we also need to get distance from our past and not ruminate on it.

is the 'new beginning' it can offer — and the newness of the moment is the real value of time.

The word שמחה / *Simchah* / joy contains the letters that spell the word מחה / *Machah* / 'erase' (as in, ומחה אדנ-י ה׳ דמעה מעל כל-פנים / "and Hashem will erase the tears away from all faces" *Yeshayahu*, 25:8). Often, the 'erasure' of a memory or a grudge, or the 'forgetting' of a tenacious attachment to the past, allows us to be more fully present and experience the joy of the infinite moment.

What we should always remember is that the only true moment is 'now', and any moment that is co-opted for wallowing in the past or fantasizing of the future is a stolen opportunity for life growth, radical Teshuvah, and joyful spiritual awakening.

Chapter Three

VERBALIZING TESHUVAH: CLEANSING SPEECH

A CURSORY OBSERVATION OF THE LITURGY OF YOM KIPPUR REVEALS THE COPIOUS AMOUNT OF TEXT DEDICATED TO CONFESSION, TO וידוי / *Viduy* / VERBAL AND AUDIBLE CONFESSION OF SIN. Hopefully, not every transgression enumerated was actually performed by the individual reciting these *Tefilos* / prayers, but it is more about the collective, "*We* have transgressed." Even so, the question is, why spend so much time *Davening* / praying in a posture of confession?

To understand the nature and purpose of Viduy, let us begin
with the Rambam's words regarding Teshuvah in general.

THE MAIN COMPONENTS OF TESHUVAH

First, what are the strict Halachic definitions and components of Teshuvah? Writes the Rambam, ומה היא התשובה. הוא
שיעזב החוטא חטאו ויסירו ממחשבתו ויגמר בלבו שלא יעשהו עוד שנאמר יעזב
רשע דרכו וגו'. וכן יתנחם על שעבר. וצריך להתודות בשפתיו ולומר ענינות אלו
שגמר בלב / "What is Teshuvah? The sinner shall cease sinning,
and remove sin from his thoughts (this is called עזיבת החטא /
Azivas haChet / letting go from the ways of sin). And he shall
wholeheartedly resolve not to revert back to it (this is called
קבלה / *Kabbalah* / acceptance for the future, to act differently),
as it says, 'Let the wicked forsake his way.' So, too, he shall be
remorseful for what was past (this is called חרטה / *Charatah* /
regret for the past)... It is, moreover, essential that his confession shall be by spoken words of his lips, and all that which
he concluded in his heart shall be formed in speech" (*Hilchos
Teshuvah*, 2:2).

In other words, Teshuvah entails a few basic components:
a) עזיבת החטא / *Azivas haCheit* / letting go of one's old paths
of behavior, b) קבלה על להבא / *Kabbalah* / acceptance for the
future, and c) החרטה על העבר / *Charatah* / regret for the past. In
addition, one also needs to verbalize the above as וידוי / *Viduy*
/ confession, for confession is to speak with words what one
resolved in his heart. He needs to speak words expressing his
Azivah, his Kabbalah, and his Charatah. This is what consti-

tutes Viduy; essentially, it is a verbal declaration of the Teshu-vah one senses in his heart.

With the following words, the Rambam begins his treatise on the laws of Teshuvah: כל מצות שבתורה בין עשה בין לא תעשה אם עבר אדם על אחת מהן בין בזדון בין בשגגה כשיעשה תשובה וישוב מחטאו חיב להתודות לפני הא-ל ברוך הוא / "All commandments of the Torah, whether they be mandatory or prohibitive, if a man violates any one of them, either presumptuously or erroneously, when he will do Teshuvah and turn away from his negative ways, he is obliged to confess before Hashem, blessed is He." כיצד מתודין. אומר אנא השם חטאתי עויתי פשעתי לפניך ועשיתי כך וכך והרי נחמתי ובשתי במעשי ולעולם איני חוזר לדבר זה. וזהו עקרו של ודוי / "And how is the verbal confession made? The one confessing says, 'I beseech You, O Great Name! I have sinned; I have been obstinate; I have committed profanity in front of You, particularly in do-ing such and such. Now, behold! I have regretted it, and I am ashamed of my actions, and I will never relapse into this thing again.' This is the עקרו / Ikaro / main component of Viduy."

A few observations should be mentioned:

A) It is possible that, according to the Rambam, there is no Mitzvah or Chiyuv / obligation to do Teshuvah; rather, "When he will do Teshuvah and turn away from his negative ways, he is obliged to confess." The Chiyuv, then, would not be Teshu-vah per se, but rather confession.[*]

[**] The Mitzvah is not Teshuvah; rather, it is Viduy. In the words of the Ram-bam, in *Sefer haMitzvos*, Mitzvah 73, היא שצונו להתודות על העונות והחטאים שחטאנו לפני הא-ל ולאמר אותם עם התשובה / "(The 73rd Mitzvah is) we were

commanded to confess sins that we have sinned, in front of Hashem, and verbalize them *with* Teshuvah." The simple reason is that the act of Teshuvah itself is just a reconfirmation and recommitment to the world of Mitzvos. We are given the Mitzvos as commandments, even though they are also 'strands' of love and connection, and a command must not be broken, but if in fact it was broken, then obviously, as part of *Kabbalas Ol /* accepting upon ourselves the Yoke of Heaven, the Mitzvos, we need to immediately let go of such deviant behaviors and refocus and recommit to uphold them. So it is not an option or a separate Mitzvah; rather, it is an integral part of keeping all the Mitzvos. Thus, the *Mitzvah* is Viduy (Although note the language of the Rambam, *Hilchos Teshuvah*, 7:3: אל תאמר שאין תשובה אלא מעברות שיש בהן מעשה כגון זנות וגזל וגנבה. אלא כשם שצריך אדם להתוודות ...לשוב. מן הכל צריך לחזר בתשובה. This suggests that the Mitzvah is actually Teshuvah). See also *Minchas Chinuch*, Mitzvah, 364: ח הרהמ"מ דמ ד"נלע ולכאורה דהמ"ע דכאן אינו התשובה רק הוידוי בפה דזגה"כ היא דאם מתנחם מהחטא צריך להתוודות בפיו ככל מ"ע שתלוי בדיבור... ואם מתחרט בלב יש לו כפרה מה שהתשובה מכפר אבל אין תלוי בכלל בוידוי דברים רק דהיא מ"ע בפ"ע ואם לא עשה כן ביטל מ"ע של וידוי אבל התשובה נתקבלה ומכפרת. See also, *Shu'T Mishpat Kohen*, 128. *Kiryas Sefer*, Hilchos Teshuvah. *Likutei Biurim*, Tanya, p. 40. The Meshech Chochmah asks how there can be a separate Mitzvah of Teshuvah, for even without this Mitzvah, a person is obligated to perform all the Mitzvos, so what is the extra obligation of Teshuvah? And he answers that the Mitzvah of Teshuvah is the Viduy: *Meshech Chochmah*, Vayelech.

Alternatively, it could be argued that the specific Mitzvah of Teshuvah is the concept of Charatah for past behavior, whereas the obligation to perform all Mitzvos is more connected to the future and Kabbalah. Note the words of the Tosefos Yom Tov: ונ"ל כי התשובה היא החרטה וההכנעה כי הם עיקרי התשובה. והוידוי בלי הכנעה אינה כלום: *Avos*, 4:11. Perhaps Rabbeinu Yonah is suggesting the same when he writes, כי אחרי שובי נחמתי ואחרי הודעי ספקתי על ירך. ענין נחמתי החרטה והצעה כי עיקר התשובה במרירות הלב: *Sha'arei Teshuvah*, 1:18. Or, כי עקרי התשובה לפי מרירות הלב: *Ibid*, 3:217. Although the simple meaning is that Teshuvah needs to be done with great remorse, not that remorse is necessarily the main component of Teshuvah. Yet, see *Tanya*, Chap 17: כי באמת, אי אפשר לרשעים להתחיל לעבוד ה' בלי שיעשו תשובה על העבר תחלה – לשבר הקליפות שהם מסך מבדיל ומחיצה של ברזל המפסקת בינם לאביהם שבשמים, על ידי שבירת לבו ומרירת נפשו על חטאיו... והיא בחינת תשובה תתאה.

The Mitzvah of Viduy is Min haTorah: Rambam, ibid. *Toras Kohanim*, Bechukosai. Smag, Mitzvah 16. *Sefer haChinuch*, Mitzvah 374. Smak, 53. *Sefer*

Teshuvah itself is not and cannot be a 'separate' Mitzvah, as Teshuvah is merely having regret over veering from the path and committing to the path of Torah and Mitzvos.

Moreover, the regret, desire and commitment of Teshuvah cannot be a Mitzvah. *Mitzvah* means a 'command', and Teshuvah means an inner desire to change. An inner desire cannot be 'commanded'. If Teshuvah were a Mitzvah, it would not be we, ourselves, wanting to change, rather, we would do it because it is commanded, and hence it would not be defined as Teshuvah. Imagine a young child lashing out at his mother, and his father commanding him, 'Tell your mother you're sorry.' If the child listens to his father and says 'I'm sorry' to his mother, it is obviously not Teshuvah. He is simply 'apologizing' because his father told him to do so. Real Teshuvah comes from within the person who transgressed, with a strong, authentic sense of regret and resolve. To tell Hashem you are sorry because you are commanded to do so is not Teshuvah. This is the reason why Teshuvah cannot be a 'Mitzvah' in the opinion of the Rambam.

B) Viduy comes *after* the Teshuvah, as it says: 'One should do Teshuvah and then confess.' Viduy, according to the Rambam, is the culminating and final expression of one's Teshuvah.*

Chassidim, 20. See also, *Kerisus*, 12a. *Zohar* 3, p. 122a. Other sources write that Viduy is only a Mitzvah *mi-d'Rabbanan* / from our sages: *Mahari Perlo*, Sefer haMitzvos, Rasag, 3, Parsha 42. p. 374–375.

** On the verse לעשתו ובלבבך בפיך מאד הדבר אליך כי־קרוב / "For this thing is very close to you, in your mouth and in your heart, to do it" (*Devarim*, 30:14), says the Ramban, this refers to Teshuvah; in your heart you can desire Te-

C) Viduy consists of verbalizing one's sentiments of the heart: 'I confess that I transgressed, I regret it, and I am committed to doing right in the future.'

Yet, these are the words of the Rambam regarding Yom Kippur and the idea of Viduy on Yom Kippur: יום הכפורים הוא זמן תשובה לכל ליחיד ולרבים והוא קץ מחילה וסליחה לישראל. לפיכך חיבים הכל לעשות תשובה ולהתודות ביום הכפורים / "Yom Kippur is a time of Teshuvah for all, the individual and the collective. And it (Yom Kippur) is the goal of exoneration and forgiveness of the People of Israel. Therefore, all are obliged to do Teshuvah and to confess on the day of Yom Kippur" (*Hilchos Teshuvah*, 2:7). הודוי שנהגו בו כל ישראל אבל אנחנו חטאנו (כלנו) והוא עקר הודוי / "And the Viduy (text) that has been accepted by Klal Yisrael contains the passage 'but we have (all) transgressed,' and this is the עקר / *Ikar* / main component of Viduy" (*Ibid*, 8).

---

shuvah and thus speak the words of Viduy: בפיך ובלבבך הוא ענין הודוי על התשובה שהזכיר למעלה, ואמר, כי המצוה הזאת, על התשובה נאמר שהוא מצוה בה, כמו שאמר ושבת עד ה' א-להיך, ואמר לא נפלאת היא ולא רחוקה, כי אף בהיותם בארץ אויביהם בגלות והם נדחים ונפוצים יכולין הם לשוב בתשובה בכל מקום שהם, אף אם היו בסוף העולם קרוב אליך הדבר מאד בפיך ובלבבך לעשותו. In other words, תסכים במחשבתך ותגמור בלבך ותתודה בפיך / "Resolve in your mind, conclude in your heart, and then confess with your mouth": Rabbeinu Bachya (ben Asher), quoting the Ramban, *ad loc*. Thus, first one does Teshuvah, then Viduy. Yet, the Pasuk says ומודה ועזב ירחם / "And one who confesses and lets go of them (his sins) will find mercy (from on High)": *Mishlei*, 28:13. This suggests that first comes Viduy and then Teshuvah. Or, first Charatah, then Viduy, and then Azivus haChet — הזכיר תחלה ומודה. על החרטה והוידוי. ואח"כ ועזב: Rabbeinu Yonah, *Sha'arei Teshuvah*, Sha'ar 1:13. Furthermore, Rabbeinu Bachya ibn Pakuda writes that it is through speaking the words of Viduy that one arouses (deeper) Teshuvah: *Chovos haLevavos*, Sha'ar haBechinah, 5.

From the above quote, it seems that:

D) On Yom Kippur there is a *Chiyuv* / obligation upon us all to do Teshuvah and to say *Viduy* / confession.

E) The Viduy comes after the Teshuvah, for 'one does Teshuvah' and then 'one confesses.'

F) The main component of Viduy is to say "I (we) have transgressed," an admission of transgression.

Curiously, points D and F seem to be in contradiction to points A and B. It seems that regarding all the days of the year, there is no *Chiyuv* / obligation to do Teshuvah, but rather a Chiyuv to do Viduy. Whereas, on Yom Kippur, there seems to be a Chiyuv both to do Teshuvah and to say Viduy. Regarding all the days of the year, the Viduy is a verbal expression of what the reciter is sensing in his heart, regretting the past and resolving for the future, whereas on Yom Kippur, it seems that the עקר / *Ikar* / main component of Viduy is just the verbal admission of sin.

The second question is easily resolved.*

---

* Although this does not answer why the *Nusach* / formulation of the Viduy prayer omits the idea of *Charatah* / regret and *Kabbalah* / acceptance, and we only recite, "We have sinned."

Technically, it is possible that the Viduy service in our Yom Kippur Tefillah corresponds to the Viduy of the Cohen Gadol on Yom Kippur (וידוי יום הכפורים. צוה יוצרינו לכהן גדול שיתודה על חטאת יום הכפורים...תולדה למצות עשה צוו חכמים שכל ישראל יתודו בין איש בין אשה ביום הכפורים: *Sefer Yere'im*, 263, 1:2. Indeed, Viduy is recited ten times (in Tefillah) corresponding to the ten times that the

The truth is the main components of Viduy are to speak about one's *Charatah* / regret and one's *Kabbalah* / acceptance and resolve for the future. When the Rambam writes that on Yom Kippur אבל אנחנו חטאנו (כלנו) והוא עקר הודוי / "(Saying) 'We have (all) transgressed' — this is the main component of Teshuvah," it is not to exclude regretting and accepting. Rather, since previously he has already established that Viduy entails

Cohen Gadol recited the Divine Name. See *Levush*, Orach Chayim, 620). If so, we are simply praying the words that the Cohen Gadol said, and thus our Viduy is a part of Tefillah and not an actual 'act of Teshuvah' There is no reason for Charatah and Kabbalah if it is not an actual process of Teshuvah. (Although, this explanation would not address the Nusach of the Viduy on the night of Yom Kippur, when there was no Viduy by the Cohen Gadol, as there were no offerings. And in general, the Rambam clearly learns that the Viduy is a part of the Teshuvah of Yom Kippur: יום הכפורים הוא זמן תשובה לכל...לפיכך חיבים הכל לעשות תשובה ולהתודות ביום הכפורים — *Hilchos Teshuvah*, 2:7. *Minchas Chinuch*, Mitzvah 364).

On a deeper level, perhaps the answer is that because of the intensity and power of the day, even a lighter form of Teshuvah is sufficient: note Mabit, *Beis Elokim*, Sha'ar haTeshuvah, 15. The Rambam writes, אף על פי שהתשובה והצעקה יפה לעולם. בעשרה הימים שבין ראש השנה ויום הכפורים היא יפה ביותר ומתקבלת היא מיד ... במה דברים אמורים ביחיד אבל צבור כל זמן שעושים תשובה וצועקין בלב שלם / "Even though Teshuvah and calling out (to Hashem) are desirable at all times, during the ten days between Rosh HaShanah and Yom Kippur, they are even more desirable and will be accepted immediately...To whom does the above apply? To an individual. However, with regards to a community, (Teshuvah and calling out to Hashem) are accepted *whenever* it repents and cries out wholeheartedly" (*Hilchos Teshuvah*, 2:6). This seems to suggest that throughout the year for Teshuvah and Tefillah to be accepted בלב שלם / wholeheartedly is required, on Yom Kippur even less than such, is also considered Teshuvah — דהתם מיירי בעשרת ימי תשובה אבל בשאר ימות השנה צריך שיהיה בלב שלם: *Rebbe Akivah Eiger* on the Rambam. Perhaps the same applies to Viduy — that on all other days of the year, Teshuvah requires Charatah and Kabbalah, but on Yom Kippur, Charatah and Kabbalah are not required.

various properties, he thus does not go into all the details again here (And this is also the simple *Peshat* / literal meaning of the Gemara — תו — אמר מר זוטרא: לא אמרן, אלא דלא אמר: אבל אנחנו חטאנו אבל אמר: אבל אנחנו חטאנו לא צריך. דאמר בר המדודי: הוה קאימנא קמיה דשמואל, והוה יתיב, וכי מטא שליחא דצבורא ואמר: אבל אנחנו חטאנו, קם מיקם, אמר שמע מינה עיקר וידוי האי הוא *Yuma*, 87b. The words אבל אנחנו חטאנו are part of the entire Viduy that is said, and the essence of the entire Viduy are these words. Indeed, this is how the *Lechem Mishneh* reads this Rambam. ונראה דלאו דוקא חטאנו לבד אלא חטאנו עוינו פשענו שזהו עיקר הוידוי וכמו שכתב רבינו למעלה בריש פ' ראשון חטאתי עויתי פשעתי לפניך: *Lechem Mishneh*, ad loc).

VIDUY AS AN EXPRESSION OF TESHUVAH, OR AS ANOTHER DIMENSION OF TESHUVAH

One distinction still remains, and that is that on Yom Kippur there is a Chiyuv to do Teshuvah *and* a Chiyuv to say Viduy, whereas throughout the year the Chiyuv is to say Viduy as an expression of Teshuvah.

Throughout the year, the purpose of Viduy, as will be explored, is to reveal, express, define, and concretize our Teshuvah. A person experiences in his heart a sense of regret for the past actions, accepts upon himself a different course for the future, and then speaks about his feelings in Viduy. But there is no Chiyuv to do Teshuvah; only if one desires Teshuvah in his heart, then he must reveal these sentiments with the medium of speech.* On Yom Kippur, however, it is זמן תשובה לכל

---

* If Teshuvah or at least the Viduy of Teshuvah is a Mitzvah, why do we not recite a *Berachah* / blessing before doing Teshuvah or at least before saying Viduy? (*Beis Yitzchak*, Yorah De'ah 2, Siman 168). The simple answer is, since the 'act' of Teshuvah is in the heart as an inner resolve, and since Viduy only expresses verbally what one feels inwardly, hence no Berachah is to be said, as we do not recite a Berachah on a 'feeling' Mitzvah: *Pardos Yoseph*, Parshas Acharei Mos. Perhaps also, since complete Teshuvah is one

/ "a time of Teshuvah for all" and as such, just as on the *Yom Tov* / holy day of Matzos we need to eat Matzah, on the 'Yom Tov of Teshuvah', there is a Chiyuv to do Teshuvah. Just as on Rosh Hashanah, the *Mitzvas haYom b'Shofar* / the Mitzvah of the day is Shofar," on Yom Kippur, the Mitzvah of the day is Teshuvah.

On Yom Kippur, the recitation of Viduy is not merely there to 'reveal' the Teshuvah of the heart; rather, Viduy has its own purpose.

To understand the nature of Teshuvah on Yom Kippur, let us explore the reasons offered for Viduy in general. Why is there a need and obligation to verbalize our Teshuvah?

Teshuvah, as mentioned, is not complete until we a) articulate what went wrong in the past, and b) verbally commit to changing our behavior in the future. Why is this? Why do we need confession? Why is verbalization so integral to the process? What is the great importance of making a verbal confession or commitment, especially as it is done not in front of a person but in front of Hashem alone? Doesn't Hashem already know our thoughts and intentions? How does verbalization

---

that has been accepted on High and is, in that sense, not fully in our hands, we do not recite a Berachah. We do not recite blessings on a Mitzvah that is not entirely in our hands when performing it. Nor do we make a blessing when the Mitzvah is dependent on a recipient, such as *Tzedakah* / charity, as it is possible for the person not to want to receive the charity: *Teshuvas haRashba*, 1, Siman 18. Similar, perhaps, is Teshuvah.

facilitate, stimulate or cement the life-changing process of Teshuvah?

OVERCOMING OUR SENSE OF LONELINESS THROUGH SPEAKING

Before delving more deeply into the reason for Viduy with regards to Teshuvah throughout the year, there is something about the mere act of speaking, verbally expressing our desire for Teshuvah that is cathartic for us, and also essential to the process of Teshuvah and to *Avodas Hashem* / serving the Creator, in general. Speaking can be very soothing for a soul who feels alone and dejected and is yearning to reconnect with some sense of unity with HaKadosh Baruch Hu.

On the deepest level, we all long for connection with the Source of Life and with our core essence of self. Sometimes this longing appears as a desire for a certain object or for a sense of connection with other people — but this is actually a longing to connect with our soul and our Creator.

Often we do not realize how profound our existential need for connection with Reality is until we seem to have lost it. One of the most devastating and demoralizing feelings that arises in a healthy individual is felt when he or she acts in contrast to who they know they really are. The sense of disconnection, shame, and loneliness can seem crushing. We can, however, begin to overcome this state by articulating our feelings and our real desire, which is to 'return home' to our Source and essence.

Speech consists of sound and vibration as well as intentionality and meaning. When we speak and can hear ourselves speaking, we are both listening and speaking at the same time, as if there are two people present, a speaker and a listener. As the 'speaker', you are in the presence of a compassionate, non-judgmental 'friend' who is silently listening. As the compassionate, silent 'listener', you can heal the 'speaker' of the alienation that arose from engaging in misaligned desires. You can offer the awareness of 'another person' and relieve the 'speaker' of loneliness. Our sages advise us that if you find yourself troubled, speak to a friend (אמר חד אסי ורבי אמי רבי ,ישחנה איש בלב דאגה לאחרים ישיחנה אמר וחד מדעתו ישחנה: *Sotah*, 42b. *Yuma*, 75a). A person may feel cured merely by opening up to someone who listens, maybe even talking to himself, and listening to himself as a good friend would listen.

Of course, in Viduy we are not just speaking to ourselves but rather listening to our conversation with the Master of the Universe. When we are speaking words of confession and unburdening, we should realize that we are speaking to the greatest listener of all, the all-compassionate and life-giving Divine Presence. By opening up and communicating freely with the Infinite Listener, we create new channels to receive empowerment (Regarding speaking to Hashem, see *Sefer Chareidim*, 65. *Likutei Moharan* 2, 96, 99. *Michtavei Chafetz Chayim*, p. 86–87. שבעת הנכונה העצה לזאת אשר יהי' לבדו בלי חברת האדם בביתו או בחוץ ישפוך שיחו לפני ה'.... גם בשכבו על משכבו לבבו ממקור בוראו לבין בינו שיחתו תהי' זאת בלילות: *Maor vaShemesh*, Shabbos Shuvah. *Sur meRa v'Asei Tov*, p. 43. *Tzav v'Ziruz*, p. 327).

Being open, vulnerable, transparent, and spontaneous with our Loving Father in Heaven has tremendous spiritual, and even mental and emotional value. Speaking effortlessly and unselfconsciously to Hashem as a child speaks to his parents opens new avenues of communication. We no longer feel alone, disempowered, or incapable; rather, we feel that the challenges and obstacles in our lives seem less monumental and less frightening.

We can be completely open, honest, and vulnerable with HaKadosh Baruch Hu. We can speak whatever language is easiest for us, so that we can freely express everything that comes to mind without any sense of hesitation. Nothing is too trifling or insignificant to bring into the flow of connection with the Divine Listener. When we feel free to speak with Hashem even about superficial, mundane issues, we can be surprised by the deeper issues that emerge from the subconscious mind, arising in order to be resolved.

"Return, O Israel, to Hashem your G-d," thunders the Prophet Hoshea (2:14). Deeply, this means that we need to do Teshuvah until we can call Hashem *our* G-d. We should aspire to sense Hashem's Presence so vividly, that it is as if we are in the presence of another person; then Hashem is "Our G-d" — real and immediate to us (שצריך לשוב עד שיהיה ה' הוא הבורא אלוקיך אלהות שלך פי' שתהא כסא ומרכבה לקדושתו ותוכל לדבק בו ולדבר לפניו תפלות ותחנונים כאשר ידבר איש אל רעהו למשל כאשר תאמר ברוך אתה ה' יהיה בעיניך כאלו אתה עומד לפניו ממש בלי שום מסך *Avodas Yisrael*, Shabbos Shuvah. See also *Bnei Yissachar*, Tishrei, Ma'amar 4).

Communication that is grounded in honesty promotes greater closeness. Intimacy is greatly enhanced when we speak authentically, whether between us and another person or between us and our Creator. The more open we become, the more we can unburden ourselves of our worries, troubles, frustrations, and anxieties, and the more intimacy and 'at-one-ment' is created.

VIDUY IS A MEANS TO DIFFUSE NEGATIVITY

When we verbally acknowledge the areas in life that keep us entrapped, their energy and potency is diffused. The *K'li* / 'vessel' of speaking out our remorse and resolve to change allows us to own and master the issue we are struggling with. The problem becomes manageable when 'externalized' as words.

Unfulfilled fantasies can perpetually haunt and grip people, since desires lodged in the subconscious mind are hard to expunge and forget. Confessing shortcomings externalizes them and makes them conscious and concrete. Once they are concrete, they can be released and forgotten. We cannot forget something that we hardly remember. Until a desire is brought into the light of objectivity, it remains a fixation or a latent tendency and cannot be deliberately released. When this desire is garbed in words, it can be consciously addressed and subsequently dismissed.

If you tell the truth about something with proper intent, you dissipate the energy around it. Speaking helps you shake it off. In fact, the word *Viduy* comes from a word meaning to throw off or cast aside (וידו־ארן בי / "and cast stones at me": *Eichah*, 3:53. As the *Kesav ve-haKabalah* explains, Vayikra, 5:5).

There are various methods for releasing old, deeply entrenched negativities, but the most powerful way is simply to cease denying that they exist. Hiding from something does not remove it. Acknowledge your feelings, confess that your transgressions are real, and then declare Teshuvah.

Ultimately, confession delivers our imperfections into the 'Hands' of the compassionate Master of the Universe, the Ultimate Listener and Healer. In this way, we free ourselves of the hidden weight of subconscious guilt. As we begin to feel forgiven, we more easily forgive others, and deeply heal our past. Finally, we can move on with our lives, feeling light and clean.

These are very general reasons for verbal Teshuvah; now let us focus more pointedly on the act of Viduy and its inherent link with the remorse and resolve of Teshuvah.

SPEAKING GIVES VOICE / SUBSTANCE TO FEELINGS

On the most elementary level, speaking gives a physical expression to our subjective, and often elusive, thoughts, rendering them more objective, clear, and intelligible to ourselves.

Speaking intelligible words gives voice to our thoughts, clarifying, crystallizing and structuring them (*Chorev*, Pirkei haMitzvos, Teshuvah 2). As they exist within the mind, thoughts are often evasive, undefined, and unstructured. When they 'descend' into articulate language they are reified, and as a result, we can understand them with clarity. This coherence unveils insight regarding what we really wish to achieve. This is why, when mulling over an issue, some people speak their thoughts out loud to remember or get a better grasp of what they are contemplating.

In this way, verbalizing Teshuvah is not an act of conjuring up the sentiments of Teshuvah. Rather, it is reifying the thoughts of Teshuvah and heartfelt feelings of yearning, giving them proper 'vessels' of expression. When they become clear, we can make effective conscious choices.

WORDS MAKES THINGS REAL

Speaking about something also makes it real to us. Until we speak about something, even when we feel we know about it, somehow it is not as real. On the day of the passing of the illustrious sage Rebbe Yehudah, his students declared, "Whoever says that Rebbe Yehudah has passed away shall be pierced with a sword" (*Kesuvos*, 104a). Clearly, they were not in denial that he had passed on, and they knew quite well intellectually that he had passed away, yet they could not bring themselves to verbalize this truth. They emotionally sensed that until someone openly pronounced that he had died, he was still 'alive'. Similarly, when we hear bad news, our first response is often disbelief and denial; sometimes, we may even exclaim, 'Don't even say it!' It is as if what is not verbalized does not really exist.

Verbally articulating our feelings of Teshuvah and desire to change makes these sentiments truer for us. In the language of the Chinuch, משרשי המצוה. לפי שבהודאת העון בפה תתגלה מחשבת החוטא ודעתו, שהוא מאמין באמת, כי גלוי וידוע לפני האל ברוך הוא כל מעשהו / "It is from the roots of this commandment [that it is] because, through the verbal admission of iniquity, the sinner reveals his thoughts and opinions. Then he truly believes that all his deeds are revealed and known before G-d, blessed be He" (*Sefer haChinuch*, Mitzvah 364). In other words, while he knows in his heart that he is living in Hashem's Presence, speaking about it reveals to his mind that he is a מאמין באמת / a true believer in this.

To make the Teshuvah in our heart real, to take our regret of the past and our resolve for the future seriously, we must speak about it in detail.

Through speaking honestly to ourselves, about ourselves, in front of our Creator, we come face-to-face with our own truth. We are empowered to peacefully confront the way we have been living up until this point, as painful as it may be. Putting our inner thoughts of regret and resolve for the future 'on the table' may make us feel vulnerable, but it is the only effective way to break complacency and spiritual inertia. By pushing aside any foolish pride, honest confession gives us the ability to make real changes in our lives.

Indeed, an element of maturity coincides with the ability to verbalize our shortcomings. Bringing even our subjective shortcomings into objectivity enables us to respond to them without reactivity. Like a wise parent, we can observe where the shortcoming came from, and we can find the original spiritual, mental, emotional, or even physical deficiency that gave rise to those actions. Then we can mourn and regret them accurately, and see how much better life will be when we resolve the problem at its root.

WORDS CREATE OUR REALITY

We are creatures of speech, and we are strongly affected by all we say and hear. Ancient thinkers defined the human being as a *homo sapiens*, a 'rational animal', while others called him a 'tool-making animal', a 'social animal' or a 'worshiping animal'. Classical Torah scholars, such as Rebbe Yehudah haLevi, author of *The Kuzari*, define the human being as a מדבר / *Medaber* / 'speaking being' (On the verse ויהיה האדם לנפש חיה / "And man became a living spirit," says the Targum, this means לרוח ממללא / "a speaking spirit," ונפש המדבר: Rambam, *Pesicha l'Torah*). Language is essential to the human world, not only for communication with others, but to decipher, interpret, and contemplate our own experience. Language both influences the way we think and reveals what we think.

Our world was brought into being through the Ten Utterances of the Creator: "And Hashem said 'let there be light', and there was light." When Hashem speaks, the world responds and phenomena become real. It is the same with our utterances, for we are created in the 'image and likeness' of the Creator. We contextualize our existence and the world around us through language and 'create' our reality.

In this way, when a person speaks about his inner resolve and desire to elevate his life and no longer get dragged down into specific patterns of thought and behavior, these words have a creative power. Articulating the positive commitments of the mind and heart creates barriers that help a person not fall back into transgression. Again, in the words of the Chinuch, גם מתוך הזכרת החטא בפרט ובהתנחמו עליו יזהר ממנו יותר פעם אחרת לבל יהי נכשל בו, אחר שיאמר בפיו כזו וכזו עשיתי ונסכלתי במעשי יהיה נגדר שלא ישוב לעשות כן / "Additionally, through verbalizing the sin specifically, and through his remorse about it, he will be more careful about it on another occasion not to stumble in the same way again. Since he declares verbally, "I did such-and-such, and I stumbled in my deeds," he will have (through his words) created a fence so he will not repeat what he did" (*Sefer haChinuch*, Mitzvah 364).

VOICE AROUSES & CREATES INTENTION

קול מעורר כוונה / "Voice arouses intention" (Taz, *Orach Chayim*, 101:3. *Reishis Chochmah*, Sha'ar haKedushah, 15. *Shaloh*, Sh'ar haOsyos. *Shabbos*, 119: regarding בכל כחו / "with all one's strength," Rashi writes that it means בכל כוונתו / "with all one's intentionality," while Tosefos writes that it means בקול רם / "with a loud voice." The reconciliation of the Ritva is that verbalizing with a loud voice will arouse more intention). The more we objectify our thoughts and feelings through words the deeper our intention becomes. Even just the sound of the words arouses greater commitment and a more focused desire to change.

What's more, if one's regret and resolve to change are weak and teetering, the act of speaking about it will bring a person to a stronger desire to change. Speaking enhances feelings. Contrary to some popular opinions, if a person becomes angry, their most effective remedy may simply be to refrain from speaking about it. In most cases, speaking of anger does not resolve it; it just fans the flames and exacerbates it (Rebbe Rashab, *Sefer ha-Ma'amarim*, RaNaT, p. 5). This is true of any feeling; the more we speak about it the more real or intense it becomes. Through speaking to Hashem about our decision to make Teshuvah, our inner intention to return to harmony with the Divine Will becomes more revealed, and it becomes easier to act upon it.

If you ever have a feeling in your heart that something is amiss or that you sense a lack of fulfillment and that you are ready for change, you are open to Teshuvah. The Torah guides you in that moment to begin speaking about it, whether out loud or mentally, if necessary. The more you speak about it the greater the resolve in the heart will become,* and this intention will begin to overflow into action.

---

* This Pasuk speaks of Teshuvah: כִּי־קָרוֹב אֵלֶיךָ הַדָּבָר מְאֹד בְּפִיךָ וּבִלְבָבְךָ / "For it (Teshuvah) is very close to you, in your mouth and in your heart": *Devarim*, 30:14, Ramban, *ad loc*. First it says "with your mouth" and then "with your heart," which suggests that your heart will follow your mouth. Indeed, often it is our feelings that follow our words. See Maharal, *Derech Chayim*, Avos, 1:17. *Michtav m'Eliyahu* 4, p. 257. Rabbeinu Bachya writes that speaking the words of Viduy arouses Teshuvah. *Chovos haLevavos*, Sha'ar haBechina, 5. In this way, even if one has not yet resolved to undertake the journey of Teshuvah, the speaking of regret and resolve will bring a person to Teshuvah.

These are some of the reasons why Viduy is integral to Te-shuvah throughout the year. In fact, any time a person resolves in his heart to take up a path of Teshuvah, there is an obligation to voice these sentiments so that the feeling will become more defined and practical. On Yom Kippur, 'the Day of Teshuvah', Viduy is of another nature; there is a *Chiyuv* / obligation to ex-perience feelings of Teshuvah in one's heart as well as in one's mouth — both to feel Teshuvah and to speak Teshuvah.

VIDUY ON YOM KIPPUR

Yom Kippur is a day of *Penimiyus* / internality, inwardness. On this day, each person represents the innermost and elevated figure of the *Cohen Gadol* / the High Priest, as he enters in si-lence, alone, into the innermost chamber of the *Beis haMikdash* / Holy Temple. Inwardly 'acting out' and contemplating this scenario draws us to the inwardness of the day.

עיצומו של יום מכפר / 'The Essence of the day of Yom Kippur brings atonement." This is because, on Yom Kippur, the es-

---

* The idea of עיצומו של יום מכפר / "the essence of the day brings atonement," is the opinion of Rebbe Yehudah. Thus in the liturgy on Yom Kippur we say, למחילה ולסליחה ולכפרה ולמחל בו את כל עונותינו / "(It is a day of) Mechilah, Selichah and Kaparah, to forgive all our sins." Yet, the sages maintain that on Yom Kippur, one is still required to 'do' Teshuvah. In other words, all agree that the essence of the day brings atonement, but their debate is only whether one must also actively engage in Teshuvah, or if one can simply allow the essence of the day to create atonement without actively engag-ing in Teshuvah. In the words of the Rambam, who rules like the sages, ועצמו של יום הכפורים מכפר לשבים / "The essence of the day of Yom Kippur brings atonement *for those who return*": *Hilchos Teshuvah*, 1:3. *Likutei Si-chos*, 4, p. 1150. See also *Siach Yitzchak*, D'rush l'Shabbos Teshuvah, p. 55.

sence of self and our deepest desires are revealed. We experience many 'external' desires, and sometimes תקפו יצרו / the strength of our lower inclination overwhelms us and takes charge. Deep down, however, our innermost desire is to be one with HaKadosh Baruch Hu and to live a life of Torah, meaning and higher purpose (Rambam, *Hilchos Geirushin*, 2:20). On Yom Kippur, the manifestation of *Achas baShanah* / 'Oneness within time', our essential Oneness becomes revealed, our most essential desires become conscious. Although this desire for Teshuvah can be revealed on any and every day of the year, Yom Kippur is the 'headquarters' of this power of revelation.

Usually, Teshuvah is founded upon *Charatah* / remorse and disgust over one's past behavior, and *Kabbalah* / acceptance of a new path and resolve for a different future. In this paradigm, the regret and resolve in the heart are made real and defined through spoken Viduy. But on Yom Kippur, on the essence of all days, Teshuvah and atonement is of a much higher paradigm.

Throughout the year, Teshuvah demands that the *Gavra* / person desires to change his ways, transform himself, and

---

When exactly does the atonement take place? From the Gemara in *Kerisus*, it appears that atonement is attained the moment Yom Kippur begins and continues throughout the day (דילמא כוליה יומא מאורתא...שכל היום מכפר) : *Kerisus*, 18b). Yet, Tosefos, *Shevuos*, 13b, writes that atonement is attained at the end of Yom Kippur (ויום הכפורים אינו מכפר עד שתחשך למוצאי יום הכפורים). Today, atonement is perhaps attained right away, whereas in the times of the Beis haMikdash it was only attained after the offerings, hence by the end of the day: *Shu'T Shoel u-Moshav*, (1), 1, Siman 284.

therefore, feelings in the heart need to be expressed in words, to reveal and solidify them. The day of Yom Kippur, by contrast, is a *Cheftza* / object of Teshuvah; it is a זמן תשובה לכל / "a time of Teshuvah for all," a Mikvah in time. In other words, on Yom Kippur, everything in the cosmos returns to its Source simply because it is Yom Kippur. This includes us as well; we spontaneously return to the essence of our own soul, our perfection and wholeness.

כי ביום הזה יכפר עליכם לטהר אתכם; מכל חטאתיכם לפני ה' תטהרו / "For this day will atone for you and purify you; all your sins 'you shall purify' before Hashem " (*Vayikra*, 16:30). The simple reading of the first half of the sentence is that on Yom Kippur there is atonement and purification without our participation — and even without the Cohen Gadol's participation. The day itself brings atonement.* Yet, the second half of the Pasuk says, לפני ה' תטהרו / "...you shall purify before Hashem," implying that we do actively participate. While is true that Yom Kippur itself brings atonement, and the day is similar to a Mikvah of

---

* In the words of Rabbeinu Yonah, כי ביום הזה יכפר עליכם לטהר אתכם שהוא אמור על הטהרה שהשם יתברך מטהר אותנו מן העון ומכפר עלינו / "For on this day shall atonement be made for you, to purify you" — this speaks about the purification that Hashem, may He be blessed, is to purify us from iniquity and atone *for* us...": *Sha'arei Teshuvah,* Sha'ar 4:17. In this view, we are not purifying ourselves, rather Hashem is. However, see *Sifra*, ibid, 27 — "For this day will atone for you and purify you...": ומנין אף על פי שלא בקרבנות ושלא בשעיר היום מכפר; תלמוד לומר יום הכפורים הוא / yet the words "with Teshuvah" are then added. The *Even Ezra* and *Seforno* write, צריכים. *Kesav VeHakabalah:* תטהרו הכהן יכפר עליכם. Or as the *Kli Yakar* writes, כי לפני ה' תטהרו: אתם לטהר עצמיכם מכל חטאתיכם קודם אין יום כיפורים מכפר כ"א לשבים.

purification within time, even within a Mikvah a person will not become pure if they are still holding onto an impure object: כטובל ושרץ בידו / "Immersing while holding an impure animal in one's hand (is not effective)." Similarly, we need to let go of impurity in order to activate the purifying power of Yom Kippur.

In order for the 'magic' of Yom Kippur's healing and atonement to affect us, we need to purify ourselves and actively throw away any impurity 'in our hand'. Then the essence of the day can take hold in us and purify us. This is the deeper reason for Viduy on Yom Kippur and why it is a separate *Chiyuv* / obligation.

Participating in Viduy cleanses us and allows us to let go of our impurities, so that we do not immerse in the 'Mikvah' of Yom Kippur while holding onto an impure object. We need to cleanse our thoughts, hearts and words. In this sense, Viduy does not merely express our inner sentiments of Teshuvah; rather, Viduy is itself a form of purification. In particular, it purifies our words and the world of speech.

Throughout the year, Teshuvah is a state of turning from a path of brokenness ("broken wells that cannot hold water": *Yirmiyahu*, 2:13), decent, and spiritual darkness, and turning toward a path of wholeness, ascent, light, and meaning. It is moving away from a state of imperfection and reclaiming our innate state of perfection. We are moving from one status to another. As such, to ensure that our inner intention and resolve become certainties, we recite a verbal Viduy service in most weekday Shacharis and Minchah services. On Yom Kippur, however, our inner perfection, our *Yechidah* / deepest level of soul and innermost essence of self, is revealed. This is a movement from the inside out. Our inside is lit up and shines outwardly as Viduy. The essence of the day reveals the essence of consciousness, which is ever-pure; Viduy is just a vehicle that puts us in touch with this ever-present purity.

On Yom Kippur, there is no question of whether one's Teshuvah is real or not, as the day itself is a revelation of our essential Teshuvah. The point of the Viduy of Yom Kippur allows our inner light to shine and become revealed on all levels of self, in the 'garments' of our thoughts, feelings, and words. It allows us to let go of our impurities on the level of 'garments', so that our inner purity can "break forth like the light of day."

As explained, the first part of the Pasuk clearly says, "This day will atone for you," and this means we do not have to do anything to be purified.* Yet, the second part, לפני ה׳ תטהרו / "In front of Hashem you shall purify yourselves," clearly states that *we* need to purify ourselves. Says the Targum Yonasan, what does it mean to "purify yourselves?" קדם ה׳ תודון סורחנותכון / "In front of Hashem we need to *confess*." Viduy is the way to purify our 'garments' or 'vessels' of self.

CLEANSING OUR THREE GARMENTS: THOUGHT, SPEECH & ACTION

Each of us possesses three powers or instruments of expression: thought, speech, and action. These are our interface with the world, both in terms of input and output. However, these powers are not only the thoughts, words, and deeds themselves but also the *way* we think, the *way* we speak to express ourselves and interpret the world around us, and *how* we do what we do. These, too, are 'garments' through which we apprehend and assimilate the world and project ourselves onto the world.

Pure, noble, and holy thoughts keep the garment of thought clean; pure, noble, and holy words spoken keep the garments of our speech clean; and pure, noble, and holy action keep the garment of action clean. To allow our deepest core perfection to shine brightly — which allows the essence of the day to bring atonement — we need to ensure that our 'garments' are clean. We need to make sure that the lenses through which our soul shines forth into the world are not smudged.

In this way, thinking thoughts of Teshuvah cleanses our garments of any negative or sinful thoughts, and speaking words of Teshuvah cleanses our garments of any negative speech. In terms of action, on Yom Kippur we are removed from worldly actions, and also our thoughts of resolving to actively live out our positive potential in the year to come cleanse our garments of action (See *Sefer haIkarim*, Ma'amar 4:26. *Akeidas Yitzchak*, Sha'ar 100. *Reishis Chochmah*, Sha'ar haTeshuvah, 1).

COSMICALLY CLEANSING THE WORLD OF SPEECH, OUR WORLD

On a cosmic level as well as on a personal level, Yom Kippur is a revealing of the 'essence of the day', 'a time of Teshuvah' to the entire world. Through Viduy, cleansing our personal world of speech, we are also cleansing the entire cosmos and making Teshuvah more accessible to everyone.

Again, this is because the world was created with the *Asara Ma'amaros* / Ten Utterances, ten Divine sounds or vibrations. Through multiple 'utterances' did Hashem choose to speak the world of multiplicity into being (*Pirkei Avos*, 5:1). It is through these primordial utterances that Creation first emerges and is manifest. "Hashem said: 'Let there be *Ohr* / light,' and there was light" (*Bereishis*, 1:3). Each time there was a Divine saying, a new dimension of Creation came into being by means of the vibrations of the Hebrew letters of the name of that dimension; the letters of *Ohr* constituted the manifestation of 'light'. "Now, although the word אבן / *Ehven* / stone is not mentioned in the Ten Utterances recorded in the Torah (how, then, can we say that letters of the Ten Utterances are the life-force present within a stone?), nevertheless, the stone is animated through the Ten Utterances by means of letter permutations and substitutions...so that ultimately the specific combination of letters (which form) the word אבן / stone descends from the Ten Utterances... And so it is with all created things in the world" (Tanya, *Sha'ar haYichud ve-haEmunah*, 1).

As such, everything in this world has a distinct vibration and frequency; every phenomenon that we can observe in the world is a manifestation of its corresponding spiritual vibration. The Hebrew word for 'thing' is *Devar*, which also means 'word' or utterance. Every 'thing' is thus essentially a physical manifestation of a unique Divine word. 'Things' are *Devarim* / words that are based on combinations of letters and sounds.

Everything in the world continues to vibrate with the Divine pulse with which it was created. The 'micro' and 'macro' movements of phenomena in the world are manifestations of corresponding spiritual movements and vibrations emanating from the Creator of all Life. All dynamics and dimensions of Creation are revelations of different Divine frequencies.

The meta-expression of Divine speech is the primordial Torah: "Hashem looked into the Torah and created the world" (*Medrash Rabbah*, Bereishis, 1:1). The following verse from *Mishlei* / Proverbs refers to this primordial Torah (*Shabbos*, 89a. *Medrash Rabbah*, ibid): ואהיה אצלו אמון ואהיה שעשועים יום יום משחקת לפניו בכל-עת / "Then I was with Him as a nursling, and I was daily שעשועים / *Sha'ashu'im* / delighting, playing, always before Him" (*Mishlei*, 8:30). The word *Sha'ashu'im* comes from the *Sha'ah* / to turn. A double *Sha'ah*, as in *Sha'a-Shu'a*, means 'turning for the sake of turning', which is an act of pleasure or play, as opposed to an act of necessity. This is the level of the 'source' of the letters of the Torah as they exist in the highest realms ("always before Him"), is known as *Olam haMalbush* / the World of Garments (*Emek haMelech*, Sha'ar 1:4. *Nefesh haChayim*, Sha'ar 4:10).

In simple language, this means that the root of manifest Creation is Divine speech, and the root of all Divine speech, expression, and externalization is the World of the Garments, which is the highest, most primordial level of Torah. In this way, "The world is a *Roshem* / imprint of the Torah" ("...and the Torah is a Roshem of *Elokus* / Divinity": *Shaloh*, Shavuos, Torah Ohr, 34. *Asarah Ma'amaros*, Yonas Elem, 1). And when the world is in its perfect state, it is a direct imprint and clear representation of the Torah and the Divine frequency, but, sadly, the world can fall away from this state. And this is due to our choices.*

"Hashem, Torah and Israel are one" (quoted frequently in *Chassidus* and in Kabbalah in the name of the Zohar, although it is not actually clearly stated there: see *Zohar* 3, 73a). "There are three knots bound together: the Holy One, blessed be He, the Torah and Klal Yisrael" (*Ibid*). Two knots would be a hierarchy: Hashem, Torah and us. Three knots, though, suggest a linked triangle, in which Klal Yisrael is both 'lower' and 'higher' than Torah. In other words, we receive the Torah but also have an 'influence', as it were, on Torah. In this way, we have the power to draw down Torah, but also, to G-d forbid, smudge and discombobulate the letters of the Torah. And because the Torah is the root of Creation, our thought, speech and action can cause a defect, a fall, a disunity within all of Creation. For example, when someone steals, the letters of the Torah that state, "You shall not steal" are blurred and smudged (כי נודע אם האדם הוא חוטא

פוגם בהתורה שהוא כ"ב אותיות שנבראו בהם שמים וארץ כי על ידי החטא הוא מחסר האותיות

מן התורה העליונה אם גנב ועבר על לא תגנוב הפריד האותיות מן התורה: *Meor Einayim*,

---

* As the Torah is the meta-root of Creation, we can better understand the teaching of the Baal Shem Tov, who teaches, "When tempted to commit a sin (Heaven forbid), recite the Torah verses pertaining to that sin. Recite them with their intonations and punctuation, with fear and love, and the temptation will leave you": *Tzava'as haRivash*, 13-14. *Baal Shem Tov al ha-Torah*, Shemos, 13

Vayeitzei). And this causes a negative frequency in the entire world.

Once a person steals, the concept of theft becomes more readily available, and people have an easier time stealing. The 'smudging' of the cosmic meta-board of Torah, the Blueprint of Creation, creates a shift in the very fabric of the consciousness of the world. When this moral fabric is altered, instead of saying "do not steal," it seems to say 'steal'. The zeitgeist of the world changes, sadly, for the bad. A new 'culture virus', as it were, is released into the atmosphere and now people tend to steal more. There is an erosion of the morality of other people, when we act immorally. Our actions truly matter, not only for ourselves but for the world around us. If, G-d forbid, we steal, the letters and vibrations of Creation are provisionally changed, and this has an effect in the world. Even moral people, who otherwise have a strong conscience, can unfortunately find themselves stealing, or even just thinking that stealing is sometimes the 'right' thing to do.*

---

* The Alter Rebbe speaks about this idea in terms of angels. Thoughts, words, and actions create angelic or vibrational forces that are released into the world. If a person lies, for example, an 'angelic force' called *Sheker* / 'Falsehood' is generated. To diffuse this force, the one who lied needs to verbally declare regret and the desire to stop lying. When he does so, the letters of the word *Sheker* are disassembled and the life-force that emanated from them disintegrates and disappears: *Ma'amarei Admur haZaken*, HaKetzarim, towards the end. *Asarah Ma'amaros*, Ma'amar Chikur Din, 1, 3. *Ohev Yisrael*, Purim. Additionally, everything is multi-dimensional; everything and everyone is composed of a physical and a spiritual dimension, matter and energy, body and soul. The 'body' of a transgression is the action itself, whereas its 'soul' is the pleasure enjoyed in the act. The Alter Rebbe also speaks about how the yearning for Teshuvah, felt deep within the heart, dif-

SHATTERING OF THE LETTERS

The above is what the Baal Shem Tov calls *Sheviras haOsyos* / the Shattering of the Letters (שברי כלים והם שברי אותיות: *Ohr haEmes* (1977), p. 48, see also *Sefer haTemunah*, Os Shin). The disintegration and breakdown of the combinations of letters in the Torah that spelled "Do not steal," now cause it to *appear* to say, 'Do... steal.'

Although the 'shattering of the letters' begins on a personal, inner level, it causes an outer shattering in the world at large. To explain: our body is a physical reflection of the soul, while the soul is an individualized reflection of the Torah. The Torah reveals 248 positive Mitzvos, which correspond to the 248 positive potentials of the soul, which correspond to the 248 'limbs' of the body and their positive states of health. Likewise, the 365 prohibitions of the Torah are the 365 protective functions of our soul's immune system, and the 365 main 'veins' that channel life-force and manage the immunity in our body. In other words, the Torah is written within our psyches and within our DNA. "You shall not steal" is part of who we are.

One's 'inner Torah', ingrained within his or her being and consciousness, becomes diminished and blurred with every

---

fuses the 'soul' of the action, whereas verbalization of Teshuvah is a minor form of action (עקימת שפתיו הוי מעשה / "The movement of the mouth is like an action": the opinion of Rebbe Yochanan in *Baba Metzia*, 90b. *Sanhedrin*, 65b. Rambam, *Hilchos Sechirus*, 13:2. Although see *Hilchos Sanhedrin*, 18:2), and hence, it erases the transgressions of bodily action.

breach of a prohibition. The more accustomed to 'stealing' one becomes, the easier it is for him to steal again, compromising his natural spiritual immunity. If the letters upon his soul are heavily discombobulated and blurred, "You shall not steal" seems, even emphatically, to command him: 'You *shall* steal.' It becomes almost impossible for the habitual thief to even entertain the thought of stopping, because now, his inner Torah pleads with him to steal whenever the opportunity arises.

We matter, and our actions matter, and exert a powerful influence on the world around us. We are entrusted with the power to uphold the Torah in our thought, speech and action, or G-d forbid, to 'drop' the Torah in our thought, speech or action. Just as dropping a physical Torah scroll can damage the letters or parchment, 'dropping' the Mitzvos and guidance of the Torah can damage the collective spiritual energies and frequencies which resonate throughout the entire world. Every action creates ripple effects throughout the cosmos, and thus when a person commits a negative act, destructive vibrations or shattered letters ripple out into the world. There they become the 'source' of the spiritual and psychic atmosphere for all other creatures, rendering an imbalance in nature and a fall in the very fabric of our world. For example, in the Generation of Noach, the rampant destructive behaviors of human beings disturbed and caused the animal kingdom to behave in the exact same ways.

If a letter in a physical Sefer Torah is written with a very slight error, it can look like a different letter, which spells out a different word. This renders the entire scroll *Pasul* / defective. On a metaphysical level, knowingly and deliberately reading from this Sefer Torah could have a defective effect on all of manifestation, as the matrix of creative letters has been changed to express an energy that departs from the actual Divine revelation. Our negative or 'broken' actions can cause a holy *Os* / letter of the cosmic Torah to 'change the spelling' and channel a Pasul, harmful influence into Creation, Heaven forbid, nurturing powers of poverty, death, sin and so forth. Our task and holy obligation in Teshuvah is thus to elevate the Osyos back to their Source in holiness and wholeness. Then they will resonate accurately with their original intent and radiate goodness and blessing throughout Creation.

Teshuvah is שמשיב הדיבור לשרשו / "to return (the world of speech) to its Source" (Rebbe Chayim Chaykel of Amdur — a close disciple of the Maggid, and whose son, as Rebbe, became a Chassid of the Alter Rebbe — *Chayim v'Chesed*, Teshuvah, 14). Teshuvah, especially verbal Teshuvah, Viduy, returns fallen 'letters' of speech to their Source in Torah, in unity with the Compassionate One, HaKadosh Baruch Hu.

Teshuvah is the process of dissipating and clearing away the pollution of negativity, and generating positive, balanced, repaired frequencies instead (*Meor Einayim*, Chukas). Verbal Teshuvah, in particular, counterbalances and rectifies the fallen vibrations of speech which cause dissonance in the world. Viduy repairs the brokenness within ourselves, so our own rectified vibrations can influence the world and rebalance the energy field of the universe.

If a person has lied in the past, when he declares, "I will stay away from lies," or "I will only speak the truth," he begins to repair his inner Torah, the letters engraved within his own consciousness, and now the letters of his Torah accurately spell, מדבר־שקר תרחק / "Distance yourself from speaking falsehood" (*Shemos*, 23:7). As such, the individual is repairing his own inner Torah and returning the world of speech to its proper Source. This ensures that in the cosmic Torah, the meta-root of Creation, the creative energy of this Mitzvah remains clear and prominent. This has healing power for the person himself as well as for the entire world.

THE DIFFERENCE BETWEEN TEFILLAH AND TESHUVAH

Even deeper than positivity, the power of Viduy lies in its ability to deconstruct negativity. In general, in our daily *Tefillah* / liturgical prayers and praises, it is enough to meditatively enter a state of *Ayin* / transcendence, access the silence, the inner *Nekudah* / point of the holy words in the Siddur, and then from this silence to verbally project a new positive reality. For example, if, while saying prayers of healing, we enter into a state of Ayin in prayer, then when we simply bless Hashem for being the Healer of the Sick, we draw down healing light from Above into our world, and people heal. In this context of prayer, we need not deal with anything negative; rather, we just open channels for the light of these positive words to shine into the world.

Our positive words of Tefillah do not by themselves eliminate the 'adversary' that was created through the negative deed. However, in the act of Teshuvah, we do not merely affirm the positive. For example, if a person has stolen, it is not enough for them simply to affirm, "I do not steal," or "I am an honest person." Rather, they first need to verbally admit, for example, *Gazalnu* / "We (or I) have stolen." In this way, they can rectify the negative or damaging energy by confessing and releasing it. And then they can move on to positive affirmations.

The Early Mekubalim teach that in order to nullify a negative 'decree' or experience of suffering and turn it into a positive vibration, one must first break apart the *Tziruf* / sequence of letters of the 'word' that is experienced. For example, if one is distressed, the energy of the word *Tzarah* / 'distress' is influencing them. The person needs to break up the letters of the word *Tzarah* into its root ingredients. The root ingredient of each letter is a Yud, since graphically, this is the original point from which the letter descends and takes shape. When each letter is deconstructed and reduced to its Yud, the Yud can return to its source in the *Olam haMalbush* / World of Garments and immerse in the Oneness of Atzilus. Then *Tzarah* can re-emerge as *Ratzah* / desired, a positive reality.

In other words, just as a person emerges from a Mikvah pure and full of positive potential, the Yud of each letter can then emerge from the Oneness of Atzilus and the Olam haMalbush with a positive charge. When it descends back into the lines and shapes of its letters, realigned and rectified, the letters can naturally form a wholesome Tziruf. Instead of forming the sequence that spells *Tzarah* / distress, the letters can rearrange to spell *Ratzah* / 'desired'.

If a person is going through Tzarah because of a transgression, they need to confess the transgression through Viduy. Offering words of confession up to Hashem allows those words to 'deconstruct' into their root ingredients, and ascend to the realm of recreative Oneness. Hashem's original *Ratzon* / will for them is that they should thrive and not need to experience hardship. The words are thus offered back to the person rearranged to express redemption and positive experiences in harmony with the original Divine will. Thus, through the deconstruction of Vidui, Tzarah merges into Ayin and then re-manifests as Ratzah.

Viduy deconstructs our exile so that we can then arise and claim our redemption.

Chapter Four

REGRET OR RESET:
WHAT COMES FIRST?

A S MENTIONED, THE PRINCIPAL COMPONENTS OF TE-SHUVAH ARE *Charatah* / חרטה / REGRET AND *Kabbalah* / קבלה / ACCEPTANCE. OF COURSE, TRUE CHARATAH INCLUDES THE COMPONENT OF KABBALAH. Charatah requires recognizing the bitterness of transgression in a manner that results in 'accepting' a firm resolution — a conscious, whole-hearted commitment — not to repeat the transgression in the future.

WHAT IS CHARATAH?

Charatah is related to the word *Charitah* / engraved. It is a profound remorse that is so 'engraved' and ingrained into our consciousness that it will ensure there is almost no possibility of returning to the mistake.

Once, the Alter Rebbe offered a visceral parable to understand what true regret is (note a similar parable, perhaps heard from the Chassidim, is found in *Chazon Yechezkel*, Tefillah uMoadim, p. 417). Imagine a person is traveling in the middle of the winter with his two friends. They come across a frozen river. His two friends tap the ice and conclude that it is unsafe to traverse, as the water is only thinly frozen. However, he calculates that crossing the frozen river, rather than going around and finding a bridge, will cut their trip by many hours. He decides to walk across the river, despite their reluctance and warnings. In the middle of the river, the ice starts cracking and he begins to sink and nearly drown. Imagine the intensity of his regret; if only he heeded his friends' warnings. Just to save a few hours, he has risked his life. How foolish his decision was! It is very unlikely that he will ever make the same mistake. This is true Charatah.

It could be said there are two forms of Charatah: 'Charatah of the heart' and 'Charatah of the mind'. For Charatah to truly be effective and transformative, it needs to be 'Charatah of the heart', and not just an intellectual construct. If you decide intellectually that something is not good for you, this concept may make absolute sense, and all kinds of proof can be brought to support the belief, but it still may not make any difference in your day-to-day life. This is because one's lower behaviors and appetites are driven by what feels good or feels less bad. Therefore, for Teshuvah to be effective, our commitment must harness the power of feeling, as well. There must be an emotional component to our Teshuvah, and a visceral relationship between the mistake and the resulting feelings. If the body-mind is acutely aware of heartfelt feelings of regret and pain associated with the mistake, it will more likely avoid making that same mistake over and over again.

Charatah of the heart — regret for past negativity, for time squandered on foolishness, for life-force wasted on self-gratification — gives the body-mind focus in the present. It arouses our awe of the Creator who has given us a brief opportunity to achieve our mission in life and wants to see us use every hour wisely. Charatah of the heart gives us an ability to recalibrate our attention in life and start anew. This Charatah creates *Kabbalah* / the acceptance of a new direction in life. From another perspective, a solid Kabbalah and resolute commitment for the future is the greatest 'Charatah' there is.

WHAT COMES FIRST: REGRET OR ABANDONING THE TRANSGRESSION?

Charatah and Kabbalah are of a single dynamic; true regret begets paving a new path for the future, and radical acceptance of a new way is the essence of regret and yearning to move away from the past. And both are manifestations of עזיבת החטא / *Azivas haCheit* / abandoning destructive actions. In fact, it would seem that עזיבת החטא should naturally arise to consciousness before Charatah. It would seem that one would first let go of spiritually harmful behavior, actively step away from the addictive pull of transgression, and then proclaim, 'Enough! I regret my old ways and plan to live differently.' Indeed, this is the way the Rambam illustrates the process: ומה היא התשובה.

הוא שיעזב החוטא חטאו... ויגמר בלבו שלא יעשהו עוד... וכן יתנחם על שעבר / "What is Teshuvah? That the sinner let go and abandon his ways of sin.., resolve in his heart not to do these acts any longer (Kabbalah), and he should also regret (Charata) his past deeds" (*Hilchos Teshuvah*, 2:2). In other words, first there must be *Azivah* / abandonment of the behavior, and only then can there be a genuine, non-theoretical Kabbalah of responsibility and commitment. And then, the process can be cemented through Charatah.

According to this view, Azivah must come before Kabbalah. If you are still doing the negative acts in the present, then you cannot honestly claim that you are accepting upon yourself to act differently in the future, nor do you have authentic Charatah of the heart.

This seems straightforward, yet Rabbeinu Yonah writes (*Sha'arei Teshuvah*, 1:10-11) that there are two *Ikarim* / main ingredients in Teshuvah, and העיקר הראשון, החרטה / "The first main step is the Charatah...." Only after the prerequisite of 'regret' will the second Ikar, Azivas haCheit, be meaningful and successful. A person needs to first regret his recent behavior even before he disentangles himself from such patterns. However, this seems counterintuitive. Imagine a person feels regret over a habit of overeating, and he declares, even while storing a tub of ice cream in his freezer, that he regrets eating an entire tub of ice cream last night. Even if there is a sincere regret of the heart, perhaps it will be unproductive since he is still in the gravitational field of the desire and most likely has no escape route. In fact, generating regret while still entrapped might only create stress and guilt, which will incite another instinctual attempt to feel better through overindulgence.

Yet, both sequences can actually be appropriate and effective, and the difference is only in relation to the conditions and circumstances in which they are to be applied. A person declaring Teshuvah needs to determine whether their particular mistakes or transgressions have become ingrained habitual patterns of behavior, or if they were uncharacteristic slips.

If you desire Teshuvah because you slipped ethically or spiritually in a way that was not habitual, then the first step is Charatah. This will be effective if what you have done is foreign to how you generally live your life. The bitterness of Charatah should be strong enough to realign you and bring you back to the guidance of your conscience and moral strength. Once you are experiencing a genuine Charatah, you can proceed with Azivah and you will be in a position to prevent further occurrences.

STOP THEN REGRET

Azivah is obviously more complicated to attain when a transgression has become a habit, a compulsion or addiction, or any reaction that automatically arises whenever certain triggers or conditions are present. At this point, misaligned behavior becomes second nature, at least in relation to a specific trigger. For instance, if every time someone is tired or feels drained, he finds himself binging on sweets, he may not think he is 'addicted', but in fact, there is an ingrained habitual reaction to experiencing those conditions or sensations.

In this unfortunate predicament, Charatah will not help as a first step, because it will never be fully sincere. So long as one's subconscious mind and physiology are clinging to such behaviors, the 'positive' feelings associated with the behavior are much stronger than the Charatah he can willfully generate. He may have intense Charatah in the moment, but ultimately, when the trigger reappears, he will revert to the stronger association, the gratification. The 'negative' feeling of regret rarely has the chance to push back against the imprinted 'pleasant' or numbed feelings connected with the habitual behavior. The behavior has left the realm of conscious control, and the force of instinct will most likely override the temporary irritation of Charatah.

Certainly, Charatah that is generated by an intellectual conviction of what is right and wrong is easily bypassed by the force of sub-intellectual instinct. Even sincere apologies and expressions of regret, while they may be felt as sincere in the moment, will probably not alter your subconscious attachments. As soon as the trigger reappears once or twice, the bitterness of regret may be simply discarded again in favor of the imagined sweetness or comfort of the habit. For Teshuvah to be effective in this predicament, another approach is required.

In this circumstance, you must first engage in Azivah. The negative action, mindset, and corresponding false self-identity need to be abandoned immediately and completely. Pausing to engage in regret before Azivah can bring the temptation back into view, providing a stimulus to the sub-intellectual self to remember and yearn for the momentary comfort of the habit.*

Only once you drop and abandon the behavior, and create a sharp *Havdalah* / separation from it, can you honestly take responsibility for your past and future behavior. Only then will your feelings of regret have leverage over your conditioning. A person floundering in a river may drown if they struggle to stay above water; they must not struggle, but rather become calm and float on top of the water. A person needs to remove himself from the triggers with which he struggles and quickly rise to a place of emotional calm, stability or happiness. 'Floating' upon that higher vantage point, that higher state of consciousness, he can get a detached and comprehensive view of his situation and reconfigure his inner guidance system.

When your identity and feelings are re-wired to harmonize with the Divinity of the Mitzvah that had been habitually transgressed, you can then have real Charatah. When your feet are on solid ground and you have a distance from how you used

---

* In the words of Rabbeinu Yonah; דע כי מי אשר חטא על דרך מקרה. כי התאוה תאוה. ויחזק עליו יצרו ויתקפהו... ראשית תשובת האיש הזה החרטה... אחרי כן יוסיף בכל יום יראת ה' בנפשו. ..ויעזוב דרכו... אך האיש המתיצב על דרך לא טוב תמיד... ראשית תשובת האיש הזה. לעזוב דרכו ומחשבתו הרעה: *Sha'arei Teshuvah*, 1:11.

to live, you can then use regret to decondition your system in relation to the triggers. Then success will build upon success and propel you further along the path of righteousness. This process is consistent with the Pasuk that the Rambam brings in the teaching quoted above: כי אחרי שובי נחמתי / *Ki Acharei Shuvi, Nichamti* / After I did Teshuvah, I regretted (my deeds) (*Yirmiyahu*, 31:18).

In other words — again, with the example of habitually binging on sweets — instead of starting with regret and feeling depressed about the habit, start by not eating sweets for, say, forty days. During those forty days, there will likely be several times when the triggering conditions arise, but you will be committed to not responding to them. You will need to consider sweets illegal, or incurring a very expensive monetary fine. You may need an accountability partner, or an environment that is completely removed from your former life, in order to stick to your contract with yourself. But you must not think about regret. It is better to be inspired by your burst of effort or change of scenery and firmly decide to stop.

After this period, when you have remained 'sober' in the face of triggers and stimuli, only then should you revisit the past, feel the entire weight of your regret and grieve how you transgressed your conscience. Then, accept your new way of life for the future and commit to it.

To be abundantly clear, repeatedly applying Charatah to an ingrained negative habit or 'addiction', without stopping the actual behavior, simply leaves one with a sense of failure. If the discomfort of Charatah does not stop the behavior, it leads to frustration or hopelessness, which can greatly exacerbate the erroneous habit. Feeling low about oneself is actually the root of negative patterns of behavior. The Kotzker Rebbe once quipped, "People say that sinners sin because of *Perikas Ol* / 'throwing off of the yoke of Heaven', but I say they sin because of depression and feeling bad about themselves."

Stay away from fruitless Charatah, and just bluntly remove yourself from the trap. And do not try to remove yourself from the negative action by ramping up ill feelings within. Remove yourself out of a positive, life-affirming, hopeful, even joyful movement of self-redemption. Affirm that you have the right and power to choose how you will live, get the support you need, and then simply cut yourself free.

One of the best ways to stop a habitually negative behavior from a place of positivity is to vividly imagine that you are already a Tzadik. Picture yourself as a fully realized, wholesome, holy individual, filled with love and joy, resonating deeply with your deepest self, with your Creator and with the Divine Mitzvos. Imagine that your greatest pleasure is in *Tzedakah* / charity, *Tefillah* / prayer, and Torah; negative attachments are not part of your identity or nature. Once you are visualizing this strongly, do something to act it out and make it real, even if it seems small. Do something positive for another or for HaKadosh Baruch Hu. For example, give a small amount of money or resources to Tzedakah. Then repeat that action, and repeat it whenever possible until it becomes a new habit, supplanting the energy of a negative habit. Repeating the movement of giving can replace an ingrained pattern of greed or taking things for yourself instead of sharing.

It takes forty days to transform our nature. The forty days from Rosh Chodesh Elul to Yom Kippur are an ideal opportunity to engage in this kind of self-transformation, but regardless of the date, it is best not to postpone. Begin today; stop an old pattern of behavior and choose a new one.

Even if you feel that you are imperfect or out of tune, your essential soul is absolutely perfect, whole and holy. And there are certainly many, many good points within your personal 'conscious self' as well. When you acknowledge and amplify these good points, other strengths and positive qualities will spontaneously come into focus as well. You come from the Source of wholeness and perfection, and your natural state is Teshuvah, constantly returning to the Source of wholeness and perfection. Never give up.

The Creator of all Life desires to be close to you; in fact, throughout the month of Elul, preceding Tishrei, Hashem was in the 'field' searching for you. Then came the period of דרשו ה' בהמצאו / "Seek Hashem while He can be found" — the Ten Days of Teshuvah (*Rosh Hashanah*, 18a). And now it is Yom Kippur, the time of קראהו בהיותו קרוב / "Call to Him, as He is near" (*Yeshayahu*, 55:6). This Day of Atonement is the culmination of the whole process of Hashem's approaching us and then revealing Himself as being closer than all closeness (קרוב אתה יותר מכל קרוב: Even Ezra, *Tehillim*, 119:151). In this time of Divine Desire, do not hesitate to take up the Royal invitation and claim your birthright, your wholeness, perfection and holiness.

Chapter Five

FIVE STAGES OF TESHUVAH & THE FIVE LEVELS OF SOUL

S EXPLORED ABOVE, TESHUVAH MEANS MUCH MORE THAN 'REPENTANCE' OR 'PENITENCE'. TESHUVAH IS RESPONDING, RETURNING, AND REINTEGRATING. It restores the human being to a state of being human, to a state of integration within oneself and with the Source of All Life. This is the path and effect of Yom Kippur.

To better grasp the nature and dynamics of Teshuvah, sages throughout the ages have contemplated the Hebrew word *Teshuvah* itself, and viewed it as an acronym in order to decode its deeper meaning.

ACRONYMS OF TESHUVAH

The Arizal, Rebbe Yitzchak Luria, writes that the word תשובה / Teshuvah is an acronym for these five spiritual tools in the path of Teshuvah: תענית / Ta'anis / fasting, שק / Sak / (wearing) sackcloth, ואפר / V'eifer / (placing upon one's head) ashes, בכיה / Bechiyah / wailing, and הספד / Hesped / lamentation. The Chida, Rebbe Chaim Yoseph David Azulai, writes that Teshuvah is an acronym for תורה / Torah, שבת / Shabbos, וידוי / Viduy / confession, בושה / Bushah / bashfulness, and הכנעה / Hachna'ah / self-humbling.

Rebbe DovBer, the Maggid of Metzrich, taught his students that the verse "You shall return to Hashem Elokecha / your G-d" (Devarim, 30:2) means 'You shall turn to Hashem, the Transcendent One, until the point at which Hashem, Divine Transcendence, becomes for you Elokecha, Divine Immanence.' You should be inspired and uplifted until you reach a vantage point at which you can honestly declare that 'the Infinite is the intimate'; the Transcendent is the immanent Divine Power to which you personally relate and resonate. In other words, you shall become aware of the fact that that which is beyond you is also your inner nature.

In order to achieve and reveal this profound state of living, we must first believe that we can do so. Often, sadly, our greatest obstacle and adversary for genuine transformation is our own limited concept of our capacity. Because of this, when it comes to change, we often get in our own way. In order to step out of the way, we must place "Elokecha" or Elokim upon ourselves. *Elokim* is the Name of Hashem in the manner that it is revealed within the Tzimtzum, the perceptual Self-limitation, so-to-speak, of the Creator's infinity. This is the root of all finite realities and limitations. Therefore, the solution to self-limitation is to raise it back to its root in Divinity, the Tzimzum. By offering up our self-limitation to Hashem through Teshuvah, we trade it for the Divine Self-limitation. And since Divine Self-limitation is ultimately unreal, as Hashem is not actually limited in any way, our own limited nature becomes one with the essential Divine Infinity.

After the Maggid transmitted this teaching, his beloved student, Rebbe Zusya of Anipoli, explained that the word *Teshuvah* is an acronym for five sacred verses that help us unpack and open ourselves to the Transcendent One.[*]

ת / T: תמים / *Tamim* — תמים תהיה עם ה׳ אלוקיך / "Be sincere with Hashem your G-d" (*Devarim*, 18:13).

ש / Sh: שויתי / *Shivisi* — שויתי ה׳ לנגדי תמיד / "I have set Hashem before myself continuously" (*Tehillim*, 16:8).

ו / U: ואהבת / *V'ahavta* — ואהבת לרעך כמוך / "Love your fellow as yourself" (*Vayikra*, 19:18).

---

[*] *Hayom Yom, Tishrei* 3–8. See also Rebbe Pinchas of Koritz, *Imrei Pinchas*, p. 188. *Medrash Pinchas*, p. 84. Rebbe Zusya of Hanipoli, *Menoras Zahav*, p. 181. Rebbe Uri of Strelisk, *Imrei Kodesh*, p. 110. For the Arizal's acronym, see *Sefer Chareidim*, Chap. 63. *Reishis Chochmah*, Sha'ar haTeshuvah, 5. *Shnei Luchos haBris*, Meseches Yuma, Ner Mitzvah. Rebbe Eliezer Papo, *Pele Yoetz, Os* Tof. See also *Emek haMelech*. Sha'ar Tekunei Teshuvah, 9. For the Chida, see *D'vash l'Phi*, Ma'areches Tav, 8. *Bnei Yissaschar*, Ma'amarei Chodesh Tishrei, Ma'amar 4.

ב / V: בכל / *B'chol* — בכל דרכיך דעהו / "In all your ways, know Him" (*Mishlei*, 3:6).

ה / H: הצנע / *Hatznei'a* — הצנע לכת עם אלוקיך / "Walk discreetly with your G-d" (*Michah*, 6:8).

Let us delve a bit deeper into these five verses and understand the process of Teshuvah more fully. The five above verses suggest a precise map for deep Teshuvah. There are five levels of the soul (and generally, the number five is a major theme on Yom Kippur, such as the five prohibitions, and the five *Tefilos* / prayers, as explored earlier), and each of the verses offers a key to the progressive unshackling and de-constriction of higher levels of soul.

The fifth and highest level of the soul does not experience even a shadow of limitation, so we will explore the verses corresponding to the four lower levels of the soul, in ascending order. We will investigate the constrictions of each level, and also the remedies — the paths of Teshuvah for each.

FOUR LEVELS OF SOUL LIMITATION

1) *Nefesh* / **the Physical Self:** Physical limitations appear when we believe we cannot change because it is not in our 'stars'. We may imagine there are other forces, such as our genes and our limited longevity, health, or physical endurance, that constrict our personal development and capacity to serve the Creator.

2) *Ru'ach* / **Emotional Soul**: Emotional limitations appear when we are emotionally affected by the negative criticism of others. It occurs when we internalize feelings of weakness or unworthiness, and we begin to believe that we are incapable of being anything more.

3) *Neshamah* / **Intellectual Soul**: Intellectual limitations appear when our own thoughts and analyses get in our way. Here it is not someone else, but we ourselves, who begin thinking, 'I am unworthy and incapable of any true spiritual greatness,' or 'My life is doomed to be mediocre.'

4) *Chayah* / **Existential Soul**: Existential limitations appear when, on a supra-rational level, we believe that the whole context of our lives is limited. When we believe that the structure of reality itself is limited, whether it is because of our nature or our nurture or anything in between, mediocrity becomes the only real possibility for us. With such beliefs, we will never be able to live in a deep state of Teshuvah — at-oneness with Self and HaKadosh Baruch Hu.

FOUR LEVELS OF TESHUVAH

1) The remedy for physical limitation at the level of Nefesh is the first letter of the word *Teshuvah*, Tav. This letter corresponds to the verse תמים תהיה עם ה' אלוקיך / "Be sincere with Hashem your G-d." Chazal teach us that the first word, תמים / *Tamim* / 'sincerity in action,' means we should be simple, wholehearted, and not pay attention to stargazers (*Pesachim*,

113b). This means we should not believe we are bound by *Mazal* / luck, superstition, genetics, historical precedent, or any other aspect of the world of cause and effect. To be תמים / *Tamim* means to be 'whole, present, dedicated, readied, and focused in the now.' It means to simplify your life by focusing on Hashem rather than on lesser sources of power or guidance. When we are in a state of *Temimus* / deep focus and sincerity, we can overcome any physical and conceptual self-limitations, turn to Hashem and begin to live a better life.

Teshuvah should never be confused with bitterness or heaviness. The process of Teshuvah enlivens and empowers a person, often even increasing their health and physical resiliency. Real Teshuvah is not a stressful, exhausting, terrifying, or demoralizing experience. It never makes a person feel insignificant or guilt-ridden. Rather, it redeems, re-energizes and rejuvenates. When the pinnacle of Teshuvah is attained, it manifests as an ongoing state of wellbeing and aliveness.

When we are wholly focused on our purpose and walk through life with sincerity and simple faith, we are released from limitations within the level of Nefesh.

2) The remedy for any emotional limitation on the level of Ru'ach is the second letter of *Teshuvah*, Shin, corresponding to שויתי ה' לנגדי תמיד / "I have set Hashem before myself continuously." The first word, שויתי / *Shivisi* / "I have set," alludes to Hi**sht**avus, 'equanimity.' When we are emotionally equanimous, we do not react negatively to criticism, because we do

not feel it defines or limits us. Equanimity is the inner sense that life is as it should be; no matter what, it is always perfect and whole. Whether people praise or scorn you, it is all equal to you. It is not that you become stoic in the face of life or indifferent to people — a compliment is still a compliment, and an insult is still an insult, but these things do not matter enough to you to throw you off kilter. You remain rooted in a deeper foundation that allows you to maintain a state of emotional equilibrium even amid life's ups and downs.

From this perspective, any input arising before us from the outside is felt and experienced as an input from Hashem. As a result of this sense of Divine Presence, a person may sense an ongoing subtle joy or emotional clarity in the background of experience. There is no obstruction before the Ru'ach, and there is a free flow of our emotions as our soul returns to its Source.

3) The remedy for assumed intellectual limitations on the level of Neshamah is symbolized by the third letter of *Teshuvah*, Vav. This letter corresponds to the verse, ואהבת / *V'ahavta* in ואהבת לרעך כמוך / "Love your fellow as yourself." From this verse, we see that love must begin with self-care, but it must also extend outward to others, first to the people closest to us, then to our wider family, community, and the rest of the world. Extending and expanding ourselves through loving action gets us 'out of our heads' and breaks our limited mental judgments of other people. This verse concludes, *Ani Hashem* / 'I (G-d) am *Hashem*, the Transcendent, Infinite One.' In other

words, we must love ourselves and others simply because we are each part of Hashem's Infinity. This is the unifying vision, the soul-perspective that comes from Teshuvah on the level of intellect, the soul dynamic of Neshamah.*

4) The remedy for the perception of any 'existential' limitations on the level of Chayah is symbolized by the fourth letter in the word *Teshuvah*, Beis. This letter corresponds to בכל / *B'chol*, in בכל דרכיך דעהו / "In all your ways know Him." "In all…know" suggests the comprehensive awareness called

---

* "…As yourself" in Hebrew is כמוך / *Kamocha*, which in numeric value is 86: Chaf/20, Mem/40, Vav/6, Chaf/20 = 86. The Name *Elokim*, 'Divine Self-limitation', is also numerically 86, as is the word *haTeva* / 'the natural'. Thus, what begins as "yourself," your limited nature and self-love, expands into a paradigm of *Ani Hashem* / I am the Infinite One, the soul perspective of Unity. A 'transcendent unity' equalizes every individual, and thus when you are delimited, you can love another equally as you would love yourself.

The Mitzvah to love is to "act" lovingly — מצות עשה של דבריהם לבקר חולים. ולנחם אבלים. ולהוציא המת. ולהכניס הכלה. וללוות האורחים. ולהתעסק בכל צרכי הקבורה... אף על פי שכל מצות אלו מדבריהם הרי הן בכלל ואהבת לרעך כמוך. כל הדברים שאתה רוצה שיעשו אותם לך אחרים. עשה אתה אותן לאחיך בתורה ובמצות: Rambam, *Hilchos Avel*, 14:1. *Sefer haChinuch*, Mitzvah 243. In the words of the Ramban, "It does not register upon the heart of man to love his friend as he loves himself": Ramban, *Vayikra*, 19:17. Yet, elsewhere, the Rambam suggests that the Mitzvah to love is to actually "feel love" — היא שצונו לאהוב קצתנו את קצתנו כאשר נאהב עצמנו ושתהיה אהבתו אהבתנו לאחיו כאהבתו וחמלתו לעצמו בממונו ובגופו וכל מה שיהיה ברשות / "That is, He commanded us to love each other as we love ourselves, and that one's love and compassion for one's brother be like the love and compassion for himself regarding his money — regarding his body and regarding everything that is in his domain": *Sefer haMitzvos*, Mitzvah 206. In other words, perhaps the Rambam is talking about an actual feeling, not only an action that would represent such a feeling. A feeling of love is generated by a proactive meditation in the mind, therefore it could be viewed as something we can be commanded to produce.

Da'as Elyon / higher knowing." Higher awareness and knowing is our full alignment with the total context of reality; it is the lens through which we view the whole of our life. If we are constricted on this level, we are not aligned with our existential freedom. When we turn and align our Da'as with 'Him,' our whole existence resonates with the frequency of the Infinite One. As such, the greater context of our life is not limited, confined, or constricted, and it is completely open to Transcendent Aliveness. This is 'Teshuvah' on the level of *Chayah* / the living soul.

5) The final letter of the word *Teshuvah* is 'H' or Hei, standing for הצנע / *Hatznei'a* in the verse הצנע לכת עם אלוקיך / "Walk discreetly with your G-d." To be 'private' or alone with the Transcendent and Holy 'Other', is to be one with the One. This oneness may seem "discreet" or hidden, but it is always present as the core of who we are, the *Yechidah* / united essence of soul. This is the essence of Teshuvah and 'returning', realizing that ultimately, we never left, and there is nowhere to go. We are always one with HaKadosh Baruch Hu. Whenever we 'fall', Hashem is always picking us up, and wherever we 'fall', we are always 'falling' into the Divine embrace.

May our Yom Kippur inspire genuine Teshuvah, return to who we really are on all levels of being; physical, emotional, intellectual, and existential — with the realization of the essential Oneness that we have never left.

Chapter Six

THE CUSTOM OF KAPAROS:
BUMPING UP AGAINST DEATH

I N THE EARLY MORNING OF EREV YOM KIPPUR, THERE IS A
CUSTOM TO PERFORM *Kaparos* / 'ATONEMENTS'. THE BASIC
OUTLINE OF THE CUSTOM IS AS FOLLOWS. One holds a live
chicken and recites various verses from the Torah and other appropriate texts. Then one passes the chicken in a circular
motion over his or her head three times while saying, "This is
my exchange, this is my substitute, this is my atonement." The
chicken, which is a symbol of ourselves, is then slaughtered (in
the most humane fashion possible, as the laws of the Torah
delineate), and then the meat or its monetary value, is given to
the poor or another charitable cause (או יתן פדיונו לעניים וזה טוב יותר, לפי
שמתביישין כשנותנים להם התרנגולים: Shaloh, *Yuma*, Ner Mitzvah, 1, 15).

This contemplative experience is meant to cultivate compassion in us, and arouse similar compassion from on High. We arouse Divine *Rachamim* / Mercy and Compassion as we approach Yom Kippur, a day of utter Divine Mercy.*

A chicken is used as our 'replacement' as it were, since in Hebrew, the word for 'man' is *Gever*, and in Aramaic, the language of the Talmud, *Gever* means a rooster (*Yuma*, 20a. Rosh, *Yuma*, 8). Also, a chicken is also specifically used since chickens were not offered in the Beis haMikdash, and in this way, there will be no mistaken perception that we are offering it as a ritual sacrifice. Another simple reason why chickens were used is that during Medieval times chickens were easily available in every town and village throughout Europe. They were common and inexpensive.

In a place where chickens are not readily available or where the custom is not to do Kaparos with chickens, a bundle of coins is waved over the head instead, and then the money is given to charity.

---

* The Ramban writes, בראש השנה מתיחד במדת הדין ומנהיג עולמו וביום הכפורים במדת הרחמים והוא מאמרם מלך יושב על כסא דין וכו' ראש השנה יום דין ברחמים ויום הכפורים יום בדין רחמים / "On Rosh Hashanah Hashem is concerned entirely with the attribute of Justice and conducts His world (by that attribute), and on the Day of Yom Kippur He is concerned entirely with the attribute of Mercy. It is this which is expressed in the saying of the Rabbis: 'The King sits upon the throne of Judgment....' Thus, Rosh Hashanah is a day of Judgment with Mercy, and the Day of Yom Kippur is a day of Mercy in Judgment": Ramban, *Vayikra*, 23:24.

THE SOURCES FOR KAPAROS

The custom of Kaparos dates back to the early Geonic period (Sixth to Seventh Centuries) (יש מקומות שנוהגין לשחוט תרנגול לכפרה)
וגם שמעתי שנשאל רבינו האיי ואמר .Tur, *Orach Chayim*, 605 וכן יש בתשובת הגאונים
שכן נהגו: *Beis Yoseph*, ad loc. *Teshuvos haRashba*, 1, 395). The great Elev-
enth-Century rabbi and commentator, Rashi, speaks about us-
ing a plant and describes the particular practice as follows: A
vessel was made out of palm leaves for each of the children of
the household, and then filled with earth and fertilizer. Some
fifteen days before Rosh Hashanah, they would plant sprouts
within these pots. On the day before Rosh Hashanah, the children would take their plants, and swing them over their heads
seven times, saying, "This instead of this. This is my exchange.
This is my substitute." And then, they would cast the plant into
the sea (*Shabbos*, 81b).

Although Rashi writes about this custom, it is clear that
the custom of performing Kaparos with chickens dates back
hundreds of years before Rashi. Rashi's student, the author of
the *Machzor Vitri* (which contains a collection of Rashi's many
rulings), writes of the custom of using chickens (*Machzor Vitri*,
873. Mordechai, end of *Yuma*). Perhaps using an animal and not
a plant connects us to the idea of the *Sa'ir haMishtale'ach* /
the 'scapegoat' that symbolically carried the sins of Klal Yisrael and was sent away to the wilderness to be thrown down
a mountain. It, too, was not an actual *Korban* / offering (*Even
Ezra*, Vayikra, 16:8. Ramban, *ad loc.* Note however, *Yuma*, 64a. זו דחייתו לצוק
היא שחיטתו), and yet it helped Klal Yisrael realize atonement. The

Kaparos chicken, although certainly not a Korban, helps us realize atonement, too, as will be explored.*

---

* The Arizal teaches that on the ninth day of Tishrei, we sweeten the Gevurah of Yesod, the ninth Sefirah, via Kaparos. On the tenth day of Tishrei, which is Malchus, the tenth Sefirah, we sweeten the Gevurah of Malchus via the *Sa'ir haMishtaleach* / the goat that was sent to the wilderness.

Perhaps, on a level of *Avodah* / inner spiritual work, we can say the following: Gevurah of Yesod is aggression. Yesod is a masculine, active quality, and the negative side of Gevurah of Yesod is aggression and even blood lust. Through the act of Kaparos and the release of the chicken's blood in a controlled and holy environment, there is a sweetening of this negative trait.

Malchus is being receptive, present and settled. The negative side of Malchus, the negative Gevurah within Malchus, is depression and *Yi'ush* / giving up. Shabbos is Malchus, and Yom Kippur is 'the Shabbos of Shabbos'. The *Tikkunei Zohar* teaches that on Shabbos, there is an influence of Shabtai, a zodiac symbol that is connected with all forms of depressions and darkness. Thus, many ancient pagans who desired to connect with this influence would sit on the Seventh Day in darkness, 'give up' on life and mourn. The Torah thus tells us to do the opposite on Shabbos: light candles, eat festive meals and have *Oneg* / pleasure of Shabbos; celebrate the gift of human life.

The word *Sameach* / joyful is intricately related to the *Tzameach* / growing. As we experience the deep, peaceful joy of Shabbos, we are actually growing. And we are nullifying the negative human tendency to 'give up'.

"Man is created to toil" (*Iyov*, 5:7): the nature of the human being is to grow, to move, to do, to be active, and not only in action but in the mind as well. On Shabbos we need to rest. But rest can be positive and the source of inner joy, or it can be negative and the source of depression. When Shabbos is not observed correctly, there is a danger that it can be the source of frustration, anxiety, and even depression and 'giving up'. This is the Gevurah or Din within Malchus. An ancient *Tikkun* / rectification for this negativity was the Sa'ir haMishtaleach, the elevation of 'wildness', as will be explored later in greater detail.

THE OPPOSERS OF THIS PRACTICE

In the Shulchan Aruch in the laws of Yom Kippur, there is an extremely short chapter (605) in which Rebbe Yoseph Caro writes the following: מה שנוהגים לעשות כפרה בערב יום כפורים לשחוט תרנגול על כל בן זכר ולומר עליו פסוקים יש למנוע המנהג / "The custom regarding Kaparah on the day before Yom Kippur, by slaughtering a rooster for each male and saying verses over it, should be stopped."

Today, the title of this chapter in *Shulchan Aruch* (and we are uncertain who wrote the title) reads, מנהג כפרות בערב יום כפור / "The Custom of Kaparos on the Day Before Yom Kippur." However, in the first printings of the *Shulchan Aruch*, the title of this chapter was מנהג כפרות בערב יום כיפורים מנהג של שטות הוא / "The Custom of Kaparos on the Day Before Yom Kippur *Is a Foolish Custom*."

These are very strong words from Rebbe Yoseph Caro (if in fact he wrote the titles). He based his ruling on that of some of the great Spanish rabbis, most notably the Ramban and the Rashba, who maintained that this practice has undertones of דרכי האמורי / 'the ways of the Emorites', meaning it is irrational and superstitious. Any act or practice that has a basis in superstition is in fact forbidden by Torah law (והרשב"א כתב בתשוב' בענין הכפרה שעושין לנערי' בעי"ה מנהג זה פשוט בעירנו אע"פ ששמעתי מפי אנשים הגונים מאשכנז שכל רבני ארצם עושים כן וגם שמעתי שנשאל רבינו האיי ואמר שכן נהגו עכ"ז מנעתי המנהג הזה מעירנו וכתוב בא"ת שהרמב"ן אוסרו משום דרכי האמורי: *Beis Yoseph*, Orach Chayim, 605).

Not surprisingly, the Rambam does not write about this custom, and so the Yemenite Jews, who strictly follow the rulings of the Rambam, do not practice Kaparos.

CUSTOM PREVAILS

Yet, despite the above concerns, the prevailing custom in Ashkenazi traditions is to perform Kaparos with a chicken. In his note in *Shulchan Aruch*, the Rama, Rebbe Moshe Isserles, the 16th Century rabbi of Krakow, Poland, writes that Kaparos is a custom from the Geonic period, and וכן נוהגין בכל מדינות אלו ואין לשנות כי הוא מנהג ותיקין / "such is the custom in all these lands, and we should not change this custom, as it is an old established custom" (*Rama*, ad loc).

Yet, the worry of appearing pagan exists, and therefore, though it is preferable for a white rooster to be taken by a man and a white hen by a woman, it is strongly forbidden to make a strenuous effort to procure only a white bird, so as not to appear that one is following an idolatrous ritual of offering only white birds.

During the time of Rebbe Yoseph Caro and the Rama, the Arizal lived as well. The holy Arizal as well adapted this custom and explained its deeper symbolic and embodied undertones. When the writings of the Arizal arrived in Europe and the Sefardic communities, the practice of Kaparos became universal. Even among the Sefardim, who usually follow the ruling of Rebbe Yoseph Caro with regards to Kaparos, the prevailing custom (besides the Yemenites) is to perform Kaparos as presented by the Arizal. Today it continues to be a ubiquitous custom (וכן נוהגין בני ספרד :*Kaf haChayim*, Orach Chayim, 605:8. ועוד י"ל דהא דנהגו

בתרנגול משום כי כן נפיק ג"כ מפומיה דהאר"י ז"ל: Ibid, 22. For more contemporary sources, see *Ben Ish Chai*, Hilchos Shanah 1, Vayeilech, 3,1. *Yalkut Yoseph*, Moadim, p. 75. *Ma'amar Mordechai*, 42:1).

A DEEPER UNDERSTANDING OF KAPAROS

As mentioned, the word *Gever* means 'man' in Hebrew and 'rooster' in Aramaic. *Gever* is related to *Gevurah* / restraint, withdrawing and harsh judgment. In this way, using a rooster for Kaparos causes a transformation and sweetening of Gevurah and any harsh judgments that were in place for the coming year.

We take Gever and offer it on the ninth day of the month, nine signifying the ninth Divine attribute from within the Ten Sefiros, the attribute of *Yesod* / foundation or connectivity. Yesod is the channel through which the Transcendent Creative Light enters this Malchus and this world. Through the act of Kaparos, we sweeten the judgment within Yesod so that the Light can shine and be absorbed properly into this world.

Kaparos is (ideally) performed early, in the pre-dawn hours, as the Gevurah of darkness is about to turn into the Chesed of sunrise. This transitional hour is considered a time of great potential and *Ratzon* / 'Divine desire'. It is a special time of benevolence, appropriate for drawing out and sweetening Gevurah and *Din* / judgment with the light of Chesed.

Red represents Gevurah. We inspire to sweeten cosmic and personal Gevurah by drawing out the red blood of the chicken in the morning, when there is a powerful abundance of cosmic *Chesed* / goodness and kindness. We meditate on eradicating all harsh judgments and securing a sweet and healthy new year of living with and through Divine kindness.

BUMPING UP AGAINST DEATH

One could ask, what exactly is it that brings *Kaparah* / atonement in this ritual? Is the *Ikar* / main idea of Kaparos the *Shechitah* / slaughter of the chicken, and the Teshuvah stimulated in the person observing it? Or is the main idea the food that is produced for the poor, the atonement that comes from giving this Tzedakah? One way of exploring this question is to imagine the following scenario. If, after the participant has waved the chicken and it has gone to the slaughter, it becomes revealed that the chicken was not Kosher, or that it became un-Kosher through a mistake in the Shechitah itself — does the person need to do Kaparos again? (See *S'dei Chemed*, quoted in *Moadim u-Zmanim* 1–2, Siman 52)

Compassion towards the poor is certainly an important aspect of Kaparos. Taking your chicken, raised or purchased with your own hard-earned money, and giving its meat to the poor, is a propitious act on the day before we ask our Creator for compassion and forgiveness. But there is also value in the visceral act of holding a vibrant, living creature in your hands, and then observing its life force leaving and returning to its Creator. This is an induction into a proper mindset for Yom

Kippur, arousing us from our spiritual, mental, and emotional stupor, and instilling in us the realization that we, too, must return to our Creator, although, of course, also while alive.

On Rosh Hashanah, we contemplate our 'birth', the birthday of humanity. On Yom Kippur, we contemplate our mortality, our destined 'return' to the Source of Life, and the renewal of our life in the present moment. A thought to entertain throughout the 25–26 hours of Yom Kippur is, what if these are the last hours of my life, how should I spend them? What do I really care about? What is truly important and valuable to be, think, say, and do?

To induce us into this state of consciousness, we perform various practices on Erev Yom Kippur that allow us to 'bump up against death'. Kaparos is not, G-d forbid, a superstitious, magical, or morbid ritual. It is a time-tested practice of arousing deep symbolic significance and a tangible, bodily awareness of our own mortality, and our liability for the transgressions we have committed. Meditating on our own death can even shock us into a temporary 'ego-death', a state of *Bitul* / self-surrender that allows us to make radical Teshuvah. And this, paradoxically, brings us alive in a new way and with greater vibrancy and wholeness.

Besides sympathetically identifying with the chicken during its slaughter, the Arizal teaches that we ought to contemplate ourselves undergoing the four death penalties that the Torah prescribed for the most serious transgressions. These capital punishments are *S'kilah* / 'stoning', *Chenek* / 'strangulation', *Hereg* / decapitation', and *Sereifah* / 'burning'. In the Era of the Beis haMikdash, when the *Sanhedrin* / Council of Sages was functioning correctly, these were dramatic forms of atonement and Tikkun that were administered to souls who needed rare, radical intervention. Through these interventions, they could resolve the issues in their current *Gilgul* / incarnation and proceed to a better future Gilgul. Since the destruction of the Beis haMikdash, these have been used as a contemplative stimulation for general soul-searching and Teshuvah.

One who has already recited the verses of Kaparos and circled the chicken over his head then places the chicken on the ground before the Shochet. He tosses a little bit of dirt in its direction, and taps on it lightly with a rock in a symbolic stoning. When the Shochet picks up the bird and pulls back its head to perform the Shechitah, this is a form of 'strangulation'. The actual act of Shechitah is a type of 'decapitation'. When the chicken is cooked to be eaten by the poor, the cooking is a form of 'burning'. At every step of this process, we fully identify with chicken and feel as if we, too, are going through these experiences ourselves. This cleanses us without the use of any actual 'punishments', G-d forbid. Our negativity itself is what 'dies', while we "go on to a good, long life, and peace" (*Seder Kaparos*).

These four capital punishments correspond to the four letters in the Name of Hashem, Yud-Hei-Vav-Hei, which in turn correspond to four categories of transgressions that can obscure the brilliance of the letters of the Name and their spiritual qualities. The example transgressions below are obviously not the cardinal sins that would have incurred capital punishment; rather, they are categories that can help anyone contemplate their own life to find the areas in which they need to make Teshuvah and Tikkun. One can use these categories during the Kaparos ceremony to meditate upon specific transgressions, along with their form of 'death' or atonement.

Capital Punishment	Letter in Name of Hashem	Spiritual Quality of Letter / Example of 'Ritual' Transgression	Physical Quality of Letter / Example of 'Mundane' Act of Transgression
Skilah / Stoning	Yud	*Chochmah* / Omitting recital of the Shema twice a day	Fire / Acting in anger
Sereifah / Scalding	Upper Hei	*Binah* / Omitting putting on Tefillin on weekdays	Wind / Speaking idle talk or negative speech
Hereg / Decapitation	Vav	*Ze'ir Anpin* / Omitting to wear Tzitzis on a garment requiring them	Water / Acting on an insatiable, harmful desire
Chenek / Strangulation	Lower Hei	*Malchus* / Omitting prayer when it is required	Earth / Acting on (or refraining from acting due to) depression or laziness

TIME OF TRUTH

על שלשה דברים העולם עומד: על הדין ועל האמת ועל השלום / "Upon three things is the world founded: *Din, Emes v'Shalom* / justice, truth and peace" (*Avos*, 1:18). Rosh Hashanah is a time of *Din* / judgment, a judgment on the coming year. Sukkos is a time of Shalom, as we are all gathered, potentially, under one Sukkah (*Sukkah*, 27b), and we bring together all the various types of people, symbolized in the four species of the Lulav and Es-rog. Yom Kippur is the day of *Emes* / truth, as we come face to face with our own deepest selves and the lives we are living honestly, openly, and truthfully.

In order to help us wake up and recognize who we truly are, sometimes we need a 'shock treatment'. The visceral, even gory practice of Kaparos is one such method, among other ways of 'bumping up against death'. When we can gain a glimpse of our own mortality, it forces us to take stock of our lives and turn to Hashem, the Ultimate Emes, with *Hachna'ah* / sub-mission.

In the past, most people living in villages would own at least a couple of chickens. Raising an animal creates a 'personal' re-lationship with it, to the point that it can become 'part of the family', as it were. When the prophet Nasan offers a metaphor to distinguish the rich from the poor, he says the rich have many possessions and animals, whereas "the poor man has only one little ewe. He tended it, and it grew up together with him and his children. It used to share his morsel of bread, drink from his cup, and nestle in his bosom; it was like a daughter to him" (*Shmuel 2*, 12:3).

When someone was asked to perform Kaparos with the chicken which he had raised, fed, and nurtured, he felt the em-pathic impact of the Shechitah very personally and became deeply humbled by it.

Most of us in contemporary urban societies no longer raise chickens in our yards. To tap into the full power of Kaparos, we should hold the live chicken in our hands for a few moments, and connect empathetically to it, feel its life force, and consider its vulnerability and its instinctual 'yearning' to stay alive. This is one way to connect our life-force with the chicken's life-force, and to feel the loss of its life more personally and dramatically, so that we may be shaken out of our complacency. In this way, we can precipitate 'bumping up against death', face our own mortality, and attain a deeper level of humility.

We must go into Yom Kippur in this posture of Hachna'ah and stand exposed in front of Hashem, vulnerable, open, and honest. With deep submission we must ask ourselves, "Who am I?" "How am I living my life?" Thinking about the more uncomfortable and compromised aspects of our life within the brilliant holiness of this day, we are empowered to make *Havdalah* / separation from those aspects. Ultimately, as we conclude Yom Kippur, there is a great *Hamtakah* / sweetening of our life. The present moment becomes sharp and focused, while simultaneously, all of our past, which led up to the present moment, becomes redeemed and elevated.

BEING COMPASSIONATE

It is important to note that while the harshness of Kaparos is valuable to us if it shakes us up and awakens us, still, it is essential that the chickens are treated with complete compassion and care, creations of Hashem, as they are. We must not harm them or cause them any unnecessary pain or even discomfort during the entire process, and the Shechitah must be performed as humanely as possible, as is strictly required by Torah law.

In these days between Rosh Hashanah and Yom Kippur, when our life in the coming year is hanging in the balance, we aspire to elicit Divine compassion upon us. For this reason, we must show increased compassion toward all forms of life. כי ראוי לרחם על הבריות שירחמו עליו מן השמים / "It is appropriate to be compassionate to all creatures so that Heaven will have compassion for him" (Taz, *ad loc*). There are sources, for example, that suggest that on Erev Rosh Hashanah, we should not perform Shechitah at all (*Teshuvos Asei Lecha Rav*, 3, Teshuvah 20, p. 67). Kaparos involves Shechitah, but we need to make sure that we show compassion by treating the animal gently, not scaring it, and donating the meat to the poor. The Rama even states that the intestines of the bird are to be placed "on the roof or in a courtyard, a place where the birds are able to take them" (Rama, *Orach Chayim*, 605).

Certainly, the most impactful act of compassion we can perform is to truly wake up, atone, and turn our whole life toward Hashem. This is the intent of Kaparos, for whenever a human being wakes up and then goes on to act as an illumined Tzadik, a flow of blessing descends, and the entire world becomes more compassionate. The more of us who awaken, the more that higher awareness and righteous, compassionate action will increase. This will reach the point that even (*Yeshayah*, 11:6) וגר

‏זאב עם־כבש ונמר עם־גדי ירבץ ועגל וכפיר ומריא יחדו ונער קטן נהג בם‎ / "The wolf shall dwell with the lamb, the leopard will recline with the baby goat; the calf, the beast of prey, and the fatling together, with a little child to herd them" — with the great sweetening of all reality, may it manifest speedily and in our days.

Chapter Seven
KAPAROS FOR CHILDREN & THE UNBORN:
REWIRING THE SUBCONSCIOUS MIND & GENETICS

FOR THE CUSTOM OF KAPAROS, AS EXPLORED IN THE PREVIOUS CHAPTER, A MALE USES A ROOSTER, AND A FEMALE USES A HEN. BUT WHAT SHOULD BE DONE WHEN A WOMAN IS PREGNANT, AND THE GENDER OF THE UNBORN CHILD IS YET UNKNOWN? The Rama rules that in such a situation, the practice is to take two chickens; a hen for herself and the perhaps female fetus, plus a rooster for the possibly male fetus (*Shulchan Aruch,* Orach Chayim, 605: ולוקחין למעוברת ב׳ תרנגולים אולי תלד זכר. See also, *Bach,* 605).

Regarding this ruling, the Magen Avraham notes that the Arizal maintains that three chickens are needed for a pregnant woman (ג והאר"י לקח. The *Hagahos Maimoniyos* writes the same). Apparently, this means one hen for the mother herself, another hen for a potential female child, plus a rooster for a potential male child (ובאליהו זוטא כתבתי סמך דאין שנים יוצאין בתרנגול אחת דהא דוגמת קרבן הוא ולכפרה באין, וקיימא לן דאין שתים מביאין קרבן של חובה: *Eliyah Rabbah*, Orach Chayim, 605:8). However, we do not continue to add more chickens with the consideration that perhaps she is carrying twins or triplets, and so forth.

Why, then, according to the Rama, does a pregnant woman use only two chickens and not three? Perhaps it is because more than one person can use a single chicken for this ritual (צידה לדרך מטה משה, יש כתבו דצריכין שלוש ולא ידעתי למה אם העובר נקיבה די בתרנגולת אחת עם אמה, עד כאן, וכן כתב הב"ח: *Eliyah Rabbah*, ibid). But if that were the case, why not use one chicken for all three 'participants': the mother, a potential female and a potential male? Also, if two people can use a single chicken, why does the Arizal require three?

Regarding the ruling of the Rama, the Gra notes that the pregnant mother needs two chickens because עובר ירך אמו הוא / "A fetus is considered the 'thigh' of its mother." This statement is puzzling — why would the mother need two chickens if the fetus, regardless of its gender, is considered to be 'part of the mother', her own limb? A single hen should suffice (Although perhaps he means only one hen is needed for the mother and the potential girl, as the latter is qualitatively more a part of a single female body, while the potential boy needs his own rooster, since although he is currently like an appendage of his mother, he is qualitatively different from her even now, and he will increasingly differentiate as time goes on).

Moreover, this whole discussion brings up an important fundamental question: does a fetus need Kaparah in the first place?

WHY DOES A FETUS NEED ATONEMENT?

If a chicken is indeed being brought for the Kaparah of a fetus, we need to understand why. Certainly, a fetus has not sinned in its short, protected life, even if it could already have some sense of agency or intentionality. In fact, our sages describe life in the womb as one of a complete Tzadik (*Nidah*, 30b):

"And a lamp is lit for the unborn child above his head, and with its light, he peers out and sees from one end of the world to the other end, as it is stated: 'When His lamp shone above my head, and by His light, I walked through darkness' (*Iyov*, 29:3).... And throughout one's life on earth, there are no days on which a person experiences more bliss than during those in his mother's womb, as it is stated, 'If only I were as in the months of old, as in the days when G-d watched over me' (*Iyov*, 29:2).... And a fetus is taught the entire Torah (while in the womb), as it is stated: 'And He taught me and said to me: Let your heart hold fast to My words; keep My commandments and live' (*Mishlei*, 4:4). And as it also states: 'As I was in the days of my youth, when the company (or secret) of Elokim graced my tent'" (*Iyov*, 29:4).

Our sages also make this clear in the following debate and resolution (*Sanhedrin*, 91b):

"Antoninos asked Rebbe: 'From when does the evil inclination dominate a person? Is it from the moment of the formation of the embryo, or is it from the moment of emergence from the womb?' Rebbe said to him: 'It is from the moment of the formation of the embryo.' Antoninos said to him: 'If so, the evil inclination would cause the fetus to kick his mother's innards and emerge from the womb. Rather, the evil inclination must dominate a person (only) from the moment of emergence from the womb.' Rebbe (conceded and) said: 'Antoninos has taught me this matter, and there is a verse that supports him, as it is stated: 'Sin crouches at the entrance.' This indicates that it is (indeed only) from the moment of birth, when the newborn emerges from the 'entrance' of his mother's womb, that the evil inclination lurks.'"

As a fetus does not even have a negative inclination, and no capacity for transgression, why does including it in Kaparos imply the need for his or her atonement? On the other hand, despite this Gemara stating that there is no Yetzer haRa in the womb, there are contradictory sources in Chazal suggesting that even in the womb there *is* a Yetzer (Maharsha, *Chidushei Agodos*, ibid.[*])

---

* ויש להקשות מהא דאמרי' פ"ב דיומא ההוא עוברה דארחה ביוה"כ אתאי לקמיה דר"מ א"ל
לחישו לה ולא אלחישא קרי עליה זורו רשעים מרחם מוכח מהא ששולט יצה"ר גם במעי אמו?
ובהא יש ליישב דע"י אמו כי התם אפשר דשולט בו יצה"ר קודם היציאה אבל בולד עצמו אינו
שולט יצר הרע דא"כ היה בועט ויוצא. אך קשה מהא דדרשינן גבי ויתרוצצו הבנים בקרבה
שהיתה עוברת על פתח עבודת כוכבים והיה עשו מפרכס לצאת וק"ל.

In the Book of *Tehillim*, Dovid haMelech / King David, declares זרו רשעים מרחם / "The wicked are estranged from the womb" (58:4). Says Rashi, "From their mother's womb they become estranged to the Holy One, blessed be He, in the way that Eisav did, as it says (*Bereishis*, 25:22), ויתרוצצו הבנים בקרבה / 'And the children moved violently against each other in her womb.'" And as Rashi writes on that *Pasuk* / verse, "Whenever she passed by the doors of the Torah, Yaakov moved convulsively in his efforts to come to birth, but whenever she passed by the gate of a pagan temple, Eisav moved convulsively in his efforts to come to birth." And as the Medrash tells us, in the womb Yaakov and Eisav wished to kill each other (זה רץ להרג את זה וזה רץ להרג את זה: *Medrash Rabbah*, Bereishis, 63:6).

So which one is it? Does a fetus have or not have a Yetzer haRa? Besides the two divergent opinions among the sages, it could be understood that while a fetus does not have a Yetzer haRa, as it does not even have (full) self-awareness or the discernment and agency that allow for free choice, it is still *possible* for the fetus to become "estranged" on some level from the path of holiness and righteousness even in the womb. Hence, "The wicked are estranged from the womb."

TWO WAYS TO UNDERSTAND KAPARAH / ATONEMENT FOR A FETUS

Before exploring this further, it will help to mention that there are two general approaches to understanding bringing a Kaparah for an unborn child: 1) the atonement is actually just for the mother who is carrying the fetus, not for the fetus itself, 2) the atonement is for the fetus, but since it is only a fetus, the mother is doing Teshuvah on behalf of the child.

In a bit more detail:

Kaparah just for the mother: Even if we concede that עובר ירך אמו הוא / "A fetus is considered as the 'thigh' of its mother," still, there are two individuals: "a fetus" and "its mother." One could say that while she is pregnant it is as if *she* has two bodies or 'selves' (see *Sanhedrin*, 80a: ולד...והנוגחת אסור, היא וולדה. נגחו...אין להוכיח דעובר. *Tosefos, Baba Kama,* ירך אמו הוא דהתם היינו טעמא שהולד עצמו נהנה...והיא וולדה נגחו 47a). And herein lies the argument between the Rama and the Arizal regarding whether she needs to bring two or three Kaparos. According to the Rama, she is a female, her own body and that of the potential female body, and like a male, hence two Kaparos. According to the Arizal, she is counted as one female body, the fetus, which is potentially another female body, is another female, and the potential male is another male body, hence three Kaparos. And that is the reason she needs to bring, when pregnant, another one or two chickens for atonement, for her own Teshuvah, as she now has 'two' or 'three' bodies (*Likutei Sichos*, 22, p. 59).

Kaparah on behalf of the unborn child: Again, why would a fetus need Teshuvah? One answer could be that the child might be a *Gilgul* / reincarnation, a soul who came down to this world to create a Tikkun for a past life, and thus the mother brings a separate Kaparah for this unborn child. Still, we cannot rely on a *Sod* / mystical answer alone; to understand a Minhag or any area of Torah thought, we need to understand it on a *Peshat* / straightforward level, as well. The Maor vaShemesh writes that he heard from his Rebbe, the Noam Elimelech, that he did Teshuvah for things he did in his youth, and even did Teshuvah for the pain he caused his mother in the womb (*Maor VaShemesh,* Masei 9).

AN ADULT DOING TESHUVAH FOR ACTIONS DONE AS A CHILD

There is a question that is asked among the *Poskim* / the codifiers of law, and that is, do we, as adults, need to do Teshuvah for things we did as children? And even stronger, why do Teshuvah for 'acts' done perhaps even before the brain and personal consciousness was fully developed?

The question is also as follows. When the Torah says that a *Katan* / young child, before reaching 'the age of maturity' (12–13 years old), is *Patur* / exempt from punishment, קטן לאו בר עונשין / "the child is not punished" (*Nidah*, 45b). Does this mean that they are totally exempt from Mitzvos before their Bar or Bas Mitzvah? Or does it mean that since they are too young and do not have the proper mindset and skills to understand their actions, they are exempt from 'punishment' — but they are nonetheless technically *Mechuyav* / commanded and obligated in the Mitzvos (*Aruch l'Ner*, ibid).

There are those who maintain that children are not at all obligated in Mitzvos (*Minchas Chinuch*, Mitzvah 263, 36. *Kovetz Ha'aros,*

33:8). Others contend that with regards to positive Mitzvos, such as putting on Tefillin, a child is completely exempt, yet, with regards the refraining from negative commands, even a child is a *Mechuyav* / obligated, albeit not punished (*Pri Megadim*, Pesicha Koleles, Orach Chayim 2:3. *Shu'T Beis haLevi* 1, 14:2. *Shu'T Mishkanos Yaakov*, Even haEzra 47. See also, *Shu'T Chelkas Yoav*, Siman 1. Note, כיון דמזידה היא, תקלה נמי איכא, ורחמנא הוא דחס עלה עלה. *Sanhedrin*, 55b).

Certainly, even a child is a Mechuyav with regard to the universal laws of civility, that all humans are responsible, such as not stealing or hurting another human being (*Ohr Sameach*, Hilchos Isurei Bi'ah, 3:2).

In the Shulchan Aruch, the Rama rules, וקטן שהכה לאביו או עבר שאר עבירות בקטנותו אע"פ שא"צ תשובה כשהגדיל מ"מ טוב לו שיקבל על עצמו איזה דבר לתשובה ולכפרה אע"פ שעבר קודם שנעשה בר עונשין / "If a child struck his father or transgressed otherwise in his youth, even though he does not need to do Teshuvah when he matures, it is still good for him to take upon himself some element of Teshuvah and Kaparah, even though his sin was at an age when he was not eligible for punishment."*

It seems clear from the sources above that with regard to moral, ethical and civil behavior, even if children are not re-

---

* *Shulchan Aruch*, Orach Chayim, 343. *Sefer Chassidim*, 692. The Mitteler Rebbe, *Pokeach Ivrim*, 22. See also, *Baba Kama*, 98b. הוה עובדא וכפייה רפרם לרב אשי ואגבי ביה / "There was an incident like this one, and Rafram forced Rav Ashi, who had burned a document in his youth (Rashi), to pay damages, and he collected payment: Taz, *ad loc*. The Radbaz writes that only for monetary issues does one need to do Teshuvah and pay back what was stolen, for example, but not with regards to issues between man and Hashem: *Teshuvos haRadbaz*, Siman 2314.

sponsible for their behavior *when they are children*, when they reach adulthood and maturity, they should reevaluate their lives and do Teshuvah for any type of negative behavior, certainly those affecting other human beings. If a youngster shoplifted or insulted a friend of his, when they gain maturity and reach adulthood, optimally, they should do Teshuvah, repay what was stolen, ask forgiveness from the person insulted, and so forth. As such, the Rama is ruling that although children are exempt from punishment — and maybe even exempt from all responsibility as they do not have full *Da'as* / discerning awareness — yet, they should do Teshuvah when they are older.

The question still remains, however. Why exactly should a person do Teshuvah for a foolish action or inaction perpetuated as an innocent child? Once we understand this issue regarding a young child, we will be able to better understand the idea of Kaparah for an unborn child.

UNINTENTIONAL ACTS REVEAL WHO WE TRULY ARE

An adult's unintentional transgressions, when they were without *Da'as* / conscious awareness, fall into a Halachic category called *b'Shogeg* / 'without intention' or 'by mistake'. This kind of act is similar to the act of a child, who acts without Da'as.

The general consensus is that if someone transgressed a מצוה מדרבנן / *Mitzvah mi-deRabanan* / a Mitzvah established by our sages, and did so b'Shogeg, there is no need for them to do

Teshuvah. The reason for this is that the obligation of Mitzvos mi-deRabanan is on the גברא / *Gavra* / person and not on the חפצא / *Cheftza* / the object itself. As such, if a Gavra does an action without intention, there is no Gavra transgressing and thus no transgression (*Kesef Mishneh,* Isurei Bi'ah, 2:12. *Nesivos haMishpat,* 234:2. *Shu'T Toras Chesed,* Orach Chayim, 32. *Shu'T Minchas Elazer,* 3:12. *Asvan d'Oraisa,* Kelal 10. *Shu'T Beis Ephrayim,* 111. *Minchas Shai,* 62, and many other others. בדרבנן עבדינן מעשה והדר מותבינן תיובתא / "In matters of Rabbinic law, we carry out the practice and only later consider possible refutations": *Eruvin,* 67b. See *Nesivas ibid.* See, however, *S'dei Chemed,* 1, p. 245–246. *Mishnah Berurah,* 334:78: בין שעבר על איסור דאורייתא או על איסור דרבנן (ומיירי כשעבר בשוגג).

Mitzvos that are *d'Oraisa* / 'explicit in the Torah' are obligatory both for the Gavra *and* the Cheftza. If the person transgresses without intention, there is no Gavra consciously present, as it were — yet the actual Cheftza of the sin, the act itself, has been performed. Thus, even a b'Shogeg transgression of a Mitzvah d'Oraisa requires Teshuvah. Similarly, during the times of the Beis haMikdash, a person who committed certain wrongdoings was obligated to bring a *Korban* / 'offering' even if they acted unintentionally.[*]

---

[*] The Ramban writes, וטעם הקרבנות על הנפש השוגגת מפני שכל העונות יולידו גנאי בנפש והם מום בה / "The reason for the offerings for the erring soul is that all sins [even if committed unwittingly] produce a particular 'stain' upon the soul and constitute a blemish thereon": Ramban, *Vayikra,* 4:2. This idea will be explored further on in the text. Elsewhere, the Ramban writes (*Sha'ar haG'mul*) that a b'Shogeg is called a sinner, as he should have been more careful, as a scrupulous person would not eat something, for example, until he double checks if it is Kosher. This is similar to the words of the Rambam, שהשוגג היה לו לבדוק ולדקדק ואילו בדק יפה יפה ודקדק בשאלות לא היה בא לידי שגגה ולפי שלא טרח בדרישה ובחקירה ואחר כך יעשה צריך כפרה / "For with regard to an

On a deeper level, unintentional mistakes could require Te-shuvah because nothing happens in a vacuum. An outwardly manifest mistake could indicate an inner source or cause. As ultimately there are no 'accidents', even an unintentional act has a reason, albeit a subconscious one. A mistake could be 'unintentional' on a conscious level, yet it has deep roots in the person's subconscious 'intentions'. If a person 'accidentally' says something hurtful to another person, it is likely because they are harboring ill feelings towards them. Sometimes a person with a habit of displaying anger throws a tantrum and then remarks, 'I simply couldn't help it, I just lost myself.' It may be true that they did not consciously choose to behave that way, but their anger was triggered for a subconscious reason. Nothing is random.

If one truly wishes to understand who they are on a deep level, what they really believe in and how their inner issues are affecting their outer life, they should take notice of their accidents, unintentional acts and utterances, their 'random' thoughts and nocturnal dreams.

To see ourselves objectively and without bias or subtle dishonesty, we need to observe our reactive or impulsive behaviors, our mistakes, obsessions, slips of the tongue and unconscious habits. For example, what is our first reaction when faced with

---

inadvertent transgression, the transgressor carries a certain amount of culpability, for he should have checked and been careful. Had he examined the matter thoroughly and been careful in asking questions, he would not have transgressed. Since he did not take the trouble to examine and research the matter before acting, he requires atonement": *Hilchos Shegagos*, 5:6

an unexpected challenge, predicament or turn of events? Are
we gripped with fear, anxiety, hopelessness — or faith, truth
and hope? Such first reactions, before our social conscience or
intellect kicks in, are indicators of what is really going on within our psyche.

For this reason, from a certain perspective, an unintentional transgression demands an even greater soul searching and
Teshuvah than a premeditated or deliberate transgression. Unconscious negative behaviors overtly demonstrate that deep
down, the individual is still very much associated with negativity and with negative tendencies* even when denied by the
conscious mind.

What organically surfaces to thought is not random nor
without a source. On the contrary, there is always a context to
our daydreams, thoughts, words, actions and unpremeditated
responses; they are manifestations of where our heart and mind

---

* The Rebbe, *Likutei Sichos* 3, 944. See also, Alter Rebbe, *Ma'amarei Admur haZakein*, Ma'amarei Razal, p. 31. An unintentional act demands even
greater Teshuvah than an act that was intentionally committed: Shaloh,
Meseches Rosh Hashanah, p. 194. *Tanya*, Igeres haKodesh, Igeres 28. Unintentional misdeeds are indications of previous intentional misdeeds, as sin
draws sin: Rebbe Moshe Alshich, *Vayikra*, 4. *Pirush haGra*, Mishlei, 13:6.
Likutei Torah (Arizal), Vayikra. Unintentional negative and sinful acts indicate that one is still connected with that negativity: *Beis Yaakov* (Ish-
bitz) Shemini, p. 44a. שהוא, שעינן בלי דעת לעבור עליו ישראלי לאיש שהזדמן השוגג
מאחר מ"י הש ציווי מחמת מלעשותו שהזהיר אף דבר לאותו השתוקק מכבר שבודאי מחמת
והכפרה בשוגג עליו לעבור הזה דבר כ"ע מזדמן אליו הדבר לזה חיבור לו יש הרי לזה שהשתוקק
כבר אליו שהשתוקק מה על הוא: *Sheim MiShmuel*, Tzav. They also show a lack
of attachment and Deveikus with Hashem: Rebbe Yoseph Yavetz, *Avos*,
3.

are based at that particular moment. As a result, our mistakes show us where we need the most refocusing and Teshuvah if we truly want to grow. Our negative projections upon others also show that there is a deep connection to that negativity within ourselves. They are disowned parts of ourselves revealed outwardly.

Goodness emanates from a purely good person; the opposite of goodness can only emanate from someone who is still struggling with impurities, as the Maharal explains. Thus, "No harm befalls the righteous" (*Mishlei*, 12:21) — even accidentally, as a Tzadik is someone whose subconscious, deeper self has been transformed.

Not only will a Tzadik not accidentally insult someone, nor unwittingly commit a transgression, nor project negativity upon others, but a person living a truly holy and wholesome life will rarely attract negativity or transgression of any kind into their domain. This fact reveals two types of movement of influence: from the inside-out and from the outside-in. Just as our thoughts can move outward and influence our words and actions, our deeper, subconscious mind can move out into revealed perceptions and thoughts. In this way, no negativity emanates outwardly from a Tzadik, as well as from anyone who lives a holy, wholesome, integrated life and does not harbor negativity within.

An example of the movement of influence from the outside-in is eating food. We internalize not only nutrition but spiritual forces when we eat. "No harm befalls the righteous" means the wholesome person does not internalize negativity from the outside world. A Tzadik will not eat, even accidentally, non-Kosher food, for instance.* In contrast to the movement from the inside-out, this would seem to be outside the realm of the Tzadik's choice, as, for example, if someone served the Tzadik non-Kosher food. Yet, there are many anecdotes of righteous people unexplainably refraining from imbibing presumed Kosher food, and later the food was revealed as un-Kosher.

Goodness attracts goodness, and blessings attract blessings. Beneficial objects and events are 'attracted' to beneficial people, as it were, just as good people are attracted to good situations.

ACTIONS REPEATED OVER AND OVER LODGE INTO THE SUBCONSCIOUS

What creates a transgressive or negative pattern within the heart or mind? One major force is actions, including unintentional ones, repeated many times. Actions repeated over time create a new 'second nature',** since they eventually lodge them-

---

* According to Tosefos, this principle only applies to accidentally almost eating non-Kosher foods: Tosefos, *Chulin*, 5b. *Tosefos*, Yevamos, 99b. The Ramban argues with Rabbeinu Tam and says this principle applies to all areas of life: *Ramban, Chulin*, 7a, based on the Gemara in *Kesuvos*, 28b. See also *Yevamos*, 121a. *Medrash Tana Devei Eliyahu Rabbah*, 26. See also *Nedarim*, 10a, where it seems like this assumption holds true regarding all matters of life.

** הרגל נעשה טבע שני / "Habit becomes second nature": Meiri, *Chibur haTeshuvah*, Meishiv Nefesh, Ma'amar 1:3. *Shevilei Emunah*, Nesiv 4:2. *Shu'T Ma-*

selves in the inner psyche. There they drive automatic negative behavior or are 'burped up' from the subconscious through unintended thoughts, words or actions.

Often, people behave in a manner completely contrary to what they intellectually know to be true. For instance, say a person consciously understands that acting out of anger is damaging and "similar to idol worship." He sincerely understands that his displays of anger will erode his inner integrity, his mental and physical health, his public image, his professional life, and his family, and so on. He knows that others will ultimately treat him the way he treats them and that he will cause himself needless suffering and anguish. Yet, when 'provoked', he simply becomes angry again, as if against his own will.

Why does one allow himself to fly into a rage when he knows that it is highly detrimental to himself? What one knows on

hara miPanu, 36. Rebbe Yoseph Yavetz, *Avos*, 4:13. Shaloh, *Asarah Hilulim*, p. 317. In the words of the Ramban, וטעם הקרבנות על הנפש השוגגת מפני שכל העוונות יולידו גנאי בנפש והם מום בה / "The reason for the offerings for the erring soul is that all sins (even if committed unwittingly) produce a particular 'stain' upon the soul and constitute a blemish thereon" (*Vayikra*, 4:2). Negative repetitive acts, even when done, unconsciously and not maliciously, create a negative mindset, which gives rise to future negative acts. This is similar to a person eating poison by mistake, unintentionally. Although he is not at 'fault' (albeit, maybe he could have been more careful), he still becomes poisoned. The same is true with inadvertent, unintentional acts; the spiritual damage to the soul is the same, as such behaviors become ingrained into one's psyche and thus lead to more negativity. In the words of the Yismach Moshe, ועוד נמצא טעם על השוגג שצריך כפרה, כי כל חטא פוגע בטבע בנפש, כי אם יחתה איש בשוגג אש ובגדיו לא יישרפו. ואם יאכל אדם סם המוות בשוגג ולא ימות. לכך צריך כפרה, דהיינו לנקות ולקנח הפגימה בנפש: *Yismach Moshe*, Mishpatim.

the surface of his consciousness is not necessarily known in his deeper, instinctual levels of self.

And this is the deeper reason that we need a Kaparah for our own childhood. When we are small children, our brains are developing; neurons are making connections and associations, and patterns of coping are being solidified and fashioned. This is when behaviors are most readily ingrained and become part of the baseline functioning of our instinctual brain. In other words, someone may suffer today because of the learned and repeated behaviors of their childhood.

Even though a child does not have full *Da'as* / discernment and thus free choice or responsibility, his or her actions still contribute to the adult that they become. Certain attitudes and approaches become default modes, seemingly hard-wired into their neurophysiology. However, the work of Teshuvah rewires one's system. And this reconfiguring and recalibrating of our subconscious mind is demanded of us as we mature, if we wish to live freely without the burden of intense anxieties, angers, cravings and self-defeating behaviors. Teshuvah is a must if one wants to live a truly happy, holy, wholesome life.

IN UTERO KAPARAH

Clearly, a fetus in the womb does not have any conscious Da'as, and without Da'as, there is no ability to choose behaviors. Yet, just as we learn certain patterns of behavior in our youth and begin to solidify them, we 'learn' attitudes and even behaviors in the womb. Certain genetic 'switches' are turned on or off based on the choices our parents, principally our mother, make while carrying us. We hear the voices of people and music and media around us, we resonate with the emotions and tensions of our mother, and we are influenced by the foods she eats and her self-care and prayer. All the words, images, feelings, that make an impression on the mother, and all the Mitzvos and spiritual studies that she does, release particular chemicals in the mother's brain, which in turn affect the fetus as well.

If the mother is depressed or happy, anxious or relaxed, angry, or peaceful, it literally turns on genetic switches in the fetus and predisposes the child towards certain habits and states of mind. And this is what the Book of Tehillim means when it says, זרו רשעים מרחם / "The wicked are estranged from the womb." The mother's choices and behaviors establish the tendencies of the child (See *Maharsha*, Yuma, 83a. גם ר" יצה ששולט מוכח מהא במעי אמו ובהא יש ליישב דע"י אמו כי התם אפשר דשולט בו יצה"ר קודם היציאה, אבל בולד עצמו אינו שולט יצר הרע).

A tale is told in the Gemara. A pregnant woman smelled food and had a craving to eat it on Yom Kippur. Her family members came before Rebbe Chanina to ask how to proceed. He said to them: "Whisper to her that today is Yom Kippur." They whispered to her, but she did not accept the whisper and continued to crave the food. Rebbe Chanina then recited this verse about the baby: "The wicked are estranged from the womb," meaning, they are estranged already in their mother's womb. Indeed, she gave birth to a son called Shabsai, and when he grew up, he was known as 'Shabsai the hoarder of fruits'. He hoarded fruit during years of famine in order to inflate its price and profit at the expense of poor people (*Yuma*, 82b–83a).

In the times of the Gemara, the most famous heretic was known as Elisha *Acher* / the 'Other', the Estranged. Chazal tell us that a reason Elisha became estranged later in life, once he was already a celebrated sage, was because when he was in the womb, his mother would walk by a place of idol worship and would take in the odors and the 'smell' of idols would percolate in her body (Yerushalmi, *Chagigah*, 2:1. 9b: אמו כשהיתה מעוברת בו היתה עוברת על בתי עכו"ם והריחה מאותו המין והיה אותו הריח מפעפע בגופה. See also *Pri Chadash*, Yoreh De'ah 81:26. Note *Tosefos*, Yevamos, 109b: ואחר מתחלתו היה רע). The Gemara is suggesting that Elisha was subliminally drawn toward heresy even before he was born, although it did not manifest outwardly until much later.

Everything a pregnant mother takes into her body, mind and soul during pregnancy has an effect on the developing child. Whatever affects the mother penetrates the fetus at least subliminally and affects his or her development.

Even the mother's and father's own genetic patterns and markers inform the development of the unborn child. The unborn child inherits their 'spiritual genes' as well. Perhaps this was the root cause of Eisav's inclination toward houses of idol worship, as the genes of his grandfather Lavan had an effect upon his system even before he had developed a working *Yetzer haRa* / evil inclination.

In this way, because of the environmental, subliminal and 'genetic' influences internalized by an unborn child during this foundational period, the mother needs to bring a Kaparah for the unborn child. No one can help create a proper Tikkun for the child like the mother. Additionally, when she brings a bird for Kaparah on behalf of the child, she creates a sense of Teshuvah within herself, which automatically has a positive effect upon the unborn child.

WAYS TO RECTIFY INGRAINED NEGATIVE PATTERNS

Although genes and other subtle influences are turned on or off in the womb, and certain neurological connections are formed and established, which help determine the future character traits of the person, Teshuvah can override all of these natural determinants. Teshuvah reaches the spiritual source and root of the brain and beyond. Even from a purely scientific view, the neuroplasticity of the brain can be leveraged through Teshuvah to form new neural connections in the brain and new behaviors. New pathways in the brain can be formed according to the healthy, positive, holy, wholesome behaviors we choose. In any case, despite being predisposed to certain behaviors, we have the creative ability to overcome all instincts and tendencies through sincere inner resolve and resolute repetition of new behaviors.

When Yom Kippur, the essential day of Teshuvah, arrives, we need to consider what we need to do in order to undo these effects. What specifically do we need to do to transform our subconscious selves, and even modulate the functioning of our genes, brain, and heart? Most people will need to commit to specific repeated actions and behaviors that match and counteract their old programming.

For example, if speaking out of anger has been one of your issues, the next time you feel anger rising up, you will need to 'act calm'. In a moment you feel this is not possible, you may need to remove yourself from the interaction and run around the block. Gradually you can begin to substitute running around the block with the approach of 'acting calm', each time the stimulus arises. Eventually, you will train your mind and body to have a different reaction when circumstances seem to prompt anger. Acting calm will become your new 'instinct' and automatic response. New pathways can be created in the brain due to the way the Creator designed it.

There may be a subliminal narrative playing in our own head that tells us we are capable or not capable, a good person or not so good, successful or not, loved or not. These messages become solidified over time through believing them, repeating them and acting them out. Sadly, a parent or teacher or another impressive person may have told you that you are a clumsy person. If you believe this and experientially confirm it, it seemingly becomes who you are.

An inner voice of Kelipah masquerading as 'religious authority' could suggest that you are a sinner, incapable of Teshuvah and a good life. Even if this is not a conscious narrative, it still has a devastating effect. To counter this narrative, we need to create a positive belief and narrative. We constantly need to repeat to ourselves holy and positive sayings, such as *Elokai, Neshamah she-Nasata Bi Tehorah Hi* / "My Creator! The soul that You have given me is pure!"

One way of activating and integrating such a saying is by working with it in a verbal and auditory way. For example, one would take this phrase, set it to a *Nigun* / melody, and repeat it over and over again like a chant so that it may gradually penetrate and fill the subconscious mind, replacing the opposite message. One could also take a holy phrase or idea and make it into a visual and sensory experience. You could imagine yourself as a Tzadik; imagine the perception of wholeness and goodness emanating from your state of *Yichud* / unification with HaKadosh Baruch Hu, and then act from this place. You could imagine yourself as the Cohen Gadol serving in the Holy of Holies in awe, attaining atonement for Klal Yisrael — or another image of soul-actualization that you are seeking to manifest in your life.

Imagery registers deeper within us than words. An image lodges itself in the subconscious layer of self and informs our actions, even when we are unaware of what causes such behavior. Imagery also influences our emotional responses beneath the surface of our mind and identity.

If your internal self-image is of an unsuccessful, sinful, or incompetent person, you need to supplant this self-defeating image. You need to replace it with an empowering image of yourself as a successful, good, capable person. Actively envisioning yourself in these positive images uses the power of the creative imagination to actually create a shift in your baseline self-image.

Throughout the *Davening* / prayers of Yom Kippur, we elaborately recall the details of the *Avodah* / holy work of the Cohen Gadol in the Beis haMikdash. Today when there is no physical Beis haMikdash, our prayers take the place of the offerings and Avodah. On a deep level, we *become* the Cohen Gadol serving in the Holy of Holies; we enter our own inner Holy of Holies, the deepest place of who we truly are, the place of our stainless purity, *Deveikus* / 'absorption in Divinity', joy, wholeness and perfection. This visual and visceral contemplation is part of Teshuvah, overriding and replacing our negative or random self-images with the most luminous, elevated ones possible. In this way, we are able to reclaim our deepest selves. For the truth is, we are all, in essence, Tzadikim: ועמך כלם צדיקים / *Ve-Ameich Kulam Tzadikim* / "And all Your People are Tzadikim…" (*Yeshayahu*, 60:21. Eventually we are all (mostly) Tzadikim. Rambam, *Hilchos Teshuvah*, 3:5. וכן כל הרשעים שעונותיהן מרבים דנין אותן כפי חטאיהם, ויש להן חלק לעולם הבא, שכל ישראל יש להם חלק לעולם הבא, אף על פי שחטאו, שנאמר ועמך כלם צדיקים לעולם יירשו ארץ).

With this affirmation and realization, we bring Kaparos, so-to-speak, on behalf of our own inner child, and for ourselves as a pre-conscious fetus. Then, on Yom Kippur, we are spiritually reborn in a state of clarity and luminosity. And no negativity will emanate from a Tzadik, but only positivity — as it is stated: "And He taught me (in the womb) and said to me: 'Let your heart hold fast to My words; keep My commandments and live!'" (*Mishlei*, 4:4)

Chapter Eight
THE SECRET OF THE GOAT SENT TO THE WILD: ELEVATING THE DARK SIDE

MONG THE MANY SERVICES IN THE BEIS HAMIK-
DASH ON YOM KIPPUR, THERE IS A SEEMINGLY VERY
PECULIAR PRACTICE DELINEATED BY THE TORAH:
the *Avodah* / spiritual service of the two he-goats, sometimes
translated as 'the ritual of the scapegoat'.

"And from the children of Israel, he (Aron) shall take two
he-goats for a sin offering...shall take the two he-goats and let
them stand before Hashem at the entrance of the *Ohel Moed* /
Tent of Meeting. And he shall place lots upon the two goats,
one marked for Hashem and the other marked for Azazel. Aaron shall bring forward the goat designated by lot for Hashem,

which he is to offer as a sin offering; while the goat designated by lot for Azazel shall be left standing alive before Hashem, to make expiation with it and to send it off to the wilderness for Azazel" (*Vayikra*, 16:5–10).

THE GENERAL OUTLINE OF THE PRACTICE

Essentially, two identical male goats were placed before Aharon haCohen / Aaron the Priest, one to the right and one to the left of him. In subsequent generations, such were placed to the right and left of the serving *Cohen Gadol* / High Priest. Then a wooden receptacle with two lots, one inscribed "For Hashem" and the other inscribed "For Azazel," was placed in front of the Cohen Gadol. He would shuffle the lots and put both his hands into the receptacle, taking one in his right hand and the other in his left. If the lot 'For Hashem' came up in his right hand, the Deputy would say to him: "My master, Cohen Gadol, raise your right hand so that all can see with which hand the lot 'For Hashem' was selected." And if the lot 'For Hashem' came up in his left hand, the head of the family of Cohanim would say to him: "My master, Cohen Gadol, raise your left hand."

Then the Cohen Gadol would place the two lots upon the two goats, the lot that arose in his right hand on the goat standing to his right side and the lot in his left hand on the goat to his left. And upon placing the lot 'For Hashem' upon a goat, he would say: "For Hashem, as a sin-offering." The goat upon which fell the lot bearing the inscription 'for Hashem' was destined for a *Korban* / sacrifice. The goat upon which fell the lot bearing the inscription 'For Azazel' was afterwards sent out into the (wilderness of) Azazel (*Yuma*, 39a. Rashi, *ad loc*).

Rambam elaborates: "He ties a crimson cord weighing two *selaim* on the head of the goat to be sent to Azazel and positions it in the direction where it will be sent. And he ties such a cord on the goat to be slaughtered, hanging it over the place where it will be slaughtered… Afterwards, he would send the living goat to be taken to the desert with a person prepared for this task…[*]

---

[*] The Pasuk says ושלח ביד־איש עתי / "And it shall be sent off to the wilderness through a designated agent" (*Vayikra*, 16:21). Whether he is the *Shliach* / "agent" of Klal Yisrael or of the Cohen Gadol is debated (*Shu't D'var Avraham* 2, 8:6. *Chidushei haGriz*, Yuma. *HaGriz Al haRambam*, first letter at the end of the book. Note, אתי משלח, מצאו בשוק לכהן גדול, אומר לו איש כהן גדול עשינו שליחותך: *Yuma*, 71a). What does איש עתי / 'designated agent' mean here? Chazal learn from the word עתי / *Iti* that the agent goes on his mission even if he becomes impure (עתי אף בטומאה: *Yuma*, 66b. *Yerushalmi*, Yuma, 6:3). This means that if the one sending the goat away becomes impure, he nevertheless enters the courtyard of the Beis haMikdash while he is impure and sends it away. The obvious question is why? Yes, the person is "designated," and so he is the one who must take it out to the wilderness even if impure, but why not take the goat of the Mikdash *to him*, so that he will not bring Tumah into the Azarah? (as the *Shitah Mekubetzes* asks: Hashmatos, Kerisus, 14a. See also *Chelkas Yoav*, Orach Chayim, 29). This reinforces the idea that this Sa'ir haMishtaleach is connected with the elevation of the 'dark' side, even Tumah, as it were.

The *Meam Loez* (quoting the Ralbag, Vayikra, ibid, albeit slightly differently) writes that *Iti* means someone who is a 'master of time' (as the word עתי comes from the word עת / time), and can travel into the desert at any time, cold, heat, rain, winds. The idea of a master of time can be positive, or it can mean he is beyond the rhythm of time, i.e., of life, because he is connected to the world of death. In fact, the *Chizkuni* writes, in the name of a (lost)

(This person) would divide the crimson cord tied to the goat's horns. He would tie half to a rock and half between its two horns. He would then push it backward (off the cliff) and it would roll over and over as it plummeted. It would not reach halfway down the mountain before it was torn limb from limb" (Rambam, *Hilchos Avodas Yom haKippurim*, 3:3–7).

As this goat plunged to its death, it carried the sins of Klal Yisrael with it. By sending it away and then throwing it off the cliff, our sins were cast away and destroyed, as it were.

The Torah itself does not offer any reasons for this seemingly wild or even barbaric practice. To do such a thing on the holiest day of the year may seem counterintuitive and hard to grasp. For one thing, the *Shechitah* / slaughter of an animal must always be done in the most humane way, causing the least pain and stress to the animal. And in general, we are commanded to avoid causing unnecessary suffering to living beings. On this day, when we are confessing any acts of violence, we are asked

---

Medrash, עתי שהגיע זמנו למות תוך אותה שנה שהרי הנושא את השעיר אינו עובר שנתו / לכך היו בוררין איש שהגיע זמנו למות תוך אותה שנה וחכמת המזלות היתה קלה בעיניהם "The word עתי (which could be translated as 'whose time had come') refers to someone who was destined to die before the year is over. This would account for the fact that it was noticed that the man who had been entrusted with this task never lived out that year. We must assume that in those days people used astrology to determine who was not destined to live out the year." Indeed, the word עתי means 'his time', a man in his time, meaning that the person appointed to accompany the goat into the wild would not live out the year. See *Chida*, citing a Medrash. *Nitzutzei Oros*, Zohar 3, 63b. In other words, he is a 'dead man walking', as it were, hence connected with the world of Tumah and death.

to tie a stone to a goat and push it off a cliff in order to bring us some form of *Kaparah* / atonement. This unsettling ritual seems unlike the Torah, "Whose paths are pleasant and all her ways peaceful" (*Mishlei*, 3:17). Yet, a thorough understanding of this service reveals profound insights into the nature of Yom Kippur and Teshuvah.

STATUS OF THE GOAT TO THE AZAZEL

Our first question is, what is the status of the goat that is sent into the wilderness? Is it a *Korban* / offering? One of the two goats, as the Torah states, is clearly a *Korban Chatas* / sin offering: "Aaron shall bring forward the goat designated by lot for Hashem, which he is to offer as a sin offering." If the goat sent into the wilderness is also some type of Korban, who is it offered to? It is seemingly 'offered' to the wilderness itself, although this does not apparently resonate with the uncompromising Monotheism of the Torah.

Among the *Rishonim* / early commentators, there is a debate on this question. The Even Ezra (16:8) writes clearly, כי המשלח / איננו קרבן כי לא ישחט / "The goat that is sent away is not a Korban, as it is never ritually slaughtered." Similarly, the Ramban (*ibid*), speaking of the 'dark' forces that reside in the 'wilderness', writes, ואין הכונה בשעיר המשתלח שיהיה קרבן מאתנו אליו חלילה / אבל שתהיה כונתנו לעשות רצון בוראנו שצונו כך / "The intention in our sending away the goat to the desert was not that it should be an offering from us to it (to the wilderness and its dark forces),

Heaven forbid. Rather, our intention is (solely) to fulfill the wish of our Creator, Who commanded us to do this."

Yet, the Torah says clearly, ומאת עדת בני ישראל יקח שני־שעירי עזים לחטאת / "And from the community of the Children of Israel he shall take *two* he-goats for a sin offering" (*Vayikra*, 16:5). This means that *both* goats are to be sin offerings; even the goat that is sent to the wilderness of Azazel is a *Chatas* / sin offering (Meiri, *Yuma*, 62b) of some sort. And regarding the proof of the Even Ezra, כי לא ישחט / "The fact that the goat to the Azazel is never ritually slaughtered proves that it is not a Korban" is not an issue, for our sages have already said that הא אמרי במערבא דחייתו לצוק זו היא שחיטתו / "They say in the West (Eretz Yisrael) that pushing it off the cliff is its slaughter" (*Yuma*, 64a).*

---

* Other proofs that it is a Korban are from the fact that both goats are purchased with the monies of Shekalim, that Chazal connect the goat to Azazel with חטאות המתות, and this goat may not have a *Mum* / blemish. The Brisker Rav questions if, in fact, the goat sent to the Azazel has a *Din* / legal status of a Korban Chatas: *Chidushei haGriz*, Zevachim, 113b. See also, *Meiri*, Yuma, 62b. He is also *Mechadesh* / revealing a novel reconciliation between the two opinions regarding whether this goat is a Korban or not: up until the *Viduy* / confession service performed by the Cohen Gadol, this goat is considered to be dedicated as a Korban and all the laws of a Korban apply. Yet, once it is sent out of the Beis haMikdash it ceases to be a Korban. The Rambam writes שני שעירי יום הכפורים ששחטם בחוץ. אם עד שלא התודה עליהם חיב כרת על שניהן הואיל וראויין לבוא לפני השם לודוי. ואם אחר שהתודה פטור על המשתלח שהרי אינו ראוי לבוא לפני השם. *Hilchos Ma'asei Korbanos*, 18: 11. In other words, once the Cohen Gadol has made Viduy over the goat that will be sent into the wilderness, it is no longer a Korban.

Again, if this goat were a Korban, what kind of Korban would it be? And if it is not considered an actual Korban, it is still an essential Mitzvah of Yom Kippur, and we need to understand its unique significance.

AZAZEL BRINGING ATONEMENT

Whether the goat sent to the Azazel is an actual Korban or not, this Mitzvah does bring *Kaparah* / atonement, as the Torah states clearly: "...and it should carry all the sins" (*Vayikra*, 16:21). In the words of the Rambam (*Hilchos Teshuvah*, 1:2), "Since the goat sent (to Azazel) atones for all of Klal Yisrael, the Cohen Gadol confesses upon it as a spokesman for all of Klal Yisrael... The goat sent to Azazel atones for all the transgressions in the Torah, the severe and the light ones, those violated intentionally and those transgressed inadvertently... This applies only if one does Teshuvah. If one does not do Teshuvah, the goat only atones for the lighter sins."

In fact, the Gemara tells us that the Babylonians (Alexandrian Jews who would go to Yerushalayim for Yom Kippur) used to pluck the hair of the Azazel goat and proclaim, "Take and go forth, take and go forth," meaning, take away our sins (*Yuma*, 66a–b).

There seems to be no opinion in the Gemara for the Rambam's statement that even without Teshuvah, the mere act of sending the goat to Azazel atones for 'light sins' (as *Kesef Mishnah* asks, דלרבנן אפילו אעשה אם לא עשה תשובה אין שעיר מכפר ולרבי אפילו על החמורות מכפר בלא תשובה). What is the logic of the Rambam's ruling? Is not the whole idea of Teshuvah dependent on intention, i.e., owning one's mistakes, taking conscious responsibility for them and resolving to live differently? How could the act itself bring atonement?

THE SECRET OF THIRTY-THREE

Having himself decoded the mystery of the Azazel ritual, the Even Ezra writes, ואם יכולת להבין הסוד שהוא אחר מלת עזאזל תדע סודו וסוד שמו כי יש לו חברים במקרא ואני אגלה לך קצת הסוד ברמז בהיותך בן שלשים ושלש תדענו / "If you are able to understand the *Sod* / secret that follows the word *Azazel* (in the Torah) then you will know its secret and the secret of its name, for it has comrades in other verses in the Torah (in other words, the word *Azazel* is composed of two words, *Ez* / 'goat', *Azel* / 'goes', and indeed there are many such words in the Torah and Nach — one word composed of two words). I will reveal a bit of its secret to you in a hint: when you are 33, you will understand it" (*Vayikra*, 16:8).

What does the Even Ezra mean when he writes, "When you are 33, you will understand it"? Commenting on this Even Ezra, the Ramban writes, והנה ר"א נאמן רוח מכסה דבר ואני הרכיל מגלה סודו שכבר גלו אותו רבותינו ז"ל במקומות רבים / "Behold, Rebbe Avraham of faithful spirit conceals the matter, but I am a gossiper, so I will tell his secret, as our rabbis have already revealed this secret in many places." The Ramban then elaborates on the nature of the Azazel, as will be shortly explored. And regarding the cryptic statement, "When you are 33, you will understand it," the Ramban says this alludes to Chapter 17, Verse 7, which

is 33 verses from the above: ולא-יזבחו עוד את-זבחיהם לשעירהם אשר הם
זנים אחריהם / "...And that they may offer their sacrifices no more
to the goat-demons after whom they stray." In other words, the
secret of the goat that is 'offered' in the wilderness is connected
to the *prohibition* on offering a sacrifice to the 'goat demons',
referring to some form of demonic ritual. What exactly a 'goat
demon' is, and how this is connected to the goat which is sent
to the wilderness, will be explored later.

Yet, the *Peshat* / simple meaning of the hint of Even Ezra
is that one will have a revelation of the secret of the meaning
of Azazel at the age of 33 (as the Yavetz notes, *Mitpachas Sefarim*,
8:14. Although the Ya'avetz completely dismisses the Even Ezra). As such,
how does the age of 33 connect with the Azazel? What, in
general, does the number 33 signify, and where else do we find
this number in Torah thought?

ONE PARALLEL THE OTHER

As mentioned, the two goats brought to the Cohen Gadol
are exactly equal in appearance, size, and value (*Yuma*, 62aˈ). Yet,

---

* The Pasuk (16:7) says ולקח את-שני השעירם, and the word השעירם / 'the goats'
is written without the second Yud; it has a missing letter. When the Torah
writes about two objects with a missing letter, it suggests that they are identical — לוחת כתיב ששתיהם שוות / "The word *Luchos* (missing the Vav which
would make it plural) is written in a singular form to indicate that the two
tablets were the same (Rashi, *Devarim*, 9:10. *Medrash Tanchuma*. Although
they were not literally identical, as there is nothing exactly alike in the universe — דבן סורר ומורה לא היה ולא עתיד להיות משום דכתיב בננו זה דבעינן שיהו אביו ואמו
שוין במראה ובקומה וזה אי אפשר להיות אבל גבי בהמה מיהא יכול להיות יותר ואע"פ שאין
ממש דומות זו לזו דאמרינן בירושלמי חטה אינו דומה לחברתה מכל מקום בעין שיהו
שוין במראה ובקומה כל מה שיוכלו : *Tosefos Yeshanim*, ad loc.

one is offered as a Korban Chatas in the Beis haMikdash, with all the specific details and *Kavanos* / specific intentions that are required, whereas the other one is taken into the wilderness to be pushed off a cliff. These are practically identical animals, yet they have very divergent outcomes. The celebrated Italian *Mekubal* / Kabbalist, Rebbe Menachem Azarya deFano, writes that the five-letter word עזאזל Azazel is an acronym for את זה לעמת זה עשה / *Es Zeh Le'umas Zeh Asah (Elokim)* / "Hashem made one opposite the other" (*Koheles*, 7:14). In other words, these two goats are parallel to each other, but one represents the side of righteousness, light and order, while the other represents the opposite side, that of darkness, disorder, and chaos.

The archetype of *Te'omim* / 'twins' in the Torah is that of Yaakov and Eisav. They represent two opposite paths: the path of righteousness, goodness, and order and the 'dark' path of disorder, brute force, and barbarism. Yaakov is "a man who dwelled in tents," a gentle spiritual scholar. Eisav is "a man of the fields," a brute and powerful hunter. Klal Yisrael, the People of Israel, are named after Yaakov / Yisrael. Klal Yisrael is thus connected with the goat that is offered in the Beis haMikdash, whereas Eisav and his descendants, who are the pagan and not-yet-elevated nations of the world, are connected with the goat which was sent into the wild.

Here is a Medrash (*Bereishis Rabbah*, 65:15) speaking about these two archetypes and paradigms: "And Yaakov said to his mother, "But Eisav my brother is איש שער / hairy," a demon-like person (שער / hair is connected with שעיר / demon-goat: *Yeshayahu*, 13:21), and I am smooth-skinned person (איש חלק: *Bereishis*, 27:11)... 'Yaakov', too, becomes dirtied with sin, but when Yom Kippur comes he has a way to attain atonement... thus when it says ונשא השעיר עליו את־כל־עונתם / "and the goat shall carry upon it, their sins," this refers to Eisav. And עונתם / "their sins," can be read as עונות תם / 'the sins of the *Tam* / simple, straightforward one,' referring to Yaakov, who is called (*Bereishis*, 25:27), an איש תם / *Ish Tam* / simple person." And thus the Azazel goat (Eisav) carries the sins of Yaakov, who is now Klal Yisrael (*Ta'anis*, 5a. Regarding Eisav and Yaakov and the two goats, see also Arbarbanel on this Parsha. A slightly earlier source, also from one of the great scholars of Spain during the expulsion, is Rebbe Yitzchak Arama. He also explains that Eisav is 'the hairy one', the goat, while Yaakov embodies the quality of Eisav when he puts on the skins of a goat to receive the blessings: *Akeidas Yitzchak*, Sha'ar 63).*

The 'one goat' that is offered in the Beis haMikdash corresponds to Yaakov, and the world of *Tam* / simplicity, mindfulness, order, and civility. The parallel goat, taken to the wilder-

---

* It is for this reason that *The Zohar* (3:100b) reveals to us that the confrontation between Yaakov and the *Sar* / angel of Eisav (which is Sam-E'l, as will be further explored) occurred on Yom Kippur evening. And the actual meeting between Yaakov and Eisav, his twin, occurred on Yom Kippur, towards the evening, the time of *Neilah* / closing of the Gates on Yom Kippur. After their encounter on Yom Kippur, the one 'goat', Yaakov, goes to the geographical location "Sukkos." This means he proceeds from the Yom Tov of Yom Kippur to the Yom Tov of Sukkos. Sukkos can also refer to the Beis haMikdash, called today, in exile, "the fallen Sukkah," so the goat representing Yaakov goes to the Beis haMikdash, the place of holiness and purity. Whereas the other goat representing Eisav is sent to שעירה / Se'irah, as in שעיר / Sa'ir / goat and שער / hairy. Eisav returns to the wild, to darkness and impurity.

ness, which is the absence of civility, order, and mindfulness, corresponds to Eisav and the dimension of the wild 'goat de-mon'. And it is thus Eisav who carries away the sins of Yaakov, atoning for the transgressions of Klal Yisrael.

MEANING OF THE WORD AZAZEL

To add another layer to this mystifying ritual, even the name of the Mitzvah, *Azazel*, is a mysterious word. It is a very unique word in Tanach, and does not appear anywhere else but here. What does the word עזאזל / *Azazel* actually mean?

Chazal (*Yuma*, 67b) teach that the word *Azazel* is related to the word עז וקשה / rough and hard (*Toras Kohanim*, 16:8). Rashi further elaborates and writes that *Azazel* is comprised of two words, *Az* / strong and *E'l* / mighty. As such, *Az-Az-El* refers to the rugged, rocky, rough mountain cliff from which the goat was cast down; the word refers to a location.

Another interpretation of the word is that it refers to the goat itself, as in עז / *Ez* / 'the goat', אזל / *Azal* / 'went away', or 'the Goat that is Sent Away'.

Yet, Chazal also say, "The school of Rebbe Yishmael taught: It is called *Azazel* because it obtains atonement for the affair of עזא ועזאל / Uza and Aza'el." These are the names of הנפלים / the fallen angels (*Bereishis*, 6:4), who are also called 'demons' (The word הנפלים equals numerically זה הוא עזא ועזאל / this is Uza and Aza'el: Rabbeinu Yoel, *Sefer haRemazim*, Bereishis, 6:4). Both the Even Ezra and the

Ramban equate *Azazel* with the name of a goat spirit which was a form of pagan idol worship in the ancient world.

Rashi, commenting on the above Gemara, says, כלומר על העריות מכפר / "In other words, the goat sent to Azazel atones for all forms of deviant, illicit, carnal, and licentious behavior." In this view, the Azazel goat has less to do with abstract, external, 'objective' fallen angels and demons, but it is still very much connected to a person's subjective 'inner animal' and their indulgence in wild or 'demonic', thoughtless and irresponsible physical passions. Untamed, insatiable cravings, respecting no boundaries or human civility, are symbolized by an untamed, wild goat. Indeed, the goat deity worshiped by many ancient pagan cultures was associated with unbridled physical carnal desires, and wild, licentious behavior, as well as with fertility.

Whether the 'goat' is seen as a deity or some type of force within us, Azazel seems to be connected with 'the other side' or 'the dark side' contrary to the path of order and righteousness.

MEDRASHIC SOURCES EQUATING AZAZEL WITH DEMONIC FORCES

To add more bewilderment to the puzzle, there is a fascinating yet theologically challenging Medrash in which Chazal further equate Azazel with demonic forces. Moreover, it does seem as if the Scapegoat ritual of Yom Kippur is portrayed as some kind of 'offering' to these forces, however they are to be understood:

אמר סמאל לפני הקב"ה רבון כל העולמים על כל העכומו"ז נתת לי רשות ועל
ישראל אין אתה נותן לי רשות, אמר לו הרי יש לך רשות עליהם ביום הכפורים
אם יש להם חטא, ואם לאו אין לך רשות עליהם, לפיכך נותנין לו שוחד ביום
הכפורים שלא לבטל את ישראל שלא לבטל קרבן של ישראל, שנאמר גורל
אחד ל-ה' וגורל אחד לעזאזל / "Said the Samech-Mem (also called 'the
Angel Samael' or Sam-E'l: *Sam* / poison of *E'l* / Hashem. The Angel Samael
is also the Angel of Eisav: *Tanchuma*, Vayishlach, 8. *Zohar* 1, 170a) before
HaKadosh Baruch Hu: 'Master of the Universe! Over all of
the nations of the world You have given me permission, but
over Klal Yisrael You have not given me such license.' Hashem
said to him (the Samech-Mem): 'You have permission on Yom
Kippur to have sway over them, so long as you find among
them sin. However, if you cannot, then you have no permission.' Therefore, he (the Samech-Mem) is given שוחד / a bribe
on Yom Kippur, in order that he not cause Klal Yisrael to fail
to offer their sin-offering, as it says, 'One lot to Hashem and
one to Azazel' (*Pirkei d'Rebbe Eliezer*, 46).

From this perspective, sending the goat into the wilderness is 'bribing the Satan', giving a conciliatory gift to the Samech-Mem, the "other side."*

Via a lottery, one goat is chosen to be offered as a Korban
to Hashem and the other is sent away to be given to Azazel, the power of Samech-Mem. Says the Zohar, since the Sa-

---

* Sam-E'l is called the Samech Mem, the letters Samech (ס) and final Mem
(ם). Within the Aleph Beis, the Samech and final Mem are the only two
letters that are completely circular or self-enclosing. Hence, they represent
a closure and entrapment of the Divine flow, otherwise known as the "*Sitra
Achara* / the other side."

mech-Mem is ready to pounce and spew negativity and harmful accusations against Klal Yisrael, in order that he not have the ability to open his mouth, we give him a portion, as a form of appeasement, in this is the lottery (*Zohar* 3, p. 101b).

The Zohar gives an analogy for sending the goat into the wilderness as follows. There was once a shepherd who wished to move his sheep across the river, but then he noticed a lone wolf standing nearby, waiting to attack. He thought, 'If I start taking my sheep across the river, the wolf will attack the remaining sheep every time I cross, and will kill many sheep, certainly the younger ones.' So he took an older sheep, yet one who could still put up a good fight, and offered that sheep to the wolf. He thought to himself, 'As the wolf is busy fighting with this one sheep, I will have time to bring the rest of the flock to the other side (This parable is also recorded in *Medrash Rabbah*, Shemos, 21:7. Sending the goat to Azazel is like a master throwing a bone to his dog, so that the master can eat in peace: Rebbe Yitzchak d'Min Aco, *Meiras Einayim*, Acharei, 16:8).

Similarly, it is as if HaKadosh Baruch Hu says, 'If the Samech-Mem wants to be an accuser of Klal Yisrael on this day of final judgment, the holy day of Yom Kippur, I will keep him busy during the day with the Azazel, and like that, he will not accuse Klal Yisrael.' Sending the Scapegoat is an act of appeasement or distraction for the Samech-Mem, as it were, ensuring that he stays quiet.

The illustrious Ramban writes that since Chazal had already revealed the secret of the Azazel, he would elaborate on their teachings:

"Now, the Torah has absolutely forbidden us to acknowledge these powers as 'deities', much less to worship them in any manner. Nonetheless, HaKadosh Baruch Hu has commanded us that on the Day of Atonement, we should let a goat loose into the wilderness, gifting it to that 'prince', that power which rules over wastelands and desolate places. And this goat is fitting for it because he (that 'prince') is the master of that place, and from the emanation of his strength comes destruction and desolation, for he is the cause of the 'stars' of the sword and the blood and the wars, the quarrels, wounds and plagues, and all division and destruction. This 'prince' or power is the soul of the sphere of Mars (the 'red planet'). Its portion among the nations is Eisav (the *Adom* / 'red one' embodied in the nation of *Edom* / Rome, the inheritors of the way of war and the sword and the spilling of red blood — in whose exile we are still living).

"Among the animals, his portion is the goat, and (among the spirits) his portion is the demons. His demons are called "destroyers" in the language of Chazal, and *Se'irim* in the language of the Torah, for both he and his nation are called *Sa'ir* / goat, demon, and *Se'ir*, which is another name for Edom, the land of Eisav. Now the intention in our sending away the goat to the desert is not that it should be a *Korban* / offering from us to these powers, Heaven forbid. Rather, our intention is to fulfill the wish of our Creator, Who commanded us to do so.

This may be compared to the case of someone who makes a feast for his master, and the master commands the person making the feast, "Give one portion to that servant of mine," in which case the host gives nothing of his own to that servant,

and it is not to show him honor that he acts in that way towards him, but everything is given to the master and it is the
master that gives a gift to his servant. The host only observes
his command and does in honor of the master whatever he
commanded him to do. The master, however, out of his own
compassion for the host, wanted all his servants to derive some
enjoyment from the feast, in order that they may all speak of
his [the host's] praise and not of his shortcomings."*

In this passage of the Ramban, who clearly bases his ideas
on the Medrash and teachings of the Zohar, we notice a combination of a few themes. There is an astrological notion of
Mars being connected to war and bloodshed (האי מאן דבמאדים יהי
גבר אשיד דמא: *Shabbos*, 156a), combined with a demonological idea,
plus the historical dichotomy between Yaakov, which is Klal
Yisrael, and Eisav, which is the nation of *Edom* / Rome. Rome
is connected with the 'prince' or archangel of the nations of the
world. However, as the Ramban makes very clear, although
these constructs seem to have some type of power — of course,
lent to them by the Source of all power — that we must under-

---

* Here is the Ramban in the original Hebrew: והנה התורה אסרה לגמרי קבלת
אלהותם וכל עבודה להם אבל צוה הקב"ה ביום הכפורים שנשלח שעיר במדבר לשר המושל
במקומות החרבן והוא הראוי לו מפני שהוא בעליו ומאצילות כחו יבא חורב ושממון כי הוא העילה
לכוכבי החרב והדמים והמלחמות והמריבות והפצעים והמכות והפירוד והחרבן והכלל נפש לגלגל
מאדים וחלקו מן האומות הוא עשו שהוא עם היורש החרב והמלחמות ומן הבהמות השעירים
והעזים ובחלקו עוד השדים הנקראים מזיקין בלשון רבותינו... ואין הכונה בשעיר המשתלח שיהיה
קרבן מאתנו אליו חלילה אבל שתהיה כונתנו לעשות רצון בוראנו שצונו כך והמשל בזה כמי
שעשה סעודה לאדון וצוה האדון את האיש העושה הסעודה תן מנה אחת לעבדי פלוני שאין
העושה הסעודה נותן כלום לעבד ההוא ולא לכבודו יעשה עמו רק הכל נתן לאדון והאדון נותן פרס
לעבדו ושמר זה מצותו ועשה לכבוד האדון כל אשר צוהו האדון ואמנם האדון לחמלתו על בעל הסעודה
רצה שיהיו כל עבדיו נהנין ממנה שיספר בשבחו ולא בגנותו.

stand that there are no dual, dueling divine forces, G-d forbid. And our intention in this service was only to do the will of HaKadosh Baruch Hu, Who asked us to "give a portion to my servant (the 'prince')." Hence, "The host gives nothing of his own to that servant, and it is not to show him honor that he does this for him; rather, everything is given to the Master and it is the Master that gives a gift to his servant (through Klal Yisrael)."

But still, what does this all mean? Clearly there is no other force, as there is really "no other" besides Hashem, so who is this so-called 'servant', the 'prince of darkness'? And why the need to appease him? (הנה כמעט ח"ו שירמה הדבר לעכו"ם :*Ohr haChayim,* Vayikra, 16:7).

DRAWING LOTS & ELEVATING THE 'DARK SIDE'

In general, the service of the lottery is connected with the 'darkness' of randomness. In addition, there are a few laws unique to this *Avodah* / service that are connected with the 'left side' — a term of darkness.

Chazal tell us that טרף בקלפי, והעלה שני גורלות / "The Cohen Gadol would mix the lots in the lottery receptacle used to hold them and draw the two lots from it, one in each hand" (*Yuma,* 39a). As an Avodah in the Beis haMikdash on Yom Kippur (*Ibid,* 39b), this drawing of lots is unique. Normally, the Mitzvos of the Beis haMikdash needed to be done with the right hand, and a left-handed person was not even permitted to serve in the Beis haMikdash. Yet drawing the lots needs to be done with the left hand as well (וכשרה עבודה זו בשמאל כמו הוצאת כף ומחתה בכ"ג דיה"כ: *Tosefos Yeshanim*, ad loc).

Perhaps the use of the left hand represents an inclusion and an elevation of the 'left' or 'dark' side, as does the entire ritual of the Azazel. In fact, the word סמא"ל / Sam-E'l, is similar to the word שמאל / left (hand), as the idea of the Azazel is connected with the 'left' side (*Meiras Einayim*, Acharei, 16:8).

Another one of the main Avodas of Yom Kippur is the *Ketores* / the incense that was brought into the Holy of Holies, and done so only once a year, on Yom Kippur. Tellingly, on Yom Kippur, the Avodah of Ketores was Kosher when performed using the left hand (מאי שנא שמאל דאשכחן לה הכשירא ביום הכפורים: *Menachos*, 6b. ואי אשמעינן שמאל דאית ליה הכשירא ביום הכיפורים: *Zevachim*, 34b. The service of the Ketores, too, transforms the 'darkness' of death). On Yom Kippur, there is a 'Kashering' of the left hand.*

---

* The Rambam writes, כבר בארנו שהולכה בשמאל פוסלת בדם הקדשים ושאר העבודות. ולפיכך היה מן הדין שיוליך המחתה בשמאלו וכף הקטרת בימינו. אבל מפני כבד המחתה ועד שהיא חמה. אינו יכול לסבלה בשמאלו עד הארון. לפיכך נוטל המחתה בימינו וכף הקטרת בשמאלו / "We have already explained that carrying a sacrificial substance in one's left hand disqualifies it with regard to the blood of the sacrificial animals and other services. Hence, it would be appropriate that he should carry the fire pan in his left hand and the *Caf* / 'spoon' full of incense in his right hand (as that is the Avodah). Nevertheless, because of the weight of the firepan — and because it is hot — he would not be able to carry it with his left hand until he reached the Holy Ark (in the Holy of Holies). Therefore he should carry the fire pan in his right hand and the Caf with the incense in his left": Rambam, Hilchos *Avodas Yom haKippurim*, 4:1. On this, the *Kesef Mishnah* comments, וק"ל כיון שהולכה בשמאל פוסלת היאך הכשירו כאן מפני טעמים הללו. ואפשר דהולכה בשמאל לא פסלה אלא מדרבנן א"נ אע"ג דהולכה בשמאל בדם פסלה מדאורייתא משום דא"א שלא בהילוך בקטרת לא פסלה ובהכי אכשר רחמנא. Ei-

The deeper reason behind doing this Avodah with the left hand is that on Yom Kippur there is an elevation even of the 'other side' or the 'left side'. Manifesting the highest level of Teshuvah, Yom Kippur transforms sins into merits and 'the other side' into *Kedushah* / holiness. This is especially true of the Avodas haKetores, which consisted of eleven ingredients, eleven symbolizing the side of Kelipah, concealment and separation.*

It also included the Chelbenah, a foul-odored galbanum spice. Our sages say, כל תענית שאין בה מפושעי ישראל אינה תענית שהרי חלבנה ריחה רע ומנאה הכתוב עם סממני קטרת / "Any fast that does not include the participation of some of the 'sinners of Israel' is not a (proper) fast, as the smell of galbanum is foul and yet the verse lists it with the ingredients of the incense" (*Kerisus*, 6b). The elevation of the פושעי ישראל / 'sinners of Israel' is also a 'left hand' Avodah, as it were.

---

ther way, whatever the technical Halachic reason for this exemption and allowance of using the left hand is, from a more *Penimiyus* / inner understanding, there is a depth to why an Avodah on Yom Kippur is allowed to be performed with the left hand, as it represents the elevation of the 'left side'.

---

*There are ten Sefiros, ten refracted revelations of the One Light of Hashem. In the Sefiros of Kedushah, the *Ohr* / light and the *K'li* / vessel of each Sefirah are unified; as such, there are ten vessels and ten Sefiros. Kelipah is the world of separation, where the One Light does not penetrate and is obscured by the *Kelim* / vessels; thus, the name Samech-Mem, which are two completely closed letters, as explained earlier. As such, since the Light remains 'separate' from the vessels, there are eleven dimensions: the ten Kelim and the One Light.

GOATS, NIGHT, CONFUSION & TOHU

The Gemara tells us a story: "Rebbe Zeira once found Rav Yehudah standing at the entrance of his father-in-law's house and observed that he was in an especially cheerful mood. Rebbe Zeira understood that were he to ask Rav Yehudah about anything in the entire world, he would tell him the answer, and so he asked, 'Why do male goats walk in front of the flock and the ewes follow?' Rav Yehudah answered, 'It is just as it was in the creation of the world: דברישא חשוכא והדר נהורא / "...which at first was dark and then light followed."' Rashi explains here that male goats are typically black, and ewes are typically white (Rashi, *Shabbos*, 77b).

Rav Yehudah is alluding to the perspective that a he-goat embodies a quality of darkness. The Maharal points out (*Chidushei Agados*, Shabbos) that the word שעיר / *Sa'ir* / goat is numerically 580, the same numeric value as the phrase *haYetzer haRa* / 'the evil inclination'.

In contrast to sheep, which are seen as gentle and white, corresponding to the ideas of daytime, light and positivity, goats represent 'night', darkness, and negativity or destructive, devilish energy. One way that goats may have become associated with negativity (although, of course, they have no free choice and there can be no moral judgment upon them) is the way they graze 'greedily' and indiscriminately. If not checked, they can consume, trample and destroy all the greenery in their path, including saplings, causing land to erode. Some goats can even climb trees to consume their desired vegetation, like lust-ful people who will do anything to obtain what they crave. In these ways, wild goats were sometimes seen as threatening pests. Even today, in certain countries, government agencies encourage controlling the population of feral goats through hunting.

'Evening' in Hebrew is *Erev*, which is related to the word *Iruv* / mixed up, discombobulated. Nighttime represents an absence of clarity and distinctions; it is thus a state of confu-sion, disorder, and lack of a sense of safety, in which things are 'mixed up', as it were. Daytime is a state in which everything can generally be seen, defined and quantified. Light allows for observation, and hence there are clear distinctions, order, and a sense of safety.

In the unfolding of Creation, first darkness arose and then *from* the darkness arose light. From chaos came order; from confusion emerged clarity. Similarly, on a microcosmic level, our development from childhood to maturity is a movement from darkness, disorder, and confusion, to light, order, and clarity. We begin life in *Tohu* / the world of chaos, and gradu-ally work our way into *Tikkun* / the world of rectification and order. For the first few years of life, we are in general impulsive and messy, and a source of mess for others. We are not highly attuned to the ways of cause and effect. As we grow up, we gain focus, self-restraint and some level of being organized and mindful of cause and effect.

As a pattern, light following darkness, order following chaos, has its roots in the deepest macrocosmic level, in these origins of Creation. Prior to the Creation of this world of *Tikkun* / balance, when "There was evening, and there was morning, day one" with a separation of *Ohr* / light and *Choshech* / darkness, there was a world of *Tohu* / chaos and unclarity. Behind the scenes of the present moment as well — as our world is continuously being created — there is a state of darkness, imbalance, and unbridled and untamed forces, and an evolution into balance, order, and light.

YAAKOV & EISAV, ORDER & CHAOS, LIGHT & DARKNESS

As it is associated with the Yetzer haRa and 'dark' powers, the goat sent to Azazel is also associated with Eisav, the older twin brother of Yaakov, who is like the darkness and Tohu that is manifest before the light and Tikkun. Eisav embodies the brute, unbridled power of chaos; he is the man of the field, the unkempt, hairy, impatient, 'wild goat'. Yaakov is the cerebral, settled quality of Tikkun; order, balance, patience and healthy boundaries. As the Medrash says, ויקרא א-להים לאור יום זה יעקב. ולחשך קרא לילה זה עשו / "Elokim called the light 'day' — this is Yaakov. And the darkness He called 'night' — this is Eisav" (*Medrash Rabbah*, Bereishis, 2:3. אז יבקע כשחר אורך / "Then shall your light burst through like the dawn": *Yeshayahu*, 58:8. The word יבקע / 'burst through' has the same letters as יעקב / Yaakov).

In fact, as brought down by the Rishonim, the words אור

יום / "The light (He called) day," in numerical value, is 263, and this the same numerical value as the words זה יעקב אבינו / "This is Yaakov our father." And the words קרא לילה / "He called (the darkness) night," is numerically 376, the same value as the name *Eisav* (Rabbeinu Yoel of the Chassidei Ashkenaz, *Sefer haRemazim*, Bereishis, 1:5).

INWARD LIGHT AND DARK SIDES

In human beings, there appears to be an open and lifelong battle between one's better self, the Yetzer Tov, which desires only goodness and positivity, and the Yetzer haRa, which desires self-indulgences, meaningless material gain and power over others. It is as if we have 'twins' within us who struggle with each other: our noble 'Yaakov' self and our debased, egoic 'Eisav' self. Sometimes our better side wins and other times we succumb and our lower self takes over.

On an even subtler level, there is a battle between our conscious and subconscious self. Rebbe Yisrael Salanter, the founder of the modern *Musar* / ethical movement, calls the conscious self the 'bright', clear side and the deeper conscious self the 'dark' side.

Subconscious layers of self can be viewed, and correctly so, as the composite of our deep-seated 'memories' of every stimulus and impression we have imbibed. Every image we have seen, every sound we have heard, every smell, sensation, and even every thought and cognitive association that we have entertained, is imprinted, albeit unconsciously, on the deepest parts of our brain. This can be viewed as our deeper, more primitive, wild, primordial, 'reptilian' level of the brain and self, much like the sand and gravel or 'dirt' underneath the fertile, cultivated soil of our consciousness (It should be pointed out in passing that deeper than this layer of sand and gravel and 'dirt' is a limitless mine of gems, the true depths of being, our soul).

The Azazel, the "wild goat," is sent into the sand and gravel of the wild desert, the 'dirty', uncultivated, uncivilized subconscious levels of self, where primitive, perverse and perhaps even diabolical forces lurk. This is the realm of the untamed, unrestrained ego. If one were lost in a desert and met a snake or a prowling wild animal, it would be a situation of 'kill or be killed'. Thirsty and dehydrated in a parched wilderness, the craving for a drop of water can lead to a deadly competition. The ego-self is the realm of survival instincts, deadly battles, cravings, and competition for dominance.

In this way, Azazel represents both the cosmic force of darkness and the microcosmic representation of that 'other side' within the individual person. The Mitzvah of sending the goat to the Azazel is a Tikkun on all levels, outer and inner.

AN ACT OF TOHU / CHAOS AND CONFUSION

The Torah tells us that the Azazel goat needs to be sent אל ארץ גזרה / "to an inaccessible region" (Vayikra, 16:22), yet the word גזרה / Gezeirah more literally means 'a decree'. What would it mean to send the goat to the region of 'decree'? Chazal ask,

גזירה שמא תאמר מעשה תהו הוא תלמוד לומר אני ה' גזרתיו ואין לך

רשות להרהר בהן / "What does the word Gezeira mean? Lest you say the procedure of the Azazel (appears to be) an act of תהו / *Tohu* / chaos and confusion, the Torah states (along with the commandment), 'I am Hashem.' In other words, "I, Hashem decreed (Gezeira) this act, and you shall not question it" (*Yuma*, 67b).

If we think that this ritual is a מעשה תהו / act of Tohu, a nonsensical and irrational, or even barbaric ritual, the Torah asks us to suspend judgment. Despite what it appears to be, HaKadosh Baruch Hu clearly decreed that we perform it. We need to realize that this seeming Tohu is actually the will of Hashem.

Clearly, the most obvious aspect of Tohu is how the Mitzvah is performed — the way the goat is thrown off a cliff. Even if it were just gently sending the goat into the deadly *Midbar* / desert, it would be a demonstration of Tohu. To subject any living being to a place of spirits and demonic forces seems cruel. Even if we accept that it is the will of Hashem, we still need to ask, how could the Source of Infinite Compassion command such a deed?

GOING TO THE MIDBAR / PLACE OF HEFKER / WILDERNESS AND OWNERLESSNESS

"And he shall send it away with the designated man to the *Midbar* / desert" (*Vaykira*, 16:21). A Midbar is a place of הפקר / *Hefker* / 'ownerless' wilderness (כל מי שאינו עושה עצמו כמדבר הפקר אינו יכול לקנות את החכמה והתורה: *Medrash Rabbah*, Bamidbar, 1:7). Similarly, a Midbar is called ארץ לא זרועה / "a land that is not sown" (*Yirmiyahu*, 2:2). A place out of the reach of human toil or interaction.

A desert is also a place of חורב שממה / destruction and desolation. It is called מקום החרבן / 'the place of destruction', and is connected to the zodiac sign of *Ma'adim* / Mars, associated with blood (מפני שהיו ישראל במדבר חורב שממה...וישראל היו במדבר במקום החרבן שהוא מחלק כוכב מאדים: *Rabbeinu Bachya,* Shemos, 32:4). Ma'adim is the sign connected with Eisav.

Speaking of the journey of Bnei Yisrael in the Desert, the prophet says, המוליך אתנו במדבר בארץ ערבה ושוחה בארץ ציה וצלמות בארץ לא־עבר בה איש ולא־ישב אדם שם / "Who led us through the wilderness, a land of deserts and pits, a land of drought and darkness, a land no man had traversed, where no human being had dwelt" (*ibid*, 2:6). The desert is a place of inhumane darkness, a place not suitable for human dwelling, nor conducive for civilization (*Berachos*, 31a).

There, in that place of Hefker, we need to push the goat off a cliff, an apparently uncivilized, 'inhumane' act. As the Akeidas Yitzchak writes (*Sha'ar*, 63), the person leads the goat into the desert in a *Minhag Hefker* / a custom of 'abandonment', which 'lacks in humanity'.

THROWING A RANDOM LOT

Even the way the goat was chosen for Azazel seems to be 'Hefker' in nature, meaning random and without intention or choice. Throwing a lottery and then picking up at 'random' the two pieces seems to be an act of allowing chaos and randomness to choose. A lottery is an 'unconscious' act (Although, of course, nothing is actually random, and this is clearly true with regards to 'lotteries' in Torah — בחיק יוטל את־הגורל ומ־ה׳ כל־משפטו / "Lots are cast into the lap (on Yom Kippur, *Medrash Rabbah*, Bereishis, 98:2), and the decision depends on Hashem": *Mishlei*, 16:33. וזה מפורסם מעניין הגורל בספורי דברי הנבואה וכבר. תעמוד על זה מהחוש כי למצליחים יבא על הרוב להם בגורל היותר טוב העובר. Ralbag, *ad loc*. על הגורל כעובר על עשרת הדברות / "One who denies the effectiveness and validity of the lottery is compared to one who denies the Ten Commandments": *Shu'T Chavas Yair*, Siman 61. *Sdei Chemed*, K'lalim, 3:14. See *Teshuvhas ha-Geonim*, HaK'tzaros, Siman 57. *Divrei Geonim*, Klal 20:1).

The entire Mitzvah of the Azazel goat seems to be a Mitzvah of Tohu, as it were, a 'chaotic', 'random', 'unconscious', 'Hefker' act, done with a symbol of demonic darkness, and in a place that is devoid of humanity. This is very unusual, since the entire objective of Torah is to live in a mindful, civil, humane and beneficial way, with Kavanah, intention and attention. The Mitzvah of Azazel is "the one against the other," a practice of 'conflict', and one that leans, apparently, towards the darker, more primitive and sinister side. Certainly, dipping deeper into the unconscious, the mysterious and hidden levels beyond normative consciousness.*

---

* The Radziner writes that on Yom Kippur we 'surrender' our free choice and give ourselves over totally to HaKadosh Baruch Hu. Thus, throwing a lottery shows that even in a place beyond our Da'as and choice, we are aligned with the ultimate will of HaKadosh Baruch Hu. In his words, כי בהפעולה של הגורל מראין ישראל שיש להם חיבור בהשורש ית׳ גם למעלה מתפיסת דעתם אף במקום עליון כזה שאינו כלל בהשגת הדעת... והטלת גורל מורה על שלילת הבחירה מהדעה כי גורל הוא בלי דעת האדם אכן מאחר שישראל מוסרים את כח בחירתם להשי״ת בדעתם וברצונם לכך מראה להם השי״ת שאפילו בהטלת הגורל שהוא בלי דעתם כוונו לעומק רצונו ית׳ שהוא למעלה מבחירת דעתם: *Sod Yesharim*, Erev Yom Kippur, p. 24–25.

Appropriately, the Mitzvah of Azazel, accompanied by Teshuvah, atones for both those transgressions that were violated intentionally and those done unintentionally or unknowingly.

THE INTERNAL BATTLE BETWEEN TOHU AND TIKKUN: WILDNESS / STRUCTURE, CHAOS / ORDER

There are parts of ourselves that are civilized, settled, and cultivated, intellectually aware and emotionally aligned. This is the self of Tikkun, of creativity, positive progress and making beneficial order. There are also more primitive parts of self, beneath the 'cultivated soil', that are more connected to the inner 'naughty child' and the world of chaos and *Yetzer haRa* / egoic drive, desolation, and unconsciousness.

Impulses and fantasies, hidden lustful desires and deep-seated angers may lurk in one's subconscious, certainly if one has never done any real inner *Avodah* / work. And if not transformed and directed into wholesome, holy outlets, or if they are simply left unchecked and unguided — these primitive impulses can pop up and compel one to act in ways completely inconsistent with who he thinks he is on a conscious level.

Much Teshuvah is in replacing the bad with the good in action, speech and thought. Instead of doing negative actions, one does positive actions, instead of hurtful speech, beneficial speech, instead of unholy thoughts, holy thoughts. As desirable as these are, they are not actually *Teshuvah Sheleimah* / complete and whole Teshuvah, as they only address the conscious self. Teshuvah Sheleimah demands a total transformation of both our conscious and unconscious levels of being.

The *Ohr* / Light of Yom Kippur demands from us — and gives us the necessary strength and wisdom — to uncover and properly deal with the deepest recesses of our psyche; the good, the bad, the messy, and even the ugly.

A TIME OF TRUTH & THE IMP OF THE PERVERSE

Yom Kippur is a day when the *Emes* / truth of who we are is revealed. It allows us to deal truthfully, honestly, openly, and vulnerably with the deeper recesses of our unconscious mind. Those who have never delved into the *Avodah* / work of healing and purifying their spiritual, mental, and emotional worlds can be unsettled or even frightened when they look inside and discover what is there.

Sadly, often, faced with the 'dirty' truth of how they are manifesting their lives, an individual can fall into despair and give up. The task of honest Teshuvah seems too disturbing. Life becomes overwhelming when we begin to think about it. An inner voice whispers, 'Just let go, throw your life down the mountain; run into the wild and jump off a cliff.'

There seems to be a deep-seated 'imp of the perverse' sub-personality within people, almost like a little demon, driving them to do wrong simply because they can do it. Even worse, one can be paradoxically driven to *Mafkir Chayav* / to make one's own life *Hefker* / ownerless, and even *Chas v'Shalom* / Heaven forbid, hurt oneself.

While doing a *Cheshbon haNefesh* / soul-examination, thinking about one's life and how it is unfolding, some people may admit that there is some righteousness and goodness in their life; they observe Mitzvos, are kind to others and rightfully feel good about this. And yet, on closer examination, they may also perceive that there is still much ugliness and pettiness in their psyche; they see they are still involved with angers, lusts, and laziness. Their inner 'animal self' is still very much alive and robust, and they see that they can easily revert to self-centered transgressions, even after a very uplifting spiritual experience such as the High Holy Days of Tishrei.

This can cause a person to feel devastated and dispirited. They may think, 'After all the Avodah and inner work that I have done, I still cannot even *Daven* / pray a full service without intruding thoughts or negative thoughts,' or 'I can't seem to overcome my interpersonal conflicts,' or I'm still completely ruled by my desires.'

Such moments of honesty can compel an individual to simply say, 'This is going nowhere; I give up.' They may eventually reach the point where they consider throwing their life down a proverbial mountain. One could feel completely convinced that the only happiness and relief they can find is in running wild, trying to live in an uncivilized or inhumane realm, and figuratively jumping off a cliff: 'Let me go with my 'inner goat',

my dark side, and break away from society and the world of order, responsibility and mindfulness — because look how little
that has done for me. I will just act as I wish and let my lower
desires guide me.'

YIUSH / TO GIVE UP

The truth is, this urge to act 'freely', beyond all norms, wild
and untamed, may not be an act of *Perikas Ol* / throwing off the
Yoke of Heaven. For example, when we see a teenager slipping
from the ways of Torah, we might assume it is because they are
ruled by their animal self and reject *Kabbalas Ol* / acceptance of
the Yoke of Heaven. In truth, the urge to be wild and free can
be a sign of a struggle against depression.

As mentioned earlier, the holy Kotzker Rebbe once said,
"Most people think sinners sin because of their lack of acceptance of the Yoke of Heaven, when in truth they are simply
depressed."

Yi'ush / giving up is letting go of fighting for what matters.
When one gives up resisting what needs to be resisted and
allows the 'desert' of depression or the animal self to take over,
there is a death of sorts. There is a deadening of the will, a ceas-
ing to progress. The Torah says, "I set before you life and death;
choose life." The only viable choice is to choose life; choosing
to live consciously, mindfully, and progressively. When we let
go of choice, when we choose not to choose, we find ourselves
in the uninhabitable wilderness of Yi'ush and 'death'.*

---

* On one level, the reason a person has Yi'ush is that first he thinks he can

THROWING A BONE TO TOHU: SUBJUGATION & ELEVATION

On Yom Kippur, the day of truth, we need to reveal to ourselves the truth of where we currently stand. We reveal both our light and our dark side. On Yom Kippur, we need to acknowledge that a lower voice still exists within us. We celebrate the higher self that is light, whole, holy, orderly, the 'right hand' path of Chesed, that which is "To Hashem." We do have within us what to 'offer' to Hashem consciously and directly.

---

control 'everything', and when he realizes he cannot do this, he gives up and says he cannot control 'anything'. It seems like an either/or choice. The 'weekday' is when we may attempt to control our surroundings, while on Shabbos — or Yom Kippur, which is the 'Shabbos of Shabbos" — we let go of controlling anything in our surroundings. The ritual of the Sa'ir haMishtaleach is saying that if, on the Shabbos of Shabbos, you are still dealing with a suppressed dark side, take it away, take it to the wilderness and let it fall off the mountain. The Sa'ir haMishtaleach brings atonement for all negative actions so long as the people did Teshuvah (*Hilchos Teshuvah*, 1:2). This is because the root of all sin is really spiritual Yi'ush, as in, 'Do my actions really matter? Who cares what I do? Everything is random, and nothing really matters.' We need to throw away this way of thinking.

Sometimes life does, in fact, seem like a random lottery without rhyme or reason. We may be tempted to give up and feel we cannot control anything, and that, G-d forbid, there is no control in life at all: "There is no judge and no judgment." Yet, when Klal Yisrael is doing the will of the Creator, when we are collectively aligned with our purpose, then even the lottery shows itself to be Divinely guided. Our sages say there was a miracle with the lottery when Israel was doing the will of the Creator and that the words "To Hashem" always came up appropriately in the right hand of the Cohen Gadol (*Yuma*, 39a). In other words, when Teshuvah is complete, we realize that nothing is random, there is no reason for Yi'ush, and Hashem is always guiding our personal and collective history.

And there is also within us a lower, chaotic, destructive side, the 'left hand', indirect path of Gevurah, our inner 'scapegoat'.

When he was young, the famous *Mashpia* / spiritual mentor, Reb Nisan Neminov, once asked his Mashpia — my great grandfather, the legendary and extraordinary *Oved Hashem* / servant of Hashem, Reb Zalman Moshe haYitzchoki, זצ״ל, why he smoked. This was in the early 1900s when people were not yet aware of the physical harms of smoking. "Does smoking seem to be giving into one's *Taavos* / desires of the body?" Reb Zalman Moshe responded, "Sometimes you need to throw the dog a bone so it will stop barking."

'Sending our inner scapegoat to Azazel' is a bribe, as it were, given to the Samech-Mem, which is also the Angel of Death and our own Yetzer haRa: הוא שטן הוא יצר הרע הוא מלאך המות / "The Satan, the Yetzer haRa and the Angel of Death are one" (*Baba Basra*, 16a. כי המזיקים הם שעירים והם היצר הרע: *Yaaros Devash*, Derush 6, 11). The metaphor used by Chazal is of throwing a bone to the lower self, the Eisav within, to distract it and satisfy it. By owning and sending away our inner Tohu, it becomes busy with itself and then self-destructs in its own desert of emptiness. Alternatively, it is giving our dark side an outlet and, in fact, giving it some form of 'nourishment'.

In the spiritual, mental, emotional Avodah of 'inner wild goat', there are thus two levels: 1) Acknowledging and subjugating the Yetzer haRa in a way that ultimately leads it to its own self-destruction, and 2) Nourishing the Yetzer haRa in such a way that elevates and transforms it into good.*

LEVEL ONE: ACKNOWLEDGMENT OF THE YETZER HARA LEADING TO ITS DESTRUCTION

On the first level, Yom Kippur is a time of ultimate truth and honesty. Inwardly, this means it is a day to acknowledge one's 'dark side', one's barbarism, darkness, depression and untamed lust and anger; one's Yetzer haRa. Normally, a person prefers to sweep these darker parts of self and their attached struggles under the rug. On Yom Kippur, we do a meticulous self-inventory. While we acknowledge our strengths, we also need to acknowledge and accept our lowliness and dark rebel-

---

* Ultimately, the Samech-Mem itself can be transformed. The Toldos Yaakov Yoseph teaches that the negativity of the Samech-Mem, spelled in full, is סמא"ל / Sam-E'l, can be 'sweetened' or transformed by the power of the Divine name סא"ל / Sa'al, one of the 72 three-letter Names of Hashem. See also Rebbe Moshe Dovid Valle, Sefer haLikutim 21. When we meditate on Sa'al, it can help us overcome the darkness of Kelipah, open the closed letters of Samech and Mem, and liberate the sparks of purity that were swallowed up and trapped within them: Toldos Yaakov Yoseph, Parshas Vayakhel. The name Sa'al is the 45th Name in the 72 Names sequence. These 72 Names are derived from the words, Vayisa Yisrael haLaila…, "Yisrael traveled by night…" (Shemos, 14:19-20), implying that they have the power to override and transform darkness by revealing the light within. The first, last, and first letter from each verse forms a name. These letters are to be pronounced or visualized with their natural vowels — Aleph with a Kamatz, Beis with a Tzeirei, and so forth. סא"ל is also numerically 91, the Yichud between the Name of Hashem (26) and the Name Ado-noi (65) = 91. This Yichud represents the integration of the Higher Reality where there is only Light, and the lower reality where darkness is possible.

liousness, our inner scapegoat. We submit to the fact that we have this quality; we grab it by its horns, as it were, take it out into the dark, wild desert, and push it off a cliff.

Genuine Teshuvah demands that we acknowledge our entire self. If we do not acknowledge the Sa'ir, the Eisav within us, its lurking subconscious darkness will burst forth and hurt us. What is swept under the rug and not dealt with will eventually resurface and manifest with vengence and even violence (Hence, precisely on Yom Kippur, the holiest day of the year, the Yetzer haRa can be most pronounced — אמר ליה אליהו לרב יהודה אחוה דרב סלא חסידא, אמריתו: / "Eliyahu אמאי לא אתי משיח והא האידנא יומא דכיפורי הוא ואבעול כמה בתולתא בנהרדעא the Prophet said to Rav Yehudah…You have wondered why the Moshiach has not arrived. Why? Is it so surprising? Isn't today Yom Kippur, and yet relations were had with several virgins in Nehardea": *Yuma*, 19b).

On Yom Kippur, we submit to the fact that we, in some ways, are still on the level of *Chelbenah* / galbanum, the foul-smelling herb in the *Ketores* / incense offered in the Beis haMikdash. Generally, a person may temporarily sweep his 'imp of the perverse' under the rug, but on Yom Kippur, one needs to hold it, name it, and then throw it away and observe its destruction.

This, then, is what the Medrash, Zohar and Ramban mean regarding appeasing the darker side on Yom Kippur. If we do not acknowledge this part of ourselves on this day and let it be self-satisfied and self-consumed, it will surface in the future and cause much greater havoc. If we do not do this on Yom Kippur, our Teshuvah will not be *Shaleim* / complete.

LEVEL TWO: ACKNOWLEDGMENT OF THE YETZER HARA LEADING TO ITS TRANSFORMATION

On level two, acknowledging the negativity within and throwing it away leads to its redemption and transformation.

As room is opened for the hidden, unconscious parts of self to become revealed within the positive and holy context of this day, we honor and give voice to our wild and untamed side of self. We embrace any Yi'ush or desire to avoid the divine nobility of our *Tzuras Adam* / human form. We acknowledge any yearning to give up the fight, surrender to the animal soul within, and live freely without responsibility. Even deeper, we give this part of us an outlet of expression within a context of Kedushah and by means of a Mitzvah. We affirm that there is room for this Yetzer within a certain holy context. This elevates the good within it.

Although on the surface the Mitzvah of sending this negativity off into a wasteland may look superstitious and barbaric, this is how *Din* / harsh judgment and the inner adversary is mitigated. We give this Tohu side of self a small, controlled outlet, a minor appeasement, and as a result, our Yetzer does not bother us. Once this has been achieved, its negativity can even become sweetened and changed into an expression of positivity.

THE MIDDLE PATH OF APPEASEMENT: DISTRACTION

In the depiction of the Zohar above, a shepherd takes an old sheep and throws it to the wolf so that he can carry all his other sheep to the other side of the river. This appeases the wolf and distracts it as a first step in a wider strategy. At this point, one is neither 'destroying' the wolf nor 'transforming' the wolf.

Within ourselves, the body and its natural desires and urges for food, procreating, expansion, protection, and so forth are connected to the world of Tohu, raw energy. Our mind and soul are connected to the more civilized, orderly, tender world of Tikkun.

Our bodies have needs, and so do our mind and spirit, and sometimes these two seem to clash. For example, in your mind and soul, you want to *Daven* / pray with focus, but your body is hungry, and it keeps pulling your attention from the prayer toward the desire for food. Or, say you would like to get up early in the morning to study Torah, but your body is exhausted, and you feel you cannot get out of bed. Even if you manage to overpower the body and get out of bed, the body will continue to vie for attention, distracting you from learning. The stress of this conflict will make it even harder to get up the next morning. What can be done?

Here, 'appeasement' is needed, meaning to distract the body with some satisfaction or reward. For instance, you could 'offer' your body a delicious, stimulating cup of coffee when you wake up early. Your body may respond by getting out of bed; it knows that some satisfaction lies ahead, so it may not put the brakes on what you truly want to do. Even if your body is getting up for the delicious coffee, your mind and soul will be allowed to learn, and 'everyone' is happy.

This is one reason that Chasidim drink alcohol, in an appropriate amount, setting, and time. The soul wishes to join a late-night *Farbrengen* / 'gathering' conducive to spiritual breakthroughs, contemplate wisdom, and dance and sing before HaKadosh Baruch Hu — but the body wants to go to bed or to a type of gathering that is less elevating. By offering the body a little to drink when it joins the Farbrengen, it accepts the effort of staying up and attending the gathering. This small 'sacrifice' to the cravings of the animal soul pays off, especially when the Yetzer haRa is subdued and nullified in the holy atmosphere of the Farbrengen.

THE BAAL SHEM TOV ON DISTRACTION

In order to advance beyond our limits in any discipline, certainly in spiritual disciplines, we need הסכמת האיברים / 'the consent of our limbs'. We need the permission of our body in order to ensure that it will not distract us (although the 'self' includes the body, heart, mind and soul; there is no intention to suggest an actual split between any of these aspects). Without this consent, as the Baal Shem Tov teaches, sometimes a person wants to Daven with passion and fervor, and his mind, heart, and spirit are on board, yet, in the end, he cannot get himself to Daven deeply because "his limbs are heavy" (*Amud haTefillah*, 66. *Ohr Torah*, Ekev).

Here is another powerful teaching from the holy Baal Shem Tov on the subject (*Baal Shem Tov*, Bereishis, 165:1. *Toldos Yaakov Yoseph*, Chukas):

"My master, the Baal Shem Tov, explained that when a person does good and there is no negativity (within the goodness he is doing), the Yetzer haRa taunts him. This is not so when the Yetzer haRa sees that there is a mixture of good and bad in the deed; then the Yetzer lets him go. But then the deed is already done (without the obstruction of the Yetzer), and afterward, the person can (freely) act *l'Sheim Shamayim* / for the sake of Heaven alone. This is as our sages say (*Avodah Zarah*, 70a), 'Yisrael are thieves....' Why? Because one needs to 'steal' the Da'as (and deceive) the Yetzer haRa in every performance of a Mitzvah, as it says (*Tehillim*, 119:59), 'I have calculated my ways and returned my feet to Your statutes.' This means that in every Mitzvah or act of *Kedushah* / holiness, one (usually, at least subtly) calculates *his* ways — *his* benefit in doing it, which is materialism (subtle negativity). But then afterward, "I return *Raglai* / my feet to Your statutes." *Regel* / foot alludes to *Hergel* / habit, for even though one is habituated to act *not* purely l'Sheim Shamayim (and he does so), one can then turn around and act l'Sheim Shamayim (thereby deceiving the Yetzer haRa *twice*). And this is (*Tehillim*, 119:62) 'In the middle of the night I arise,' i.e., from my desire for personal benefit. For it is not easy to *immediately* wake up (from the spiritual slumber of attachment to personal benefit) and act l'Sheim Shamayim. But in the middle of the 'night', when I wake up to take care of *my* natural needs, I can at that time overpower nature — *within* natural matters and in the middle of natural sleep...."

Similarly, in general, it is not possible to have Tov without a small element of Ra. For example, if a person tries to Daven with fervor and it is purely for HaKadosh Baruch Hu, still, afterward, he will think, 'I Davenned well!' Even if he does his 'good deed' in private, with nobody seeing him, he will still be seeing himself and detract slightly from the goodness with pride. There will always be some small point of self-centeredness in an attempt to achieve holiness. If you really want to do a Mitzvah *Lishmah* / for the sake of Heaven, you should acknowledge the Yetzer haRa in a way that 'feeds' it. In other words, you should give it a part of your Avodah — at least once a year on Yom Kippur.

The raw energy of physicality does not actually want you to sin; it wants to feel alive. It wants to dance and display *Katnus* / spiritual 'smallness'. If we simply suppress or bypass our Katnus and attempt to enter directly into *Gadlus* / spiritual expansiveness, Katnus will eventually come back to negatively influence our consciousness and behavior.

Say you propose to add to your daily Avodah by reciting an extra portion of Tehillim after each Shacharis. You might feel some Katnus and resistance coming from your animal self; it just wants to relax and chat with people at that point in the day. 'What am I going to get from reciting Tehillim?' it asks. 'Am I at least going to feel good, maybe get a spiritual high, maybe there's some reward?' The way to add to your Avodah is to let the animal self be involved; perhaps sing the verses quietly if that brings elated feelings. Perhaps reward your 'animal body' with a piece of cake after the Tehillim. If we do not acknowledge the Sa'ir, the raw energy of the body and include it before letting it go, it will continue to complain and distract us from our Avodah. By throwing the ego a bone, we pull the rug out from under it. It accepts the small 'profit', loses interest in resisting, and departs.

On Yom Kippur, the day that we are most true to ourselves, we acknowledge that we have done a couple of wild, 'stupid' things in our lives; we stand there and feel it. 'Holding onto' the goat in this way is not meant to suppress it or punish it or make it feel uncomfortable; it is to give it attention there in the light of the Beis haMikdash, the light of our higher self. After a little while, it simply leaves and disappears into the empty abyss. By feeding the 'inner beast' in a holy way, giving it some of the attention that it craves, it is nourished, and then it leaves us alone, retreating into the empty wilderness.

This is the deeper meaning of the teaching in Chazal that לעולם יעסוק אדם בתורה ובמצוה אפילו שלא לשמה, שמתוך שלא לשמה בא לשמה / "A man should always occupy himself with Torah and good deeds even if not *Lishmah* (with the intention to connect with Hashem or to grow), for doing so will (eventually, at least) lead to doing them for their own sake" (*Pesachim*, 50b). The word לעולם / "always," seems to suggest that this is the way a person should always serve Hashem — and yet the first part of the sentence is about service that is שלא לשמה / 'not for the sake of Heaven'. Why should we "always" serve Hashem even when it is "not" actually for Hashem? It is because if we do not feed the body what it needs, it will distract us and not allow us to focus and what we wish to focus on. If we are learning Torah, it will not allow us to have true Kavanah. Thus when we are serving Hashem, we "always" need to include what is "not (directly) for the sake of Heaven," for this too is ultimately "for the sake of Heaven."

SEEMINGLY GIVING INTO THE BODY ON THE WAY TO THE AZAZEL

A similar idea is expressed in a teaching by our sages regarding the sending of the goat into the wild.

The individual who was dedicated to take the goat to the cliff was fasting while walking in the dry heat of the desert in Tishrei. He would become thirsty. Chazal tell us that on his way through the desert to perform the Azazel ritual, booths with shade, water and some provisions were prepared for him to stop, take some shade, a drink and a bite of food. At every booth, those waiting for him in the booth would say to him, הרי מזון והרי מים תנא מעולם לא הוצרך אדם לכך אלא שאינו דומה מי שיש לו פת בסלו למי שאין לו פת בסלו / "'Here is food, here is water if you need it.' It was taught that no man who escorted the goat ever needed this food and water. However, they would offer it to him anyway because one who has bread in his basket is not similar to one who does not have bread in his basket" (Yuma, 67b).

In other words, when a person is fasting, the body fights for food and drink, and this can be very distracting to the Avodah of Yom Kippur. Yet, the mere fact that the body knows that it *could* drink, if necessary, strengthens it. This is without actually 'feeding the beast', as it were, rather merely letting it know that it could have what it wants. Then the body stops fighting with the mind to give it food and drink and becomes a vehicle for the Avodah.

Here is how the *Talmud Yerushalmi* describes this dynamic: אומר לו הרי הרי מזון והרי מים לייפות את כוחו למה שאין יצר הרע תאב אלא דבר שהוא אסור לו כהדא רבי מנא סלק למבקרה לרבי חגיי דהוה תשיש א"ל צחינא אמר ליה שתה שבקיה ונחת ליה בתר שעה סלק לגביה אמר ליה מה עבדת ההיא צחיותך א"ל כד שרית לי אזלת לה / "At each booth, a person calls to him, 'Here is food, here is water,' in order to strengthen him. Why? The *Yetzer haRa* / the egoic evil inclination desires only what is forbidden to him.[*] As the following: On Yom Kippur, Rebbe Mana went to visit Rebbe Chaggai, who was weak. Rebbe Chaggai told Rebbe Mana, "I'm thirsty." "So, drink!" responded Rebbe Mana, giving him permission to drink on Yom Kippur due to his illness. Rebbe Mana left, and after some time, he came back to visit him. 'How is your thirst?' he asked. Rebbe Chaggai told him, 'The moment you permitted me to drink, my thirst went away!'" (*Yuma*, 6:4)

This is a deep psychological insight, if someone tells himself he must fast, an inner rebellion is triggered, and it makes him think about nothing but food. What one resists persists. The moment he stops resisting and tells himself that he can eat or

---

[*] Note Tosefos regarding the present exploration — נראה — גדול המצווה ועושה דהיינו טעמא דמי שמצווה ועושה עדיף לפי שדואג ומצטער יותר פן יעבור ממי שאין מצווה שיש לו פת בסלו שאם ירצה יניח: Tosefos, *Kiddushin*, 31a.

drink if he needs to, the hunger subsides, and the fast becomes easier. This is a subtle form of 'feeding' the Samech-Mem, the body or Tohu — or actually 'tricking' it, so to speak.

Similarly, you can distract your body by suggesting that it will get what it craves later, in another few minutes. For example, if you are in the middle of Davening and suddenly a hunger for food comes up (and food can be a metaphor for any other bodily desires), instead of pushing it away, say, 'I hear your need, I will take care of you in a few moments, just allow me now to focus on my Davening.' Or, perhaps even affirm that you *could* stop and have one of your favorite foods right now, but it will be more enjoyable to eat in a relaxed manner when your Davening is over. This is a way to 'nourish' the instinctual energy of the body and its urges without actually surrendering to it. In all likelihood, once the Davening is over, the insistence of the animal self will have subsided because it mainly just wanted your attention and care, and this was already provided.

BEFORE AND AFTER THIRTY-THREE

'Before the age of 33' and 'after the age of 33' represent two approaches to becoming free from the negativity of the Yetzer haRa: a) subjugation and destruction, and b) elevation and transformation.

Generally speaking, the age of 33 is seen as an age of transition, an age that studies suggest, and many people claim, to be their happiest. Around this time, one is transitioning from 'youth' or 'young adulthood' into their midlife. There is something unique about this year, as also evidenced in the teachings of Chazal:

א"ל ההוא מינא לר' חנינא מי שמיע לך בלעם בר כמה הוה א"ל מיכתב לא כתיב אלא מדכתיב אנשי דמים ומרמה לא יחצו ימיהם בר תלתין ותלת שנין או בר תלתין וארבע א"ל שפיר קאמרת לדידי חזי לי פנקסיה דבלעם והוה כתיב ביה בר תלתין ותלת שנין בלעם חגירא כד קטיל יתיה פנחס ליסטאה / "A certain heretic said to Rav Chanina: 'Have you heard how old Bilam / Balaam was when he died?' Rav Chanina said to him: 'It is not written explicitly in the Torah. But from the fact that it is written: "Bloody and deceitful men shall not live half their days" (*Tehillim*, 55:24), this indicates that he was 32 or 34 years old, less than half the standard 70-year lifespan.' The heretic said to him: 'You have spoken well, I myself saw *The Notebook of Bilam* and it was written therein: 'Bilam the Lame was 32 years old when Pinchas the highwayman killed him'" (*Sanhedrin*, 106b).

Bilam is a man of 'blood and deceit', a man of lechery. He even sleeps with his donkey (*Avodah Zarah*, 4b), and brews diabolical schemes to cause the downfall of Klal Yisrael by tempting them to licentious behavior. Appropriately, when Bilam was asked what his punishment was in the afterlife, he responded that he was being 'cooked' in boiling semen (אמר ליה דיניה דההוא גברא במאי אמר ליה בשכבת זרע רותחת: *Gittin*, 57a).

Through the teachings of Chazal, the above statement from the obscure *Notebook of Bilam*, and later, the writings of the holy Arizal, we know that the name 'Bilam' is a code name for many different people. Through *Gilgulim* / reincarnation and other associations allusions, 'Bilam' refers to many dubious characters in history, such as Lavan and others. And up until the age of 33, each of those characters was filled with 'blood, deceit, and lechery', at which point they promptly died or were killed (see *Ben Yehoyadah*, Sanhedrin, ibid. See also, *Sanhedrin*, 107b, and *Sotah*, 47a: "She has narrow eyes").

To make these ideas relevant to our own lives, we can contemplate the nature of our own first 32 years of life and the youthful energy and immaturity that still clings to us when we are older than that. The age of 33 represents our turning point and decision to commit to Avodas Hashem and 'kill' or put an end to any 'blood, deceit, and lechery' or active negativity and selfishness lurking within us. Just as a young person must, at some point in the maturing process, acknowledge, subdue and discard his Tohu, his raw, egoic, physical energy, we need to *periodically* acknowledge and subdue our Tohu. The more one feeds self-centered urges, the more 'hungry' they become (משביעו רעב: *Sukkah*, 52b). Each year, Yom Kippur gives us an opportunity to confess how these urges are still running in the background of our system — no matter our age — and cast them into the abyss.

At some point in 'growing up', a transition needs to occur; maturity needs to set in, and mindfulness needs to dominate. G-d willing, sooner rather than later, one needs to become more detached and objective about his sensations and urges and develop the strength not to follow every impulse that arises. At this point, when maturity has been firmly established, the energy of one's 'wild side', inner chaos, and physical cravings can and should be harnessed and integrated into a context of holiness and wholesomeness. Even the more base human instincts and desires can be elevated, channeled away from harm toward beneficial purposes, and given higher, holy outlets.[*]

Elevating our Tohu is only applicable and viable after a literal or metaphorical transition from youth to maturity. Only once we have the spiritual acumen and mental and emotional stability can we safely transfer the raw energy of Tohu into *Kedushah* / holiness and Avodas Hashem. Without real maturity, there is a worry that the individual will become *Farchapped* / lured in, sucked into the world of *Kelipah* / negativity, and swallowed up within the *Kochos haTumah* / the forces of impurity. One could become reinvolved in the ways of 'blood, lust, and deceit' and other forms of depravity, Chas v'Shalom.

---

[*] Note the teaching of Yalta: כל דאסר לן רחמנא שרא לן כוותיה / "Any item that the Merciful One prohibited to us, He permitted to us a similar item": *Chulin*, 109b. Perhaps a similar idea is expressed, the allowance for an outlet, in the Mitzvah of sending away the mother bird. The Gra writes, ומצות שילוח הקן הוא אכזריות גדולה / "The Mitzvah of *Shiluach haKan* is an incredibly cruel commandment": *Pirush haGra*, Mishlei, 30:17. He repeats the idea in several places. In fact, there are many earlier sources for this idea as well. Yet, clearly, here the point is that we should feel sickened and horrified so that our *Rachmanus* / compassion is aroused, and this arouses Rachmanus from on High — דאמר קב"ה חס על דא לא לא אמר ולא כלום. מאן דחס שבק אימא ובנהא ואזיל ליה. ומה דאימא מתרכא מן הקן דילה מה היא אומרת אוי שהחרבתי את ביתי ושרפתי את היכלי והגליתי בני לבין האומות ועל דא ירחם הקב"ה דהא רחמנא לא אשתכח אלא הכי: *Zohar Chadash*, Ruth, 29a–b. See also, *Tikkunei Zohar*, 23a. *Ya'aros Devash* 2, Derush 6. *Imrei Noam*, Berachos, 33b. Thus, even if one does not need the chicks or the eggs, there is still a Mitzvah to send away the mother: *Shu'T Chavas Yair*, Siman 67. See, however, *Shu'T Chasam Sofer*, Orach Chayim, Siman 100, who strongly disagrees.

Everything created by HaKadosh Baruch Hu has its appropriate place: אין לך דבר שאין לו מקום / "There is nothing that does not have its *Makom* / space" (*Avos*, 4:3). Everything has its 'place', and כל מה שברא הקדוש ברוך הוא בעולמו, לא בראו אלא לכבודו / "Everything that HaKadosh Baruch Hu created in His world, He created for His Honor" (*ibid*, 6:11). Even the wild, uncivilized energies in the world and within our own psyche, can be expressed in a way that gives Kavod to Hashem.

Hashem is the יוצר אור ובורא חשך / *Yotzer Ohr u'Vorei Choshech* / "the One Who forms light and creates darkness" (*Yeshayahu*, 45:7). Just as Hashem created the place of civility, order and Da'as, Hashem also created the desert, the darkness called *Alma d'Charuvah* / 'the World of Destruction'. There, the *K'vod Hashem* / glory of Hashem is not observable to the untrained or unstable eye, as its powerful, disorderly forces can seem to eclipse its light. Similarly, we might not even fathom how the Glory of Hashem could ever arise from the great undisciplined powers within the human soul.

These powerful forces from the World of Destruction, rooted in the World of Tohu, fuel all negative desires such as lust and anger, which apparently obscure the Infinite Light of Hashem. When a person, however, does full Teshuvah and observes the K'vod Hashem hidden within his own soul, he will then be able to harness these powers from upon a base of spiritual maturity 'beyond the age of 33'. He will be able to draw vigor and vitality from them in order to serve Hashem. He will then know experientially and viscerally that Hashem alone is the Source of both Ohr and Choshech, that עשה שלום ובורא רע; אני ה' עשה כל-אלה / "I create Shalom and (the appearance of) negativity; I, Hashem, create *all* of these" (*Yeshayahu*, ibid).

Both the 'goat of Light' and the 'goat of darkness' need to be brought to the Beis haMikdash, and placed "in front of Hashem." There is a place for both of them, although the Avodah performed with the 'goat of darkness' will soon proceed with its removal from the Beis haMikdash and from the civilized world. This Mitzvah needs to be completed 'outside' the Makom set aside for expressions of Kedushah. There is room for *Vildkeit* / wildness and even *Shetus d'Kedushah* / holy folly — just where and how these qualities are to be expressed needs subtle attention and mature wisdom.

Having both goats stand in the Beis haMikdash represents an open acknowledgment and 'confession' of the existence of these opposite qualities in us. It also represents a waiting period in which we assess whether we can currently bring the 'dark side' into our service 'within the borders' of the inner 'Beis haMikdash' or not. When the lottery is cast, and we realize we cannot elevate both 'goats' directly, we must do another type of Mitzvah, one that is done outside the normal borders of Kedushah, as it were. For example, we might leave the holy atmosphere of the *Beis Medrash* / Torah study hall and ride in funny-looking trucks with blaring lights through a 'wasteland' of materialism on Fifth Avenue, announcing loudly that Tefillin is available to be put on. In this way, we can harness and utilize that 'loud', unconventional, uncontainable, youthful brazenness for Kedushah.

LIGHT FROM DARKNESS

The Arizal teaches (*Likutei Torah*, Arizal, Parshas Acharei) a *Sod* / secret of the Azazel. Azazel means the *Ez-Azel* / "the goat that goes"; it is the back side of Kedushah that "goes" down to the 'hell realm' of the Samech-Mem. When it is sent into the desert, it descends to a spiritual world called *Metzulos Yam* / Depths of the Sea, and all the way down to the *Tzal-Maves* / Shadow of Death. Anything that has *Chayus* / life is connected to unification and Kedushah, whereas Maves is separation and Tumah. And yet, the term *Tzal-Maves*, teaches that there are two levels of *Kelipah* / endarkening 'shell' or obstruction of light: *Tzeil* / shadow and *Maves* / death.

A superficial layer of Kelipah is called *Tzeil* because it obstructs the Light of Life like a shadow or a silhouette. This is also called *Kelipas Nogah* / 'a glowing shell'; an obstruction or partial obstruction of light which nonetheless emits or admits some light. The deepest level of Kelipah is called *Maves* / 'death', or a humanly irreversible obstruction. If a person is in a psychological or spiritual state of Tzeil, feeling and acting like a silhouette of their humanity, they may seem 'unreal' or disembodied — but they can be rescued, elevated and revived by finding points of light in them and magnifying these points. If a person is in the deeper state of Maves, they may be 'too far gone' for a human being to rescue them. Only the Creator Himself can revive the dead. On the other hand, the Creator's will is manifested through a correctly performed Mitzvah.

Kelipas Nogah is half *Tov* / good and half *Ra* / bad. Ever since Adam ate from the Tree of Knowing Tov v'Ra, these two forces are *M'urav* / mixed and tangled in the other. Thus, every good deed has an element of Ra or ego, and every sin also has a hidden element of Tov. If a person does something negative in a Kelipas Nogah situation, it becomes Ra. When a person does a Mitzvah that includes a Kelipas Nogah, the Ra can be converted into Tov. This contributes to the fixing of humanity's eating from the Tree of Knowledge of (the Mixture of) Good and Bad.

We stand the two goats in front of the Cohen Gadol (symbolizing Hashem's Oneness). Through the Mitzvah of the lottery, the Cohen Gadol enacts a sifting of the Tov from the Ra. There's an awareness of the separation of Tov and Ra with the revelation of what he has in his right and left hands, and the act of placing the lots on each goat and proclaiming "To Hashem" and "To Azazel." Then there is a full separation, and the Tov goes up to Hashem while the Ra goes down to Azazel.

A *Chidush* / novel insight of the Arizal is that the *Ez* / goat descends to that place of Tzal-Maves in order to transform the 'adversarial' force there into an 'advocate' by releasing the positive side within the Tzeil. This works because the Ez, too, is a *Klipas Nogah*. As above, we cannot elevate a *Kelipah Tameyah* / a completely impure Kelipah at all,* but a Kelipas Nogah can

---

* We cannot transform a Kelipah directly or through our own Avodah. For example, we cannot deliberately nullify and transform an unkosher food. We are not allowed to convert an unkosher broth into a kosher one by pouring into it 60 times its volume in kosher broth. Rather, *Bitul* / nullification of its prohibited status has to occur on its own. This is in some ways

be elevated under certain conditions, by extracting the positive from it. Inwardly, the Ez has two sides, a hidden side of light and positivity, and a revealed side of darkness and negativity. The light hidden in the Ez combines with the light hidden in the Tzeil of Tzal-Maves, and together these lights nullify the darkness of Maves. In this way, this service extracts the light and positivity from the Ez and the Tzal-Maves and reveals its Divine purpose.

When someone falls into sin, the side of Tumah is strengthened. In order to make Teshuvah and return to balance again, the bond of Kedushah that has been broken has to be even stronger and higher than before. The light that is extracted from the 'chemical reaction' of the Ez colliding with the Tzeil is a higher light, as in "the advantage of light that *comes from the darkness.*" This is the new, higher bond with Kedushah that we achieve on Yom Kippur.

THE UNITY OF DARKNESS & LIGHT

ויהי־ערב ויהי־בקר יום אחד / "And it was *Erev* / evening, and it was *Boker* / morning, *Yom Echad* / Day One" (*Bereishis*, 1:5). Why is it called 'Day One', and not 'the First Day', which would be the conventional way to list something in an ordinal series? Indeed, the Torah enumerates the rest of the days of Creation as the 'second day', the 'third day', and so on. Says, the Medrash,

similar to the service of the Sa'ir haMishtaleach, which we cannot perform of our own volition, as we only do it to fulfill Hashem's command, without our own intention or choice. This service also functions by means of a lottery, meaning that we are not choosing the goat which will be sent to 'Heaven' or to 'hell'; HaKadosh Baruch Hu is the one choosing.

Yom Echad / 'Day One' refers to Yom Kippur (יום אחד, שנתן לו הקדוש ברוך הוא, ואיזה זה, יום הכפורים: *Medrash Rabbah*, Bereishis, 2:3).

On the *Yom Echad* / Day of Oneness, the *Achas baShanah* / Oneness manifesting within time, we need to stand in front of HaKadosh Baruch Hu fully, and with the two sides of ourselves. We place our whole self in the holiness of this day — both the *Erev* / 'evening' part, our dark, unclear, unhealthy Tohu side, and the *Boker* / 'morning' part, our *Lichtike* / lit up, clear, *Tikkun* / orderly, whole side.

Yaakov is our *Boker* / 'enlightened'* traits, and Eisav is the *Erev* / 'endarkened' traits. To achieve at-one-ment, both 'goats', Yaakov and Eisav, stand before HaKadosh Baruch Hu, one to be offered on the *Har haBayis* / Temple Mount and one to be 'offered' in the 'netherworld'.

Yaakov becomes Yisrael / Israel when he is victorious over the angels of Eisav, but on a deeper level, this occurs when he is able to integrate and unify the positive, raw power of Tohu into his own life of Tikkun. It is fascinating that *The Zohar* teaches the confrontation between Yaakov and Eisav was finally resolved at the time of the Neilah Prayer, in the culmination of Yom Kippur (וישב ביום ההוא עשו לדרכו אימתי בשעת נעילה: *Zohar* 3, p. 101b).

---

* Yaakov is connected to the word בקר / *Boker* / day, as in אז יבקע כשחר אורך / "Then shall your light burst through like the dawn": *Yeshayahu*, 58:8. The word יבקע / 'burst through' has the same letters as יעקב / Yaakov. Eisav, by contrast, is connected to the night and darkness, as in the dark-colored *Sa'ir* / goat.

In this final twilight service of the Yom Echad, the *Yechidas haNefesh* / 'oneness of souls' is completely revealed.

In other words, Yaakov is victorious over his own inner 'spirit of Eisav' and is transformed into Yisrael, and this occurs soon after the offerings of the two goats symbolizing Yaakov and Eisav. And now, instead of Yaakov representing Daylight-consciousness alone, he becomes 'Yisrael'. The word ישראל / Yisrael equals 541, which is the sum of the words אור / *Ohr* (207) plus וחשך / *v'Choshech* (334). Klal Yisrael becomes a people that is able to integrate, in a wholesome way, both the side of light and the side of darkness.

As the day of Yom Kippur is unfolding, we stand in front of HaKadosh Baruch Hu with our whole self so that we can achieve total Teshuvah, total transformation, even the lowest parts of who we are. Maybe not every part of us is currently *Ra'ui* / fitting to be brought into the 'Beis haMikdash', but it too is an offering.

On the deepest level, the 'negative' forces that we 'appease' on Yom Kippur are not some external, objective agents of negativity, nor even substantial inner obstructions of the Infinite Light. For there are ultimately no forces or dynamics 'outside' of Hashem, but rather אין עוד מלבדו / *Ein Od Mil'vado* / "There is no existence other than Hashem" (*Devarim*, 4:35). The sending away of the 'dark side' within us is ultimately to integrate it in Divine Oneness.

When we are 'older than 33', having *Da'as* / acute awareness, stability and maturity, we can learn to give the dark side
an elevated outlet within 'Mitzvah'. Then a) this 'lower' dimension of ourselves does not disturb our 'higher' dimensions, and
this allows us to do our Avodas Hashem. And b) from a deeper
perspective, both dimensions can come together in a holistic
Avodas Hashem — the borderless Light of Tohu within the
Vessels of Kedushah.

And this is the 'secret' that is only revealed "when you reach
33."

PART THREE:

Customs & Tefilos/Prayers for Yom Kippur

Chapter One
ATTAINING THE FORGIVENESS OF OTHERS & FORGIVING

Y OM KIPPUR BRINGS ATONEMENT FOR ACTIONS OR NON-ACTIONS BETWEEN MAN AND HIS CREATOR, BUT NOT FOR OFFENSES THAT WERE PERPETRATED BE-TWEEN ONE HUMAN BEING AND ANOTHER. Every interpersonal violation against another human being is actually three: it is a transgression against the other, against oneself, and against the Creator. Forgiveness from others should be sought throughout the entire year. Erev Yom Kippur, however, is a time when atonement looms large, and it is customary to ask *Mechilah* / forgiveness from any person that one may have offended throughout the year.

Upon committing an offense against another human being, one must first ask for their forgiveness. Until forgiveness is granted, Teshuvah remains incomplete. For example, even if a thief returns what he had stolen, his Teshuvah is incomplete until he has been forgiven by the other or until he has made a sincere effort and requested forgiveness at least three times.[*]

If the aggrieved is reluctant to forgive after three sincere, humble requests, one should, in front of witnesses, ask another two times. After this, one should *not* continuously ask for forgiveness; rather, he should declare publicly that he has sincerely attempted to engender his forgiveness and move on.

In general, to refrain from forgiving someone who is asking

---

[*] *Baba Kama*, 60b. Rambam, *Hilchos Teshuvah*, 2:9: אינו נמחל לו לעולם עד שיתן לחברו מה שהוא חייב לו וירצהו. אף על פי שהחזיר לו ממון שהוא חייב לו צריך לרצותו ולשאל ממנו שימחל לו / "(However, sins between man and man; for example, someone who steals), he will never be forgiven until he gives his colleague what he owes him and appeases him. Even if a person restores the money that he owes [the person he wronged], he must appease him and ask him to forgive him." Although the Rambam also rules, אינו דומה מזיק חברו בגופו למזיק ממונו. שהמזיק ממון חברו כיון ששלם מה שהוא חייב לשלם נתכפר לו / "A person who damages a colleague's property cannot be compared to one who injures his physical person. When a person who damages a colleague's property pays him what he is obligated to pay him, he receives atonement": *Hilchos Chovel u'Mazik,* 5:9. This seems to suggest that just by returning the money or damage, he receives atonement. Yet, earlier, he ruled that he must appease him as well. The *Lechem Mishnah*, ibid, asks this question and offers an answer: וי"ל דשאני גזלן דנתהנה מאותה עבירה ועוד שציער הרבה לנגזל שלקח ממנו בעל כרחו אבל מזיק הממון שלא נתהנה מהיזק ההוא אלא שהזיק לו ולמזיק לא באה הנאה ממנו לא נצטער כל כך הניזק כמו הנגזל כיון ששלם לו היזקו די. Or perhaps, in terms of the laws of Teshuvah, Teshuvah is not complete without appeasement.

in sincerity is cruel, though in certain instances, as will be explained, it is justifiable. If we choose to go through life unforgiving and feeding our anger toward those who have hurt us, we end up carrying the negativity with us wherever we go, and we thereby place the power to choose and move forward in the very hands of the very person who has hurt us.

In Hebrew, the word *Simchah* / 'joy' contains the letters that spell the word *Machah* / 'erase'. We experience more joy when we let go of resentments and erase old grudges. First, we have to forget. Then, once negativity is erased, a healthy equilibrium can be restored, and we can endeavor to transform our inner state into joy.

Teshuvah completes our past, creates our future, and connects our consciousness to HaKadosh Baruch Hu in the Eternal Now. When a person steals, for example, Teshuvah includes returning the stolen objects. Making amends in this way helps him complete his past, and recontextualize it in a positive way. It also helps to create a better future and reestablish his lost connection and the 'stolen opportunity' of his connection with Hashem's Presence.

THE THREE PARTIES HURT

As mentioned, when one inflicts harm upon another human being, he is actually transgressing three different forms of connection to wholeness and genuine being: 1) he separates himself from the conscious awareness of HaKadosh Baruch Hu, 2) he places a false separation and barrier between himself and the other person, and 3) he internally separates himself from his own higher potential and true self. To fully experience forgiveness and the power of Teshuvah, this person needs to reestablish and repair all three of these ravaged connections.

FORGIVING ONESELF

Let us begin with the third category, repairing our relationship with ourselves. In order to be able to move on with our lives after doing the proper steps of Teshuvah — *Charatah* / remorse and *Kabbalah* / acceptance, as explored earlier — we need to stop condemning ourselves and cultivate a consciousness of forgiveness and unconditional positive self-regard. Only when we learn this is our Teshuvah complete and empowering. Forgiving ourselves is a crucial component in this process. Doing so helps us complete our past so that it does not invade and crowd out the infinite possibilities of the ever-unfolding present.

This state of Teshuvah gives us the freedom to be in the present without feeling imprisoned by the past. We feel forgiven and healed when we wholeheartedly surrender our foolish hope, our 'if only' daydream. The past is done and was meant to be. What we can do now is redeem our past through present actions and higher consciousness.

We need to attribute all that has transpired in the past to Divine Providence, but with regards to the present and future, everything should be seen as dependent upon our free will and our right to choose. This is a psychologically liberating and energizing perspective: let the past be, and at the same time, take up the responsibility of free choice for the present and future.

FORGIVING OTHERS, NOT FORGETTING

When on the receiving end of a negative act, we need to learn the art of forgiveness and letting go. If someone has wronged you, although the ramifications of their actions may still stimulate pain, once they have asked for your forgiveness, it is up to you whether to open up the channels of healing or not. Closing your heart and carrying a grudge can be quite exhausting and even worse than the original wound.

If you go through your life feeding your anger toward the offender, you end up carrying the negativity with you wherever you go. You thereby place your power of choice and moving forward in the hands of the very person who hurt you. Holding onto anger is more harmful and has more power over you than the offense itself. Forgiveness is the way to release your involvement with the offender and the offense; you have a choice to expunge their hurtful influences from your system.

Forgiveness does not mean forgetting. In fact, it is often beyond our control whether we forget or not. We cannot demand of ourselves that we forget, yet we can certainly choose to forgive.

The truth is, forgetting is usually based in selfishness, while forgiving is based in selflessness. It is empowering to work on forgiveness and not to focus on forgetting. When you say to someone, "Forget about it," or "Don't worry, I already forgot about it," you are essentially saying that their actions do not matter to you, and that is why you were able to move on. There is a hidden but disempowering self-importance and anger in this attitude. To forgive is to selflessly move on with your life even if their actions did matter to you, and even when it still hurts. Forgetting is usually 'for getting', for the purpose of getting something from the other person — namely a false sense of power.

Forgiving is 'for giving', for the purpose of giving something. When you forgive, you may still be very much aware of the other, their actions, and your own feeling of loss, yet you give the person a free gift: an increased power to do Teshuvah.

When forgiveness is given not for any personal, financial, physical, or psychological benefit, it is pure unconditional compassion. This highest level of forgiveness is not a logical calculation, as in, 'I might as well forgive that person so that I can feel better (or so I can be a better person, or so I can encourage him to do Teshuvah).' Rather it is an act of pure selfless giving.

THE THREE TYPES OF OFFENSES AGAINST OTHERS

In offending others, whether bodily, emotionally or psychologically, there are three types of offenses: 1) an offense committed against you that can be compensated to some extent, 2) an offense committed against you that is 'irrevocable' in nature, 3) an offense committed against you which is not directed *to you* as an individual and hence your compensation is irrelevant.

In case 1, forgiveness is usually obligatory. In case 2, forgiveness is commendable. In case 3, forgiveness is forbidden, for you were not the victim.

To explain: Case 1 is where a wrong was directed towards you and has been compensated, and now your forgiveness is obligatory. For example, say 'Person A' steals money from 'Person B', but then he repays the full amount and asks for forgiveness. As long as 'A' is asking forgiveness with seriousness, 'B' is required to forgive him. 'B' is allowed to test the sincerity of 'A's remorse by making him ask for forgiveness on three separate instances. But once he has requested forgiveness three times, there is a Torah obligation to forgive.

Case 2 is where a wrong was directed towards you but where the damage done is irreversible, and you have the right to forgive or not forgive. For example, 'A' has spoken slander against 'B' in front of others, and now feels remorseful and asks 'B' for forgiveness. Since the words spoken against 'B' are irretractable, forgiveness is optional although preferable, for if 'B' does not forgive, however, he will end up clinging to the hurt and living with detrimental anger.

Case 3 is where an offense was committed against you, but not to you as an individual and hence compensation is irrelevant and forgiveness is 'forbidden'. We cannot forgive someone for a wrong they have inflicted upon another person; we are not allowed because it is not our place. The only person who can grant forgiveness is the one who was hurt, and only for the deed that was directed at him. There are instances when someone acts negatively in a way that, on the surface, seems to be directed at you, but is really directed toward your family or your larger community, as in anti-semitism, or to someone else for whom you were mistaken. In these cases, it is forbidden and impossible for you to forgive.

> *Rebbe Chayim of Brisk, the celebrated Nineteenth-Century sage, was once traveling alone on a train when two well-dressed young men approached him. Thinking he was a poor beggar, they began to poke fun at him. When the train arrived in Brisk, they realized, to their dismay, that the person they had been harassing was none other than the famed Rabbi of Brisk. In great haste and contrition, they approached the Rabbi and pleaded for his forgiveness. Reb Chayim, however, refused to forgive them. He said that his refusal stemmed not from a desire to cling to the negative experience but rather from his lack of authority to forgive. He explained that it was forbidden for him to forgive, since the person they had harassed was not the same person who was asked for forgiveness. They had offended a poor beggar, and now they would have to find such a man, and in fact, they would have to find all the poor beggars of the world and ask them all for forgiveness.*

Upon being forgiven by oneself and others and feeling lighter from it, we are now ready to enter Yom Kippur and attain forgiveness from the Master of the Universe and bask in the Light of HaKadosh Baruch Hu for the 26 hours of utter transcendence.

Chapter Two
FESTIVE MEALS BEFORE & AFTER YOM KIPPUR

EREV YOM KIPPUR, THE NINTH OF THE MONTH OF TISHREI, IS A MINOR *Yom Tov* / HOLIDAY. THIS FACT IS EXPRESSED IN THE OMISSION OF *Tachanun* / PENITENTIAL PRAYERS, AND ALSO IN THE FESTIVE MEALS THAT ARE EATEN ON THIS DAY.

This day is an intermediary that links the 'transcendent' fast day of Yom Kippur with all the other 'mundane' days of the year. It contains elements of eating, as on all the regular days of the year, and fasting, as on Yom Kippur. As such, there is a Mitzvah to eat on this day, and yet, *Chazal* / our sages tell us, "One who eats and drinks on the Ninth (and fasts on the Tenth), the Torah considers him as if he has fasted on the Ninth and the Tenth" (*Berachos*, 8b. *Yuma*, 81b). In other words, eating on this day is comparable to fasting, and in this sense, it is a kind of unity of eating (mundane or immanence) and fasting (transcendence).[*]

On Erev Yom Kippur, there is a Mitzvah to eat lavishly. In practice, this means there should be two sit-down meals with bread (see *Minchas Chinuch*, 313), one around midday and the other closer to the end of the day. The simple 'reasons' that there is a Mitzvah to eat well on the Ninth are a) that we should have energy and proper focus for our prayers and Teshuvah on the Tenth when we are fasting, and b) that the fasting does not harm us (Rashi, *ibid*. Rosh, *Yuma*, 8:22. In the words of the Tur, וציום שיאכלו וישתו תחלה כדי שיוכלו להתענות ושלא להזיק להם העינוי משל למלך שהיה לו בן יחיד וגזר עליו להתענות יום אחד וצוה להאכילו ולהשקותו קודם כדי שיוכל לסבול: *Orach Chayim*, 604. (Other Rishonim argue that feasting makes it harder to fast: *Shibolei haLeket*, Siman 307). Hence, women are just as obligated as men in this Mitzvah. And the Mitzvah of eating is by day not on the night prior — שהסעודה אינה עד למחר: Rashi, *Kesuvos*, 5a (Although see Rashi, *Nedarim*, 66b, עד אותה לילה שיצום למחר ואותה הלילה מותר לאכול בשר. See also, *Ha'amek Sha'alah*, 169. *Pri Chadash*, Orach Chayim, 604. Yet, as known, the 'Rashi' on Nedarim is not from Rashi himself). Or perhaps feasting is a 'separate' Mitzvah that is time-bound, and

---

[*] The reason this feasting is considered like fasting (afflicting the body) is perhaps related to the way we might eat, as 'over-eating' can be experienced as a form of 'affliction'. צריך לאכול בערב יום הכיפורים אכילה גסה ולהרבות באכילה ושתיה כשיעור שני ימים כמו שכתוב בספרים קדושים, וכשאוכל אכילה גסה הוא עינוי, ונמצא שיש לו גם כן בחי' יום הכיפורים / "One should eat and drink heavily and abundantly on Erev Yom Kippur, like the amount he would eat in two days, as is written in the holy Sefarim. And when this heavy eating is an *Inuy* / affliction or discomfort for him, he is also experiencing an aspect of Yom Kippur": *Meor Einayim*, Ha'azinu.

women are thus exempt: *Shu'T Rebbe Akivah Eiger,* Siman 15. Most opinions are that women are obligated: *Shu'T Kesav Sofer,* 112. *Chochmas Shlomo,* 604. *Minchas Chinuch,* ibid. *S'dei Chemed,* Yom Kippur 1/5. The Torah says regarding Yom Kippur, ועניתם את נפשותיכם / "You shall afflict your souls." The word נפשותיכם / 'your souls' is plural, suggesting that we afflict our soul on the Tenth by fasting from food, and 'afflict' our soul on the Ninth through eating: *Shaloh,* in the name of *The Zohar,* Yumah, Sod Achilah b'Erev Yom Kippur).

We also eat on the Ninth to make a distinction from the Tenth (*P'risha,* Orach Chayim, Siman 604:2). Either way, these simple reasons for the extra meals are connected to the day of Yom Kippur itself and to Teshuvah.

We are moved to celebrate and express joy for the amazing gifts of Teshuvah and atonement which HaKadosh Baruch Hu gives us on Yom Kippur. It is just that on Yom Kippur itself, we refrain from food, and so to celebrate the joy of the Yom Tov of Yom Kippur,* we feast lavishly on Erev Yom Kippur.

---

* *Sha'arei Teshuvah,* Sha'ar 4:8–9: נתחייבו לקבוע הסעודה על שמחת המצוה בערב יוה"כ. See also Ritva, *Rosh Hashanah,* 9a. According to the *Shelitos,* Rosh Hashanah and Yom Kippur are days of *Simchah* / joy — אבל הני כיון דאית בהו שמחה ואע"ג שאין בו שמחה דאכיל ושתי' : *Shelitos Rav Achai Gaon,* 15. כרגלים דמו ומפסיקין מכ"מ יש בו שמחה גם בפועל ע"פ ד"ת וכדתנן שלהי תענית לא הי' יו"ט לישראל כט"ו באב וכיוה"כ כ' ובנ"י יוצאות וחולות בכרמים כו: *Ha'amek Sha'alah,* ad loc. Although see *Gilyoni haShas,* Moed Katan, 19a. In fact, many Geonim were of the opinion that in the text of our Tefillah (and Kiddush), we should refer to Rosh Hashanah and Yom Kippur as days of Simchah — Tur, *Orach Chayim,* 582: אבל רב שר שלום כתב אומר בב' ישיבות בר"ה וביה"כ בין בתפלה בין בקדושה מועדים לשמחה חגים וזמנים לשון את יום הזכרון הזה...וכ"כ רב פלטוי גאון זצ"ל...וכ"כ רב שמואל בן חפני מנהג ב' ישיבות לאומרו. Certainly, Yom Kippur is not meant to be a sad day. So much so that the sages changed the location of the 'red thread' so as not to cause people to be sad on Yom Kippur — תנו רבנן : בראשונה היו קושרין לשון של זהורית על פתח האולם מבחוץ, הלבין היו שמחין, לא הלבין היו עצבין ומתביישין. התקינו שיהיו קושרין על פתח אולם מבפנים / "The Sages taught: At first they would tie

red strip to the opening of the Entrance Hall on the outside. If the strip turned white, they would rejoice. If it did not turn white, they would be sad and ashamed. When the Sages saw that people were sad and distressed on Yom Kippur, they established that they should tie it to the opening of the Entrance Hall on the inside": *Yuma*, 67a. There seems to be some ambivalence regarding the opinion of the Rambam. The Rambam writes, אבל ראש השנה ויום הכפורים אין בהן הלל לפי שהן ימי תשובה ויראה ופחד לא ימי שמחה יתרה / "But there is no Hallel on Rosh Hashanah and Yom Kippur because they are days of repentance, awe and fear — not days of excessive joy": *Hilchos Chanukah*, 3:6. From the words לא ימי שמחה יתרה / "not days of excessive joy," one can deduce that they are not days of "excessive" joy, but days of regular joy nonetheless. Although one can argue that the Rambam just writes those words שמחה יתרה / "excessive joy" not to imply that regular joy is relevant on Rosh Hashanah and Yom Kippur, rather, since he is talking about the laws of Hallel, and Hallel is only said when there is שמחה יתרה, and thus Rosh Hashanah and Yom Kippur are excluded, but in truth they are not days of regular שמחה / joy as well. No matter which opinion, all agree that Yom Kippur is a day of joy for HaKadosh Baruch Hu, a day when the garbage is removed from the Castle. Here are the words of the Medrash: ימים יוצרו ולא אחד בהם: זה יום הכפורים לישראל לפי שהיתה שמחה גדולה לפני הקב"ה שנתנו באהבה רבה לישראל משלו משל למה הדבר דומה למלך בשר ודם שהיו עבדיו ובני ביתו מוציאין את הזבלים ומשליכין אותו כנגד פתח בית המלך וכשהמלך יוצא ורואה את הזבלים הוא שמח שמחה גדולה. לכך נדמה יום הכפורים שנתנו הקב"ה באהבה רבה ובשמחה. ולא זו בלבד אלא בשעה שהוא מוחל לעונותיהן של ישראל אין מתעצב בלבבו אלא שמח שמחה גדולה. לכך נאמר כה אמר ה' אלקים להרים ולגבעות לאפיקים ולגאיות באו ושמחו שמחה גדולה שאני מוחל להם לעונותיהם של ישראל / "'Though many days will be fashioned, He chose one of them' (*Tehillim*, 139:16)... This refers to Yom Kippur; HaKadosh Baruch Hu was extremely happy when He gave this day to Israel with great love. A Mashal for this is given. It is like a king of flesh and blood, when his servants and children took out the garbage, they threw it in front of the entrance to the king's palace. And when the king went out, he saw the garbage and became very elated (because they had cleaned their quarters). Such is Yom Kippur, which Hashem lovingly and joyfully gifted to Israel. Furthermore, at the time when He forgives the sins of Israel, He has no sadness in His heart; rather, He rejoices greatly, as it says (*Yechezkel*, 36:4): "Thus says Hashem Elokim to the mountains and hills, to the streams and valleys, 'Come and rejoice with Me, for I forgive the sins of Israel!': *Tana D'vei Eliyahu Rabbah*, 1:3. Note that the Arizal draws a parallel between the days between Rosh Hashanah and Yom Kippur and the days of *Chol haMoed* / 'minor holy days'

Yom Kippur is a time of Teshuvah, of making a *Tikkun /* repair on, and elevation of, the entire past year in general. On Erev Yom Kippur, when there is a Mitzvah to eat, we have the ability to create a specific Tikkun on all the eating of the entire year.

PURIM & EREV YOM KIPPUR

The Zohar teaches that Purim is linked to Yom haKi-*Purim*; they are equivalent to each other, and in fact Purim is in a way even 'higher' (*Tikkunei Zohar*, Tikkun 21). These two Yamim Tovim parallel each other in that Erev Purim is a fast day and Purim is a feast day, while Erev Yom Kippur is a feast day and Yom Kippur is a fast day. As such, the fasting of Yom Kippur corresponds in some way to the feasting of Purim. As eating is a higher level of elevation and transformation, Purim is higher than Yom Kippur itself, as it were.

On Yom Kippur, transcendence is 'exclusive'; to enter the transcendence of Yom Kippur, we need to 'exclude' our 'human' state and stop eating, whereas the Light of Purim is so lofty that it can even penetrate the lower levels of physicality, even the level of eating. Furthermore, the eating of Erev Yom Kippur connects us with the level of Transcendence that is 'inclusive' of the revealed joy of Purim (the Rebbe, *Likkutei Sichos*, 24, p. 572).

As such, one should eat with joy and great relish on Erev

---

between the days of full Yom Tov: *Ya'aros Devash*, Derush 1. See also, in the name of the Ramak, *Ohr Tzadikim*, 36:3.

Yom Kippur. Rebbe Levik, the esteemed and holy father of the Rebbe, would, throughout the year, only eat using one hand. On Erev Yom Kippur, he would use both hands to eat (*Sichas Erev Yom Kippur 5745*). In this way, we could say he was 'doubling' his feasting. Alternatively, he was engaging the right hand of *Chesed* / the 'kindness' and expansiveness of 'doubly feasting', as well as the left hand of *Gevurah* / the 'withholding' act of 'doubly fasting'. And thus, in a certain sense, he was celebrating both the essence of Purim and the essence of Yom haKippurim at the same time.

This is the power of our celebratory feasts on Erev Yom Kippur.

Chapter Three
KREPLACH

M ANY HAVE THE CUSTOM TO EAT *Kreplach* DURING THE MEALS ON EREV YOM KIPPUR, SMALL PACKETS OF DOUGH FILLED WITH MEAT. TRADITIONALLY, THESE ARE PLACED IN SOUP, LIKE A DUMPLING.

Although the word *Kreplach* is a Yiddish version of the word meaning 'pastry', nothing is by happenstance and without *Hashgachah* / Divine providence. Kreplach are traditionally eaten on Hoshanah Rabba and on Purim as well; hence the root of the word *Kreplach* (K-R-P) is an acronym for (Yom) **K**ippur, (Hoshanah) **R**abba, **P**urim.

On a more exoteric level, the simple reason we eat meat covered in dough is that Yom Tov is defined by a prohibition to do mundane work (ששת ימים האלו שאסרן הכתוב בעשיית מלאכה ...הן הנקראין ימים טובים: Rambam, *Hilchos Shevisas Yom Tov*, 1:1). On Yom Tov, there is also a Mitzvah to be joyful, and since, generally, even today, meat is a luxury and brings festivity, we eat meat on Yom Tov. On Erev Yom Kippur, as well as Hoshanah Rabbah and Purim, we technically *are* allowed to do work. We can drive and, if necessary, even go to work on these days, yet they are also semi-Yamim Tovim. As such, we endeavor to eat meat on these special days as well, just covered over to indicate that these days are not *full* Torah-based Yamim Tovim.

There is, however, a deeper reason, and one particularly connected to Yom Kippur. Meat is 'dead', and red meat in particular also represents the world of *Gevurah* / severity and harsh judgment. White flour and dough mixed with pure, transparent water, the basic ingredients of Kreplach, represent the world of *Chesed* / kindness and expansiveness. Wrapping meat in dough prayerfully expresses the sweetening of all judgments and severities.

As we are about to enter the day of the final judgment of the Ten Day from Rosh Hashanah to Yom Kippur (Hoshanah Rabbah, being the final "seal"), the judgment of our entire year to follow, we celebrate this day by eating Kreplach. By doing so, we demonstrate the *Emunah* / faith and *Bitachon* / trust that we will be judged favorably (see Alter Rebbe, *Ma'amarei Admur haZaken*, Inyanim, p. 180), and that our lives, the whole world, and all of reality will soon be sweetened.

Chapter Four
MIKVAH IMMERSION

A S EXPLORED EARLIER, YOM KIPPUR IS A PROVERBIAL 'MIKVAH OF TIME', A DAY WHEN WE ENTER THE 'MIK-VAH OF HASHEM'. Another *Remez* / hint at the waters of the Mikvah is the fact that the idea of Selichah and Mechilah is connected to the world of water, fluidity and flow. Being able to forgive others (which is a prerequisite to enter Yom Kippur, enabling us to ask for forgiveness from HaKadosh Baruch Hu) is to be malleable, flowing and less rigid.

Appropriately, there is a very well-established *Minhag* / custom of Mikvah immersion on Erev Yom Kippur (Rosh, *Yuma*, 8:24. *Shibbolei haLeket*, 283. *Manhig*, 52. Tosefos, *Berachos*, 22b. Tur, Mechaber, *Orach Chayim*, 606:4). So important is this immersion that

Rebbe Saadiah Gaon (882–942), the great leader and sage, suggests (although, this is not the law) that one recite a *Berachah* / blessing on this immersion (Although, generally we do not recite a blessing on a Minhag: *Sukkah*, 44b. Yet, when a custom has inherent positive value on its own, we do recite a blessing: *Tosefos*, ibid. *Shu'T Avnei Nezer*, Orach Chayim, 452).

It is brought down in the name of the great Tzadik Rebbe Yehudah haChasid (1150–1217) that we should immerse three times in the Mikvah on Erev Yom Kippur, corresponding to the three descriptions that the Torah employs for 'transgression': *Cheit* / unintentional misdeeds, *Avon* / intentional transgressions, and *Pesha* / negative actions done in spite.*

What's more, there is a custom among Chasidim to immerse on Erev Yom Kippur three separate times: once early in the morning before Kaparos, once before Minchah, and once right before the final meal before the beginning of the fast. The widespread custom to immerse before the Minchah prayers is to ensure that Minchah, which includes the recital of Viduy, is performed in purity.

---

* Also corresponding to the three times the word *Teharah* / purity appears in the Torah portion that describes the Yom Kippur service: *Vayikra*, 16:19-30. *Sefer Chassidim*, 394. *Reishis Chochmah*, Sha'ar haAhavah, 11. Additionally, the word *Mikvah* appears in the Torah exactly three times: *Bereishis*, 1:10, *Shemos*, 7:10, and *Vayikra*, 11:36. Many other sources speak about these three immersions on Erev Yom Kippur, including *Sefer Rokeach*, Yom Kippur, 214; *Shulchan Aruch*, Orach Chayim, *Magen Avraham*, 606:8, *Shulchan Aruch haRav*, 606:12, *Aruch haShulchan*, ibid, and *Mishnah Berurah*, ibid.

Immersing in water is an enactment of a state of non-being, the inner space in which one can transform their being; hence it is vital to immerse in a Mikvah before Yom Kippur. Teshuvah is a radical transformation of self; we become a new self, and before this can happen, we need to let the old self return to nothingness in the Mikvah.

THE THREE DIMENSIONS OF THE MIKVAH & THE THREE NAMES OF HASHEM

There are three basic elements to the structure of a Mikvah: A) the 'ground' you are standing on, the floor of the Mikvah pool, B) the water that surrounds you and the four walls of the pool, and C) when you are immersed, the surface of the water above your head, which is the 'roof' or 'crown' of the Mikvah.

Corresponding to these basic elements, there are three prominent Names of Hashem. A 'Name' is a modality of revelation and Divine interaction with Creation, and we immerse in these Names, as it were, when we immerse in the Mikvah.

1) Havayah – the Yud-Hei-Vav-Hei, which is also called *Hashem* / the Name, or the 'Tetragrammaton'.

2) Ado-noi – the Name of Hashem as it is pronounced today.

3) Ehe'yeh – "I am" or "I will Be," the Name Moshe experienced at the Burning Bush.

The Name Havayah represents Infinity. The four letters of the Name, Yud-Hei-Vav-Hei spell the words *Hayah* / 'it was' (past); *Hoveh* / 'it is' (present); and *Yehiyeh* / 'it will be' (future). Embodying these four letters, it expresses the Infinite Timeless One.

The Name Ado-noi represents the Creator's mastery of Creation. The name of Hashem is pronounced today as *Adonoi*, and in this way, Ado-noi is the 'finite' container that contains and gives us access to Hashem, the Infinite One. The Name Ehe'yeh is a Name related to 'potentiality', or a future 'becoming'.

These Divine Names represent cosmic creative forces of HaKadosh Baruch Hu, so to speak, and they are also reflected in the microcosmic man who is created in the Divine Image, as it were. Inwardly, the reflection of these Names in our lives is as follows: 'Hashem' represents our Neshamah, our 'infinite' soul, the layer of self that is part of Hashem: כי חלק י-ה-ו-ה עמו / *Ki Chelek Yud-Hei-Vav-Hei Amo* / a part of Hashem is His nation" (*Devarim*, 32:9. *Tanya*, Iggeres haTeshuvah, 5). Our souls are essentially One with Hashem, and this is our 'infinity', so to speak. The Name 'Ado-noi', relative to our life, is our 'ground', where we stand presently. The name Ehe'yeh is our future, who we are becoming.

These three Names are also reflected in the three dimensions of the Mikvah:

A) Ado-noi is like a container or the ground, the floor of the pool that you are standing on before you immerse. This is your self-image in the present moment. It is your identity, for better or worse; your life as it currently appears. Say someone's self-image is a business person. There is an undertone of limitation or even negativity in this image, as it does not capture who they really are, but rather only what they do. If they are highly attached to this image, when someone else suggests that they are not good in business, they will fume in anger or fall into self-doubt and depression.

B) The four walls of the Mikvah, and the water swirling around you, are reflections of the element of 'Hashem', Infinity. This element is beyond you and actually beyond your grasp, imagery, or contextualization; water is impermanent, fluid, ungraspable, and in this sense, transcendent. Also, the Torah gives no account of the creation of water — it transcends being a particular 'thing', as it were. As you submerge beneath the waters, you have a subtle experience of letting go of your 'manifest being', your strong sense of self. Under the water, you are no longer a separate 'creation', attached to a self-image — certainly not a negative self-image. Your self-definitions blend into the water, and you stop being a business person. There is no business to do underwater, no business attire, no conversations, no clocks or computers, no money, and no finite self. There, you are just a pure *Neshamah* / soul. Thus, underwater, you experience a moment of Infinity and a loss of attachments and habits. The Mikvah is a 'reset button' for your life.

C) While underwater, the water above your head, the 'roof' of the water, is like a skylight through which you will emerge into a new experience of yourself. As you rise out from under the water, you experience a reflection of the name *Ehe'yeh* / 'I Will Be."* You are being reborn from the womb of the Mikvah and you have a fresh beginning in life, an open potential; you can choose who you will be. As you exit the water, you are purified of your past identity. Now you can don your fresh, clean Yom Kippur garments and walk into a whole new life.

We cannot dwell underwater, and likewise, we should not attempt to live without a sense of identity or definition. If you find yourself manifesting as a good business person, one that makes money and gives Tzedakah and helps others, then by all means, take on this role and do good things with your money and influence. Just don't get so caught up in this finite image of self to the extent that you forget or lose focus on who you really are. You are part of Hashem, a Neshamah that 'has' a body and a role and purpose. You 'are' not your body, your role, or your activities. As underwater, you have realized you are not your self-image; now, when you emerge from the Mikvah, you have

---

* The word *Mikvah* in numeric value is 151, which is the value of the 'filled' name of Ehe'yeh. There are four letters in the Name Ehe'yeh: Aleph-Hei-Yud-Hei. To 'fill' this word, these letters themselves are spelled out in the following way: Aleph/1, Lamed/30, Pei/80=**111**. Hei/5, Hei/5=10. Yud/10, Vav/6, Dalet/4=**20**. Hei/5, Hei/5=**10**. 111+10+20+10=**151**. Another way of 'filling' the word is to multiply the values of the letters, as such: Aleph is 1, and 1x1=1. Hei is 5, and 5x5=25 (1+25=26). Yud is 10, and 10x10=100 (1+25+100=126). Hei is 5, and 5x5=25 (1+25+100+25=151): Arizal, *Sha'ar haPesukim*.

an open opportunity to connect with a healthier and more positive self-image.

Our purpose is not only to be our infinite self without images or tasks. We do have a 'finite self', and we each have a purpose that demands exercising our special talents and strengths. When we emerge from the Mikvah of infinity, we re-enter the world and dress ourselves in purpose, purity and positivity.

THREE MOVEMENTS OF GROWTH

The three elements of the Mikvah's structure are related to the three essential steps we need to take in order to grow and move forward in our life in all situations, certainly in the process of Teshuvah and Yom Kippur.

A) The first step is *Hachna'ah* / submission; acknowledging where we stand at the present moment. What is our current self-image, what is our 'floor', where are we in life?

B) The second stage is *Havdalah* / separation, meaning letting go and unburdening ourselves from our attachments and finite self-images. Let go of your old self, and feel enveloped in the infinity of your Neshamah and the Infinity of Hashem.

C) The third stage is *Hamtakah* / sweetening, recollecting and reconnecting with our self-image from a healthy space. This corresponds to the Name Ehe'yeh.

THE NAME YA'BOK

The three Divine Names above are also connected with the sacred Name יבוק / *Ya'bok*. This Name is an acronym for יחוד / *Yichud* / Unity, ברכה / *Berachah* / Blessing, and קדושה / *Kedushah* / holiness. In numerical value, the Name *Ya'bok* is 112, the same as the three Names of Hashem which are being explored:

Hashem: Yud/10, Hei/5, Vav/6, Hei = 26

Ado-noi: Aleph/1, Dalet/4, Nun/50, Yud/10 = 65

Ehe'yeh: Aleph/1, Hei/5, Yud/10, Hei/5 = 21

26+65+21=112 (*Ya'bok*)

In our personal lives, this acronym describes three steps parallel the three stages of Hachna'ah, Havdalah and Hamtakah. First, we need to perform a *Yichud* / unification with ourselves as we are right now, then see ourselves and our entire life as a *Berachah* / blessing, and finally, to reach and integrate a higher level of *Kedushah* / holiness.

Hachna'ah / submitting to the fact that you need to change	*Yichud* / uniting with yourself as you are now
Havdalah / separating from negativity	*Berachah* / transcending the past by immersing your consciousness in infinite positivity and blessings
Hamtakah / sweetening, or transforming negativity into positivity	*Kedushah* / integrating and acting on a new level of positivity and holiness in life

A SIMPLE MIKVAH KAVANAH — MEDITATION & INTENTION

Based on all of the above, we can delineate a simple Kavanah which we can contemplate as we immerse in the Mikvah.

Before preparing to immerse in the Mikvah, begin by noticing what you are wearing. Feel the weight of your clothing, and perhaps the slightly 'soiled' quality of the fabric. View your life as it is right now, 'unite' with it and own it. Submit to the perception that you want to become fresh and new. Imagine each piece of clothing as an extraneous layer of your identity, inhibiting the authentic expression of who you are and what you were born to be. As you undress, sense each layer dropping away, one after the other, until you are unclothed, free of all unnecessary covering.

A Mikvah should be entered slowly; rather than jumping into it, slowly walk down the steps into the pool. The water receives you gently until you are completely enveloped and held.

As you are standing on the floor of the pool, sense it as the presence of the Name Ado-noi, cosmically and microcosmically, the finite foundation of all that you are in the present. As the water begins to surround your body take notice of the four sides of water enveloping you. This is the presence of the Name of Hashem, the Yud-Hei-Vav-Hei, Hashem's Ineffable Name. You are not merely in a 'ritual pool', you are in Hashem's infinite, open arms: "The Mikvah of Israel is Hashem." Feel the overwhelming embrace of HaKadosh Baruch Hu.

Notice the contrast between the actual hard or solid, firm floor and the swirling, light fluidity around you.

Walk deeper into the Mikvah and immerse yourself completely in the water, sensing your feet leaving the finite floor beneath you. Now you are weightless, soaring in the boundless expanse around you. You are separate from all negativity and no longer attached to any finite self-image; you blend into formless, infinite positivity and blessing.

As you emerge from the waters, notice yourself moving through the surface, as if through a skylight in the roof of the waters, and emerging a new you. You are full of potential; the sky's the limit. As you are moving out of the dip, notice that all you had shed in the dressing room, and deeper, everything you have let go under the water, moving back towards you. It no longer appears heavy and inauthentic but is rather more transparent and fluid, an essential part of who you are — familiar and necessary. You recognize all that was you is all that needs to be you, in a sweetened, holy, and integrated way.

As you emerge from the Mikvah, notice how calm and pure you feel. You have been cleansed on a soul level, and you are re-entering the world with a deeper sense of sweetness, positivity, and holy purpose. And now you are ready to enter the sacred, transcendent day of Yom Kippur, a day of intimacy with your Creator.

INTENTIONS FOR MIKVAH

Name	Attribute	Mode of Being	Identification	Element of Mikvah
ADO-NOI	Divine Finite	Manifest Being	Current Self	Floor of Mikvah
HASHEM	Divine Infinity	Unmanifest Being	Self-Transcendence	'Surrounding' Water or Walls
EHE'YEH	Divine Creative Potential	Manifesting or Becoming	Potential Future Self	'Roof' of Water (when re-emerging)

Chapter Five
AVINU MALKEINU / OUR FATHER OUR KING

O UR SAGES TELL US THE FOLLOWING STORY: מעשה ברבי אליעזר שירד לפני התיבה, ואמר עשרים וארבע ברכות ולא נענה. ירד רבי עקיבא אחריו ואמר: "אבינו מלכנו אין לנו מלך אלא אתה. אבינו מלכנו, למענך רחם עלינו", וירדו גשמים / "Once Rebbe Eliezer descended to serve as prayer leader before the ark on a fast day. He recited 24 blessings but was not answered. Rebbe Akivah descended before the ark after him and said: '*Avinu Malkeinu*, our Father, our King, we have no king other than You! Our Father, our King, for *Your* sake, have mercy on us!' Rain immediately fell" (*Ta'anis,* 25b). We are told that Rebbe Akivah was actually answered from on High because of his own forgiving nature, yet, since he was answered by saying this phrase, *Avinu Makeinu* / "Our Father, Our King," this phrase was later adapted as part of our liturgy. Over time, many more short prayers beginning with the words *Avinu Malkeinu* were composed.

The power of these words lies in the dual aspect of the phrase, relating to HaKadosh Baruch Hu both as a Father and as a King. *Avinu* / our Father is a cry of yearning of a child for his father, a yearning of love. *Malkeinu* / our King is a call of a servant to his king, a call of duty and responsibility.

Our souls are rooted in Divine Unity, and we are truly a part of the One Above. As far as our souls are concerned, Hashem is our Parent, our Source of existence and love. Our bodies, however, labor in a universe of apparent separateness, a world of distance and estrangement. On its own, the best that the body can sense is to feel like a servant serving its master. Although the servant may have a very important position in the king's court, as a minister even, there is always a measure of distance in the servant-king dynamic, which reflects the reality of our physical body and physical world.

HASHEM IS OUR KING, WHO IS ALSO OUR FATHER

Here is a Chassidic tale that illustrates this point.

Once, it was common for a farmer to hire a teacher to teach his children Torah. When Rosh Hashanah and Yom Kippur came along, the teacher would leave for his hometown, and so the father would substitute and teach his own children.

With the teacher, the children would behave nicely, but

with their father, perhaps not so much. Soon, the father would lose control of the classroom and announce, "From now on, no one can say, 'Tatty, please, can I do this,' or 'Tatty, can I do that.' From now on, as long as we are in this room, I am not your father; I am your teacher."

Control was regained in the classroom, and as a teacher, the father became stricter and stricter. One day, as he was teaching his class with strict discipline, his youngest child burst out crying. He asked the young boy, why are you crying? "I am crying because I want to tell my father to tell my teacher not to be so strict."

And so, we declare, "Our Father, Our King…." 'Please see us, judge us, as we truly are, as Your Children and You as our Father.' Yet, on an even deeper level, it is actually the will of Our King to reveal the 'Father' within the 'King'.

DIVINE GAME OF HIDE AND SEEK

Life is a game of hide and seek: Hashem hides, and we seek.

Once, the young son of the Maggid of Mezritch came crying to his father, saying that he was playing a game of hide-and-seek with his friends, and he and one friend hid in really good hiding places and were not found. But having waited for hours to be found, they finally emerged from the hiding places only to discover that the friend who was

seeking them had stopped looking for them a long time ago. He had given up and gone home. The boys were heartbroken that while they were hiding, excitedly expecting to be found at any moment, no one was even seeking them. At this point, the Maggid himself started crying and declared that HaKadosh Baruch Hu has the same complaint.

Our task is to seek and find Hashem. But where does Hashem hide, as Hashem is everywhere and within everything and "There is no place void of Him"? So perhaps an alternative metaphor is the game of peek-a-boo. Peek-a-boo is a game in which the parent is obviously not really hiding. Even though toddlers already have 'object permanence', they cooperate with the illusion of their parent's 'disappearance' and laugh with relief when the parent's face is suddenly revealed from behind his or her hands. So too, Hashem covers His all-compassionate identity with the guise of an awesome and almost indifferent King who judges strictly by the Book. And it is true that Hashem is our King, but then we pull on His hands and are delighted to suddenly see Him again as our loving Parent.

In this way, we seek to unveil the compassion of 'Our Father' within the stern voice of 'Our King'. We are the small child who climbs into the king's arms, pulls the mask or daunting crown off and cries, "It's Tatty!" And this, of course, is exactly what the King had been waiting for all along.

THERE IS ONLY HASHEM

On the deepest level, when we say the words אבינו מלכנו אין
לנו מלך אלא אתה / "Our Father, our King, we have no King but
You," we are declaring, 'Yes, You are our King, and You are
our Father, but we really just want You.' We don't just want a
manifestation or mask, we want the 'You' that can manifest as
either Father or as King. We want You as You are in Yourself,
transcendent of these outer appearances. We want YOU.

Hashem's 'appearances' or attributes are very different: *Av
she-Machal al K'vodo, K'vodo Machul* / "A father can forgo his
honor," as the prototype of a father having *Rachamim* / compassion for his children, and his compassion overrides his need
for honor. *Melech she-Machal al K'vodo, Ein K'vodo Machul* /
"A king cannot forgo his honor," for a king, by definition, demands awe and honor (HaMaknah, *Kidushin*, 32b). Yet, Hashem
can be both our Father and our King because Hashem remains
the *Atah* / 'You' behind these different appearances. 'Father' is
Hashem's appearance of Rachamim, and 'King' is Hashem's
appearance of *Din* / judgment. Hashem is the common de-
nominator and essence of both these attributes.

In the *Nusach* / liturgy throughout these days of Rosh Hashanah and Yom Kippur, we repeatedly plead, כרחם אב על בנים
כן תרחם עלינו / "Just as a father has compassion on his children,
have compassion on us (Note *Tehillim*, 103:13: 'כרחם אב על-בנים רחם ה
על-יראיו).*

---

* Although Rosh Hashanah is more about Din whereas Yom Kippur is *Ra-*

One question that may come to mind is, why do we mention specifically a fatherly compassion when a mother's compassion could be stronger (In general, מפני שהנשים רחמניות הן: *Megilah*, 14b. Although see *Mabit*, 1, Siman 339. *S'dei Chemed*, Aleph, Klal 144. *Mishpat Tzedek*, 1:23)? If our only goal in this prayer is to elicit compassion, perhaps it would be more effective to appeal to Hashem's motherly attribute: "Just as a mother has compassion...."

Love, and hence honor, arise in a child towards his mother more naturally, whereas *Yirah* / fear and awe are more natural for a child to feel towards his father (*Kidushin*, 30b–31a). During this period, called the *Yamim Noraim* / Days of Awe (the term has been used for centuries, see Ra'avyah, Berachos, Siman 39: 1), Hashem is appearing to us as the Melech, instilling Yirah. Thus, we are turning to the Holy One and saying, "True, You are our Mel-

---

chamim / Divine Compassion — בראש השנה מתיחד במדת הדין ומנהיג עולמו וביום הכפורים במדת הרחמים והוא מאמרם מלך יושב על כסא דין וכו' ראש השנה יום דין ברחמים ויום הכפורים יום רחמים בדין / "On Rosh Hashanah He is concerned entirely with the attribute of Din and conducts His world [by that attribute], and on the Day of Yom Kippur He is concerned entirely with the attribute of Rachamim. It is this which is expressed in the saying of the Rabbis, "The King sits upon the throne of Judgment etc." Thus Rosh Hashanah is a day of Judgment with Mercy, and the Day of Yom Kippur is a day of Mercy in Judgment" Ramban, *Vayikra*, 23:24. In fact, there is a debate in the Poskim if in the *Mi-Shebeirach* prayers on Yom Kippur we should say, *LiCh'vod Yom haDin*, or *LiCh'vod Yom haKippurim* rather than 'Yom haDin', as Yom Kippur is pure *Rachamim* / Divine Compassion: See *Sha'ar haKolel* on the Alter Rebbe's Siddur, Chapter 26:5. The nine days from Rosh Hashanah through Erev Yom Kippur, are a time of self-excavation, evaluation, and inner work. In nine days, there are 216 hours (9 x 24 = 216), which is the numerical value of the word *Gevurah* (Gimel/3, Beis/2, Vav/6, Reish/200, Hei/5 = 216) — the idea of constriction and *Din* / Judgment. These nine days are days full of the beneficial constriction of self-judgment, and then comes Yom Kippur, the day of expansive forgiveness and Divine Rachamim.

ech, and we are Your subjects, but You are also our Father, and fathers have compassion even when their children make mistakes. So be our King, but please do so with unlimited compassion, as *our Father* the King.

Chapter Six

"L'DOVID: HASHEM IS MY SALVATION"

I T IS CUSTOMARY TO RECITE CHAPTER 27 OF THE BOOK OF TEHILLIM FROM THE BEGINNING OF ELUL, THE MONTH DEDICATED TO INTROSPECTION IN PREPARATION FOR THE NEW YEAR, UNTIL THE END OF THE HOLIDAY OF SUKKOS. This custom is attributed to third-generation students of the Arizal and today has become widespread.

In this chapter, the Name of Hashem appears 13 times, and this is connected with the Thirteen Attributes of Mercy awakened during this auspicious time. Another reason we recite this chapter is that it contains references to all the major *Yomim Tovim* / Holidays that start off the new year.

Its opening, "Hashem is my light…" refers to Rosh Hashanah, the beginning of the renewed light that comes into the world at the beginning of the year. "…And my salvation" refers to Yom Kippur, a time of Teshuvah and spiritual redemption. "He will conceal me in the hidden places of *Sukko* / His tent" obviously refers to Sukkos when we sit in *Sukkos* / huts, reminding us of the 'tents' of the Clouds of Glory and of the literal 'tents' in which we dwelled while wandering in the Desert for 40 years.

"Hashem is my light and my salvation, whom shall I fear? Hashem is the strength of my life, of whom shall I be afraid" (Pasuk 1). 'Light' and 'strength' are two different forms of Divine revelation within this world. Hashem manifests to us as 'our Light' when we walk in the higher path, the path of light free from transgression. However, Hashem manifests to us as 'our Strength' after we have transgressed and fallen from the higher path, for then we need extra strength to climb back up again.

Prior to surrendering to our ego or negative tendencies, the idea of falling is but a distant fear. We operate in a constant state of light. Everything is clear and unambiguous. Our lives are filled with clear meaning and purpose. We are unencumbered by dichotomies and anxieties. However, sadly, if we end up surrendering to our lower selves even temporarily, the light and clarity may become obscured. We may no longer feel empowered. Doubts, uncertainties, and even worse, self-doubt and uncertainty in our self set in. Courage is lost. And so we turn to Hashem and say, 'I have lost my strength; *You* are my strength. Only You can give me the *Koach* / power and the courage to stand up again and face life without fear, to recalibrate and reclaim who I truly am.'

Maybe we are carrying our light and clarity, and our moral and spiritual convictions, or maybe we have dropped them slightly. Either way, Teshuvah, reclaiming our birthright, is always an available choice. Hashem is forever extending a hand, as it were, to assist us in the process of self-transformation and re-unification. We are never alone and certainly never abandoned.

While reciting this chapter of Tehillim, we should keep in mind that whatever level we have attained, even if we personally live in a very light-filled existence, we should never forget that there are others who struggle in darkness. We should also use this Tehillim to *Daven* / pray for those people, and we should seek to inspire them with the light and strength that we have.

Chapter Seven

THE THIRTEEN ATTRIBUTES OF MERCY

FTER THE EPISODE WITH THE GOLDEN CALF, AS MOSHE IMPLORED DIVINE FORGIVENESS FOR THE NATION, he was told that Hashem will always answer a heartfelt recitation of the *Yud-Gimmel Midos haRachamim / *Thirteen Attributes of Mercy.

In the *Tanach* (Torah, Prophets, and Writings), we find the Thirteen Attributes portrayed twice:

- As related in the *Book of Shemos* (34:5–7): "Hashem, Hashem, Keil, merciful and gracious, slow to anger, abundant in loving-kindness and truth, remembering kindness for thousands (of generations), forgiving iniquity and transgression and sin (of those who repent); but not clearing the guilt (of those who do not repent, rather), passing along the sins of the fathers onto the children to the third and fourth (generations)."

• As related in *The Book of Michah* (7:18–20): "Who is a *Keil* / G-d like You? Who bears transgression and pardons the wrongdoing of the remnant of His heritage? (He) does not sustain His anger forever, for He desires loving-kindness. He will once more have compassion on us (and) forget our transgressions, and (He) will hurl all our sins into the depths of the ocean. (O Hashem,) grant truth to Yaakov (and) loving-kindness to Avraham as You vowed to our forefathers long ago."*

Chazal tell us how Hashem revealed the Thirteen Attributes of Mercy to Moshe: מלמד שנתעטף הקדוש ברוך הוא כשליח צבור, והראה לו למשה סדר תפלה. אמר לו כל זמן שישראל חוטאין יעשו לפני כסדר הזה ואני מוחל להם / "This teaches that the Holy One, Blessed be He, wrapped Himself (in a Talis) like a prayer leader and showed Moshe the structure of the order of the prayer.

He said to him: Whenever Klal Yisrael transgress, let them act before Me in accordance with this order (let the prayer leader wrap himself in a Talis and publicly recite the Thirteen

---

* The Thirteen Attributes from the *Book of Michah* come from a place where there is no Din: *Zohar* 3. p. 131a. There are also the Thirteen Attributes of *Arich Anpin* / Extended Divine Face, and the Nine Attributes in *Zeir Anpin* / Small Divine Face: *Sha'ar haKavanos*, Derushei Chazaras Amidah, 5. *Eitz Chayim*, Sha'ar 13:9–11.

Attributes of Mercy), and I will forgive them" (*Rosh Hashanah*, 17b).

The above suggests that all we need to do to draw down the Thirteen Attributes of Mercy is don a Talis and recite these words (*Sefer Hafla'ah. Bnei Yissachar*, Ma'amrei Elul, Ma'amar 2:4). Yet, many Mekubalim write (Rabbeinu Bachya, *Shemos*, 34:7. Rebbe Moshe Alshich, *Bamidbar*, 14:20. *Tzror Hamor*, Ki Tisa, 34:5. Shaloh, *Asarah Ma'amaros*, Ma'amar 7 in the name of the *Reishis Chochmah*, Sha'ar haAnavah, 1) that these attributes need to be actively emulated (יעשו / "*Let them act* before Me in accordance with this order") in order to elicit them. A classic work of *Mussar* / ethics, *Tomer Devorah* by Rebbe Moshe Cordovero, elaborates on these attributes (following the order according to Michah, which the *Zohar* calls the "higher rungs of Mercy") and explains them in a personal manner, as follows:

1. "Who is a *Keil* / G-d like You!" This phrase describes the tremendous 'giving' quality* of our Creator, as it were, to withstand humiliation (and continue giving even to one who insults Him). The Divine force that animates and sustains existence is never withdrawn, even when the recipient of this life-giving force chooses to harness this very force to transgress and hurt or destroy. In our emulation of this quality, we should show patience even when humiliated by someone else, and

---

* These so-called Divine Attributes are not meant to be understood literally as qualities of the Infinite One, but rather as means by which Hashem acts and governs the world: Rambam, *Moreh Nevuchim*, 1:52. Rebbe Menachem Rikanti, *Peirush al haTorah*, Parshas Vayechi. *Shomer Emunim*, HaKadmon, 1.

demonstrate composure even when the people we have been kind to turn their backs on us. Even then, we should remain patient and not withhold our kindness from them.

2. "Who bears transgression": Hashem practices tolerance, thus allowing the negative forces created by mankind's negative actions, speech, or thoughts to be sustained, while not allowing them to destroy the perpetrator, thus giving him a chance to return and do Teshuvah. So too, we should be tolerant, even when a wrong has been done to us, and wait until our fellow has a chance to rectify his error.

3. "And pardons the wrongdoing": Out of Infinite love, Hashem forgives and cleanses. We, too, should aspire to help those in need of Teshuvah, and seek to assist them no matter what it takes.

4. "Of the remnant of His heritage": Our personal pain is Hashem's pain because we are "His heritage." Hashem is in pain *with* us, so to speak. We should strive for such empathy; we should feel others' pain as our own and love them as ourselves because they are part of us.

5. "(He) does not sustain His anger forever": And so, too, we should not hold onto our anger even when there is good reason to be upset with our fellow.

6. "For He desires loving-kindness": Hashem seeks goodness within all people, overlooking their negative behavior and

remembering their good deeds. When we feel upset because someone has wronged us, we need to look deeper and find something positive and good within that person.

7. "He will once more have compassion on us": One who was distant from Hashem on a revealed level, but has returned, has a special place in Hashem's eyes. We, too, should aspire not to nurture anger towards a person who has previously upset us, but rather to show even more love and compassion.

8. "(And) forget our transgressions": In the Creator's eyes, a negative action does not negate a positive one; and each person is accorded reward for the good done. So too, we should not allow the negativity of any person to overwhelm their positivity so that we see only the bad. On the contrary, we should suppress the (perception of the) bad, leave it behind and firmly place the good of that person in front of us.

9. "And [He] will hurl all our sins into the depths of the ocean": In Hashem's eyes, negativity is superficial; when the peel is thrown away, the good is revealed. We, too, should remember that each person is good at the core, and when we see even bad people suffering, we should show them pity.

10. "(O Hashem) grant truth to Yaakov": Hashem shows compassion even to those who do not know how to conduct themselves beyond the letter of Torah law (the lower level of Yaakov). We, too, should train ourselves to always treat others with integrity and truth.

11. "...(And) loving-kindness to Avraham": Hashem walks with those who conduct themselves as Avraham, going beyond the literal interpretation of the law; Hashem shows them extreme kindness beyond measure. So too, we should show extreme kindness and patience, especially to such people.

12. "As You vowed to our forefathers": Even the unworthy receive from the Creator's boundless abundance because Hashem has promised to their forefathers to take care of their offspring. When we encounter people who perpetrate acts of evil, we should not show anger, only mercy. We should remind ourselves that they, too, are the children of Avraham, Yitzchak, and Yaakov.

13. "Long ago": Even when the merits of our ancestors have been spent, and we do not have any personal merits, G-d forbid, Hashem remembers and recalls all our goodness and good deeds from the day of our collective birth (the Exodus from Egypt). So, too, if we see a person who is apparently devoid of any positive trait or deed, we should remind ourselves that there was a time when this person was young, pure, and innocent and certainly did some good deed.

Our behavior here below arouses the Divine attributes Above, since what is Above is a reflection of what is below. Working on perfecting these qualities within us arouses the Divine qualities Above and opens them to us below.

AROUSING AND DRAWING DOWN KESER / CROWN

The Thirteen Attributes correspond to the 10 Sefiros up

until Keser, plus the three levels within Keser. The Keser of HaKadosh Baruch Hu is His will and desire that we should exist. This will is deeper than all Divine emotions and *Seichel* / intellect.

The 13 Attributes of Mercy are sourced within the Sefirah of Keser and specifically in *Atik* / 'the Ancient', the primordial inner realm of Keser. The *Idra Rabbah* speaks of Atik as being a Divine 'Eye' with no left side, meaning no left eye, no *Din* / judgment. Furthermore, this single Eye does not have lids; it is always open, always joyful, smiling and enjoying, and always seeing us and all of Creation with pure lovingkindness (*Zohar*, 130a. This single eye is similar to those of the *Dagei haYam* / fish of the sea, which have no eyelids or eyelashes; certainly, Atik, the Source of everything, does not need any *Shemirah* / protection and is like an open eye: *ibid*). This is the way HaKadosh Baruch Hu sees Adam and Chavah when they are still in the Divine closeness, or non-separation, of Gan Eden: *Vayar Elokim ki Tov* / "And the Creator saw that it was good" — this is the "Face" of goodness, of pure *Chesed* / kindness and love.

Seeing something as outside yourself is an act of 'distancing'. Because Hashem is 'seeing His Creation', it means that we are separate from Him, as it were. Yet, the Divine seeing from the 'perspective' of Atik is one of goodness and love, which overcomes all sense of separation and a sense of distance.

By contrast, the lower level of *Zeir Anpin* / 'the Miniature Divine Face' maintains a sense of distance and includes 'two eyes': the opposites of left and right, Chesed and Din, light and dark (*Idra Rabba*, 136a). This means the revelation of Hashem's 'Face' within this world of relativity fluctuates and changes. Sometimes HaKadosh Baruch Hu appears like a "strong, young warrior" and sometimes like a "compassionate elder" (Rashi on *Shemos*, 20:2. *P'sikta d'Rab Kahana*, 12:4) This fluctuation is basically a paradigm of Din, as it is the way Creation is observed as if 'outside of its Creator' or 'outside Gan Eden', in a mode of separation. When Creation feels itself being 'seen' in the mode of Zeir Anpin, there is the potential for tension and alienation, sin, pain, and 'earning bread by the sweat of one's brow'.

Let's understand these two types of seeing, being seen from the Atik perspective versus seeing from Zeir Anpin perspective, in terms of human life. The world is created by 'being seen' by Atik — *Vayar Elokim.* That is, Creation emerges into being with the sense of being a separate entity through this original experience of being seen. Similarly, as infants, our independent sense of self — as distinct from being an extension of our mother — begins to emerge when we perceive our mother gazing at us. In other words, the emergence of selfhood develops when we see ourselves being seen by another, when we look into our mother's eyes and see her looking at us. And more specifically, the quality of that gaze, *how* we are originally seen, forges our identity, our sense of who we are in the world. Seeing someone looking at us with unconditional love, despite our 'separation' from them, shapes how we see and experience ourselves.

When we were infants, our mother or original caregiver hopefully looked at us without any Din, with fully open eyes, as it were, and full of lovingkindness and smiles of affection and delight. Hopefully, our sense of existence identity then began to crystallize as essentially 'good' and loveable. And G-d forbid, if the reverse was true, if the first time we looked up and saw our mother looking at us, it was with judgment, anger, disinterest, or lack of focus, then our identity may have gelled in the sense of being unloved or undeserving of attention.

Nevertheless, if, for whatever reason, one did not get proper 'seeing' from their mother or primary caregiver, there is still hope. One needs to find a friend, spouse, rebbe, teacher, or healer that can either recreate or reinforce the sense of being 'seen' with unconditional love and compassion. It is never too late to re-create one's life in this way. Ultimately, we also need to turn to HaKadosh Baruch Hu, our ever-present all-loving Parent, in order to be re-birthed and reaffirmed.

By turning in Teshuvah to HaKadosh Baruch Hu, we draw upon ourselves the 'Eye' of Atik, which sees us without any Din, just absolute love and openness, exclaiming, 'It is good!' We realize on a very primal level that it is indeed good that we exist. And this is the Tikkun for any *Aveirah* / transgression — to draw down the 13 Attributes of Mercy, the 'vision' of Atik. On Yom Kippur, which is a day of pure *Rachamim* / Divine compassion, we must awaken within ourselves a sense of how

HaKadosh Baruch Hu truly sees us — with an unblinking 'Eye' of unconditional, unwavering, unending love and mercy.

May we see ourselves and others as essentially good, and inspire them to see themselves as essentially good. This is how to draw compassion and blessing into this world and to know and feel that we are blessed and capable of positive change.

Chapter Eight

YIZKOR / REMEMBERING

AFTER THE DESTRUCTION OF THE SECOND BEIS HA-MIKDASH, A CUSTOM DEVELOPED TO RAISE UP THE MEMORY OF OUR ANCESTORS SO THAT THEIR MERITS SHOULD STAND BY US NOW AND FOR OUR OFFSPRING IN THE FUTURE.

Every Yom Tov when the Torah reading speaks of offering charity, those who have lost a parent recite Yizkor and commit to offer Tzedakah in the memory of their beloved ones. Certainly, this is not intended to induce melancholy or sadness, as Yom Tov is a day of inner joy. Rather, it is to remember our parent or parents, think about them and their impact on our lives, and reciprocate by doing a positive action here below in their honor.

TIME TO RECEIVE AND GIVE FORGIVENESS

Yom Kippur is a day of Divine forgiveness. Prior to Yom Kippur, we ask for and offer forgiveness to one another, and on Yom Kippur itself, as well. As we remember our parent or parents, it may be a good time to ask their souls for forgiveness if you feel you need it from them. Perhaps you will be able to ask forgiveness for something that you never had a chance to ask forgiveness for when they were alive. In any case, this day of 'letting go' is certainly a good time to forgive them, if they need your forgiveness for any harm or wrong, G-d forbid. In this way, their memory will serve only as a blessing.

OUR ACTIONS BELOW AFFECT OUR PARENT(S) ABOVE

Torah calls Yom Kippur 'Yom *haKippurim*', which is *Kippur* / 'atonement' in the plural, indicating that it is a day of atonement both for the living and for those that have passed on.*
Hence, on Yom Kippur, we invoke the memory of our ancestors for a dual purpose: that we can be sustained through their holy memory, and also that with our positive actions, we will elevate their souls on high.

---

* As explained earlier, Yom Kippurim is a *plurale tantum*, a noun that appears only in the plural form and does not appear in the singular, to denote an abstract idea, such as, in this case, the idea of atonement. Yet on a deeper level, this day is called *Kippurim* because it brings atonement for the living and those who have passed on: *Ba'eir Heitev*, Orach Chayim, 622:8 (ולכן נקרא יה"כ בלשון רבים ר"ל לחיים ולהמתים. מהרי"ו).

Everything that exists on the physical plane corresponds to what exists on the spiritual plane, as the physical is a reflection of the metaphysical. When two people are related on a physical level, say a parent and a child, it is because they share the same soul-root in the source of all souls.

This means that although our actions can and do impact the entire world, those who are most affected by what we do are the souls most closely connected to our own soul. Thus, when children in this world give charity in honor and merit of their departed parents, this action can affect the ascension of the parents' souls above.

In our world, where body and soul are joined, there are choices. In the next world, where souls exist without bodies, there are only the effects of our choices. As a result, only in our world can people truly grow, expand and develop. There is always room for change and space to leap into new and unexplored realities. For this reason, any movement in the world of souls is dependent on the actions we take, or actions we refrain from taking, in this life. After '120 years', whatever level of integration our soul has with the Source of Life — whatever measure of the light of our soul merges with the Source of All Light — is contingent on what we have done or refrained from doing during our physical life.

This world is the cause, and the next world is the effect. This world is founded on Chesed, openness, forgiving, and a place of second chances. The place of our 'destination' as it were, the world to come is the world of Gevurah, judgment and strict order, a place of rewards and consequences. That world is a place without free choice, for our World to Come is just a consequence of our actions during this life. There is no movement or development there. And yet, since our souls below are intricately bound up with our ancestor's souls above, our actions below do propel movement and growth above, as it were. When we do something noble in memory of our loved ones, not only are we ennobling ourselves, but we are essentially causing an elevation for their souls, an elevation that would otherwise not be available for them.

We fill their void, as it were, allowing their soul to ascend into higher realms of existence and well-being. At the same time, our deeds done in their honor fill the void that their passing has left us.

Repeating the words of Yizkor alone is not sufficient; we ought to commit ourselves to do good, including giving to charity, in their name and for their benefit. Then we can be certain that the effects of our remembrance will be felt by them spiritually, and we, too, will be elevated in very tangible ways.

Chapter Nine

THE TEN MARTYRS

ONE OF THE MOST PAINFUL TRAGEDIES OF OUR HIS-
TORY OCCURRED DURING THE DESTRUCTION OF THE
SECOND BEIS HAMIKDASH WITH THE MURDER OF
SOME OF OUR GREATEST SAGES AT THE CRUEL HAND OF THE
CONQUERING ROMANS.

This incident became known as the *Asarah Harugei Malchus*
/ the Ten Martyred by the occupier government. The gist of
the story, as recorded in the liturgies of Yom Kippur and Tisha
b'Av, is as follows. Once, a sadistic Roman ruler questioned ten
Jewish sages: "What should happen to a man if he is found
kidnapping one of his brothers and selling him into slavery?"

They immediately answered him, "That kidnapper should die."
He then informed them that the Jewish people had yet to pay
for the sin of the sale of Yoseph by the other 'ten' sons of Yaakov (as Binyamin was not at all involved in the sale), and that he would
correct this oversight. The story then describes in very graphic
language the savage torture and execution of the Ten Sages.

THE DEATH OF TZADIKIM

A poetic tragic account of the Asarah Harugei Malchus is
recited twice a year: on Tisha b'Av, the day of national mourning for the destruction of the First and Second Batei haMikdash, and on Yom Kippur. On Tisha b'Av, this is part of the
Kinos / lamentation service, whereas on Yom Kippur, it is part
of the *Selichos* / 'forgiveness' service. One could ask, how does
contemplating the torture and murder of ancient holy sages
elicit forgiveness for us today?

There are two teachings in Chazal regarding the death of
Tzadikim / righteous ones in general. One says, שקולה מיתתן של
צדיקים כשריפת בית אלוקינו / "The death of Tzadikim is equivalent
to the burning of the Beis haMikdash" (*Rosh Hashanah*, 18b). It
thus makes sense that we recite the story on Tisha b'Av. The
other teaching says, מיתתן של צדיקים מכפרת / "The death of Tzadikim brings atonement" (*Moed Katan*, 28a); hence we recite it on
Yom Kippur.

It could be said that the death of great sages is an even
greater reason to mourn than is the destruction of the Beis
haMikdash — and so the recital adds relevance to Tisha b'Av.

However, on Yom Kippur, we do not recite it for the purpose of mourning but rather to elicit the *Zechus* / merit of these holy souls and to draw down forgiveness and atonement.

THE META-HISTORICAL NARRATIVE

It should be pointed out that in actuality, although they did all perish at the hands of the Romans, the Ten Martyrs did not all die at the exact same time or place. For example, Rebbe Yishmael the Cohen Gadol was killed at the end of the Second Beis haMikdash period, while Rebbe Akivah was gruesomely murdered by Hadrian decades after that Destruction, sometime after the Bar Kochvah revolt.

One point of relevance for mentioning Rebbe Akivah's death on Yom Kippur is that we know that it actually occurred on Yom Kippur. Indeed, when we mention Rebbe Akivah's death on this day, we should have *Kavanah* / intention that it is happening on this day, in the present moment, and right in front of us. As such, clearly the reason for this recitation goes beyond drawing down atonement. It is also in order to impart a deep spiritual principle and truth.

It is not by chance that the numerical value of the Hebrew names of the ten sons of Yaakov involved in the sale equals 2,858, which is the same as the names of the Ten Martyrs. Nothing is mere coincidence, and everything is Divinely orchestrated; when two words or concepts are related numerically, this is an outer indication that they are inwardly related. Of course, this numerical correlation is not what links them together, rather, they share a deeper commonality, and the numerical correlation is but a Divinely serendipitous reflection of that commonality.

WORLD OF SOULS

In our fragmented world, we perceive differentiation within time and space; from our linear perspective, the past is gone, the future has yet to come, and all that exists is the fleeting present. Also, from this physical point of view, the places where the Ten Martyrs were murdered are some distance from where we are located in space. But there is a deeper and higher view in the universe — one of absolute oneness, in which there is no real differentiation in time and space, no past, no 'fleeting present' and no future, no beginning, middle or end, no here or there. In that reality, everything exists in the ever-present 'now' and in the omnipresent 'here'.

The world of souls functions in that non-linear, unfragmented reality. Reincarnation — by which some souls incarnate again into this world in order to rectify past mistakes and retroactively affect souls that manifested here years ago — can only be understood from a perspective of a non-linear reality. Thus, the ten sons of Yaakov, who sold their brother Yoseph into slavery, were later reincarnated as the Ten Martyrs in order to create a Tikkun, to rectify their past deeds and elevate their souls.

Generally, *Gilgul Neshamos* / transmigration of souls or 'reincarnation', means that the entire soul that existed in one body descends into another for the purpose of rectifying or completing past life experiences. But the type of incarnation described in the story of the Ten Martyrs is different — to be more accurate, it should be called *Ibbur* / 'impregnation', rather than 'reincarnation'.

IBBUR / IMPREGNATION

During the course of one's life, a person may become spiritually 'impregnated' with an additional soul for a short period of time. This soul is like a guest within the host person, achieving what it needs to on earth and then departing. Sometimes such a soul visits a body in order to assist the host; at other times, it does so for its own purpose, to live once again through certain physical experiences and, as a result, achieve a sought-after elevation.

Of course, the ten sons of Yaakov did Teshuvah during their lifetime for the sale of Yoseph, as the Torah clearly portrays their regret and remorse. Yet, on the high level that they were on, even a slight blemish needs a Tikkun. A speck on a white garment shows, whereas a speck on a darker garment does not, and they were on a very high level of purity where every tiny blemish shows. And so they entered the bodies of these ten sages who were then martyred, and they received their Tikkun through that harrowing experience of *Mesiras Nefesh* / self-sacrifice.

From the perspective of oneness, ever-present 'now-ness' and omnipresent 'here-ness', *Ibbur* / impregnation has another level of meaning. Perhaps it could be said that when we are reciting the account of the Ten Martyrs, we are in some sense experiencing these events here and now, as in the intention for the recital of Rebbe Akivah's death, in particular. And ultimately, not only are these events happening 'here and now', but there is no separation at all between us and them. In the recital, we become the Ten Martyrs; we receive an Ibbur of their souls, as it were, and their Mesiras Nefesh is a Tikkun and atonement for our own lives.

DUAL NATURE OF LIFE UNFOLDING

While it is true that the ten sons of Yaakov plotted to do harm to their brother, ultimately, as Yoseph himself conceded, their deeds served the greater plan: "Although you intended to harm me, Hashem intended it for the good, in order to accomplish... that a vast people be kept alive" (*Bereishis*, 50:20). Indeed, if Yoseph had not become the vizier of Egypt, his family would have succumbed to hunger. There are multiple dimensions to everything that occurs in life. Sometimes, what seems negative and destructive from a surface perspective is really positive or the source of something constructive.

In the context of Yom Kippur, this story reminds us that we can reach a higher level of Teshuvah, a Teshuvah out of love, where our past misdeeds are transformed into merits. What seemed previously totally negative and unredeemable, now, in its new context, is viewed in a positive light. Obstacles become rungs of a ladder that allow us to climb to a higher plane.

Our faults become the seeds of virtues.

Chapter Ten

AL CHEIT

W E REPEATEDLY RECITE A PRAYER OF REPEN-
TANCE ON THIS DAY CALLED *Al Cheit*, WHICH
CONTAINS A FULL LIST OF POSSIBLE SINS, such
as, על חטא שחטאנו / "For the sin we committed before You, by
talking slander," and על חטא שחטאנו / "For the sin we committed
before You, in intimate immoralities...." With such a list of
negative actions and many terrible sins, a couple of questions
come to mind. Are we really so sinful? Why should I repent
for sins, many of which I did not commit? Should I take this
list personally?

Traditionally, parts of *Al Cheit* are sung, and this may make it seem as though we are not taking the whole list personally. However, the reason we sing them is because Teshuvah is a Mitzvah, and a Mitzvah should be done with joy. Furthermore, when *Al Cheit* is recited in the quiet Amidah prayer, it is said in a somber mode, suggesting that we are indeed taking it personally. Only during the repetition of the Amidah are parts of it sung, seeming to imply that when it is said collectively, we have the *Zechus* / merit of the *Tzibur* / congregation, and hence the certainty of forgiveness.

Still, in the list of transgressions, there are things that we most likely have not done; why do we recite the whole list and pound our chest? We are taught, "Just as we ought to know our shortcomings, we should also know our value." In other words, just as it is important for us to acknowledge where we have failed in order that we can take responsibility and seek to amend our behavior, so, too, it is important that we do not belittle ourselves by assuming responsibility for something we have not done. A person who keeps on knocking him or herself down with harsh self-criticism will not have the strength to get up. This is especially true if there is, in fact, no reason to be critical in the first place.

Most people, it could be argued, are guilty of very subtle forms of each sin listed. For example, most people have "shed the blood" of another person by embarrassing them. Likewise, most people have committed "idolatry" by expressing anger. But even if this is true, what about the noble Tzadikim who have not committed these sins in any shape or form? Why do they also recite this list of sins on Yom Kippur?

Another question might be asked: is this the right time to be confessing our sins at all? Can it be that on this holiest of holy days, gathered in a holy place with holy people, there is nothing better to talk about than these base behaviors? And are we not supposed to have already examined our behavior, confessed our sins and expressed all our regrets, in the month of Elul, in preparation for Rosh Hashanah and Yom Kippur? Are we not finished with the lower Teshuvah and now involved in the higher Teshuvah of love?

VERTICAL & HORIZONTAL TRANSCENDENCE

Yom Kippur, as explored, is indeed a day of love and transcendence, of vertical upward movement into a clear, weightless state of angelic experience. We rise above the need to eat, drink, and all other human activities of survival and perpetuation. Considering this, it is even more perplexing that we should speak of terrible sins while we are, or aspire to be, in a higher, angelic state.

The answer is that transcendence can be experienced vertically and horizontally. Vertical transcendence is an upward and inward movement into the Infinite Light of Hashem. Such inwardness can make one detached from society and people, as well as from bodily needs. Yet Yom Kippur is also about *horizontal* transcendence, meaning, transcending oneself by being open and at one with others.

על חטא שחטאנו / "for the sins we committed...." Note that the language is not singular, as in, the sins "I" committed. The use of the plural "we" is, on a deeper level, an expression of personal transcendence. We are able to transcend our focus on the 'I 'of self and connect to the collective "we."

When we recite the *Al Cheit* and ask forgiveness, it is, of course, hopefully not for our literal personal transgressions that we ask; rather, it is for all the transgressions, on any level, of all of Klal Yisrael. We are saying, 'I share their struggle and feel their existential lack as my own.' Because of the principle of *Arvus* / interpersonal responsibility and because of our focus on personal transcendence on this day, the pain of all others is my pain; their Tikkun is my Tikkun. And, of course, their joy is my joy.

It may be that I am personally transcendent of all such lowly behaviors, yet, my transcendence expands 'horizontally' as well. I am open to feeling other people's struggles and darkness (*Likutei Sichos*, 19, p. 303).

CREATING A TIKKUN FOR THE WORLD CREATED BY LETTERS / DIVINE SOUNDS

Al Cheit follows the order of the Aleph-Beis; we first recite two sins that begin with Aleph and then two transgressions that begin with the letter Beis. The simple reason for this literary technique is in order to avoid the impression that only the listed transgressions have been committed and nothing else. If it were a simple list of transgressions, it would imply that only these and not others were committed, whereas employing the letters of the Aleph Beis symbolizes an inclusion of all other possibilities that begin with a given letter.

On a deeper level, *Al Cheit* follows the Aleph-Beis in order to create a Tikkun for the world, which is continually being created through the letters of Divine speech. The Hebrew letters contain all the sounds and vibrations of Creation, and thus all phenomena and events.

Every negative action, word or even thought, as explored earlier, causes a cosmic 'smudge' in the letters in the supernal Torah where these negative actions are written or hinted at. For example, "Do not steal" can appear to become "*Do* steal...." As the Torah is the blueprint and source of reality, the collective consciousness then begins to feel as if stealing is normal and even healthy. The world becomes affected by a spiritual or cultural 'virus', until stealing is ubiquitous.

Sadly, such cultural viruses are all too common; it takes only one mentally unstable youngster, perhaps infected through contact with hateful propaganda, to go on a shooting spree at school (Heaven protect us and have mercy) — and then multiple similar events start happening, one after the next. Yet, while this is true of evil, it is actually much more true of positivity and holiness. By saying the *Al Cheit* for all possible transgressions 'from A through Z', and doing Teshuvah for everything and for all people, we are empowering all human beings to make Teshuvah. And we are recalibrating the letters of the cosmic Torah, as it were, to feed this world with a tendency to nobility and true goodness.

We are repairing the spiritual acoustics of the world, so-to-speak, so that the world can resonate with the cosmic letters and words that articulate its ultimate purpose and reveal Hashem's Presence here in this world.

COMMITTED BEFORE YOU

Each confession in *Al Cheit* is preceded by the phrase, "For the transgressions שחטאנו לפניך / that we committed in front of You...". The greatest sin is our forgetfulness and loss of focus on the fact that our lives are lived לפניך / "in front of You." Indeed, if we really knew and consistently felt that we are 'in front of Hashem", we would experience too much awe and love to commit any willful transgressions. And the deepest Teshuvah is awakening the awareness and awe of being "in front of You" at all times.

There is Teshuvah of details, "I have committed this... and committed that...," but there is also Teshuvah of the bigger picture. Underneath all the details is a bigger contextual issue of not living לפניך / 'in front of You'. As we are saying the *Al Cheit* we need to ponder, 'Is my life oriented towards HaKadosh Baruch Hu? Am I living with the awareness of being in the presence of Ultimate Greatness? Is my basic and fundamental desire to live in the Presence of my Creator? Do I know deep down that I am always being seen and cherished by the Omniscient, Omnipresent One? Am I truly engaging my gifts and greatness to the best of my ability?

Becoming aware of the bigger picture — that there is a King and Master of the Universe and that we are living in His Presence — will stimulate and energize us to serve Him joyfully and create a dwelling place for Him here, in this world.

Chapter Eleven
THE STORY OF YONAH

DURING THE MINCHAH SERVICE, WE READ *THE BOOK OF YONAH* (ONE OF THE *Trei Asar* / TWELVE PROPHETIC BOOKS). This text tells the story of the Prophet Yonah as he is designated by Hashem to bring the city of Nineveh to Teshuvah, and yet initially resists the assignment.

We read this story as Yom Kippur is coming to a close to teach us that it is never too late to change our ways. As for the people of Nineveh, Teshuvah was always a possibility, and it had the power to alter the course of even the harshest Heavenly decrees.

The great city of Nineveh, an Assyrian city with a population of over 120,000 people, was notoriously corrupt. Assyria itself was the arch-enemy of Israel during the Age of the Prophets. Yet Hakadosh Baruch Hu desired to give its citizens a chance to mend their ways, and Yonah was sent to warn them of the dire consequences of their negative actions and arouse in them a positive resolve to change their ways.

Feeling overwhelmed and overburdened by his Divine mission, Yonah chose to run away instead, and jumped on a ship sailing out to sea.

Often, we human beings act in a certain way, whether directed by a subconscious reaction or a response to certain stimuli, and yet because the mind needs to rationalize everything, we invent reasons for our actions, post facto. These intellectual reasons, of course, are not the real root cause of our behavior. If, unknown to you, laughing gas were released into a room that you were in, and you began laughing, your mind would come up with several reasons why the room itself was humorous.

Chazal tell us that Yonah gave reasons for his flight as follows. If, in fact, the people of Nineveh would change their ways and be spared, then they would declare that his prophetic prediction of domesday was false to begin with, or that Divine judgment does not exist. He also reasoned that if they succeeded in mending their ways, it would reflect negatively on Klal Yisrael, who were constantly being reprimanded for their negative behavior, and who had not mended their ways (*Pirkei d'Rebbe Eliezer*, 10).

Yonah had boarded a ship only to find himself in the middle of a turbulent storm. Aboard the ship, everyone prayed intensely while Yonah sat on the side. When it became understood that he was the cause of the raging sea, he told them to throw him into the water in order to save the ship. Reluctantly, they did so, and the sea was calmed.

Once overboard, Yonah was swallowed by an enormous fish, and still alive inside, he prayed to HaKadosh Baruch Hu. His prayers were answered, and the fish spit him out. Finally accepting his mission, he went to Nineveh and chastised the city's inhabitants for their harmful ways. The city was inspired; they unanimously did Teshuvah and were spared.

A literal reading of the story teaches us many things: about the human tendency to flee our responsibilities, about our tendency to justify and rationalize our avoidance of responsibility, and of course, about the power of Teshuvah.

Everything in the Torah has at the very least four levels of meaning: 1) *Peshat* / simple or literal, 2) *Remez* / allegorical or symbolic, 3) *Derash*, implied or interpretive, and 4) *Sod* / secret or mystical. Each level of meaning is not intended to supplement or exclude the others; rather, it includes and supports the others.

Yonah was a literal man, but as the name *Yonah* / dove suggests, it also refers to our soul, our pristine self (*Zohar* 2, 199a. Gra, *Yonah*, 1:1. The Zohar also mentions a holy Yonah, which corresponds to the final letter in the Name of Hashem, the Shechinah: *Tikkunei Zohar*, 9a. In general, the bride in the book of *Shir haShirim* / the Song of Songs, which is Klal Yisrael (and the Tzadikim), is compared to the dove. See also *Shir haShirim Rabbah*, 1:15. *Berachos*, 53b. *Sanhedrin*, 108b. יונה – ישראל, שנאמר יונתי תמתי: Rashi, *Sotah*, 11b).

In *Shir haShirim*, the dove is the image used to describe the loving and loyal lover, who is deeply enamored with her spouse and looks only to him and is attached only to him.

Our soul is a loyal lover of her Groom. Our love for HaKadosh Baruch Hu is pristine and pure. On the journey of life, our soul 'descends' into this material, manifest realm and becomes embodied and enclothed within a carrier, a 'ship'. This is a metaphor for the body, which carries the soul through the journey of life, directed by the captain, the soul's higher wisdom.

In a harmonious existence, the body, soul and higher wisdom are joined as one; the ship, the soul, and the captain work in synchronicity with each other. To live in such total alignment between soul, body and mind means to live fully. The body and soul are likened to a blind and a lame person working in unison (*Sanhedrin*, 91b). The soul on its own is lame. It sees purpose, but lacks the tools to actually do anything. The body on its own is blind. It may be able to go where it wants but has no inkling where to go. In short, the soul empowers us to see, but it is the body that actually gets us there. The body moves about, but it is the indwelling hidden spirit that directs the movement. Together, in harmony, they join and can become the best of friends.

Our task is to steer our ship toward the 'city', toward our worldly environment and surroundings, with a goal to transform them. We choose the seas upon which we sail our ship — they can be the waters of Torah or the waters of passion, greed and self-aggrandizement.

Often, there are people who direct their ships far away from the city, from others and from civilization. They shy away from their environment and attempt to avoid their spiritual responsibilities. Some of us run away from our responsibilities toward others even by immersing ourselves in Torah study at the expense of assisting them in learning. Others are so engrossed in their own small lives that it is a detriment to those around them.

Of course, city life can be difficult (ישיבת כרכים קשה: *Kesuvos*, 110b), and certainly when the population is debased. In the latter case, it may be correct to separate oneself from that city and society.*

---

* In the words of the Rambam, וכן אם היה במדינה שמנהגותיה רעים ואין אנשיה הולכים בדרך ישרה ילך למקום שאנשיה צדיקים ונוהגים בדרך טובים. ואם היו כל המדינות שהוא יודעם ושומע שמועתן נוהגים בדרך לא טובה כמו זמננו. או שאינו יכול ללכת למדינה שמנהגותיה טובים מפני הגיסות או מפני החלי ישב לבדו יחידי / "Likewise, if a person is in a state or city where evil customs prevail and where the people are not following the righteous ways, he should go to a place where the inhabitants are righteous and follow the way of the good. If all the states known to him, or of which information has reached him, are followers of a path that is not good, even as it is in our own times, or if he is unable to migrate to a state whose rules of conduct are good, either on account of military operations or on account of sickness, he should isolate himself and live in seclusion": *Hilchos De'os*, 6:1.

Nineveh represents exactly such a society, one gone astray, an entire civilization gone off course. In this place, the *Yonah /* dove, the pure soul, finds it difficult to live there and rightfully refuses to go there. Yet, this is exactly what Hashem demanded of Yonah. Sometimes our souls must go on a mission of self-sacrifice by a kind of Divine mandate. Sometimes it is not our first choice. Sometimes we feel a definite holy *Shelichus /* sacred mission calling us to go and save a 'city', and then afterward retreat, if appropriate.

Sadly, there are sleepy 'souls' who shy away from their responsibility when they see others struggling in their *Avodas Hashem /* serving Hashem and tell themselves 'It's not my problem.' Sadder still, it often seems that only tragedy brings us closer to the truth of who we are and what our purpose is; only stormy waters and being 'swallowed by a fish' lead to introspection and self-evaluation. Tragedy seems to break down the ego and our resistance to change much more than joyful experiences, which generally tend to reinforce our arrogance.

At times the captain of our ship, our soul's *Seichel /* intelligence and *Yetzer Tov /* good inclination, calls to us, trying to awaken us to how we have been living and to the lies that we have been telling ourselves. This inner voice of moral and spiritual clarity rouses us, "How can you be sleeping so soundly? Stand up and call out to Hashem!"

But to awaken to life and its purpose can be daunting, certainly, if one is simply cruising through life on autopilot. Drastic life changes may wreak havoc on one's internal narrative, and the task may seem so overwhelming that one may consider himself unworthy and incapable. And so, as Yonah in the story, we tell the captain and his sailors: 'Throw me overboard — I give up, I simply cannot do this!'

And so Yonah, our soul, is thrown into the sea. As soon as we hit the water, we are swallowed by a huge fish. On one level, the 'belly of the fish' represents the casket of one's burial. Not being able to steer back to land, one literally drowns from the responsibilities and burdens of life's journey. On a deeper level, in terms of our life's journey, the 'fish' is an inner disquiet that stirs and 'swims' far below our conscious mind.

Fish, in Hebrew, is *Dag*, which is related to the word *Da'agah*, meaning 'worry' (*Tikkunei Zohar*, 53, *Kaf haChayim*, Orach Chayim, Siman 583:9. In fact, in *Nechemyah* (13:16), the word *Dag* / fish is once spelled Da'ag: והצרים ישבו בה מביאים דאג וכל-מכר ומכרים בשבת לבני יהודה ובירושלם). Before the last strand of light is eclipsed, as we are swallowed up by the oblivion and abyss, a Divine worry awakens within us, as it were. This is the voice that pulsates deep within us, reminding us that there is still a possibility for us to realize and actualize our true potential and step up to life.

This inner, spiritual existential 'worry' nags and goads us to return to our responsibilities and not give up on life. Deep within the belly of our physical worries and existential anxieties, a small glimmer of light emerges in the form of a fear that we will finally run away from our very selves. Suddenly we find ourselves ejected back onto the land.

Ultimately, like the Prophet Yonah, we too return to the 'city', learn to live authentically, and inspire others to Teshuvah and to live their purpose as well.

Sometimes it is our 'failures', our being thrown overboard — and even our deep worry over these failures — that allow us to return to land and our mission, and become infinitely more whole and complete than we were before. The Gemara says that a person does not fully grasp something until they have first stumbled in it (אין אדם עומד על דברי תורה אלא אם כן נכשל בהן: *Gitin*, 43a). Ironically, there is only one way to success, and that is through 'failure'.

When you are successful, you are whole and complete, but unfortunately, you cannot break out beyond your own uni-verse. When everything seems perfect, your life follows a rigid pattern; you tend to rest in your sense of completeness and contentment. When you fail, you are broken. You look around yourself and say, "This is worthless. I feel as if I am confined in the belly of a fish! I must get out; I must go beyond this level." Now you have the strength to escape, and to grow and expand into the Infinite. The shell of your finite limitations is broken, the fish spits you out onto dry land, and you are empowered to act.

Your Teshuvah has now given you the amazing ability to go beyond the limits of being 'whole and complete'. In the words of *The Zohar* (1:129b), you have come back to life "with increased invigoration." You have reached a new way of being, and in this newness, you serve the Infinite One with limitless vigor and passion. And now your mistakes are revealed as merits, and your seeming failures and limitations are revealed as infinite successes.

והאמר ריש לקיש גדולה תשובה שזדונות נעשות לו כזכיות

And behold, Resh Lakish has said:

"Teshuvah is great, for with it even intentional sins are made into virtues for you!" (*Yuma,* 86b)

Epilogue
NOW WHAT?
AFTER YOM KIPPUR

FTER 25–26 HOURS OF INTENSE *Davening* / PRAYING, SELF-REFLECTION, AND TESHUVAH, THROUGHOUT WHICH WE HAVE STOOD IN AN ANGELIC POSTURE AND REVEALED OUR UNSTAINABLE ESSENCE — the very first words we utter, as we begin the *Ma'ariv* / Evening Service, are והוא רחום יכפר עון / "And Hashem is Compassionate; may He forgive our sins!" What sins? We have just been forgiven and attained utter purity; what could we have possibly done in the short moment between the conclusion of Yom Kippur and the beginning of Ma'ariv?

WITH YOM KIPPUR COMES GREATER AWARENESS

A story of Rebbe Saadiah Gaon, the great Ninth Century Babylonian sage, may shed some light.

Once, he was asked by his students why he was in a constant state of Teshuvah, always immersed in introspection and pushing tirelessly to better himself. He replied that on one of his many trips, he spent a night at an inn, and the innkeeper, a pious individual, treated him very kindly as he did all his guests. The next morning, when the innkeeper saw a huge crowd gathered at his inn to greet the celebrated sage, he realized who his guest was. Sometime later, with a bitter heart, the innkeeper came to ask forgiveness from Rebbe Saadiah for the way he treated him. "But why are you apologizing?" Reb Saadiah asked, "You treated me so kindly." The inn-keeper replied, "No, I treated you as I would all other guests, but had I known who you were, I would have treated you as is fitting for a man of your stature."

This experience, Reb Saadiah said, initiated him into a constant state of Teshuvah. As he explained, "Every day that I live, I gain knowledge, awareness and understanding. Every day I realize that compared to my previous understanding, there is much more room to grow. Every day, indeed every moment, calls for new levels of return."

New possibilities, undiscovered spiritual opportunities and knowledge are opened to us with every new day. With greater understanding of the "stature" of HaKadosh Baruch Hu and Torah, can come a renewed understanding of our own true potential. We learn how much more we can improve and how much further we can grow. We realize we cannot just treat the present day as we would treat all other days. Every day is a *Gadol*!

If ever there was the perfect time to resolve and accept upon ourselves a greater and more profound level of Teshuvah, it is the day after Yom Kippur. And so, at the end of this awesome day, we immediately begin the process of Teshuvah all over again. As we reenter the dimensional world after Yom Kippur, a path of aliveness and growth is open to us, a continuous, ever-evolving movement toward Hashem, toward one's true self and toward others. It is now up to us to walk this path, one step at a time.

And yet, there is an even more profound reason why we beseech HaKadosh Baruch Hu and say, והוא רחום יכפר עון / "May the Merciful one forgive our sins...."

TESHUVAH FOR THINKING THAT OUR TESHUVAH WAS INEFFECTIVE

While it is true that in the moment after the conclusion of Yom Kippur one cannot realistically commit any negative actions, as there is no real time to act, one could, in that short window, entertain an insidious and devastating negative thought: 'Did Yom Kippur really work? Have I really been forgiven?' The greatest sin in the world at that moment would be to feel that 'Maybe all this *Avodah* / spiritual work was a waste of effort, for I will surely go back to my old ways before long.'

Or, 'Perhaps the "essence of the day" did not atone in my case; maybe forgiveness was not granted.'

Just in case we momentarily entertained this terrible thought, and even if we did so subconsciously, we now immediately turn to Hashem again and plead, "May the Merciful one forgive us!" 'Forgive us for thinking that we may not be forgiven! Forgive us for doubting ourselves, for doubting You!'

"HASHEM HAS ALREADY ACCEPTED YOUR AVODAH"

As Yom Kippur comes to a close, says the wise Shlomo haMelech / King Solomon, a Heavenly Voice rings out and declares, לך אכול בשמחה לחמך ושתה בלב טוב יינך כי כבר רצה האלקים את מעשיך / "Go your way, eat your bread with joy and drink your wine with a merry heart, for Hashem כבר / 'has already' accepted your work" (*Koheles*, 9:7). And for this reason, the night following Yom Kippur we eat and are joyous (*Shulchan Aruch*, Orach Chayim, 624:7).

After a full day of receiving atonement we need to sense that כבר רצה / Hashem has indeed "already accepted" our *Tefilos* / prayers, and we are forgiven. We are lighter and freer, for there is a sense that כבר / we have "already" attained a posture of wholeness and holiness; we are already at the goal.

If, after Yom Kippur, you feel a sense of joy, elation, a lightness of being, or being freed of the weight of your past negative actions, this is not merely because you did not eat for 25 hours, rather it is a symptom of something deeper. Your soul knows that you have been forgiven simply because Hashem says, "Today is a day of atonement." Our mind may question the logic of such a statement, but our soul knows.

If, on the other hand, we feel down, depleted, exhausted and empty after Yom Kippur, perhaps *that* is because we have not eaten for 25 hours. Those feelings do not mean that the day was just a waste of time, nor that our Teshuvah was not accepted, nor that Hashem does not have the power to atone for us, Heaven forbid. In case we have made such an erroneous interpretation of our sensations, we quickly turn back to prayer: "Please forgive us for the sin of possibly thinking that we are not forgiven."

YIUSH IS THE GREATEST OBSTACLE FOR GROWTH

Truly, the most destructive *Kelipah* / concealment and hindrance to genuine growth is self-doubt and *Yi'ush* / despair, giving up hope. A person cannot move forward with despair. There are those who doubt their abilities, and then there are those who doubt themselves as people. Sometimes such crippling doubts arise because of one's past actions and sometimes because of their upbringing or conditioning. In any case, to rid ourselves of self-doubt and lack of belief in ourselves and our future, we have to always remember that if Hashem, the Master of the Universe, thinks that we are worth creating and sustaining at this very moment, then we are certainly worthy.

There is also a point where one must simply move on. True, one needs to deal with the past, but also not to let the past crowd out and colonize the present. There is no question that we need to fix what was wrong or broken, but this focus cannot take over our entire life. Sometimes we need to stop looking at the past and see the present and envision the future, to *turn from evil and do good*. At such a point, we must pivot from focusing on the 'imperfect self' and begin instead to inhabit our eternally 'perfect self'. When we fall, we should never give up hope and tell ourselves we are a failure. We need to get back up and learn to cut our losses, at least for the time being, in order to move on toward our ultimate goal.

To be forgiven means to be released from the weight of your past actions. When your negative past no longer blocks your entry to the gift of the present, you can be sure that you have been forgiven. This release can occur in a tangible psychological and even physical way. It is not that you are relinquishing ownership of those past actions or that you are simply throwing them away. Rather, you acknowledge those actions as 'my problems', while at the same time, you acknowledge that, "That was then, and this is now. I *am* forgiven. I *can* live freely here, now."

"BEFORE ME," NOT "IN ME" OR "ME"

These sentiments of self-worth and feeling forgiven are not in contradiction with the wise words of Dovid haMelech / King David who said, וחטאתי נגדי תמיד / "My sin is *in front of me* constantly" (*Tehillim*, 51:5. Fascinatingly, Dovid was forgiven for his 'sin' on Yom Kippur: *Zohar*, Hakdamah, 8b). If you transgressed and did Teshuvah but still feel burdened by the effects of your actions, if you still feel inadequate, unworthy, doubtful or hopeless because of what you have done, then your actions are no longer "in front of" you, rather they are buried *within* you. And even more devastating, they 'are' you, in as much as you still identify with them, and they therefore seem to define who you are as a person.

One's past can sometimes be overwhelmingly heavy, like an anchor holding one down to the *Metzulos haYam* / the dark depths of the sea. By obsessing over the past, you give it permission to keep you from living your best life in the present.

Following the episode of the Golden Calf, according to Rashi, we were asked to establish and erect the *Mishkan* / Tabernacle as atonement. Moshe told the people to bring the materials for building the Mishkan, and we, swept up in the emotion of Teshuvah, began to bring everything we possibly could. Finally, the wise elders came to Moshe and said, *Marbim haAm l'Havi* / "The people are bringing more than enough..." (*Shemos*, 36:5). Aside from the literal meaning that there were physically enough materials, the Torah is saying that the inner work of Teshuvah was already "enough": 'Stop beating yourselves up, it is enough already, move on. Affirm the truth that HaKadosh Baruch Hu is infinitely forgiving and loving; say to yourself: *I am His creation, and therefore I am surely not outside of His love.*'

In the times of the Beis haMikdash, when there was an open revelation of Hashem's Presence in the world, and certainly within the Beis haMikdash, one would bring an offering for atonement. If their Teshuvah and offering was accepted on High, an image of a lion of fire would appear suspended over the altar (*Zohar* 3, 240a). Today, we do not have a physical Beis haMikdash, yet, many Tzadikim reveal that the sensation of lightness and joy that follows Teshuvah is in fact the sign from Heaven that your Teshuvah has been received.

As Yom Kippur is coming to a close, we sound a great blast of the Shofar announcing that the day is over and we should go celebrate and feast (מה שתוקעים במוצאי יוה"כ אינו אלא להודיע שהוא לילה ויאכילו את בניהם שהתענו וגם להכין סעודת מוצאי יוה"כ שהיא כעין י"ט: Tosefos, *Shabbos*, 114b. Smag, Siman, 69).

It is a time of great joy, as we are not only forgiven by, but betrothed to, our Beloved (ביום חתונתו זה מתן תורה / "On the day of his wedding" this is the giving of the Torah." This is in reference to the day the Second Luchos were given, Yom Kippur: *Ta'anis*, 26b, Rashi, *ad loc*). Now we are ready to go wrap ourselves in our Beloved's Embrace, the Sukkah, and celebrate the seven days of *Sheva Berachos* / wedding feasts, which are the seven days of Sukkos, *Zeman Simchaseinu* / "the time of our joy." This is why we have a custom to construct our Sukkah on the night after Yom Kippur, immediately following the breaking of our fast, or at the very least, we speak about our plans for building a Sukkah.

We have moved from pleading, crying, and beating our chest in remorse, to now carrying our Lulav in triumphant pride. We shamelessly move out of our home into the Sukkah to live publically with our Beloved. In our ecstasy, we have no fear of the elements and celebrate our forgiveness and intimacy openly, in view of neighbors or passersby. Our Simchah, our song and our dance, express our full acceptance, our complete certainty, and our wholehearted belief in Hashem's total forgiveness. All reality has been renewed and sweetened; we and our Beloved are one, with each other and with the world.

זה־היום עשה ה׳ נגילה ונשמחה בו:

"This is the day that the Infinite One made; may we rejoice and be happy on it." (*Tehillim*, 118:24)

Other Books by Rav Pinson

RECLAIMING THE SELF
The Way of Teshuvah

Teshuvah is one of the great gifts of life. It speaks of a hope for a better today and empowers us to choose a brighter tomorrow. But what exactly is Teshuvah? How does it work? How can we undo our past and how do we deal with guilt? And what is healthy regret without eroding our self-esteem? In this fascinating and empowering book, the path for genuine transformation and a way to include all of our past in the powerful moment of the now, is explored and demonstrated.

THE MYSTERY OF KADDISH
Understanding the Mourner's Kaddish

The Mystery of Kaddish is an in-depth exploration into the Mourner's Prayer. Throughout Jewish history, there have been many rites and rituals associated with loss and mourning, yet none have prevailed quite like the Mourner's Kaddish Prayer, which has become the definitive ritual of mourning. The book explores the source of this prayer and deconstructs the meaning to better understand the grieving process and how the Kaddish prayer supports and uplifts the bereaved through their own personal journey to healing.

UPSHERNISH: The First Haircut
Exploring the Laws, Customs & Meanings
of a Boy's First Haircut

What is the meaning of Upsherin, the traditional celebration of a boy's first haircut at the age of three? Why is a boy's hair allowed to grow freely for his first three years? What is the deeper import of hair in all its lengths and varieties? What is the meaning of hair coverings? Includes a guide to conducting an Upsherin ceremony.

A BOND FOR ETERNITY
Understanding the Bris Milah

What is the Bris Milah – the covenant of circumcision? What does it represent, symbolize and signify? This book provides an in depth and sensitive review of this fundamental Mitzvah. In this little masterpiece of wisdom – profound yet accessible —the deeper meaning of this essential rite of passage and its eternal link to the Jewish people, is revealed and explored.

REINCARNATION AND JUDAISM
The Journey of the Soul

A fascinating analysis of the concept of Gilgul / Reincarnation. Dipping into the fountain of ancient wisdom and modern understanding, this book addresses and answers such basic questions as: What is reincarnation? Why does it occur? And how does it affect us personally?

INNER RHYTHMS
The Kabbalah of MUSIC

Exploring the inner dimension of sound and music, and particularly, how music permeates all aspects of life. The topics range from Deveikus/ Unity and Yichudim/Unifications, to the more personal issues, such as Simcha/Happiness and Marirus/ sadness.

MEDITATION AND JUDAISM
Exploring the Jewish Meditative Paths

A comprehensive work encompassing the entire spectrum of Jewish thought, from the sages of the Talmud and the early Kabbalists to the modern philosophers and Chassidic masters. This book is both a scholarly, in-depth study of meditative practices, and a practical, easy to follow guide for any person interested in meditating the Jewish way.

————————

TOWARD THE INFINITE

A book focusing exclusively on the Chassidic approach to meditation known as Hisbonenus. Encompassing the entire meditative experience, it takes the reader on a comprehensive and engaging journey through this unique practice. The book explores the various states of consciousness that a person encounters in the course of the meditation, beginning at a level of extreme self-awareness and concluding with a state of total non-awareness.

————————

THIRTY – TWO GATES OF WISDOM
into the Heart of Kabbalah & Chassidus

What is Kabbalah? And what are the differences between the theoretical, meditative, magical and personal Kabbalistic teachings? What are the four paths of interpreting the teachings of the ARIzal? What did Chassidus teach? These are some of the fundamental issues expanded upon in this text. And then, more specifically, why are there so many names of G-d and what do they represent? What are the key concepts of these deeper teachings?

The book explores the grand narrative of the great chain of reality, how there was and is a movement from the Infinite Oneness of Hashem to a world of (apparent) duality and multiplicity.

THE PURIM READER

The Holiday of Purim Explored

With a Persian name, a masquerade dress code and a woman as the heroine, Purim is certainly unusual amongst the Jewish holidays. Most people are very familiar with the costumes, Megilah and revelry, but are mystified by their significance. This book offers a glimpse into the hidden world of Purim, uncovering these mysteries and offering a deeper understanding of this unique holiday.

EIGHT LIGHTS
8 Meditations for Chanukah

What is the meaning and message of Chanukah? What is the spiritual significance of the Lights of the Menorah? What are the Lights telling us? What is the deeper dimension of the Dreidel? Rav Pinson, with his trademark deep learning and spiritual sensitivity guides us through eight meditations relating to the Lights of the Menorah, the eight days of Chanukah, and a fascinating exploration of the symbolism and structure of the Dreidel. Includes a detailed how-to guide for lighting the Chanukah Menorah.

PASSPORT TO KABBALAH
A Journey of Inner Transformation

Life is a journey full of ups and downs, inside-outs, and unexpected detours. There are times when we think we know exactly where we want to be headed, and other times when we are so lost we don't even know where we are. This slim book provides readers with a passport of sorts to help them through any obstacles along their path of self-refinement, reflection, and self-transformation.

———

THE FOUR SPECIES
The Symbolism of the Lulav & Esrog

The Four Species have inspired countless commentaries and traditions and intrigued scholars and mystics alike. In this little masterpiece of wisdom both profound and practical - the deep symbolic roots and nature of the Four Species are explored. The Na'anuim, or ritual of the Lulav movement, is meticulously detailed and Kavanos,, are offered for use with the practice. Includes an illustrated guide to the Lulav Movements.

———

THE BOOK OF LIFE AFTER LIFE

What is a soul? What happens to us after we physically die?

What is consciousness, and can it survive without a physical brain?

Can we remember our past lives?

Do near-death experiences prove immortality?

What is Gan Eden? Resurrection?

Exploring the possibility of surviving death, the near-death experience and a glimpse into what awaits us after this life.

(This book is an updated and expanded version of the book; Jewish Wisdom of the Afterlife)

THE GARDEN OF PARADOX:

The Essence of Non - Dual Kabbalah

This book is a Primer on the Essential Philosophy of Kabbalah presented as a series of 3 conversations, revealing the mysteries of Creator, Creation and Consciousness. With three representational students, embodying respectively, the philosopher, the activist and the mystic, the book, tackles the larger questions of life. Who is G-d? Who am I? Why do I exist? What is my purpose in this life? Written in clear and concise prose, the text, gently guides the reader towards making sense of life's paradoxes and living meaningfully.

BREATHING & QUIETING THE MIND

Achieving a sense of self-mastery and inner freedom demands that we gain a measure of hegemony over our thoughts. We learn to choose out thoughts so that we are not at the mercy of whatever belches up to the mind. Through quieting the mind and conscious breathing we can slow the onrush of anxious, scattered thinking and come to a deeper awareness of the interconnectedness of all of life.

Source texts are included in translation, with how-to-guides for the various practices.

SEVEN PATHS TO LOVE, LIFE, PURPOSE & SERENITY:

A Book on the Sheva Mitzvos

SOUND AND VIBRATION:
Tuning into the Echoes of Creation

Through our perception of sound and vibration we internalize the world around us. What we hear, and how we process that hearing, has a profound impact on how we experience life. What we hear can empower us or harm us. A defining human capacity is to harness the power sound -- through speech, dialogue, and song, and through listening to others. Hearing is primary dimension of our existence. In fact, as a fetus our ears were the first fully operating sensory organs to develop.

This book will guide you in methods of utilizing the power of sound and vibration to heal and maintain mental, emotional and spiritual health, to fine-tune your Midos and even to guide you into deeper levels of Deveikus / conscious unity with Hashem. The vibratory patterns of the Aleph-Beis are particularly useful portals into our deeper conscious selves. Through chanting and deep listening, we can use the letters and sounds to shift our very mindset, to induce us into a state of presence and spiritual elevation.

THE POWER OF CHOICE:
A Practical Guide to Conscious Living

It is the essential premise of this book that we hold the key to unlock many of the gates that seem closed to us and keep us from living our fullest life. That key we all hold is the power to choose. The Power of Choice is the primary tool that we have at our disposal to impact the world and effect change within our own lives. We often give up this power to outside forces such as the market, media, politicians or peer pressure; or to internal forces that often function beyond our conscious control such as ego, anger, lust, greed or jealousy. Making conscious, compassionate and creative decisions is the cornerstone of living a mature and meaningful life.

MYSTIC TALES FROM THE EMEK HAMELECH

Mystic Tales of the Emek HaMelech, is a wondrous and inspiring collection of stories culled from the Emek HaMelech. Emek HaMelech, from which these stories have been taken, (as well as its author) is a bit of a mystery. But like all good mysteries, it is one worth investigating. In this spirit the present volume is being offered to the general public in the merit and memory of its saintly author, as well as in the hopes of introducing a vital voice of deeper Torah teaching and tradition to a contemporary English speaking audience

INNER WORLDS OF JEWISH PRAYER
A Guide to Develop and Deepen the Prayer Experience

While much attention has been paid to the poetry, history, theology and contextual meaning of the prayers, the intention of this work is to provide a guide to finding meaning and effecting transformation through the prayer experience itself.

Explore: *What happens when we pray? *How do we enter the mind-state of prayer? *Learning to incorporate the body into the prayers. *Discover techniques to enhance and deepen prayer and make it a transformative experience.

This empowering and inspiring text, demonstrates how through proper mindset, preparation and dedication, the experience of prayer can be deeply transformative and ultimately, life-altering.

WRAPPED IN MAJESTY
Tefillin - Exploring the Mystery

Tefillin, the black boxes and leather straps that are worn during prayer, are curiously powerful and mysterious. Within the inky black boxes lie untold secrets. In this profound, passionate and thought-provoking text, the multi-dimensional perspectives of Tefillin are explored and revealed. Magically weaving together all levels of Torah including the Peshat (literal observation), to Remez (allegorical), to Derush, (homiletic), to Sod (hidden) into one beautiful tapestry. Inspirational and instructive, Wrapped in Majesty: Tefillin, will make putting on the Tefillin more meaningful and inspiring.

SECRETS OF THE MIKVAH:
Waters of Transformation

A Mikvah is a pool of water used for the purpose of ritual immersion; a place where one moves from a state of Tumah; impurity, blockage and death— to a place of Teharah; purity, fluidity and life.

In SECRETS OF THE MIKVAH, Rav Pinson delves into the transformative powers of the Mikvah with his trademark all-encompassing perspective that ranges from the literal, Pshat observation and Halachic implications of the texts, to the allegorical, the philosophical, and finally, to the deep secrets of the Mikvah as revealed by Kabbalah and Chassidus.

This insightful and inspirational text demonstrates how immersion in a Mikvah can be a transformative and life-altering practice, and includes various Kavanos—deep intentions—for all people, through various stages of life, that empower and enrich the immersion experience.

THE MYSTERY OF SHABBOS
Shabbat Rediscovered

Delving into the transformative power of Shabbos. With an all-encompassing perspective that ranges from the literal, Pshat observation and Halachic implications of the texts, to the allegorical, the philosophical, and finally, to the deeper secrets as revealed by Kabbalah and Chassidus, creating an elegant tapestry of thought and experience. THE MYSTERY OF SHABBOS is a profound meditation on the meaning of Shabbos and demonstrates the physical, emotional, mental and spiritual possibilities available and given to us with the gift of Shabbos. Studying and contemplating this inspired text on the depths of Shabbos will unveil a redemptive light in your experience of the Seventh Day -- and by extension, every day of your life.

THE SPIRAL OF TIME:
A 12 Part Series on the Months of the Year

VOL 1: THE SPIRAL OF TIME:
Unraveling the Yearly Cycle

Many centuries ago, the Sages of Israel were the foremost authority in the fields of both astronomical calculation and astrological wisdom, including the deeper interpretations of the cycles and seasons. Over time, this wisdom became hidden within the esoteric teachings of the Torah, and as a result was known only to students and scholars of the deepest depths of the tradition. More recently, the great teachers, from R.Yitzchak Luria (the Arizal) to the Baal Shem Tov, taught that as the world approaches the Era of Redemption, it is a Mitzvah / spiritual obligation to broadly reveal this wisdom.

"The Spiral of Time" is volume 1 is a series of 12 books, and serves as an introductory book to the basic concepts and nature of the Hebrew calendar and explores the special day of Rosh Chodesh.

_____

VOL 2: THE MONTII OF NISAN:
Miraculous Awakenings from Above

The month of NISAN is the first month of the lunar cycle of the year, a month that brings in the spring and a month of redemption. Spring represents a time of plenty, abundance, sunshine, hope, and possibility. Redemption, on whatever level, feels palpable and accessible. In spring, the world is redeemed from the cold winter, the flower is redeemed from the tree, the grass from the earth, and we too feel that redemption is possible. A whole complex of ideas, including newness, redemption, going out of Egypt, and being freed from slavery, is intricately bound with the idea of Aviv / spring and the powerful month of Nisan.

_____

VOL 3: THE MONTH OF IYYAR:
EVOLVING THE SELF
& The Holiday of LAG B'OMER

The month of IYYAR is the second month of the spring, a month that connects the Redemption from Egypt in Nissan with the Revelation of Torah in Sivan. The Chai/ Eighteenth day of the Month is the day we celebrate the Rashbi (Rabbi Shimon Bar Yochai) and the revealing of the hidden aspects of the Torah. This is the 'Holiday' of Lag b'Omer. The book explores the unique quality of this special month, a month that has a Mitzvah of counting the Omer every day. In addition, the book explores the roots and significance of the mystical 'holiday' of Lag b'Omer. Including the customs & Practices of Lag b'Omer, such as, bonfires, bows & arrows, parades, Upsherin, and more.

VOL 4: THE MONTH OF SIVAN:
The Art of Receiving: Shavuos and Matan Torah

Sivan is the third month of the lunar cycle. One is a singularity. Two is division. Three is harmony, a unity that synthesizes individuality and multiplicity, Heaven and Earth, Spirituality and Physicality. During this month we celebrate Shavuos and the giving of the Torah, the ultimate expression of the unity of the Above and Below and we aspire to connect with the Keser/Crown of Torah that Transcends and yet includes all Worlds. Learning how to truly receive Higher wisdom in our Lower faculties is the mental, emotional, and spiritual exercise of the month.

VOL 5: THE MONTHS OF TAMUZ AND AV:
Embracing Brokenness –
17th of Tamuz, Tisha B'Av, & Tu B'Av

Each month and season of the year, radiates with distinct Divine qualities and unique opportunities for growth and Tikkun.

The summer month of Tamuz and Av contain the longest and hottest days of the year. The raised temperature is indicative of a corresponding spiritual heat, a time of harsher judgement and potential destruction, such as the destructions of the first and second Beis HaMikdash, which began on the 17th of Tamuz and culminated on the 9th and 10th of Av.

A few days later, on Tu b'Av, the darkness is transformed and reveals the greatest light and possibility for new life. During these summer months of Tamuz and Av we embrace our brokenness so that we can heal and transform darkness into light.

VOL 6: THE MONTH OF ELUL:
Days of Introspection and Transformation

Each month of the year radiates with a distinct quality and provides unique opportunities for growth and personal transformation. Elul, as the final month of the spring/summer season is connected to endings. Elul gives us the strength to be able to finish strong, to end well. Elul also serves as a month of preparation for the New Year/Rosh Hashanah.

We inhale our past year, ending with wisdom and then we also gain the wisdom to begin anew and exhale a positive year into being. The mental, emotional, and spiritual objective of this month is introspection and the reclaiming of our inner purity and wholeness.

VOL 7: THE MONTH OF TISHREI:
A Time of Rebirth & Upward Movement

Each month of the year radiates with distinct Divine qualities and unique opportunities for growth and spiritual illumination. As Tishrei begins the new yearly cycle, it is an appropriate month to introspect, reflect and resolve to move forward and preserve moving forward into the more inward months of the winter. This month creates the space to unburden ourselves from our negativities, and enter a more sacred, grounded sacred space. In Tishrei we are given the gift of forgiveness and then the ability to truly regain our space and inner joy.

VOL 8: THE MONTH OF CHESHVAN:
Navigating Transitions, Elevating the Fall

Directly on the heels of the inspiring and holiday-filled month of Tishrei, Cheshvan is a month that is quiet and devoid of holidays. In the month of Cheshvan we use the stored up energies of the previous months to self-generate our inspiration and creativity and provide ourselves with the strength to rise up after a fall. In Cheshvan we are entering into a stormier, wetter and colder season. It is a month of transition. The mental, emotional and spiritual objective of this month is to weather the transitions, learn to self-generate and stand tall. And if we do fall, we use the quality of this month to get back up and do so with more conviction, strength, wisdom and clarity.

VOL 9: THE MONTH OF KISLEV:
Rekindling Hope, Dreams and Trust

Kislev is the final month of the fall. Throughout this month, daylight progressively shortens, and the temperatures drop. Towards the end of the month, at the darkest hour, the winter solstice arrives and we begin the celebration of Chanukah. We commemorate the miracle of a small jug of oil that burned for eight nights, and as we celebrate, daylight expands. In the month of Kislev-despite the darkness, or perhaps because of it-we have the ability to tap into the Ohr HaGanuz, the hidden light of hope that rekindles our dreams and aspirations.

VOL 10: THE MONTH OF TEVES:
Refining Relationships, Elevating the Body

The quality of Teves is generally harsh—much like its counterpart

Tamuz in the summer, thus the tendency for many is to hunker down, retract, curl up and wait for the month to pass by, only to reemerge when the harshness has dissipated. Think for a moment about the 'easier' months of the year, which, like gentle waves in the ocean, carry us where we want to go. We can ride these energies easily and they can propel us forward effortlessly, we just need to go with the overall flow, so to speak. The harsher months, on the other hand, can be compared to the more powerful waves that emanate from the belly of the ocean, which come forcefully crashing down and can easily drown a person before they even realize what has happened. However, those who want to utilize the momentum of the powerful energy that is available during such times can, with caution and creativity, harness these intense waves and ride them higher and farther than other, more gentle circumstances may allow. However, harnessing the power of Tohu, the raw energy of the body, does in fact need to be approached with great care and attention.

VOL 11: THE MONTH OF SHEVAT: ELEVATING EATING
& The Holiday of Tu b'Shevat

Each month of the year radiates with a distinct Divine energy and thus unique opportunities for growth, *Tikkun* and illumination. According to the deeper teachings of the Torah, all of these distinct qualities, opportunities and natural phenomena correspond to a certain data set. That is, the nature of each month is elucidated by a specific letter of the Aleph Beis, a tribe, verse, human sense, and so forth. The month of Shevat is particularly connected to food and our relationship to bodily intake. During this month we celebrate Tu b'Shevat, the New Year of the Tree, and aspire to create a proper and physically/emotionally/spiritually healthy relationship with food.

VOL 12: THE MONTH OF ADAR:
Transformation Through Laughter & Holy Doubt

Each month of the year radiates with distinct Divine qualities and unique opportunities for growth and spiritual illumination. As Adar concludes the monthly cycle of the year, as well as the solar phenomena of the winter, it is an appropriate month to think about our essential identity, before moving out to meet the world come spring. This month we strive to create a healthy relationship with holy humor, unbounded joy, and a general sense of lightness of being. Through the work of Adar we transform negative, crippling doubt and uncertainties into radical wonderment and openness.

———————

ILLUMINATED SOUND:
The Baal Shem Tov on Prayer

In the year 1698 a great light was revealed to the world with the descent of the holy soul of the Baal Shem Tov. In time, the Baal Shem Tov became one of the most important and influential teachers of Torah in all of history, and the founder of Chassidus.

Amongst the vast repository of profound and revolutionary teachings of the holy Baal Shem Tov, the teachings on the path of Tefilah / Prayer are the most elaborate. The teachings of the Baal Shem Tov on Tefilah include some of his most innovative expressions, or Chidushim. Tefilah is the essential and central tenet from which all other teachings flow.

In this masterful and practical text, Rav Pinson revives the awe-inspiring and transformational teachings of the Baal Shem Tov, and illuminates his unique path to Tefilah.

———————

A CALL TO MAJESTY:
The Mysteries of Shofar & Rosh Hashanah

The Shofar is the preeminent symbol of Rosh Hashanah, waking us up to a time of deep introspection and celebration. But why do we blow the Shofar on this most special of days? While the Torah decrees that the Shofar must be blown, it does not provide a reason. On the deepest level, the Shofar is of course beyond reason altogether, and yet, from within its shape, sound and story, a constellation of "reasons" emerge. Rebirth. Responsibility. Radical Amazement. On a primal vibrational level, the Shofar calls each of us to a place of deeper consciousness and community as we crown the King of All Creation.

THE CALL TO MAJESTY delves deeply into the world of Rosh Hashanah and its primary Mitzvah, the sound of the Shofar. Weaving together a multi-dimensional tapestry of practical, allegorical, philosophical, and mystical ideas and implications, the teachings collected herein empower us all to answer the higher calling of the Shofar.

THE HAGGADAH:
Pathways to Pesach and the Haggadah

"In every generation a person must regard oneself as having gone out of Mitzrayim / Egypt." This means that when recalling the Exodus, which occurred thousands of years ago, we also need to envision ourselves as being taken out of Mitzrayim and freed from enslavement.

Introducing the Haggadah and the themes of Pesach, this book delves into the greater context of the Festival and the Seder, allowing us to tap into the profound inspiration and Koach / power that Pesach and Seder Night offers.

Printed in the USA
CPSIA information can be obtained
at www.ICGtesting.com
LVHW011511270823
756442LV00032B/308/J